*The Elizabethan Privy Council
in the Fifteen-seventies*

The ELIZABETHAN PRIVY COUNCIL *in the* FIFTEEN-SEVENTIES

Michael Barraclough Pulman

UNIVERSITY OF CALIFORNIA PRESS

BERKELEY · LOS ANGELES · LONDON

1971

University of California Press
Berkeley and Los Angeles, California
University of California Press, Ltd.
London, England
Copyright © 1971, by
The Regents of the University of California
International Standard Book Number: 0–520–01716–1
Library of Congress Catalog Card Number: 73–115497
Printed in the United States of America
Designed by Dave Comstock

For My Father
In Memory of My Mother

Contents

Author's Note   ix

Acknowledgments   xi

Abbreviations   xii

I Introduction   3

Part I *The Necessity of Counsel*

II Origins   9

III The Councillors   17

IV The Presentation of Advice   52

Part II *The Executive Function: Positive Aspects*

V The Councillors as Executives   67

VI Supervision and Management   80

VII Matters of State and Matters of Commonwealth   114

VIII The Working Process   150

Part III *The Executive Function: Negative Aspects*

IX Interference with the Law   175

X Financial Failings   182

XI Playing with Piracy   188

XII The Muster Mess   196

XIII Enforcement   202

Part IV *The Council's Achievement*

XIV Conclusion   235

Bibliography   253

Index   269

Author's Note

ALL quotations are *verbatim et literatim.* The capitalization, however, both there and elsewhere, is my own, the principle I have attempted to follow being the unoriginal one of not using upper case for the first letter of any word within a sentence unless for some specific reason. This inevitably produces an odd effect now and then, but I have at least tried to be consistent in practice even if I have not succeeded in being so in logic. Punctuation and paragraphing of quoted material are also mine.

Acknowledgments

SOME books may be the result of a private inspiration worked out in solitude. This is not one of them. It is the product of the cooperation and effort of many, although, of course, no one but myself should be held responsible for its faults. I therefore take this opportunity to express my gratitude to all the archivists whose collections are listed in the bibliography and who have been unfailingly courteous and kind: without such helpful people as E. K. Timings at the Public Record Office I should never have gotten beyond the printed sources; Dr. G. R. Elton, whose personal interest in my work, although I was never formally his student, helped keep me going through the miserable London winter of 1962–63, when concern for anything except survival was frequently on the point of being frozen out of me; Sir John Neale, Professor Joel Hurstfield and the members of their seminar at London University, who shivered with me, week in, week out, that same inclement season, to my profit, notwithstanding our discomfort; Sandy Popson, Andy Byrne and Sarah Stapleton, who typed and Jim Jones, who proofed; Joe and Barbara Eaton, who set me on a tack I would never have taken without them and Mat and Barby Delafield, who did so much to keep me on it; Tom Barnes, my teacher and friend, to whom I owe more than I can express; my father and stepmother, Maurice and Edith Pulman, partners in this enterprise and devoted parents always; and Raymond Calhoun, who read or listened to and commented so perceptively on the manuscript in all its various preliminary versions that my debt to him falls in a category of its own.

Princeton, the University of California at Berkeley, the Social Science Research Council and the Woodrow Wilson Foundation have all been extremely generous with financial aid.

I thank you all.

Abbreviations

Add. MSS	British Museum, Additional Manuscripts
AHR	The American Historical Review
APC	The Acts of the Privy Council of England, new series
BM	British Museum
Cokayne	The Complete Peerage
CPR	Calendar of the Patent Rolls
CSP Foreign	Calendar of State Papers Foreign
CSP Spanish	Calendar of Letters and Papers Relating to English Affairs Preserved Principally in the Archives of Simancas
DNB	Dictionary of National Biography
EHR	English Historical Review
HLQ	Huntington Library Quarterly
PRO	Public Record Office

The Elizabethan Privy Council
in the Fifteen-seventies

Chapter I

INTRODUCTION

 HE Privy Council was a dominating feature of the English political and social landscape in the sixteenth century. It included in its ranks the most important men in the country. To be a councillor was to be recognized publicly as a very great man, not only by the common people, but by one's peers as well. To be left outside the privileged circle—as, for example, Sir Walter Raleigh was, notwithstanding all his fame and the queen's affection—was to be excluded from the only deliberations that really mattered as long as Elizabeth occupied the throne. Above all, the overwhelming importance in its own time of the Privy Council is amply attested to by the tendency of scholars at the present to refer to it alone as "the government," an epithet to which, properly, it is only entitled in association with the monarch.

The council's power was clearly discernible and widely felt. The range of its concern was immense. It ordered appointments to and expulsions from the commission of the peace. It supervised the operation of the national militia. It saw to the intermittent raising of money and its continual disbursement. It intervened in both domestic and overseas trade and commerce. It was constantly involved in diplomatic activity. It was preoccupied with the maintenance and employment of the navy. It sat in judgment. And when the mortal Elizabeth, who had summoned it into being in the first place as long ago as 1558, went to her rest in 1603, in the act of surviving her, of watching over the peaceful assumption of the vacated Tudor throne by the Stuart rather than any other, less generally acceptable heir, of seeing England safely past what could well have been one of the more dangerous points in its history, the council attained the highest pinnacle of its prestige.

To consider the history of the Privy Council over the entire forty-five year reign of Queen Elizabeth I would be the task of a lifetime, for its relics are exceedingly numerous and widely scattered. The attempt to do so has not been made here. Attention, rather, focuses on an expanded decade of the fifteen-seventies, extending from 1568 to 1582. There are several reasons for the selection of this particular period. The membership of the council was relatively stable throughout—of the thirteen men in office at its beginning, eight remained at the end—and, as a governing body, it had had, ten years after the queen's accession, time to settle down as a team which can be thought of as truly Elizabethan. Then, too, the seventies were critical years for England. The Queen of Scots fled her own country and became Elizabeth's prisoner-guest in 1568, causing an international and domestic crisis that was to continue to simmer ominously and occasionally to erupt dangerously until Mary's eventual execution in 1587. Fifteen hundred sixty-nine saw Anglo-Spanish amity, such as it was, severely tested as a result of the English queen's seizure, when the ships carrying it were blown into English ports by channel storms, of a cargo of bullion borrowed by the Spanish king from Genoese banks to pay his army in the Netherlands. Late in the same year there was a rebellion in the north. And in 1570, after nearly twelve years of hesitation on the part of his predecessors, Pope Pius V finally excommunicated the heretic daughter of Henry VIII and Anne Boleyn. But the system of government was not yet being subjected to the stresses and strains of actual war with Spain, and the council's role in English life can therefore be assessed on the basis of how it handled the country's affairs during a period of relative "normalcy," a period, moreover, when the pattern was set that was to characterize the operating methods of the English state for the rest of the century and beyond.

The seventies saw four secretaries of state in office at various times. Three of them—William Cecil (Lord Burghley), Sir Francis Walsingham and Sir Thomas Smith—have left copious evidence of the different ways in which each filled the position, and this provides the opportunity to view in detail the role of one of the council's most important members. Two of the most interesting clerks of the council—Robert Beale (whose voluminous papers, relating in part to his tenure of the post, have largely survived) and Edmund Tremayne—were appointed early in the decade. And the Privy Council registers, sparse up to 1570 and missing altogether between 1582 and 1586, have come down to us more or less intact for the period with which we are here concerned.

These sources of information, along with many others listed in the bibliography, reveal the Elizabethan Privy Council as an institution with a distinct identity and a character all its own, which the following pages attempt to describe. They are divided into four main sections. The first traces the origins of the council and shows what it had come to be by Elizabeth's time. What it was obviously has a lot to do with who its members and employees were. The councillors' personalities and predilections, their ages, titles or lack of them, social position and wealth, and relations with the queen and with each other are examined here. Next comes a survey of the council's positive achievements—of the things it did *well*, rather than simply an account of its multitudinous activities categorized according to the nature of the matters being dealt with. Those things, in contrast, it did less effectively, or even downright badly, along with what it did *not* accomplish but which it might have attempted, are reserved for part three. Last, in part four, an overall assessment is made of the council's position, both in its own time and in the broader context of the Western experience.

What happened to it after 1603, especially as the later years of Elizabeth's reign are not dealt with here, is, strictly speaking, another story. Yet it would be as pedantic and pointless to deal with the sixteenth century council in isolation from its future as to talk about it without reference to its past. Despite its brief moment of glory at the death of its sovereign, the council declined in power and influence thereafter—along with the monarchy itself. No subsequent king or queen wielded the scepter with the authority of the Tudors. Yet the seemingly powerful council did not rise to the occasion and replace the Crown as the dominant element in English public life. It lived on and continues to do so. It retains, even now, judicial functions of some importance, and a meeting of the Privy Council is the first official function attended by each successor to the throne. But the council's survival is essentially a formal one; as a political force it has long since been moribund. Why such a fate should have overtaken so apparently hale and hearty an organism is one of the most important and certainly the most fascinating of the problems with which this study has been concerned. And it is hoped that the outcome—the discovery, in part, that the nature of the council's power in the sixteenth century contained the seeds of its own eventual decline—will contribute to a deeper understanding of the whole broad subject of English constitutional development during the exciting and important century which separated the burgeoning England of Elizabeth from the mature Augustan consummation of the age of Anne.

Part I
The Necessity of Counsel

Chapter II

ORIGINS

HE thoroughly organized institution which we know as the Elizabethan Privy Council was not a startlingly original creation of the queen who acceded to the English throne in 1558. Its origin is directly traceable at least as far back as the Norman Conquest. It was out of the original council, the *curia regis* of William I, that most of the great offices of the English state in the later sixteenth century had gradually evolved. The original functions of the chancery, of the exchequer and of parliament had been functions of the *curia*, or of individual members of it. The chancellor had been the head of the king's secretariat; the treasurer had been responsible for the handling of the royal finances; and it had been the duty of the *curia* as a whole to confer with and advise the king whenever he chose to consult it. But the Court was itinerant, and remained so, to a certain extent, at least until the sixteenth century. With the passage of time and the continued increase in the business of the government, such functions came to require a fixed base, a place where records could be kept, where clerks could set up an office, and which would constitute a recognized center on which persons having business with a particular branch of the king's government could converge. This was no sudden development. Each department became detached from the peripatetic king and his council at different times. But by the end of the fifteenth century, the process had long been completed, and the chancery and the exchequer, along with the courts of the common law, were firmly and permanently established in various parts of Westminster Palace. Parliament continued to meet occasionally at places outside London somewhat longer than the other two; but by the time the king presented the commons with St. Stephen's Chapel as a regular place of meeting halfway through the sixteenth century, the action merely confirmed a Westminster location already traditional for much of the previous two hundred years.[1]

This splintering of the original council into departmental fragments did not, of course, preclude the continuing necessity for the sovereign, who retained the initiatory and mandatory power over his proliferating departments of state, to seek assistance in his tasks of government from a group of close advisers. Throughout the Middle Ages, these advisers con-

---

1. A. F. Pollard, *The Evolution of Parliament* (London, 1920), 333.

stituted a royal council known at various times (sometimes, according to different authorities, at the same time) as the *magnum concilium*, the *concilium privatum*, the *secretum concilium*, the *bonum, sapiens, totum* and *plenum concilium*, simply as the *concilium*, as the *curia*, and even as the *parliamentum*. By whatever name it was known, however, this council was usually a council attendant on the person of the king, and it experienced a great deal of variation in plenitude of power, which tended to vary in inverse proportion to the personal authority of the incumbent sovereign. It appears to have reached its zenith during the days of the minority and incapacity of Henry VI, having previously declined to its nadir under such a strong monarch as Henry V. The effective Edward IV, too, kept his council so tightly under his control that until very recently it had hardly been thought of as having existed at all.[2] These too-neat formulae for political equilibrium (a powerful sovereign is flanked by a weak, and probably large council; weakness in the kingship is countered by a small, powerful council) could easily be upset, however, and often were, by a variety of complicating factors. The prolonged absence from the country of even a dominant ruler tended to enhance the stature of the council in much the same way as royal incompetence, and disagreement and faction among the members of an otherwise unthreatened ruling group to create a situation in which it was relatively easy for a substitute sovereign, probably one of the council's own members, to subvert its authority with his own.[3]

The reign of Henry VII, and the early part of that of Henry VIII, when the king was content to delegate the great mass of his prerogative to an almost omnipotent chief minister, continued this pattern in its most simple form. Confusion still existed, at least in Henry VII's time, and continued to a certain extent in Henry VIII's, at least as clearly as can be made out through the medium of the surviving documents, between such various manifestations of the council as the *magnum concilium*, the *concilium privatum*, and so on. This continued imprecision in nomenclature is perhaps a result of the early Tudor council's size. C. G. Bayne estimates that 225 people are known to have been referred to, at one time or another, as king's councillors between 1485 and 1509. Of these, forty-three (19 percent) were peers, forty-five (20 percent) "courtiers," sixty-one (27 percent) churchmen, twenty-seven (12 percent) diverse

2. J. R. Lander, "The Yorkist Council and Administration, 1461–1485," *EHR*, LXIII, January 1958, 46.

3. James F. Baldwin, *The King's Council in England during the Middle Ages* (Oxford, 1913), 1–208.

lawyers and forty-nine (22 percent) officials.[4] Such gigantism is partly explained by the fact that the council then "covered not only all the ground occupied by the Privy Council of a century later, but also the extensive domain of the Elizabethan Star Chamber and court of Requests."[5] It also included such legal officers as the solicitor-general and the attorney-general, who were no longer, under Elizabeth, members of the inner circle, and the judges of the common law, who were also, with the late exception of Sir John Popham, excluded by Elizabeth from her council table. But even when the legal members, not to mention the clerics, are subtracted from the total, the council of Henry VII was still huge in comparison with Elizabeth's. And there is no very convincing evidence that there existed in any meaningful sense a group of "inner councillors" who were more consistently consulted than the rest. Henry had his close associates (such as Giles, Lord Daubeny, Sir Reginald Bray, Sir Richard Guildford and Sir Thomas Lovell), and there were a few particularly high officials of the state who owed their position in the council to their rank outside it.[6] But the king seems to have consulted whoever happened to be at Court and within easy reach when a matter of importance arose on which he felt he required advice. This "council attendant" seems to have had little definition, and its advice, when asked, to have been taken only when it suited the king to do so.[7] Henry VII ruled in a strongly personal but essentially unoriginal way, and the association of the advice of the council with the authority of the sovereign in formal proclamations is not often found in those dating from Henry VII's reign.[8] It was prestigious to belong to the council; the council exercised wide judicial functions, which have left many more traces than its advisory and executive activities; but it was not intended by the king to be an executive body, and it was very much his creature. Elizabeth, too, was to dominate her council, but not in the same way. The difference can be summed up by noting one example in particular where the practice of the first and last of the Tudors markedly diverged: Henry VII "in person satte in counsell [not only on] the xth of July . . . 1486" but as a regular occurrence, presiding over routine meetings sometimes attended by as many as thirty-four people.[9] Elizabeth, on the other hand, never sat in on

---

4. C. G. Bayne, *Select Cases in the Council of Henry VII* (London, 1958), xxix.

5. *Ibid.,* xlii.

6. *Ibid.,* xl.

7. *Ibid.,* xliii.

8. *Ibid.,* xlv.

9. *Ibid.,* l.

an ordinary meeting, at least not one dealing with the kind of matters recorded in the Privy Council register, and the most fully attended later sixteenth century meetings rarely exceeded an attendance figure of twelve or so. Elizabeth may have curbed her council, but only after she had given it its head; Henry rode his on a very short rein from the start.

In 1509, the dour and diligent founder of the Tudor fortunes died and was succeeded by a youth of seventeen. Henry VIII was not only young, but enamored of his position and little inclined to devote himself to the work by which his father had consolidated the family's by this time uncontested right to the throne of England. The result was immediate: the power vacuum created by the removal of the old and potent king was filled, owing to the heir's inexperience and lack of interest in the actual business of government, by a working council, chosen perhaps by that now old, but still capable *grande dame*, the Lady Margaret Beaufort, the new king's grandmother. However chosen, the nine men selected were in fact all close associates and councillors of Henry VII, and this "council attendant," released from the controls the old king had kept on it, blossomed forth into something which looks extremely like the Privy Council which eventually succeeded it. It met, apparently, with some frequency, and, according to the evidence of the *Letters and Papers of the Reign of Henry VIII*, dealt with a wide variety of business. Also like the later Privy Council, it remained, as it was created, small and efficient. But it was doomed by the rise in Henry's favor of a new and individual executive of the King's personally unexercised authority, Thomas Wolsey, and it met for the last recorded time on February 14, 1514.

This proto-Privy Council did not die—or at least the idea behind it survived. The king always retained "councillors" about his person whom he certainly regarded as his "Privy" Councillors and whom he felt completely free to consult on any matter which interested him at any particular moment. Nevertheless, during the period of the dominance of Wolsey, like Henry VII a hard working and painstaking administrator himself, it certainly shriveled once again from lack of nourishing responsibility. The great council, which W. H. Dunham calls the Whole Council, the immediate descendant of that enormous advisory body which had surrounded Henry VII, took on a revived, and, as it turned out, a sunset importance, as a useful agent in the implementation of Wolsey's policies. At its largest, attended by fifty or sixty members, this council constituted rather "a pageant than a functional organ of government" before which Wolsey could, and did, parade before his king his successes in governing the kingdom on Henry's behalf. However, even under Wolsey such large gatherings were unusual, and the regular function of "all the king's

Whole Council" was to meet, in term-time, in the star chamber, and act as "a court of peremptory and equitable justice." It was this manifestation of the council that was the ancestor of the high court of the Star Chamber, abolished in 1641.[10]

Between 1509 and 1527, this council comprised 116 members: twenty-one peers (18 percent), twenty-nine prelates (25 percent), thirty-six knights (31 percent), one esquire and twenty-nine lawyers (25 percent). The core of this body, the members who sat in the Star Chamber more often than anyone else, and transacted most of the business of doing justice there, were the Lord Chancellor, the Lord Treasurer, the Lord Privy Seal, and the chief justices of the common law courts. Attendance usually ranged between twelve and eighteen, although even the presence of two or three was sufficient for their actions to be effective and officially recorded in the *acta consilii*. But such superficial resemblances to the later Privy Council are coincidental and misleading, and the records fail to mention any concern with the kind of domestic matters that are the stuff of the later register. The continuity, on the other hand, with the practice of the previous reign is unmistakable.[11] Throughout the fifteen twenties, we are still faced with a situation essentially unchanged. It is not until the following decade, when Henry VIII had brought about the fall of Wolsey and begun to exercise the royal authority himself, that we come upon what seems a new phenomenon in English history: the survival of an effective, organized council in the very shadow of a well-established and potent kingship. Henry resorted once more to the use of a small executive council while looking around for a new chief minister, and the eventual replacement of Cardinal Wolsey by Thomas Cromwell did not lead this time to its emasculation, as had Wolsey's accession to power earlier. The council, on the contrary, flourished under Cromwell. Indeed, it was to do so for most of the succeeding sixty or seventy years, and did not wither away into insignificance as it had tended to do during periods when the monarchy had been the most dynamic element in the state.[12]

The explanation for this unexpected development is to be found partly in the personalities of the first two Tudors. Henry VII, while obviously not socially *nouveau*, was nonetheless the first of his particular branch of the royal family to wear the crown. Politically he was not secure until at

10. W. H. Dunham, "Henry VIII's Whole Council and its Parts," *HLQ*, VII, November 1943, 7 *et seq.*

11. Dunham, "Wolsey's Rule of the King's Whole Council," *AHR*, XLIX, July 1944, 644 *et seq.*, and "The Members of Henry VIII's Whole Council, 1509–27," *EHR*, LIX, January 1944, 187 *et seq.*

12. G. R. Elton, *The Tudor Revolution in Government* (Cambridge, England, 1959), 324.

least 1500; psychologically he probably never made it to a sufficiently safe harbor to be able to exercise his power with the insouciance that goes with deep-rooted confidence in oneself and one's position. The first Tudor monarch hugged his power to his bosom. He had made his own way in the world and was prepared to be his own minister in order to prevent anyone else from sharing or stealing away the glory of his triumph and personal satisfaction in a job well done. For Henry VII a council was to be talked to; it was not to be allowed to govern. He had earned that right, and fully intended to exercise it himself.[13]

Henry VII's successor, Henry VIII, was not without insecurities of his own. He feared both rivals and disease.[14] But he *was*—and knew he was—the product of the "union of the roses." He had by far the best claim to the throne of any of his contemporaries, strong enough to convince himself of his absolute right to the crown. And he was, at least compared with his father, both lazy and pleasure-loving. He was only too happy, provided he retained ultimate control, to delegate his authority and let someone else do the day-to-day work of government. The "reigns" of Wolsey and Cromwell and a willingness to allow the council to play a functional role in the implementation of the royal will were the result.[15]

G. R. Elton has called Henry VII "a royal business man." In fact both the father, Henry VII and the son, Henry VIII, fit the description, although they actually operated in different ways. Henry VII, having made his own way to the top, continued to work as hard when he got there as he had throughout his earlier career, keeping a sharp eye on everything and everyone, trusting little to subordinates, doing as much as possible of the work of government himself. Henry VIII, on the other hand, acted, in modern terms, as the chairman of the company of England and his council constituted his working board of directors. This difference between the habits of the founder of the Tudor fortunes and those of his heir provided the atmosphere in which a new type of council could, and indeed did, come into being. It did not, however, actually give it birth. The Privy Council did not just happen. It was invented and the credit for its invention cannot be given to Henry VIII. That credit goes to Thomas Cromwell, the man whose innovative genius his ungrateful master probably appreciated only after he had had to get along without it.

Cromwell's effect upon the council was profound. Sometime between

---

13. Kenneth Pickthorn, *Early Tudor Government Henry VII* (New York, 1967), 33.

14. J. C. Flügel, "On the Character and Married Life of Henry VIII," in *Psychoanalysis and History* (Englewood Cliffs, N.J., 1963).

15. J. J. Scarisbrick, *Henry VIII* (Berkeley, 1968), 43.

1536 and 1537 he created, out of the old amoebic, almost amorphous medieval institution, the small, structured, permanent Privy Council, whose first recorded meeting took place on August 10, 1540. By 1540 it had a staff of its own; it began to hold regular meetings and the proceedings at these meetings were henceforth recorded in a register. The later fifteen thirties can, therefore, be said to be the time when the Privy Council as the remainder of the sixteenth century was to know it came into existence. In 1540 it consisted of nineteen persons: eight peers (46 percent), five clerics (26 percent) and six knights (28 percent), all the peers, except three, holding offices of state or within the household. With the exception of the clerics, this composition is similar to that of the Privy Council under Elizabeth, and it is this type of council which Henry VIII retained to assist him, in however subservient a capacity, from the time he finally dispensed with Cromwell until his death. It was "as nearly a board of advisers, policy makers, and ministers of state as the contemporary lack of ultimate definition would allow," and in 1547 it numbered twenty-nine.[16]

From the death of Henry VIII until the accession of Elizabeth in 1558, the council again underwent a series of vicissitudes, but even so, this time, it never showed signs of losing its identity. Bequeathed by Henry to his minor son, a council of sixteen "executors" was to constitute a board of regency to govern until the new king came of age. But the circumstances were not conducive to the success of an experiment in government by committee ("the Privy Council without the king was as unfinished an administrative machine as a modern cabinet without a premier") and one of its members, Lord Hertford, quickly came to dominate the rest much as Henry VIII himself had. However, although the letters patent which created him Lord Protector also set up a new Privy Council of twenty-five and gave him the authority to appoint new members, the newly promoted Duke of Somerset made few actual changes in the composition of the council he had inherited, and the Duke of Northumberland, his successor as Lord Protector, increased its numbers only slightly. During the period of the latter's supremacy it consisted of seven peers, seventeen commoners and only two prelates (a foretaste of Elizabeth's almost complete secularization), although at one point its numbers did rise to thirty-three. Under Northumberland, as under Somerset, large or small, the Privy Council exercised little authority on its own, but it was not until the death of Edward VI and the accession of his Catholic sister Mary that it underwent a revolution which changed its character completely.[17]

---

16. Elton, 316–369; Dorothy M. Gladish, *The Tudor Privy Council* (Retford, 1915), 24.

17. Gladish, 24–25.

Several of the Edwardian councillors retained their places under Mary. Most of them were men either sufficiently nonpolitical or indispensable to find themselves still there after another death in the Tudor family and the accession of its last member to bear the name. Among such were the Marquess of Winchester and the Earl of Arundel. And the council grew again. By March 1554, membership numbered forty-four, and meetings were sometimes attended by as many as thirty-three or thirty-four of them. The first reaction to such an unwieldy number was the development of committees, and the second, after Mary's Spanish marriage, the reduction, on the initiative of Philip, of the working members to six or eight. Even so, at Mary's death her council still numbered thirty-eight, and her encouragement of cliques and cabals within it had contributed seriously to that decline of good government which so characterized her reign.[18]

The long range significance for the development of the Privy Council of the years between 1553 and 1558 is procedural. While at no time during the Middle Ages had the council possessed an authenticating instrument of its own, its authority had often been cited for the issue of instruments under the Great and Privy Seals. Letters from the council regularly went out bearing the Signet, affixed by the secretary, whose relations with the council, at least from the fifteenth century on, were intimate. By the sixteenth century, however, the Privy Seal was the most commonly used instrument for this purpose. It never became the council seal and nothing else. It sufficed, nonetheless, for the purpose, until May 20, 1555, when the council acquired its own. The earliest known document to be sealed with it is dated almost a year later, and a similar seal has been in use ever since.[19]

Thus, by the time of the accession of Elizabeth, the Privy Council was already well established as an institution in its own right, with clerks, a register and a seal. There is nothing to indicate that the new Queen ever contemplated anything so drastic as its suppression. But there was no single precedent for its composition and organization that she was bound to follow, and it remained to be seen what previous example, if any, she would make her guide for the future.

---

18. APC, VI, 499–504; Gladish, 29; Elton, *England under the Tudors* (London, 1955), 214.

19. L. W. Labarree and R. E. Moody, "The Seal of the Privy Council," *EHR*, XLIII, April 1928, 194–197.

Chapter III
THE COUNCILLORS

UEEN Elizabeth "began her reign the xvijth of Nov[ember], 1558 . . . being Thursdaye . . . her highness then being at her manour of Hatfield in the county of Hertforde." It was at Hatfield, three days later, that she held the first meeting of her Privy Council. From the beginning, the precedent she followed for its size was that set by Thomas Cromwell. She decided, like him, that to be manageable such a body must be small, and small as it started out, it gradually grew even smaller. The originally selected twenty-one members quickly proved too many. In 1568 they had been reduced to fifteen and, although there had been a slight temporary increase to eighteen ten years later, by the end of the reign the council was barely half the size it had been at the beginning.[1] Scarcely two years after the accession, the Marquess of Winchester confided to Sir William Cecil his opinion that "ther shall never appere a staied councell till you have a smaller nombre and a perfitt trust of the prince in them. And in the mean tyme all good councellors shall have labor and dolor without reward."[2] The history of the council in the 1570s shows, therefore, that Elizabeth was willing to profit by advice (however round about the way it reached her) when the virtues of earlier practices were confirmed by the lessons of experience.

Only fifty-eight men served her in a formal advisory capacity during the forty-five years she reigned, and twenty-five of these held office between 1568 and 1582. They were:

Sir Nicholas BACON	Knight	
Sir Thomas BROMLEY	Knight	
Henry Carey	1st Baron	HUNSDON
William CECIL	1st Baron	BURGHLEY
Sir James CROFT	Knight	
Ambrose Dudley	1st Earl	of WARWICK
Robert Dudley	1st Earl	of LEICESTER
Edward Fiennes {	9th Baron	CLINTON and Saye
	1st Earl	of LINCOLN

1. APC, VII, 3, November 17 and 20, 1558; 479–483, list of members appointed through December 1570.

2. Samuel Haynes, *A Collection of State Papers . . . left by William Cecil, Lord Burghley* (London, 1740), 361, the Marquess of Winchester to Cecil, August 24, 1560.

Henry Fitzalan	19th Earl	of ARUNDEL
Sir Christopher HATTON	Knight	
William Herbert	1st Earl	of PEMBROKE
Thomas Howard	4th Duke	of NORFOLK
William Howard	1st Baron	HOWARD OF EFFINGHAM
Sir Francis KNOLLYS	Knight	
Sir Walter MILDMAY	Knight	
William Parr	1st Marquess	of NORTHAMPTON
William Paulet	1st Marquess	of WINCHESTER
Thomas Radcliff	3rd Earl	of SUSSEX
Francis Russell	2nd Earl	of BEDFORD
Sir Ralph SADLER	Knight	
Sir Henry SIDNEY	Knight	
Sir Thomas SMITH	Knight	
George Talbot	6th Earl	of SHREWSBURY
Sir Francis WALSINGHAM	Knight	
Dr. Thomas WILSON	Ll.D.[3]	

(Names in capitals are those normally used here.)

These men—among whom there were no ecclesiastics—had a number of things in common, but were nonetheless distinct individuals, with personalities and qualities of their own, so the character of the council as a whole was a composite one.

The two most obvious similarities shared by the members of Queen Elizabeth's Privy Council are that without exception they were gentlemen and educated. Some, admittedly, were more or less gentle and better or worse educated than others. Sir Nicholas Bacon, a product of Corpus Christi College, Cambridge, went on from there to read law at Gray's Inn and then embarked on the legal and administrative career for which he had been preparing himself. He was fundamentally a nonpolitical, highly trained professional man who made good in his chosen field. In addition to being a member of parliament in Henry VIII's time, he had obtained the attorneyship of the court of Wards by the time of the death of the king and kept it throughout the two succeeding reigns. It was primarily his expert knowledge and the breadth of experience he had by then acquired in this manner that led Queen Elizabeth to appoint him head of the chancery in 1558, a post he retained without controversy and to which he lent considerable distinction until his death in 1579. Yet apparently because his father had been only a lowly sheep-reeve, Elizabeth

---

3. APC, VII, 479–483; VIII, 468–471; IX, 450–452; X, 499–501; XI, 518–520.

never regarded him as sufficiently distinguished to be worthy of the title Lord Chancellor. He was known, instead, simply as Lord Keeper of the Great Seal. There was, however, no question as to his gentility, which his ability and diligence had earned and his knighthood merely confirmed.[4] Comparatively new as his family may have been to the ranks of those who had no need to labor for their living on the lands they owned, Sir Nicholas Bacon himself was manifestly quite as good a gentleman as the Earl of Arundel, whose pedigree stretched back to the eleventh century.

The earl was far from being as academically accomplished as the Lord Keeper. His intellectual attainments were nothing compared with those of, say, Dr. Wilson, who, having attended Eton as a boy, graduated from King's College, Cambridge, as a young man, and received the degree of Ll. D. from the Italian University of Ferrara in 1559, was probably his most highly educated colleague.[5] Arundel was probably tutored at home and from there went straight into the household of Henry VIII at the age of fifteen. Yet he had all the schooling a member of the upper class of the time was considered to need. He was described by a contemporary as "not unlearned," built up a personal library of some merit and was a member of the Elizabethan Society of Antiquaries. If few of the other councillors came close to sharing Wilson's erudition, none fell short of Arundel's quite respectable intellectual attainments and thus within the group an interchange of ideas could, and did, take place in an atmosphere of open-minded sophistication.[6]

All the members of the council were also landowners, some very great indeed. The Earl of Bedford's family, the Russells, had been vastly successful in accumulating properties in the west country even before they advanced into the ranks of the gentry. Then, shortly after they successfully cleared this important social hurdle, Henry VIII enriched them further, when the monasteries were dissolved, with the gift of confiscated Church lands in the London area.[7] The Earl of Pembroke's territorial wealth was also Tudor-bestowed and centered on Wilton, his magnificent country home in Wiltshire. The Earl of Shrewsbury possessed enormous estates in the midlands and north. And the Duke of Norfolk, greatest magnate of all and already predominant in the east, aimed at extending his holdings in the northern part of the country too by marrying the widow of the great Dacre of the north as his third wife and then proceeding to

4. DNB, Bacon, Sir Nicholas.
5. DNB, Wilson, Thomas (1525?–1581).
6. DNB, Fitzalan, Henry; Cokayne, I, 250–252, Arundel, Earl of.
7. Gladys Scott Thomson, *Two Centuries of Family History: A Study in Social Development* (London, 1930), 35–127.

unite *his* children with *hers* to bring the Dacre lands to the Howards permanently. On a somewhat lesser scale, the Earl of Leicester was a proprietor in Carmarthen, Cardigan, Brecknock, Rutland, Lancashire, Yorkshire and Warwick. Sir Nicholas Bacon had property in Norfolk, Wiltshire, Hampshire, Suffolk, Bedfordshire, Cambridgeshire, Essex, Northamptonshire, Oxfordshire and London. William Cecil, Lord Burghley, built houses on his Northamptonshire, Middlesex and Hertfordshire acres, and as for Sir Christopher Hatton, listing the gifts of land showered on him by his queen would take one into Kent, Surrey, Dorset and Northamptonshire before one had properly begun. All the others were established somewhere: the Earl of Warwick in Leicestershire and Warwickshire, the Earl of Arundel in Surrey and Sussex, the Marquess of Northampton in Northamptonshire and Essex, Sir James Croft in Hereford, Sir Thomas Bromley in Shropshire, Sir Henry Sidney and Lord Hunsdon in Kent, Lord Clinton and Thomas Wilson in Lincolnshire, Sir Ralph Sadler in Hertford, Sir Francis Knollys at Rotherfield Grays in Oxfordshire and Sir Francis Walsingham at Foot's Cray in Kent and later at Barn Elms, Surrey. Lord Howard of Effingham straddled both counties. Hampshire's most prominent personage was the Marquess of Winchester. And Sir Thomas Smith, when away from Court and not off on some diplomatic mission, could usually be found at Theydon Mount in Essex, not far from the Earl of Sussex at the old royal palace of Newhall.[8]

Perhaps more than any other single factor, the possession by these individuals of so many manors in virtually all the shires of England provided the foundations of the enormous power they exercised as a group—as the Privy Council. They not only owned land, they lived on it—or at least on some part of it—and their residence there provided them with intimate knowledge of local people and conditions. They knew what positions of responsiblity were coveted for the prestige that attached to occupying them and which were undesired because the duties outweighed the status they conveyed. Every gentleman who was not one already, the council knew, wanted to be a justice of the peace, while no one wished to be a sheriff; but they also realized who would make the most efficient magistrate and who best could assume the financial burdens and fulfil the obligations that went with being the titular head of a county. As councillors, their views on such matters carried more weight than anyone else's when it came to deciding actual appointments.[9] Appointments to and removals

---

8. These territorial details are culled from the sources cited elsewhere in this chapter under the names of the various individuals involved.

9. J. E. Neale, *The Elizabethan House of Commons* (New Haven, 1950). Neale cites numerous examples of conciliar intervention in local affairs.

from the commission of the peace were executed by the Lord Chancellor or Lord Keeper,[10] but the council did not hesitate to interfere in this routine procedure. One letter to the Lord Keeper might instruct him to add the Earl of Southampton to the commission for Hampshire, another tell him to remove Sir Richard Lee and Sir Rafe Rowlett.[11] Similarly, although it was the queen who made the final choice of sheriffs each year, the council nominated the three men per county from among whom one was eventually pricked, and even in making her selection, Elizabeth was not acting entirely without conciliar advice. In 1575 she postponed the pricking until Burghley's return after a brief absence from Court.[12]

The councillors' landed status, therefore, is of enormous importance in explaining the successful working of the entire Elizabethan administrative system. It gave them power over those on whom the Crown had to rely (in the absence of a paid bureaucracy) to carry out its orders, power which complemented perfectly the influence over royal policy they had acquired on their appointment as the queen's official advisers. They could manipulate the gentry because their suggestions carried weight with the queen; their suggestions were listened to by Elizabeth because of their standing in the countryside.

This two-sided situation is reflected in the other things that all the members of the Privy Council had in common: inclusion in commissions of the peace and membership in parliament. All the Privy Councillors were justices of the peace, often in more than one county, and those who were not automatically summoned to sit in the house of lords as peers of the realm in their own right used their local standing to have themselves elected to the house of commons.[13]

Councillors and the number of counties (or county subdivisions) in England and Wales in which each was justice of the peace:

Bacon	all 56	Bedford	9
Bromley	2	Sadler	2
Hunsdon	7	Sidney	18

10. Edward P. Cheyney, *A History of England from the Defeat of the Armada to the Death of Elizabeth* (New York, 1926), II, 317.

11. APC, VIII, 267, July 12, 1574; VII, 194, February 10, 1564.

12. BM, Lansdowne MS. 20, no. 53, Walsingham to Burghley, November 6, 1575.

13. Neale, 351. These figures for the counties and subdivisions in England and Wales are derived from two *libri pacis* in the PRO, SP.12/93ii (1573) and SP.12/121 (1577), which can be consulted for full details.

Burghley	all 56	Smith	2
Croft	11	Shrewsbury	11
Warwick	4	Walsingham	2
Leicester	11	Wilson	2
Lincoln	4		
Arundel	3		
Hatton	1	Norfolk,	
Pembroke	3	Howard of Effingham,	
Knollys	1	Northampton,	
Mildmay	2	and Winchester	
Sussex	2	were all dead by 1573	

Councillors Sitting in the House of Commons, 1568–1582:[14]

	1571*	1572*	1576	1581
Croft	Herefordshire————————————————			
Hatton				Northamptonshire
Knollys	Oxfordshire————————————————			
Mildmay	Northamptonshire————————————————			
Sadler	Hertfordshire————————————————			
Smith	Essex————————————————			
Walsingham			Surrey————————————	
Wilson				Lincoln (City)——

*new parliaments

The councillors also set an example they expected others to follow by serving as Lords Lieutenants. In December 1579 there was at least one councillor's name and usually three or four at the head of the lists of those made responsible for the military strength of the country at the county level on that particular occasion. The association of councillor and county is consistently what one would expect from what has been said already about the location of their holdings, but the number of counties for which a single councillor is designated varies from a maximum of twelve in the case of the Earl of Leicester down to one in those of Ralph Sadler, Walter Mildmay and Francis Knollys.[15] This variation points up the fact that most of the actual work was done by others, but, even so, the councillor who had himself been appointed Lord Lieutenant was ultimately the man held to account for how well his deputies did his job, and the council did not hesitate to inform even the Lord Admiral himself that

14. Most of this information is available in the DNB, but I am also indebted to the History of Parliament Trust for giving me access to their unpublished biographies of councillor members of parliament.

15. PRO, SP.12/133, no. 14, December 1579; Hatfield House, MS. 156, ff. 117–118, November 20, 1569.

"her majestie doth fynde fault with your slacknes . . . . and therefore hath willed us againe to praye your lordship to give present order accordinge to our former letters."[16] A councillor given a job—any job—was obviously expected, by both queen and colleagues, to do it.

Other common characteristics were confined to particular segments of the council. Although all were generally included in the frequently, if loosely employed phrase "lords of the council," one distinction regularly made by their contemporaries was between the "lords," or peers and the "others," or commoners.[17] But there were subdivisions even within these groups. The peers alone, for example, fall into three fairly distinct categories. Some could be described as belonging to the old nobility, others as Henrician promotions and a few—a very few—as the Elizabethan creations.

In 1568 the old nobility, in a council of fifteen, had five representatives. They were the Duke of Norfolk, the Earl of Arundel, the Earl of Lincoln (by virtue of his rank as ninth baron Clinton and Saye), the Earl of Pembroke and Lord Howard of Effingham.

Of these the Duke of Norfolk was the most eminent and the only peer of his degree left in England. He was not particularly competent. Sent north with Sadler and Croft in 1559 to see to the defense of Berwick, and young and inexperienced though he was, he aired very definite ideas about the best way of conducting English policy toward Scotland and France, none of which showed an appreciation of diplomatic realities or chimed with official views of the situation. Instead of intervening militarily in Scotland, as Elizabeth was doing with great success, he wanted her to marry an Austrian archduke—whose lineage even the high-stomached Howards respected—and intimidate France that way. This suggestion was irresponsible enough, but at least he was not yet a councillor. There was much worse to come when he became one, for he ultimately got so foolishly involved with the affairs of the Queen of Scots that he was convicted of treason in 1572 and thereupon paid for his incapacity with his head.[18]

The Earl of Arundel, though older, was hardly wiser than Norfolk and equally inept at politics. Lord Deputy of Calais and Lord Chamberlain

16. BM, Harleian MS. 703, f. 43, the council to the Lord Admiral, March 31, 1586.

17. Cambridge University Library, MS. Gg. 5. 36, 26–32, "a letter from the lordes and others of the counsell . . . to Sir Humphrey Gilbert," no date.

18. Neville Williams, *Thomas Howard Fourth Duke of Norfolk* (New York, 1964); DNB, Howard, Thomas III, fourth Duke of Norfolk; Cokayne, IX, 622–624, Norfolk, Duke of.

to Henry VIII, his testing time came with the death of the king. A sensible man would then at least have made up his own mind where his fundamental loyalties lay. Arundel, instead, vacillated from faction to faction and, after seeming to work for the succession of Lady Jane Grey while actually supporting the claims of Mary Tudor to the throne, ended up without a firm foothold in any camp. Given a chance to shine once more by Elizabeth, he failed miserably to redeem his reputation, compromising himself once again, this time, like Norfolk, by allowing himself to become involved with the dubious ambitions of Mary Stuart.[19]

Neither Norfolk nor Arundel, as their behavior testifies, can be called successful conciliar appointees. Yet neither their selection nor their failure to justify it bears witness to a lack of judgment on the queen's part. She needed them. Great landlords holding feudal sway over a significantly large number of her subjects, partisans of her dead and Catholic sister and suspected opponents of the re-established Church of England—by raising them to be her councillors she associated them actively and compromisingly with the new regime. Better to have them at hand where she knew what they were doing than have them brooding treacherously over their exclusion from power on their own potentially dangerous domains. Even so, Arundel appeared at council meetings comparatively rarely during the latter part of his life and was, indeed, never an assiduous attender.[20] Elizabeth used Norfolk and him as long and as much as she felt she safely could, but when the advantage gained thereby came to be outweighed by the risks of trusting them too far, she faced the situation realistically, removed the one completely from the scene and reduced the influence of the other.

There were more positive reasons for the inclusion in the ranks of the council of the other three descendants of aristocratic ancestors. The Earl of Lincoln had been a close friend of Henry VIII. He had secured himself in the king's favor by marrying and thus respectably providing for Henry's ex-mistress, Elizabeth Blount, mother of Henry's illegitimate son, the Duke of Richmond. Clinton (as he then still was) served in an active capacity in Henry's fleet and was made Lord High Admiral of England by Edward VI in 1550. Like so many others, he appeared to go along with Northumberland's attempt to make Jane Grey queen, but nevertheless managed to make his peace with Mary, who was only too glad to make use of his naval experience when she became involved in King Philip's continental wars. She restored the Lord Admiralship, of which he had been temporarily deprived, to him in 1558. Created earl by Elizabeth,

19. DNB, Fitzalan, Henry; Cokayne, I, 250–252, Arundel, Earl of.
20. APC, VIII, 468; IX, 450; X, 499; XI, 518.

who fully appreciated his sterling qualities, Lincoln was an altogether much more open and attractive, not to say mature, person than either Arundel or Norfolk and owed his 1558 councillorship to his competence rather than to his descent or territorial holdings.[21]

Both the Earl of Pembroke and Lord Howard of Effingham shared many of Lincoln's qualifications for such employment. Pembroke, although his title was only bestowed by Edward VI, traced his ancestry back well into the fifteenth century, through his father, the illegitimate son of the first Earl of Pembroke of the previous creation. Nominated by Henry VIII as one of the Privy Council of twelve who were to govern during the minority of Edward VI, Pembroke shifted nimbly from support of Somerset to Northumberland to Mary, who made him a councillor again, in spite of the fact that he was a Calvinist. Mary also made him Lord President of the Council in the Marches of Wales, which he had also been in her brother's time.[22] He was kept on the council by Elizabeth in 1558.[23]

Howard of Effingham, great-uncle of both the queen and her Duke of Norfolk, was the son of that Thomas Howard who had been the *second* Duke of Norfolk. Like Pembroke, his ancestry, not his title, marks him off as old nobility. He had been employed by Henry VIII on a variety of diplomatic missions prior to being convicted of misprision of treason in 1541 for reputed involvement in the troubled affairs of Queen Catherine Howard. Henry, however, liked him and pardoned him. He held office under Edward VI. And Mary made him Lord Admiral (during Lincoln's brief time in eclipse) and a member of her Privy Council. He had the foresight, however, notwithstanding the favor Mary showered upon him, to protest against the harsh treatment meted out to her sister, and this sensible precaution and inexpensive gesture paid off handsomely. He retained all his offices when the sinned-against princess became queen herself in 1558.[24]

By 1582 there were two other scions of ancient peerage families on the council: the Earls of Sussex and Shrewsbury. Sussex was the great proconsul of Elizabeth's reign, with a wide experience of responsibility behind him by the time of her accesson. Having made his maiden diplomatic voyage to arrange a marriage, which never took place, between Edward VI and the daughter of Henry II of France, he switched horses

---

21. DNB, Clinton, Edward Fiennes de; Cokayne, VII, 690–693, Lincoln, Earl of.

22. DNB, Herbert, Sir William, first Earl of Pembroke of the second creation; Cokayne, X, Pembroke, Earl of.

23. APC, VII, 483.

24. DNB, Howard, Lord William, first Baron Howard of Effingham; Cokayne, V, 9–10, Effingham, Lord Howard of; APC, VII, 479–483.

sufficiently smartly at the time of the young king's death for Edward's successor to feel enough confidence in him to employ him in the negotiations for her own much-wanted union with the prince of Spain. His efforts on this occasion were more successful, and Mary continued to make use of him, as Lord Deputy of Ireland, where she sent him in 1556. He returned to England at Mary's death, but Elizabeth continued him in the position until he was permitted to resign at his own request in 1564, feeling himself both maligned behind his back and insufficiently supported by the government. Nonetheless, he had proved himself a vigorous administrator and was soon at work again, in a similar capacity, as Lord President of the Council of the North. This assignment involved him in the suppression of the northern rebellion in 1569. Between these two appointments he had been employed once more on diplomatic business of a matrimonial nature, this time being sent to Vienna to work for the betrothal of Elizabeth to the Archduke Charles of Austria. It came to nothing; indeed few of Sussex' assignments seem to have ended on a particularly happy note, and there was much criticism at Court, of which Sussex himself was fully cognizant, of the conduct of his Irish and northern administrations. Even so, he received his reward eventually in being sworn as member of the Privy Council on the next to last day of December 1569, at the age of forty-three.[25]

Shrewsbury, too, earned his seat at the council table, but his is in many ways a special case. His council membership was essentially, uniquely, honorary, granted because of his long and faithful service as the jailer of the Queen of Scots. But since he was not in the first place selected at random for that unpopular yet vital task, it is legitimate to regard his suitability for the custodianship of Mary Stuart as the real, underlying qualification for his council membership. He was a great landowner, as we have seen, whose northerly territories provided him with a variety of places for keeping his prisoner and endowed him with provincial power and influence on the scale of that enjoyed by Norfolk and Arundel and Bedford and Pembroke. Unlike the former pair, however, he was generally acknowledged to be absolutely loyal. Like his father—who had preceded him as a royal intimate and adviser—he served a dynasty and a regime, not religion and personal ambition, and these things taken together make it plain that Shrewsbury was far from unworthy of the honors and the responsibility that Queen Elizabeth thrust upon him.[26]

25. DNB, Radcliffe, Thomas; Cokayne, XII, part i, 522–525, Sussex, Earl of; APC, VII, 408.

26. DNB, Talbot, George, sixth Earl of Shrewsbury; Cokayne, XI, 712–714, Shrewsbury, Earl of.

Under the heading "Henrician promotions to the peerage" can be listed three men who sat on the council in 1568: the Marquesses of Winchester and Northampton and the Earl of Bedford, of whom only Bedford was left in 1582.

Winchester is one of the most attractive figures of the earlier sixteenth century. Eighty-one in 1568, his own age equalled that of the dynasty he served. Of mere gentle birth, he had been actively involved in administration from at least 1512, when he held the sheriffwick of Hampshire, an office he was to hold again in 1519, 1523 and 1527. By the last date he was already one of Henry VIII's close advisers, and by 1546 he was Lord President of the council. But the career which must have especially commended him to Elizabeth did not begin until he helped to depose Somerset in 1550 and thereupon received the symbolic white staff of the office of Lord Treasurer. He was to retain it until his death in 1572. It was Winchester who headed the commission that carried out those financial reforms, planned under Edward VI, which were not actually implemented until Mary's reign. So complete was the dominance he had achieved over the national finances by 1558 that Elizabeth, in immediately appointing Winchester to her council, overlooked the fact that he had been one of those who had been assigned in her sister's reign to convey her to the Tower. She found him, in spite of his age, a man of considerable personal charm and this probably helped her remember only good things about him. But he never gave her reason to regret her choice.[27]

William Parr, first Marquess of Northampton, owed the favor which he had received at the hands of Henry VIII—he had first been made a Privy Councillor as early as 1543—in large measure to the fact that he was the brother of Catherine Parr, the king's last wife. This relationship did him no harm under Edward VI, for the boy had been fond of his stepmother, but it worked to his disadvantage under Mary, whose relationship with the Queen Dowager had been, to say the least, cool. Northampton had been far too prominent in the counsels of Lord Protector Somerset, far too friendly with Northumberland and far too closely involved in the abortive attempt to divert the succession to the Suffolk line for him to ingratiate himself easily with Katherine of Aragon's daughter. She pardoned him, but declined to restore the lands and titles that his treason had cost him. So he was known again as plain Sir William Parr until January 1559, when his other step-niece reinstated him, having already admitted him to her Privy Council on her accession. The gesture

27. DNB, Paulet, Pawlet, or Poulet, William, first Marquis of Winchester; Cokayne, XII, part ii, 757–762, Winchester, Marquess of; Frederick C. Dietz, *English Public Finance 1558–1641*, second edition (New York, 1964), 6–7.

seems to have been primarily sentimental. Northampton was probably the council's most colorless member.[28]

The Earl of Bedford was also one of Elizabeth's original selections. His extensive possessions alone qualified him, like Norfolk and Arundel, for consideration, but he had other assets as well. He had been both a member of parliament for Buckingham (before acceding to the title) and sheriff of Bedfordshire. After being involved in Wyatt's plot aimed at replacing Mary by Elizabeth, he had confirmed his claim to be considered for preferment whenever the Catholic interlude should be over by escaping to Geneva in 1555 and returning only at a time of acute national danger to assume the Lord Lieutenancy of Cornwall, Devon and Dorset. That the Earl of Bedford was a man of upright, incorruptible and pacific character without an apparent enemy in the world was an assumption contradicted by none, and it earned him the lasting respect and affection of both his fellow councillors and the queen.[29]

Up until 1568, Elizabeth herself had made only one councillor a peer —Robert Dudley, granted the earldom of Leicester in 1564—and by 1582 she had created only three others. Dudley's brother Ambrose became Earl of Warwick. Henry Carey was raised to the baronage as Lord Hunsdon. And William Cecil was finally promoted to be Lord Burghley in 1571.

If Leicester's peculiar, and certainly unique position in the group of advisers closest to Elizabeth was not entirely owing to the astrological coincidence of their having been born in the same hour, it was nonetheless largely based on the enduring hold he had on her affections. Of practical, official or diplomatic experience qualifying him for a position on the council he had little or none. It is not even possible with any certainty to establish any relationship between him and Elizabeth other than friendly acquaintance before her accession at the end of 1558. But thereafter, Lord Robert Dudley, notwithstanding his marriage in 1550 to Amy Robsart, rose rapidly to a position in regard to the queen which, owing to her continuing single state, came to be of great domestic and international importance, to say nothing of covert scandal. The queen decided not to marry him. The suspicious circumstances surrounding the too-convenient death of his wife made the prospect of such a match even more unacceptable to her other associates than it had been previously. But Dudley remained at Court and became a great deal more than a mere "closet favorite." Although he was still resented by Elizabeth's more professional

---

28. DNB, Parr, William, Marquis of Northampton; Cokayne, IX, 669–674, Northampton, Marquess of.

29. DNB, Russell, Francis, second Earl of Bedford; Cokayne, II, 75–76, Bedford, Earl of.

advisers as an ambitious upstart of little capacity, her affection established him as a power to be reckoned with, and after his appointment to the council sometime in 1562 his "faithful attendance and regular attention soon drew him into the heart of all state business."[30] Yet prior to his elevation he was given no office of any importance higher than that attaching to his mastership of the horse, which he retained until his death in 1588.[31]

Ambrose Dudley's career before he came to sit at the council board, on the other hand, had been a distinguished one, and the fact that he did not join his brother there until 1573—fifteen years after the beginning of the reign and ten after Leicester's appointment—makes it clear that he did not owe his promotion, when it came, either to his own personal association with the Princess Elizabeth when they had both been intimates of Edward VI or to fraternal influence. Warwick had been pardoned by Mary, along with his brothers, for involvement in their father's attempt to retain his own power upon Edward's death by denying Mary her rights to the succession. They had fought hard for her in France. And Warwick was sent there again in 1562, this time by Elizabeth, as leader of an expedition to help the Protestants of Le Havre against the besieging Catholics. Here he received the injury which permanently affected his health, interfered with his active life as the soldier he was by temperament as well as by training, and eventually killed him. Because of his injury he had to be granted permission to retire to his house to recuperate even before the northern rebellion was properly over, leaving the Lord Admiral, with whom he shared the command of the southern army, to supervise the discharge of the troops they had marched northwards and whose services were no longer needed. He was nonetheless apparently able to exercise effectively the duties imposed on him by the mastership of the ordnance to which the queen had appointed him in 1560, and he was both a member of the commission instructed to look into the affairs of the Queen of Scots in 1568 and one of the judges at the trial of the Duke of Norfolk in 1572. Above all a professional military man, the Earl of Warwick was also a staunch but unfanatical adherent of the reformed religion, and this commended him to both Burghley and the queen.[32]

Hunsdon was the son of Anne Boleyn's sister Mary. He was a member of parliament for Buckingham between 1547 and 1555 and sufficiently

30. Wallace MacCaffrey, *The Shaping of the Elizabethan Regime* (Princeton, 1968), 136.

31. DNB, Dudley, Robert, Earl of Leicester; Cokayne, VII, 549–552, Leicester, Earl of; Elizabeth Jenkins, *Elizabeth and Leicester* (New York, 1962).

32. DNB, Dudley, Ambrose, Earl of Warwick; Cokayne, XII, part ii, 400–404, Warwick, Earl of.

in favor to receive grants of land from Edward VI, but his career as a
servant of the state appears to have begun only in 1558. Knighted that
year, made captain of the band of gentlemen pensioners in 1561, he was
sent in 1564 on an embassy to present to the French king the Garter he
had himself received three years earlier. In 1568 he was invested with the
post of warden of the east Marches over against Scotland and made governor of Berwick, which he was to remain for the rest of his life. As
governor of Berwick Hunsdon came to play a major role in the suppression of the rebellion of the northern earls in 1569, and in the same
capacity he acted throughout his northern career as one of the government's main contacts with the various parties and factions constantly
jockeying for position, not only within their native Scotland, but *vis-à-vis*
the queen and council of England in addition. Hunsdon became one of the
"lords and others" in 1577.[33]

William Cecil, Lord Burghley, in spite of having to wait out the first
twelve years of the reign before his elevation to the house of lords, was
the first of all the councillors, both in order of appointment and in terms
of influence with the queen. Cecil had been educated at St. John's College, Cambridge and was a member (although not a barrister) of Gray's
Inn. His rise between 1547 and 1553 had been phenomenal. Continuing
the betterment of the family fortunes begun by his grandfather earlier in
the century, William Cecil became first a master of Requests, then private
secretary to Somerset and emerged, after a brief period of imprisonment
consequent upon the latter's fall, to be made one of the secretaries of state
and a Privy Councillor by Northumberland. He saw fit to remain in
England during Mary's reign, but did not manage to retain the official
posts he had held under Edward. Even so, if Mary could not forgive his
support of her rival (however reluctant it had been) to the extent of
retaining him in those posts to which he was to be so rapidly restored by
her successor, she nevertheless was quite content to make ample use of his
services as a diplomat. Throughout the reign, Cecil was careful to remain
in close, albeit cautious touch with the suspect Princess Elizabeth and
reaped his reward immediately on Mary's death. He was Queen Elizabeth's chief minister from the first.[34]

---

33. DNB, Carey, Henry, first Lord Hunsdon; Cokayne, VI, 627–629, Hunsdon, Baron.

34. DNB, Cecil, William, Lord Burghley; Cokayne, II, 428–430, Burghley,
Baron; Conyers Read, *Mr. Secretary Cecil and Queen Elizabeth* (New York,
1955); B. W. Beckingsale, *Burghley. Tudor Statesman, 1520–1598* (London,
1967); A. L. Rowse, "Alltyrynys and the Cecils," *EHR*, LXXV, January 1960,
54.

Although all these men bore hereditary titles and were at the same time members of the council, the two things were not, and did not become synonymous. Although more than half—eight out of fifteen—of Elizabeth's councillors in 1568 were peers, as compared with a slightly lower proportion ten years earlier—nine out of twenty-one—the apparent trend towards a solidly noble council did not continue. Ten years later, in 1578, it had indeed been slightly reversed: exactly half the councillors by then were titled, while half were not. Nor were all peers members of the council. There were fifty-seven of them in 1558, forty-eight of whom were not on the council.[35] For no one was a title alone enough to gain the inner sanctum, nor was a title the automatic consequence of admission to the council or the usual reward for service there, even long years of it. Possession of a title could help further a man's ambition, but in all cases, much more important than lineage and name were such things as territorial influence, enjoyed by Norfolk, Arundel, Bedford and Pembroke particularly; length of service to the dynasty, most strikingly exemplified by Winchester; commitment to the Protestant religion, most uncompromising in the cases of Bedford and Northampton; strong personal loyalty to the queen herself, displayed especially by Howard of Effingham, Shrewsbury, Warwick, Leicester and Burghley; and the competence in serving the state evidenced by almost all.

If some of the councillors were peers, some of the peers and many of the rest were also officials. Certain offices may be considered as occupying the heights commanding the Tudor administrative landscape. These were the treasury, the chancery, the principal secretaryship, the admiralty and the most important positions in the royal household. The Lord Treasurer was not the first in order of precedence among the great officers of state, but his department was the kingpin of the national administrative machinery and his importance was consequently great. The Marquess of Winchester retained the post throughout the sixties and on into the early part of the next decade; during the greater part of the seventies and up until his death in 1598, it was occupied by his successor, Burghley.

The chancery housed the Great Seal, the most prestigious authenticating instrument, next to act of parliament, of the state. Sir Thomas Bromley, the last member of the council to be appointed before the register breaks off in 1582, took charge of it in succession to Lord Keeper Bacon, whose path to the top of the legal profession Bromley followed remarkably closely. Bachelor of the civil law in the University of Oxford, 1560, barrister of the Inner Temple, retained by Lord Hunsdon

---

35. APC, VII, 479–483; Lawrence Stone, *The Crisis of the Aristocracy* (Oxford, 1965), 99.

and patronized by Cecil, this extremely professional lawyer reached the first high point in his career in 1569 when he was made solicitor-general. His rise thereafter seems to have been entirely owing to luck and force of personality. Attorney-general Gerrard, his superior in professional standing, was awkward and retiring in personal relationships, whereas Bromley was not only a man of the world but a politician. He was counsel for the Crown at the trial of the Duke of Norfolk in the early 1570s and when, at the end of the decade, the chancery had been left so long without a head following the death of Sir Nicholas Bacon that the business of administration was beginning to grind to a halt, the queen eventually allowed herself to be persuaded that Bromley was the best man for the job. He was made Lord Chancellor—the offspring of an already distinguished legal family, his birth was considered to be "better" than Bacon's—and sworn of the Privy Council in April 1579.[36]

The principal secretary was quite as important an individual as the Lord Chancellor. He controlled the use of that other crucial symbol of authority, the Signet, and by performing the secretarial function for both queen and council, he constituted the most vital link between the two. Cecil's immediate successor in the office, on his own move to the treasury, was Sir Thomas Smith. Smith was a self-made man. From a grammar school in Essex, he arrived at Queen's College, Cambridge *before* reaching the ripe old age of thirteen. As such precocity sometimes foreshadows, his most lasting fame depends upon scholarship. He became Regius Professor of civil law at the age of thirty and is the author of *De Republica Anglorum*, one of the most famous of the few sixteenth century treatises on English government. But early in his academic career he became involved in university and college administration, and this led him into the national political arena, where he became Edward VI's principal secretary during the period of dominance of the Duke of Somerset. At the time of Somerset's overthrow, Smith, too, fell from power. He had already acquired, however, the useful friendship of William Cecil, which ultimately proved one of his greatest assets. Smith was in many ways a carping, complaining kind of man, and he completely failed to win Elizabeth's respect, at least during the earlier part of his career in her service. His tactless conduct of an important diplomatic mission to France between 1562 and 1566 seemed to confirm him as conscientious but ineffectual; both the queen and her councillors actually laughed together over his pedantically detailed dispatches. Yet Cecil had him recalled to the council in 1571 and made secretary again the following year, probably on account of his amply

---

36. DNB, Bromley, Sir Thomas (1530–1587).

demonstrated capacity for taking pains.[37] Smith was, however, by this time in failing health, and a second secretary was soon added. This was Sir Francis Walsingham.

Walsingham's formidable qualifications for such employment were more widely recognized than Smith's and infinitely more appreciated by his sovereign. King's, Cambridge, had been his college and Gray's his Inn of Court. An overt and enthusiastic Protestant, he had thought discretion the better part of valor when the Catholic Mary succeeded her Calvinist brother and had gone abroad. It was time well spent. He devoted much of his time to the study of Roman law at the University of Padua, which also gave him a perfect opportunity to learn something about statecraft, Italian style. Also, he met many people, thus laying the foundations for that network of information-gatherers, access to which was to make him, on the accession of Elizabeth and his subsequent return to England, so useful to his patron, William Cecil. As a member of parliament for Lyme Regis he broadened his experience in domestic affairs, but with his obvious qualifications for diplomacy he was soon sent to Paris, originally as a subordinate of Sir Henry Norris, to ask for Huguenot toleration and latterly as ambassador in his own right, as the character of the negotiations changed, to seek a satisfactory arrangement that should culminate in a marriage between Queen Elizabeth and the Duc d'Anjou. If his success in the conclusion of the treaty of Blois in April 1572 was somewhat clouded by the events of St. Bartholomew's Day four months later, this was not Walsingham's fault. He was recalled the following year, not in disgrace, but in order to make greater use of his talents and experience at home. He was appointed principal secretary on December 21, 1573.[38]

Thomas Wilson's official career began shortly after Queen Elizabeth's accession. His qualifications for state employment were unique. He had spent the years between 1555 and 1560 on the continent, during which time he had not only received his Ll. D. but had been interrogated and tortured by the Inquisition. By the time he returned to England he had acquired highly valuable firsthand knowledge of European conditions and Catholic attitudes. He had also once been tutor to the children of William Cecil's good friend, the firmly Protestant Duchess of Suffolk, and was on friendly terms with Robert Dudley, all of which meant that he had valuable friends at Court. The avenue to preferment was open, and a man who had prepared himself more thoroughly than most proceeded to

37. DNB, Smith, Sir Thomas (1513–1577); Mary Dewar, *Sir Thomas Smith* (London, 1964).

38. DNB, Walsingham, Sir Francis; Conyers Read, *Mr. Secretary Walsingham and the Policy of Queen Elizabeth*, 3 vols. (Oxford, 1925); APC, VIII, 169.

walk it. It was this appropriately experienced Wilson, an advocate in the court of Arches and a master of Requests, who was assigned to examine, employing the threat of torture if necessary, the associates of the Duke of Norfolk who were in the Tower in 1571 and 1572, suspected of being involved in treason; who was appointed to the commission instructed to provide for the better regulation of commerce in the latter year; who was sent on missions to Portugal in 1567 and the Netherlands in 1574 and 1576; and who was finally summoned to the council as a principal secretary on the death of the incumbent, Sir Thomas Smith, in 1577.[39]

The significance of the office of Lord High Admiral stems from the importance to an island of its navy. Her fighting ships and the sea were not simply England's first line of defense against attack from without, but also the only national armed force having any kind of continuous existence between emergencies. There was no permanent land force and so no permanent army chief. There was always, however, a navy of sorts with, always, a Lord Admiral at its head; the Lord Admiral throughout the first half of Elizabeth's reign was always Lord Clinton (later Earl of Lincoln) and the Lord Admiral was always on the council.

The royal entourage had lost some of the power it had wielded under Henry VII. Yet since the monarch was still the most important single person in the realm and her Court the focus of the ambition and national pride of so many of her subjects, the Household was still a crucial, although easily overlooked element in the Tudor system. The queen had to be provided with a suitable environment to live and work in and that environment then had to be exploited. Its provision and maintenance were the function of the Lord Steward and his under-officers, the treasurer and the comptroller of the Household; its exploitation was the responsibility of the Lord Chamberlain and his department. In practice, of these four, the comptroller and the Lord Chamberlain seem to have been the most important (since Elizabeth apparently left the posts of Lord Steward and treasurer of the Household vacant during the seventies and sixties respectively, prior to her appointment of Knollys as treasurer in 1570 and Lincoln as Lord Steward in 1581), and both the Lord Chamberlain and the comptroller of the Household were always councillors. The Lord Chamberlain was, successively, Lord Howard of Effingham and the Earl of Sussex. The comptroller was Sir James Croft.

Croft is perhaps the most baffling of the men who clustered closest around Queen Elizabeth. Suspicion of double-dealing attached to him from the beginning of his career to its end at his death in 1590. The King

---

39. DNB, Wilson, Thomas (1525?–1581).

of Spain's ambassador was firmly convinced that Croft was sufficiently his friend to be willing to betray English secrets of state; others suspected it. Yet Elizabeth herself apparently trusted him, and the explanation of why he was selected for membership of the council in the first place and of how he retained his seat in spite of such long-lasting calumny (if calumny it was) seems to lie primarily in the uniqueness of his relationship with her. They were not quite contemporaries—he was already sitting in parliament when she was only eight—but their personal association went back to their young adulthood, which had been a particularly trying time for both of them.

It was not that James Croft was the only friend of Elizabeth's younger days to sit, eventually, on her council. Sir Henry Sidney and the Earl of Warwick were actually much closer to her in age. Like her, they had been part of the group gathered around her brother, the young king Edward VI. Nonetheless, Elizabeth had been only fourteen when Edward acceded to the throne, whereas Sidney was eighteen and Warwick nineteen. She was separated from them by four and five then "long" years difference in age. Elizabeth was still a child, even if a precocious one, and a royal child at that; they were young men of the world, ahead of her in concerns and interests, behind her in rank. Such a situation is not exactly conducive to intimacy. When all were older, they could be expected to be, as indeed they appear to have been, linked by the ties of shared recollections; but they were hardly bound by having survived mutually feared and similarly apprehended dangers when much of the world must have seemed in league against them. James Croft and Elizabeth Tudor were. Both had lived through the faction-ridden days of the later years of Henry VIII and of the reign of the last male heir of the line without too much difficulty. Croft, indeed, had been sufficiently in favor to be appointed Edward VI's Lord Deputy in Ireland. But the fortunes of both plummetted from the moment of the accession of Mary to such a depth that they ultimately found themselves imprisoned concurrently in the Tower for their mutual adherence to the new religion and all it stood for, with absolutely no assurance that they would ever, either of them, get out.

It seems entirely credible that a permanent, trustful and lasting attachment should thereupon have sprung up between these two still young people suffering similar indignities in a common cause. At all events, Croft's lasting favor with Queen Elizabeth seems to date from their common experience of jail, and on the latter's accession it certainly brought him the governorship of Berwick and the wardenship of the Marches over against Scotland. The two did not always go together, and the wardenship may have been given him at the instigation of Ralph Sadler, who recommended him to Cecil—Croft was definitely a competent, if crusty individual—and thus helped launch a career seemingly set fair for the future. A dramatic interruption of Croft's upward progress, however, occurred in 1560, when he was abruptly dismissed for supposedly having been carrying on a treasonable correspondence with the Scots, and for six years his public fate hung in suspense. But whatever may have been the truth of the accusations against him, he was still "in fair esteem with all who knew him," including the queen, and in 1566 he was sworn a member of the council at the same time as he received his Household post.[40]

The comptroller of the Household oversaw the receipt of funds and their expenditure on the ceremonial, managed by the Lord Chamberlain, that custom prescribed and political insight dictated must hedge a king. The functions both thus filled were evidently so vital to the smooth operation of the monarchy that, along with the Lord Chancellor or Lord Keeper, the principal secretaries and the Lord Admiral, they were the only officials, throughout the reign of Elizabeth, who sat at the council board, along with the Lord Treasurer, *ex officio* rather than simply on account of their own particular virtues.

There were a number of other positions often held by Privy Councillors, but without this apparently unbreakable relationship between office and council membership. Elizabeth's first Lord Treasurer, Winchester, was old, and his successor, Burghley, constantly concerned with a much wider range of interests than the merely financial. In consequence, much of the prestige of the office of Lord Treasurer and many of the fiscal duties of its holder descended upon the shoulders of that once lowly official, the chancellor of the exchequer who, throughout the seventies, was Sir Walter Mildmay. Although a deeply religious man of strongly Calvinist inclination and an erudite and cultivated Cambridge product who had got his learning at Christ's College and his law at Gray's Inn, Mildmay was essentially an administrator and, above all, a financier trained in the school of the old Marquess. He began his official life as surveyor-general of the court of Augmentations (of which his father was then auditor) and subsequently held a series of similar posts. He concerned himself little at any stage of his career with "general politics," so the mid-century troubles, unsettling times for many of his colleagues, left him free to pursue his valuable administrative functions undisturbed. Elizabeth made him chancellor of the exchequer in 1559. He took the great step up to the council board in 1566.[41]

40. DNB, Croft, Sir James.
41. DNB, Mildmay, Sir Walter; Stanford E. Lehmberg, *Sir Walter Mildmay and Tudor Government* (Austin, 1964).

The vice-chamberlain of the Household was also usually to be found there, although his functions—which included making the logistical arrangements for the queen's progresses—hardly seem to have made such membership absolutely necessary. That the post was held successively by Elizabeth's capable cousin-in-law Francis Knollys and both favored and competent Christopher Hatton is probably sufficient explanation.

Knollys had become one of Elizabeth's "Boleyn relatives" by marrying Catherine Carey, the daughter of Mary Boleyn. He had carried out his first Court function in 1539, attending on Anne of Cleves when she arrived in England to marry Henry VIII. The following year he was made a gentleman pensioner. His fervent Protestantism patently did him no harm in Henry's eyes and was a positive recommendation while young King Edward lived. But on Edward's death, Knollys saw fit to leave the country and spent most of the five years of Mary's reign on the continent in Geneva and Strasbourg, returning to profit by the accession of his wife's first cousin to the throne. His worldly experience, his Protestantism and his family connection all presumably combined to suggest him to Elizabeth as one of the earliest appointees to her council.[42]

Hatton did not join him there for nearly twenty years. Educated at Oxford, where he took no degree, and a member of the Inner Temple, where he appears to have acquired only a modicum of jurisprudence, Hatton, like Leicester, to begin with owed his rise to his personal attractions. Once Hatton had caught the eye of the queen and been appointed to the band of gentlemen pensioners in 1564, the facts most profusely recorded about him relate to acquisitions of land and lucrative, though hardly time-consuming, office rather than to the accumulation of experience through the practice of a career of any sort. He was, however, a member of parliament in 1571 and 1572 and his membership provided him with a knowledge of parliamentary practice and personalities that was put to use to the great advantage of the Crown later on when he became one of the most effective and respected of the government spokesmen in the house of commons. He also became, eventually, a good Lord Chancellor, in spite of his earlier failure to complete his legal education, thereby proving, as Robert Kennedy did as attorney-general of those United States of which his brother was president, that he was capable as well as favored for non-professional reasons. Elizabeth simply did not like and, what was even more politically important, was not attracted by incompetent men. To be a personal favorite of hers, therefore, as Hatton certainly was, was not at all a *dis*qualification for advancement in the service of the state,

42. DNB, Knollys, Sir Francis.

but quite the opposite. Her earlier choice of councillors amply demonstrates this and the success of Hatton's career after his admission to their ranks in 1577 merely confirms it.[43]

Few other of those offices not carrying with them automatic membership of the council were as closely or consistently associated with it as the vice-chamberlainship in Hatton's and Knollys' day, although many other councillors held many other official positions. Shrewsbury was Earl Marshall, Leicester master of the horse, Hunsdon governor of Berwick and Ralph Sadler and Henry Sidney chancellor of the duchy of Lancaster and Lord Deputy of Ireland respectively.

Sadler's career can be viewed as a personal expression of the council's institutional history from Henry VIII's time onwards. Trained in the household of Thomas Cromwell, he succeeded his master as principal secretary, along with Thomas Wriothesley, in 1540, continued with apparent security in the royal service for the next seven years and was one of those intended by Henry VIII to govern in the name of his minor son. Yet Sadler disappeared from public view not long after the death of the old king and remained out of sight until the accession of Henry's younger daughter. He was a strong supporter of the Duke of Somerset and seems to have shared Somerset's official, though escaping his personal fate. Sadler was not an ambitious man, at this point or later; perhaps he felt no need to be, since, if rumor did not exaggerate, he was the richest commoner in England. He stayed quietly at home in the country during Mary's reign, which he was never loath to do whoever wore the Crown; even after his recall to public life by Elizabeth in 1558 it was only rarely that he actually put in an appearance at the council's deliberations, but he served long and effectively, as we shall see, in other ways.[44]

Sir Henry Sidney, having been close to Edward VI as a gentleman of the Privy Chamber, was implicated in Northumberland's vain efforts to prevent the succession of Mary Tudor. Yet as queen the latter trusted him so far as to send him with the Earl of Sussex to negotiate her intended marriage with the Prince of Spain who, as King of England, eventually stood godfather to Sir Henry's eldest son, King Philip's famous namesake. In 1556 Sidney asked to be allowed to go overseas again with Sussex, this time to Ireland, where he acted as deputy whenever Sussex saw fit to be absent from his post as, for example, he did when he went

---

43. DNB, Hatton, Sir Christopher (1540–1591); Nicholas Harris Nicolas, *Memoirs of the Life and Times of Sir Christopher Hatton, K. G.* (London, 1847); Eric St. John Brooks, *Sir Christopher Hatton* (London, 1946).

44. DNB, Sadler, Sadleir, or Sadleyer, Sir Ralph; Arthur J. Slavin, *Politics and Profit. A Study of Sir Ralph Sadler 1507–1547* (Cambridge, 1966).

back to England on Mary's death. Sidney remained in Ireland until 1559 and then, when Sussex was in Vienna on his diplomatic mission, the new queen made him Lord President of the Council in the Marches of Wales, which he remained until his death. (Sussex was furious because he claimed Elizabeth had promised the Welsh post to him; but he soon got the Lord Presidency of the north instead). The Welsh office was not a very exacting one and Sidney managed to spend much time at Court. He was temporarily banished at the instigation of Burghley in 1561 for being too openly enthusiastic about the possibility of a marriage between the queen and Lord Robert Dudley. His disgrace, however, was short-lived. He appears to have been a healthy and happy, hearty sort of man who usually got along with everyone, and in 1562 he was back in favor, being sent almost immediately thereafter to Scotland to exercise his talent for creating good feeling where good feeling was needed more than almost anything else. In 1565 he went to Ireland again, this time as his own master, although limited in his effectiveness by the parsimony of the queen and the tendency of the council to think it always knew better than the man on the spot what was to be done in any given situation. These two considerations actually resulted in Sir Francis Knollys being detailed shortly after Sidney's departure to investigate his proceedings and, although Knollys exonerated him absolutely from any accusations of malpractice or incompetence, the sniping from England never really ceased for long, and none of Sidney's spells of authority in Ireland (1565–1567, 1567–1571 and 1575–1578) came in for any of the appreciation they seem to have deserved. All this time he continued as Lord President of Wales as well and was promoted to the council in 1573.[45]

In addition to office-holding, one thing further that a great number of the councillors, both noble and otherwise, had in common was family relationship. Of the twenty-five men who advised her between 1568 and 1582, no fewer than eighteen were related to each other and to the queen (see table 1). Some of these ties of blood and links by marriage were close. Walter Mildmay and Francis Walsingham were brothers-in-law, as were Henry Sidney and the Earls of Warwick and Leicester. Leicester married Francis Knollys' daughter, as the Duke of Norfolk did the Earl of Arundel's, the Earl of Pembroke the Marquess of Northampton's and the Earl of Warwick the Earl of Bedford's. Howard of Effingham and Sussex were uncle and nephew. And, in addition to Hunsdon, the queen called three lords "cousin" meaning more than simply "peer of the realm": the Duke of Norfolk, with whom she shared a

45. DNB, Sidney, Sir Henry.

common great-grandfather, and Howard of Effingham and Sussex, her great-uncle and first cousin once removed respectively. Other connections were more distant, such as that between Elizabeth Tudor and Walter Mildmay. It is true that the link between these two was a notably tenuous one. Nonetheless the marriage of Leicester to Knollys' daughter and the union of Sir Henry Sidney's son Philip to secretary Walsingham's daughter Frances meant that both the queen and her chancellor of the exchequer appeared in the extremities of the Sidney family tree, and the only eight councillors it seems impossible to associate even this remotely with anyone else are Burghley and Bacon (themselves related through their marriages with sisters), Smith, Wilson, Hatton (who died unmarried), Bromley, Croft and Sadler. There was some sort of family connection, however slight, among all the others—that is, between almost three-quarters of the council and the queen. This made for a community feeling among those who governed England that had direct political consequences because it helped them work together in harmony.

The closest relationship, of course, will never prevent a falling out between incompatible people; the bitterest quarrels are, notoriously, family feuds. But kinship among the great, especially in an age of passionate interest in genealogy and deep-rooted consciousness of social distinction, could not in itself have had an adverse effect upon the association of men as convolutedly interconnected as the Earl of Bedford and the Marquess of Winchester or the Earl of Pembroke and the Earl of Leicester. If Pembroke himself could not sort out his own relationship to his more royally favored colleague, his wife probably knew only too well that it was through *her* sister, Catherine Parr, who had married Leicester's wife Lettice's grandmother Mary Boleyn's sibling Anne's widower, who was, of course, none other than Henry VIII; and Winchester's women could, if they felt so inclined, prove at least to their own satisfaction that *their* connection with the queen—through the old Marquess's second wife's first marriage with a Sackville who was a Boleyn on his mother's side— was closer than the Bedfords', who could establish a link with the queen's mother's family only by "going through" their Sidney and Dudley and Knollys relations on the way. Gossamer-light they may seem. Indeed, they often prove to be so for poor relations whose richer cousins see no profit to be reaped by even remembering they exist at all. Yet such spidery genealogical chains can bind like hoops of steel when there is advantage to be gained by exploiting them and where virtually all the other forces at work in a given social situation are centripetal rather than centrifugal. Such was the case at England's Elizabeth-centered later sixteenth century high place of royal government, the Court.

Table 1 Queen Elizabeth and Her Privy Councillors, 1568–1582
(Names of Councillors Appear in Capital Letters)

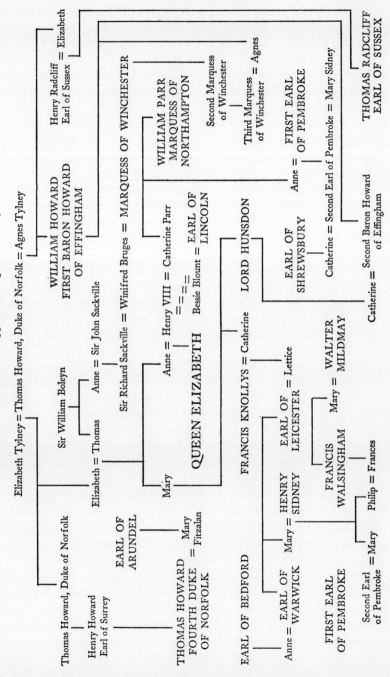

The Knollys-Carey-Boleyn circle is a notable example of this type of positive connection between family and politics. Their relationship with the queen did the surviving Suffolk sisters, Lady Catherine and Lady Mary Grey, the heirs to the throne according to the will of Henry VIII, no good whatever—rather the opposite; but Elizabeth was as personally attached to her relatives on her mother's side as she was contemptuous of those remaining on her father's. Henry Carey, Lord Hunsdon, her maternal first cousin, was the male nearest to her by blood on either side and his marriage with Hunsdon's sister, one of Elizabeth's closest women friends, had brought Francis Knollys almost as close. But neither owned his position on the council primarily to his royal relationship, even if they derived their peculiar intangibility from it. What is truly significant about their connection with Elizabeth is that it was of that degree which is sufficiently distant to avoid the obligations and sometimes embarrassing affections of closer kinship, yet near enough to conduce to a comfortable intimacy if the cousins in question happen to like each other and get along together. Cousinship is an association which can degenerate into unfamiliarity, even hostility, or ripen into friendship according to the temperaments and circumstances of the parties concerned. In these instances, kinship coincided with compatibility, and on the whole this was generally true of conciliar family relationships. Even closer affinities than those between Knollys and Hunsdon and the queen certainly seem to reflect, as they were to some extent the product of, harmonious feelings within a particular group. At all events, the ties of blood, friendship, marriage and religious sentiment joining the Earls of Warwick, Leicester and Bedford to Sir Henry Sidney, Sir Francis Walsingham and Sir Walter Mildmay, and to Knollys and Hunsdon as well, although perhaps less intimately, were as evident in their own time as they are now. And the Burghley-oriented Earl of Sussex' lack of sympathy with this puritan sept of the ruling clan is perhaps the exception that proves the rule. His wife Frances was Sir Henry's sister, yet Sussex' politics certainly tended to be more middle of the road than those of the Sidney set in general.

Complete harmony was hardly to be expected, even in so comparatively small a group. It would have been unnatural, hence unstable; and there was, of course, a variety of differences of opinion and taste among the inhabitants of this select circle, as Sussex' rather wary relationship with his wife's family suggests. Notwithstanding the settlement of 1559, religion, for one thing, was still to some extent a divisive force. The ambiguity of the thirty-nine articles—even though they were not enacted into law until 1571—added to Elizabeth's lack of interest in peering into the souls of her associates any more deeply than she cared to into those of her lesser subjects, contributed to this. A few, such as the Duke of

Norfolk and the Earl of Arundel hankered, or were suspected of hankering after the good old Catholic days.[46] Some, like Burghley, Sadler, Hatton, Croft, Sussex, Bacon and Hunsdon, hewed to the middle way, showing no more interest in polemical controversy than the queen herself. Others—Walsingham, Knollys, Bedford, Warwick, Mildmay, Sidney and, to a degree, Leicester—were more or less passionately Protestant, advocating outright English assistance to those whom they regarded as their co-religionists on the continent, and working—like Sir Walter Mildmay, who founded Emmanuel College, Cambridge, primarily to turn out their type of cleric—for the further purification of the Church of England at home. Such a variety of religious feeling was all bound to cause dispute, and did. On the one side were Burghley and the queen, refusing to be moved by "sentiment" to support causes they failed to see either as being any of England's business or capable of being turned to her national advantage; on the other, Walsingham and those of his ilk, bewailing the imminent end of everything for lack of adequate commitment to the defense of international Protestantism.[47] Sometimes the tension seemed unbearable. Religious disagreements were exacerbated by personal and political antagonisms. Burghley and Norfolk were at odds in mid-1569.[48] Burghley and Leicester sparred with each other in 1575.[49] Warwick and the Lord Admiral were on one side and Sussex on the other, with Sadler and Mildmay in the middle, trying to reconcile them in a quarrel arising out of the organization of the suppression of the northern rebellion in late 1569, early 1570.[50] Francis Knollys "motche offended my Lord Chamberlayne" and "others" in 1568.[51] Burghley was comparatively willing to placate the Queen of Scots whenever possible, while to Francis Walsingham and his supporters she never ceased to appear as the incarnation of evil.[52] Burghley and his adherents were inclined to think Francis Drake's

---

46. The Spanish ambassador at least hoped that Norfolk's third wife, Elizabeth (an avowed Catholic, who heard mass every day), might convert her husband to the old religion and Norfolk himself was fully conscious of "how ready my enemies be to count me papist," Williams, 127 and 131.

47. Conyers Read, "Walsingham and Burghley in Queen Elizabeth's Privy Council," *EHR*, XXVIII, January 1913, 34.

48. Edmund Lodge, *Illustrations of British History*, II (London, 1791), the Earl of Sussex to Burghley, May 15; BM, Cotton MS. Titus B. ii, f. 336, Burghley to the Earl of Sussex, May 27, 1569.

49. BM, Lansdowne MS. 21, f. 38, the Earl of Northumberland's account of the Earl of Leicester's speeches to him against Burghley, February 1575.

50. BM, Add. 33593, f. 27, Sadler to the queen, November 26, 1569; f. 92, Sadler to Cecil, January 1; f. 105, Sadler to Mildmay, January 9, 1570.

51. BM, Cotton MS. Caligula C. i, f. 236, December 3, 1568.

52. Read, "Walsingham and Burghley," 48.

Spanish plunder ought to be returned in the interests of a quiet international life; those who leaned towards Walsingham and Leicester's point of view were rather in favor of making much of the returned circumnavigator of the globe and disregarding the displeasure of the King of Spain.[53] Cecil warned the Earl of Huntingdon not to speak too freely of their friendship since this in itself would be likely to cause "some mislyking" in "others."[54] Conyers Read found signs of dissension between Walsingham and Burghley as early as 1576. And Mrs. F. M. G. Higham, in her useful book on the secretaries of state, talks of "a distinct split in the council" at large after 1578.[55] Like the rest of mankind, Elizabeth's ministers were lower than the angels.

Like other men, too, they differed in age. The Marquess of Winchester was already seventy-six when the Duke of Norfolk became his colleague at twenty-seven. The others came somewhere in between these two extremes (see table 2).[56]

The considerable gap between the ages of the oldest and youngest councillors can easily be overemphasized, however. Even a quick glance at Table 2 gives one the impression that the Elizabethan council was neither very old nor very young, nor both, but rather middle-aged to elderly, according to whether we look at the ages of its members from a twentieth or a sixteenth century point of view. Statistics derived from these figures bear the conclusion out, and these are especially revealing when seen in comparison with the age of the queen herself at the same chronological intervals (see table 3).

The queen, while young and inexperienced as when older and possibly wiser, manifestly wanted as councillors, not personal friends, her own contemporaries, but men who had advanced to an age of responsibility and had had time and opportunity to acquire a sense of historical perspective. That she simply did not appoint a man to her council until he had reached that period in his life when he could be expected to perform the functions expected of him in a sober and considered manner is made even plainer by the fact that about half the members of the council were appointed in their forties and more than three-quarters of them between the ages of thirty-six and fifty-seven. Even the favorite Leicester and the magnate Norfolk had to wait. As a result, they were all of a sufficient, yet (with

53. *Ibid.*, 44.

54. Huntington Library, Hastings MS. 1302, Burghley to the Earl of Huntingdon, October 28, 1569.

55. F. M. G. Higham, *The Principal Secretary of State: A Survey of the Office from 1558 to 1680* (London, 1923), 48.

56. These figures are all taken from the DNB, and the statistics on the next few pages are all derived from them.

Table 2
Ages of Elizabeth and Her Councillors, Eldest to Youngest,
in the Decades 1558 to 1578

	1558	1568	1578	On appointment or accession
Winchester	71	81	—	71
Pembroke	57	67	—	57
Sadler	51	61	71	51
Bacon	49	59	69	49
Howard of Effingham	48	58	—	48
Arundel	47	57	67	47
Lincoln	46	56	66	46
Smith			[65]	58
Northampton	45	55	—	45
Knollys	44	54	64	44
Burghley (Cecil)	38	48	58	38
Mildmay		48	58	46
Croft		48	58	46
Hunsdon			54	53
Wilson			54	53
Sussex			52	43
Bedford	31	41	51	31
Shrewsbury			50	43
Warwick			50	45
Sidney			49	46
Bromley			[48]	49
Walsingham			48	43
Leicester		35	45	30
THE QUEEN	25	35	45	25
Norfolk		32	—	27
Hatton			38	37

Table 3
Average and Median Ages of Queen and Council

Date	Average age of council	Median age of council	Queen's age
1558	49*	44*	25
1568	51*	51*	35
1578	55	55	45
On appointment or accession	42*	42*	25

*In calculating these figures the Marquess of Winchester was excluded because his age was so much greater than any other's. His inclusion, however, would increase the average and median ages of the council in 1558 to only 50 and 51 years, and in 1568 to 53 and 56, and would raise the average and median ages of councillors on appointment to 45 and 49.

the exception of Winchester) not too great an age to feel themselves "*of an age*" and for the actual ages of particular individuals to be a matter of little moment. Thus, as a group in this too they were similar, in spite of individual differences. They were almost ageless, and they aged together, with the queen.

Likewise, differences over public matters, whether arising from personal rivalries and animosities or out of policy disagreements and religion, should not be exaggerated. Even the crisis within the council in 1569, revealing as it is of discontents, can be viewed as testifying to the existence of a fundamental harmony that contributed greatly to overall institutional effectiveness. The story is complicated in detail, but its outlines seem clear enough. Norfolk and Arundel, increasingly resentful of what they regarded as Cecil's anti-Catholic attitudes, were plotting, with the intermittent connivance of Leicester, the principal secretary's ouster. Cecil, however, outmaneuvered them all. He dropped hints (particularly about Norfolk's ambitions to marry the Queen of Scots) to Elizabeth who sprang smartly to her chief adviser's defense. He placated the vacillating Leicester. He even "bought off" Norfolk himself, possibly by promising to use his influence as master of the court of Wards to ensure a favorable verdict on a case (that involving the lands of Norfolk's step-children) in the outcome of which the duke had a strong personal interest. Above all, "he was at special pains to secure the endorsement of the Privy Council to his actions," and did so very effectively, with what must surely have been gratifying results.[57] From 1569 on, Cecil's primacy in the counsels of Queen Elizabeth was not merely established—it had been that all along—but accepted. "Neither queen nor council could do without him."[58] They had never been able to; now, however, the fact of their dependence had been demontrated in such unmistakable fashion that it became an actual source of strength, rather than, as it had been earlier, a potential cause of weakness.

Membership of the same church should not be underestimated as a cohesive factor either. All the Privy Councillors, much as some of them wanted to change it, were communicants of the Church of England, acknowledging Elizabeth as its supreme governor. They attended its services, were married by its ministers, had their children baptized according to its rites and were buried with pomp and pageantry beneath often vulgarly pretentious monuments within its walls. Admittedly those who pray to-

---

57. Conyers Read, *Mr. Secretary Cecil and Queen Elizabeth* (London, 1962), 444. This interpretation of Cecil's role in the crisis of 1569 is essentially Read's, described in detail in chapter XXII.

58. Read, 454.

gether do not always stay together, but at least they speak each other's language and that rarely contributes actively to division.

A list of their various burial places both calls to mind the particular role of Queen Elizabeth's deceased advisers as living links between Court and individual "countries" and reflects the council's general character and history.

Some were interred, as one might expect, in the great national pantheons. Many more, equally typically, lie at home. A few, such as Dr. Wilson (who desired no monument and whose gravesite is consequently unknown) and the Duke of Norfolk (the notoriety of whose resting place still proclaims his treason) fill up odd corners of the earth.

All the councillors (here listed in alphabetical order according to family names) were buried in ground consecrated by the Church of England:

Bacon	Old St. Paul's
Hatton	Old St. Paul's
Pembroke	Old St. Paul's
Walsingham	Old St. Paul's
Lincoln	St. George's Chapel, Windsor
Bromley	Westminster Abbey
Hunsdon	Westminster Abbey
Croft	Westminster Abbey
Burghley	Stamford Baron
Warwick	The Beauchamp Chapel, Warwick
Leicester	The Beauchamp Chapel, Warwick
Arundel	The Collegiate Chapel, Arundel
Norfolk	The Chapel of the Tower of London
Howard of Effingham	Reigate
Knollys	Rotherfield Grays
Mildmay	St. Bartholomew the Great, Smithfield
Northampton	St. Mary's, Warwick
Winchester	Basing
Sussex	Boreham, Essex
Bedford	Chenies
Sadler	Standon
Sidney	Penshurst
Smith	Theydon Mount
Shrewsbury	Sheffield
Wilson	St. Catherine's Hospital

Personal disagreements were usually short-lived and there were no consistent political factions. In 1569 Antonio de Guaras reported that

Norfolk, Winchester, Pembroke, Arundel and Howard of Effingham—
the older generation, one might add—did "not agree in religion or other
things" with Northampton, Leicester, Bedford, Sussex, Lincoln, Cecil,
Bacon, Mildmay, Sadler and Knollys—the younger men, for the most
part—who "all oppose the others, especially on sectarian points."[59] This
puts Leicester, Sussex and Cecil all on the same side, something which
was definitely not always justifiable; but the fact that such a breakdown
—not quite the same as that assayed a few pages ago—could be made
at all nicely emphasizes how councillors could oppose each other on one
thing and be in concert about something else.

Then, too, their squabbles often sound rather petty. Knollys was
something of an old woman who could prissily, if not altogether convincingly protest he did "not envie favorr shewed to yll men" and
pompously pontificate on the happiness "of that realme where virtue is
honorred and vice is brydled."[60] Sussex was a chronic complainer. His
letters reflect a man who got some kind of definite satisfaction out of
feeling aggrieved, and Burghley repeatedly had to try and pour oil
on the waters he troubled by his resentments. Sussex on one occasion la-
mented loudly that he was "kept but for a brome, and when I have done
my office to be throwen owt of the dore. I ame the first nobel man hathe
ben thus used," which Burghley attempted to counter by asserting he
knew no one "endowed with better partes" than Sussex, whose "worthynes
only maketh me affectionated to hym."[61] The Burghley attitude is the
more significant—and the more widespread. The state papers are full of
letters gushing with good feeling. The Earl of Bedford continually and
convincingly evinced his and his wife's affection and friendship for
Burghley and Lady Burghley, and Walsingham was firmly bound to his
predecessor as secretary by enduring bonds of gratitude and professional
association. Sir Walter Mildmay was "ever as glad" of Sir Ralph Sadler's
well doing "as of myn owne."[62] "I can saye no more but that I owe my
selfe and all that I have unto your Lordship," Francis Walsingham wrote
to Burghley.[63] The Lord Admiral assured Mildmay, most fervently, that

59. CSP Spanish, II, no. 151, p. 204, Antonio de Guaras, probably to Alba's
secretary Albornoz, October 24, 1569.
60. BM, Cotton MS. Caligula C. i, f. 166, Knollys to Cecil, September 12,
1568.
61. Hatfield House, MS. 4, ff. 100–101, BM, M.485/1 (microfilm), the
Earl of Sussex to Cecil, January 23, 1570; BM, Add. MS. 33593, f. 70, Cecil
to Sadler, December 26, 1569.
62. BM, Lansdowne MS. 21, no. 19, Mildmay to Burghley, November 25,
1575.
63. BM, Cotton MS. Vespasian F. vi, f. 107, Walsingham to [Burghley],
July 13, 1572.

he would regard Mildmay's son, who accompanied him north with the commendations of the Earl of Leicester in 1569, as his own.[64] Mildmay spoke of himself as being "greatly beholding" to Burghley in 1576.[65] "I will love and honor you," Hatton promised the Lord Treasurer in his typically florid style, "as your virtue byndithe me"; and Sussex reminded him that "I have wrytten playnly, and I write playnly, and I will write playnly to you so as by my dealyngs with you you shall take no hurte nor I dyshonor."[66] The latter's feeling was amply reciprocated by Burghley. "I knowe no noble man in the erth," as he put it, "more to my harty contentation, and this I wryte even moved with the best vayne in my hart."[67] But this particular relationship has been recognized by almost everyone familiar with the period. What has not been so often noticed, but is in this context even more significant, is the evidence of friendship between the Earls of Sussex and Leicester. This was not confined to any particular period, but spread out over much of their association. "I most hartyly thank you for your gentle and friendly remembrances," wrote Leicester in 1560.[68] In 1568 he referred to "the frendshipp that ys now betwene your Lordship and me."[69] Even if the "now" implies an interruption of amity that no one would deny, the "ys" affirms its ultimate resumption if not continuance. In any event the rapprochement persisted. In 1577 Leicester did Sussex the good turn of warning him that although the queen had refused his invitation to visit him at Newhall because she felt that the notice he had received was too short for it to be fair for him to entertain her, "for my none opinion I beleave she wyll hunt and vysett your house," since her progress was scheduled to take her past his door.[70] In 1573 Leicester actually asked Burghley's assistance in furthering a suit to the queen on behalf of Sussex's wife.[71]

Even if all this looks somewhat one sided and supposing that these

64. PRO, SP.12/60, no. 9, Clinton to Mildmay, December 1, 1569.

65. BM, Lansdowne MS. 21, no. 51, Mildmay to Burghley, January 23, 1576.

66. BM, Lansdowne MS. 22, no. 82, Hatton to Burghley, April 26, 1576; Cotton MS. Caligula C. i, f. 324, the Earl of Sussex to [Burghley], September 11, 1569.

67. BM, Cotton MS. Titus B. ii, f. 233(2), Burghley to the Earl of Sussex, July 21, 1577.

68. BM, Cotton MS. Caligula B. ix, f. 132, the Earl of Leicester to the Earl of Sussex, July 11, 1560.

69. BM, Cotton MS. Titus B. ii, f. 328, the Earl of Leicester to the Earl of Sussex, January 21, 1568(?).

70. Ibid., f. 323, the Earl of Leicester to the Earl of Sussex, July 30, 1577.

71. BM, Harleian MS. 6991, f. 27, the Earl of Leicester to Burghley, February 12, 1573.

various protestations taken together do no more than indicate that Queen Elizabeth's Privy Councillors were at pains to keep up appearances, it is significant that the appearances they aimed at keeping up should have been those of friendship, unity and harmony. Clearly they felt it necessary to *seem* in agreement even if in fact they were not. In any case, it has been claimed that after 1585 "the feud in the council died a natural death in the face of the threat from Spain," and both the remark itself and the development it refers to show up the superficiality of the council's quarrels by providing a revealing glimpse into the profundity of its agreement.[72] The Privy Council was a small group of men who saw, almost lived with each other a great deal of the time. They were constantly— and understandably, in view of its capriciousness—jealous of royal favor shown to one, even if it were not at the expense of another. But this was only to be expected. There is no evidence that bouts of huffiness interfered with the smooth running of the machinery of state. And disagreement certainly never got so out of hand as to constitute a threat to national unity. Over a long period the various councillors got along together remarkably well, whether related or not, the ties of friendship and the obligations of loyalty binding where marriage ties did not link one man with another.

Altogether this strikes one as an extremely adult, unemotional, businesslike group of people, going about their common concerns without undue fuss and without making more scenes than were strictly necessary, yet letting their ill feeling show without restraint where it existed. This fundamentally cooperative attitude is perhaps emphasized, if anything, by a tendency to carp and whine on occasion when they felt badly done to. They were not people who hid their feelings, as is evident from the coolly formal nature of the close of a letter from Lord Hunsdon to Thomas Randolph, who had resorted to bad language in response to Hunsdon's failure to supply him with money he had been expecting.[73] But

---

72. Higham, 49. Robert Beale, in advising a would-be secretary against abetting possible feuds and encouraging the development of faction in the council, also bears witness to the prevailing lack of contention. Remember, he adjures with almost morbid, slightly regretful relish, how "debate betweene the D[uke] of Somersett and the E[arl] of Warwicke" enabled Queen Margaret, wife of Henry VI, to overthrow "her husbande, her sonne, her selfe and almost the whole realme." He hardly seems happy to have to confess—but confess he does—that "ther be no such stronge parties nowe." "A Treatise of the Office of a Councellor and Principall Secretarie to Her Majestie," printed in Conyers Read, *Mr. Secretary Walsingham and the Policy of Queen Elizabeth* (Oxford, 1925), I, 441.

73. BM, Lansdowne MS. 15, no. 3, Hunsdon to Thomas Randolph, March 26, 1572.

this was essentially harmless letting-off of steam. These twenty-five men held between them the most important offices in the state. They were firmly entrenched in positions of power in the social and political life of the country as a whole. They daily associated with each other in an atmosphere permeated by overlapping and interlocking ties of kinship, friendship, gratitude, affection, loyalty and self-interest. On the whole they ruled England with Queen Elizabeth in that climate of understanding which grew out of their having so many more things in common than there were jealousies and feuds dividing them. It is hardly any wonder that de Spes was able to report to the King of Spain in 1569 that when they really were all of one way of thinking "there is no one to oppose them in anything."[74]

---

74. CSP Spanish, II, no. 155, p. 207, de Spes to the King of Spain, November 8, 1569.

Chapter IV
THE PRESENTATION
OF ADVICE

UR partes," Cecil once remarked, "is to counsell."[1] "The q[ueen's] ma[jes]ty hath no suerty but as she hath been counselled."[2] The main purpose of the Privy Council, he was saying—as the very word councillor implies—was to give advice. Unfortunately this most fundamental of its functions is by far the most difficult to describe in detail. The advice given to the queen was usually verbal, and has, therefore, left little or no direct documentary evidence of having been given at all. Reports have come down to us that "the council is for ever sitting" and that some visiting dignitary has had several meetings with it, but information as to what was discussed and decided at these assemblies does not appear in the register for the simple reason that, when subjects of the greatest moment were under consideration, the clerk who otherwise kept the record was sent out of the room. The oath administered to each new member of the council itself prescribes such a procedure. "You shall keep secret," it adjures, "all matters committed and revealed as her majesty's councillor or that shall be treated of secretly in council."[3] There are no diaries of councillors or clerks, no notes exchanged at meetings, no detailed descriptions of who said what and when and in what tone of voice. Lack of certain kinds of evidence, however, does not mean that some concrete statements cannot be made about the way in which the Privy Council's advisory function was exercised under Elizabeth, for less obvious, but not less pertinent information than that which actual council meeting minutes would provide is relatively common. Councillors themselves, in letters about their ephemeral, everyday affairs, make unintentionally revealing comments on the abiding nature of their business; other people, in the course of dealing with specific issues, inadvertently attest to the existence of some generally accepted procedural conventions. From such unwitting testimony, several deductions can be made.

To begin with, it is clear that one of the most consistent aims of ad-

---

1. BM, Add. MS. 33593, f. 129, Cecil to Sadler, January 13, 1569.

2. BM, Cotton MS. Caligula C. iii, f. 386, Burghley to the Earl of Leicester, August 11, 1572.

3. Joseph R. Tanner, *Tudor Constitutional Documents* (Cambridge, England, 1930), 225.

viser and advised was the exclusion of outsiders from participating in the advisory process. The queen was entirely free to talk with anyone she chose about whatever she liked. In fact she rarely broached matters of state to those outside the circle of those actually sworn to advise her. When she did, it was regarded as a breach of custom. A minor storm that blew up over certain conversations she had been observed having with Thomas Heneage in 1570 attests to this. Heneage, as a result of these noticed colloquies, was accused of discussing with the queen things which were no business of his. The accusation stung him to inform Sir William Cecil that "myne owne consyens can not accuse me, that I ever gave her majesty advyse in a corner agaynst the determynacion of her cowncell, or ever opened my mowthe to her highnes in matter concernynge the publick estate or government, except yt pleased her to aske myne opinyon."[4] It is not so much Heneage's defense (his claiming, in effect, that there was no case for him to answer) that is significant, as the fact that the queen's apparently consulting him should have caused resentment among the sworn members of her council. Elizabeth had done something she ought not to have done just as surely as she herself had created the political climate in which such behavior on her part was unacceptable.

There were exceptions to this unwritten convention that the sovereign should discuss "matters concerning the public estate or government" only with her councillors. Special circumstances called for extraordinary conferences with people having expert knowledge or experience. The Earl of Sussex was consulted on important subjects and was even quarrelling with the Earl of Leicester at the council table long before he sat there in an official capacity.[5] During the crisis over Mary Queen of Scots in 1568, the council itself recommended that "consyderyng the weightenes" of the matter, the queen, as kings of England had always done, should summon "other erles . . . to heare and gyve ther advise," the term "erles" apparently including not only the actual earls of Northumberland, Westmoreland, and Huntingdon, but the Archbishop of Canterbury and the Bishop of London as well.[6] In such cases no resentment showed itself. Sussex was a great nobleman and Elizabeth's own kin; the council could hardly object to her doing what it had suggested. Heneage probably got into

4. Hatfield House, MS. 157, f. 55, Thomas Heneage to Cecil, as quoted in Samuel Haynes, *Collection of State Papers . . . left by William Cecil, Lord Burghley* (London, 1740), 602.

5. DNB, Radcliffe, Thomas, 583, column 2; Elizabeth Jenkins, *Elizabeth and Leicester* (New York, 1962), 119–120.

6. Hatfield House, MS. 155, f. 128, minutes of a council meeting, October 30, 1568.

trouble for personal reasons. He was a mere gentleman and, to make matters worse, had incurred Leicester's jealousy five years previously when he had been involved in a brief episode of romance with the spinster queen.[7] Either way—accepted or objected to—none of these exceptions to it disprove the rule that the queen should normally consult only with her official advisers. Indeed, they help confirm it. Sussex and Heneage were eventually made Privy Councillors themselves.[8] And in explicitly recommending the queen to seek advice elsewhere the council was implicitly enunciating the principle that with*out* its suggestion it would be improper for her to do so. As a rule, she did nothing of the sort. Elizabeth was frequently and openly accused of irresponsiblity in disregarding counsel given her; she was not often, even covertly, charged with seeking it in inappropriate places.

If the queen did not usually look beyond a chosen few for guidance in affairs of state, those prominent at Court who were not members of the council did not presume to offer it, at least directly, either. Busybodies and do-gooders too far beyond the royal pale to know the rules proffered gratuitous solutions to the problems of the day, but even the privileged Hunsdon recognized, prior to his being actually sworn a member of the council, that it was not his province as a mere royal official to offer opinions on policy to his sovereign.[9] Although in practice he traded on his position as a member of her family and *did* express them now and then, he was perfectly aware of his impropriety in doing so, and therefore made the gesture of attempting to disguise his presumption behind a facade of protestations of innocence. This charmingly naive habit, which presumably deceived no one, can most vividly be seen in a letter he wrote, apparently to Burghley, two years before he became a councillor in 1577. Promising he would "not omytt to let ye understand what I knowe" of northern matters, he went on to discuss the affairs of the Scottish regent and cite precedents for the taking of drastic action against the Scots in the border areas. In pointedly reminding his correspondent that local tradition demanded "a quyke man for a ded," he was patently anticipating that his pleas for permission to seek revenge would be passed on to a higher authority. Yet he felt it necessary to deny such an intent and avow that he did not "wryght thys as presumynge too gyve hyr ma[jes]tie any advyse heryn."[10] He knew the rules. He got around them—being, indeed, re-

---

7. Neville Williams, *Elizabeth Queen of England* (London, 1967), 130.
8. DNB, Heneage.
9. BM, Add. MS 48063, p. 189, "a councell geaven."
10. BM, Cotton MS. Caligula C. v, f. 37, Hunsdon to Burghley, August 24, 1575.

garded as "at least no worse than a councillor" for years before he actually was one—but in doing so acknowledged they existed. The circle of advisers girdling the queen was a closed one. Hunsdon's very breaching of it proves the point.

This closed circle, however, constantly expanded and contracted. There were few occasions when all members of the council could be found at Court and, like her grandfather, the queen turned for advice to those who happened to be there. This practice was regarded as perfectly normal and acceptable. Francis Knollys, writing to Elizabeth in 1569 from Bolton about the European implications of his assignment to guard the Queen of Scots, almost apologized for expressing his opinion. The conduct of foreign affairs, he recognized, "appertaynethe speciallie to your cownsell resident," the members of which were in the best position to see the situation overall and in its most up-to-date form.[11] Some months earlier, confessing himself, in view of his distance from the center of affairs, "a blynde bussard," the same Knollys had indicated in a letter to Cecil that he was content to "leave these matters to youe that have judgeme[nt]" and Sir Ralph Sadler, writing in like vein to Cecil, from the north in 1569, "doubt[ed] not all thinges to be well considered."[12]

None of this means that an absent councillor was obliged to keep silent. Sometimes, indeed, comments by the distant are less sanguine and give the impression the writer feels that his being away from Court means his advice is being unwisely ignored. In such instances he usually proffers it anyway. His oath, like the speech made to Cecil by the queen in the Great Hall at Hatfield at the beginning of the reign, called upon him to "give true, plain, and faithful counsel at all times," and this was easy enough to interpret as imposing a duty "to speake my conscience frelie" even when far away from Majesty.[13]

When a councillor was away from Court this duty could be performed in several ways. He could communicate, as Knollys occasionally did in 1568, directly with the queen, though this was comparatively unusual. "This is the 13th letter I have wrytten synce my comyng hether," wrote Knollys to Cecil from Bolton, "whereoff 2 unto hyr hyghnes, 1 to my lords of the cownsayel and 10 to you [have been] directed."[14] But it was done when the matter was felt to be important enough. One of Knollys'

11. PRO, SP.12/49, no. 28, Knollys to the queen, January 17, 1569.
12. BM, Cotton MS. Caligula C. i, f. 93, Knollys to Cecil, June 13, 1568; BM, Add. MS 33593, f. 107, Sadler to Cecil, January 9, 1569.
13. Tanner, 225; PRO, SP.12/49, no. 28, Knollys to the queen, January 17, 1569.
14. BM, Cotton MS. Caligula B. ix, f. 291, Knollys to Cecil, June 15, 1568.

later letters to the queen, for example, was written not only to urge her to accept her council's advice, which he felt she had been neglecting of late, but to impress upon her the importance of her holding her councillors to it if and when they showed signs of eventually backing away. Even coming from him, he knew that such outspokenness might be regarded as presumptuous, and he therefore felt obliged to defend it "because it is private and procedethe of good will."[15] Sir Nicholas Bacon, in 1577, committed his opinions to paper, not because he was away from Court on official business like Knollys, but because he was too sick to speak his mind in person as he had done frequently in the past.[16] "I had before this tyme signifyed to some of my lordes what I have thought in your matters of estate. Yet seing nowe the daunger increasing, I could not satisfye myne owne hart without an advertisement to your self."[17] Sir Francis Walsingham addressed Elizabeth directly because he wished to make his point with particular force. "For the love of God . . . Madame," he wrote her in 1575, "let not the mischiefs, that maye breake into this realme throughe that dangerouse gappe, teach your majestie over late to value the Scottishe amitie."[18] None of these communications, however, gives any indication whatsoever of urging anything on the queen which the writer knew the rest of the council would disapprove of: indeed they were all aiming at persuading her to follow courses already recommended to her by her "cownsell resident."

An absent councillor could write to the council itself. The Marquess of Winchester did in 1569, enclosing a letter from one Thomas Wentworth of Yorkshire and suggesting the council write its opinion to the President of the Council of the North on the strength of it, and the Earl of Lincoln was "so bowlde to saye my opinion to your L[ordship], I thynke my beinge here [in the north] ys but charge to her highnes" at the time of the great rebellion.[19] But this happened relatively rarely. The matter in question had to be brought up at a meeting by an individual, and therefore the sensible thing was to write to a specific person in the first place. Any

---

15. PRO, SP.12/49, no. 28, Knollys to the queen, January 17, 1569.

16. BM, Add. MS. 48065, f. 13v, Hertfordshire Record Office, Gorhambury MS. XII. B. 2, Bacon's speech in council at the end of the Michaelmas Term, 1562.

17. BM, Harleian MS. 286, f. 31, PRO, SP.12/115, no. 24, Huntington Library, Ellesmere MSS. 1183 and 1188, Northamptonshire Record Office, F (M) P. 209, Bacon to the queen, September 15, 1577.

18. PRO, SP.12/103, no. 28, Walsingham to the queen, April 12, 1575.

19. PRO, SP.12/60, no. 16, the Marquess of Winchester to the council, December 3, 1569; PRO, SP.12/66, no. 3, Clinton to the council, January 2, 1570.

councillor could write to any other for this purpose, as Walsingham did Sussex from France in 1581 to ask for help with his current mission to the French Court.[20] But the person most often addressed by the man away from Court who wished to make his feelings known to queen and council, was the secretary. Even the Lord Treasurer himself, having heard that the Archbishop of Canterbury was dying, did not disdain to request his inferior colleague "to take my proxy, for my poore voyce for the Archb[ishop] of York" to succeed him, and further examples are legion, for the secretary was the one person who almost always attended council meetings, the official most closely and continuously in contact with the sovereign herself.[21] It was to Cecil in his capacity as secretary that Knollys wrote in 1568 to advise against moving the Queen of Scots to Nottingham or Fotheringay, in case she form there in the center of the country a nucleus for papistical sedition, yet "hoolly subject[ing] this sodayne scruple of myne unto the grave consideration of my Lords of the Cownsay[le]."[22] It was to Cecil that Sadler expressed his fears for the queen's security and his anxiety that she should take steps to provide for it in 1572.[23] And it was with Cecil too, that Sir Walter Mildmay communicated to suggest that the queen retain the possession of a valuable lordship which had come into her hands with two years rent due from it.[24] The secretary thus formed the focal point on which advice from councillors not at Court converged. Standing at the point of contact between the queen and her resident council, the secretary was, partly as a result of his position, of all the councillors the one who could best give his own advice to both. He continually did so. The State Papers are full of Cecil's "treatises" and "considerations" on the problems and dangers of the time, drawn up both for his own edification and to guide him in presenting his advice to the queen and to her councillors.[25] This duality of the secretary's role is best expressed in the heading of one paper in particular: "A note of reasons remembered in counsell to move the queen's

---

20. BM, Cotton MS. Titus B. ii, f. 231, Walsingham to the Earl of Sussex, August 5, 1581.

21. PRO, SP.12/103, no. 48, Burghley to Walsingham, May 5, 1575.

22. BM, Cotton MS. Caligula C. i, f. 85, Knollys to Cecil, June 2, 1568.

23. Hatfield House, MS. 157, f. 106, Sadler to Burghley, February 28, 1572, as quoted in William Murdin, *A Collection of State Papers relating to Affairs in the Reign of Queen Elizabeth* (London, 1759), 175.

24. PRO, SP.12/83, no. 19, Mildmay to Burghley, November 26, 1571.

25. PRO, SP.12/51, no. 6, a treatise on the dangers of the time, in a clerkly hand, but much amended in Cecil's own, June 7, 1569 and PRO, SP.12/80, no. 17, "a short consideration of a long matter," entirely in his hand, August 6, 1571, are good examples.

majesty not to restore the Queen of Scottes."[26] The council was to be reminded that it had business to discuss *prior* to the ultimate involvement in it of the queen, both parts of the procedure being very much the secretary's concern.

If not all absent councillors insisted on expressing their opinions from a distance, not all those at Court, to whom they temporarily conceded their rights to be consulted, were actually conferred with about every matter on which the queen or her secretary felt she needed advice. Walsingham is unequivocal on this point. Writing to her in January 1575, he sent her letters from the Scottish Regent containing "matters of good consequences that touche your majestie's state and government and are to be used with secreacie, . . . to thend after the perusinge therof you maye make choyce of such of your cowncell as you shall thincke fitte to have the consideracion therof committed unto." Such confinement of certain consultations to certain councillors, even when others were available, was, on the whole, accepted without demur by those left out. It apparently seemed natural enough that those closest to the queen and working hardest at the day-to-day business of government should take it upon themselves occasionally to speak for all. In 1569 Cecil wrote Elizabeth concerning a possible marriage between the Queen of Scots and the Duke of Norfolk, "many causes mov[ing] . . . me at this tyme rather this short w[ay] to delyver my mynd to your gracious majesty than by oppen speche before your counsell."[27] He did this kind of thing regularly.

Even so, for Elizabeth to listen, or to seem to listen, too exclusively to a single councillor could cause him trouble, and Cecil was unwise in letting his personal influence with the queen appear too blatantly. In July 1570 he was compelled to extricate himself from a dangerous situation with respect to the rest of the council not only by denying that he had been persuading Elizabeth to keep the Duke of Norfolk in the Tower, but by asserting, along with Leicester, he had actually been advising her to release him.[28] It was a valuable lesson. Schooled by the queen herself in what she expected of them, her councillors in general bcame justifiably jealous at attempts of particular individuals to arrogate to themselves the function of giving advice that pertained to all of them as a group. And it was as a

---

26. BM, Cotton MS. Caligula C. ii, f. 71, a note in Cecil's hand, February 19, 1571.

27. BM, Cotton MS. Caligula C. i, f. 334, Cecil's advice to the queen, October 6, 1569.

28. BM, Cotton MS. Caligula C. ii, f. 25, a signed, holograph statement by Cecil, July 12, 1570.

group that their advice was sought on matters of the gravest importance to the state.

On the most special occasions, indeed, not only did the queen turn to the council resident for advice, she sent for those members who were away from the Court to appear and speak their minds as well.[29] During the period from 1568 to 1575, the unexpected and unwelcome appearance of the Queen of Scots in the north of England appears to have been the only one of sufficient importance for the "Duke of Norfolk and the Earls of Arundel and Leicester . . . to be summoned, so that a full council might decide what was to be done."[30]

But lesser crises were more frequent and also called for guidance from the absent. News having arrived at three o'clock in the morning of Tuesday, February 4, 1578 of a military disaster suffered by the Dutch, the queen sent Walsingham to London, where he was to assemble as many of the council as he could find at the Lord Keeper's house the following morning. Before the meeting could take place, however, there came further orders for them all to remove to the Court.[31] Such summonses normally went to relatively nearby councillors by messenger from the Lord Chamberlain; those farther afield were brought in to more important conclaves by a letter from the queen herself.[32] The queen sometimes sat in conference with her council on such occasions, and took part in its discussions.[33] This, however, was a rare occurrence. The result was the same whether Elizabeth had been actively engaged in its preparation or not: a point-by-point recitation of the answers to be made or things to be

---

29. Edmund Lodge, *Illustrations of British History* (London, 1791), II, 73, Burghley to the Earl of Shrewsbury, September 7, 1572.

30. CSP Spanish, II, no. 26, p. 35, da Silva to the King of Spain, May 22, 1568.

31. CSP Foreign, 1577–1578, Elizabeth I, volume 12, p. 487, no. 625, wrongly dated February 3 instead of February 4, 1578.

32. Nicholas H. Nicolas, *Memoirs of the Life and Times of Sir Christopher Hatton* (London, 1847), 97; Hatfield House, MS. 155, f. 131, drafts of the queen's letters to the Duke of Norfolk and the Earl of Sussex, in Cecil's hand, no date, and Haynes, 488, the queen to the Duke of Norfolk, November 3, 1568, 488, the queen to the Earl of Sussex, November 3, 1568 and 529, the queen to the Earl of Arundel, September 25, 1569.

33. BM, Cotton MS. Caligula C. iii, f. 199, "the opinion and advise of the queen's majestie conceav[ed] by many conferences had with hir counsell upon . . . the affairs of Scotland," January 22, 1572; BM, Cotton MS. Caligula C. ii, f. 50, description of proceedings in council, April 29, 1570; Huntingdon Library, Hastings MS. 1302, Cecil to the Earl of Huntington, October 28, 1569; PRO, SP.12/73, no. 7, the queen to Clinton, August 1, 1570.

done by her, or in her name, in response to the developments that had provoked the consultation in the first place.

This advice was arrived at after each member of the council had had
his chance to voice his opinion, and then was delivered to the queen
either formally in writing or informally by word of mouth.[34] Which way
was chosen depended on the nature of the subject that had been under
discussion. In 1568, the advice that the Queen of Scots be moved to
Tutbury and her affairs investigated, arrived at in a meeting attended by
twelve out of a current total of fifteen councillors (only Knollys, Croft
and the aged Winchester being away), was embodied in a written document.[35] This decision was relatively uncontroversial and comparatively
easy to arrive at. Its formal nature was probably owing to the desirability
of having something impressive to show to the Queen of Scots in order
to persuade her to agree more easily to the change of residence proposed
for her. The council, however, was less united on the issue of Elizabeth's
proposed marriage to the brother of the king of France.[36] It was a very
different kind of problem from that of dealing with Mary Stuart, and
involved not just a couple of major decisions, but the endless series of small
ones that went to make up a diplomatic negotiation. It is not surprising,
therefore, that no documents have survived attesting to the council's advice to the queen as to whether she should marry or not. There was no
necessity for such a formal statement, as there was in the case of moving
the Scottish queen, and such a thing would in any case have interfered
with the freedom of the negotiators to maneuver. It probably never
existed. The council was certainly consulted, certainly gave its advice continually but, as in the case of most of the subjects it discussed, without
leaving any direct evidence of what it recommended should be done.[37]

Though no detailed records of the discussion of issues at council meetings have survived, there is no shortage of evidence that individual councillors consulted each other about official matters in the course of trying
to decide what should be done. In 1575 the queen assigned Francis Walsingham, the attorney-general and the chancellor of the exchequer to
look into rumors of a plot, the dangers of which she seemed to take much
more lightly than her principal secretary. Walsingham, it turned out, was

---

34. BM, Cotton MS. Caligula C. i, f. 103, report of a council meeting, June
20, 1568.
35. *Ibid.*
36. CSP Spanish, II, no. 233, p. 291, de Spes to the King of Spain, January
22, 1571.
37. BM, Cotton MS. Caligula E. vi, f. 173, the queen to Edward Horsey,
special messenger to the French king, June 1573.

both worried and at a loss to know what to do once his and his colleagues' investigations had led to the extortion of confessions and the naming of names. Either his view of the affair or Elizabeth's might be the right one. He therefore wrote ("as one that takethe no delyght in others' troble, but [nonetheless feeling that] . . . the troble of a fewe may avoyde a general troble") to the Earl of Sussex for his help.[38] One suspects what he really wanted was confirmation of his own opinion that proceedings against a small number of people would preclude a larger tragedy, but however Sussex replied, the end result would be a recommendation tendered to the Crown by those of whom it had been originally requested only after at least one of them had sought his own advice elsewhere. Although Walsingham was insistent that Sussex should be discreet, such sub-consultation appears to have been frequent and too unexceptionable to incite critical comment—as long as it was kept "within the family."[39]

Whatever form advice took, and however it had been arrived at, the queen was as free to accept or reject it as she had been to ask for it in the first place. She did reject it, or at least did not follow it exactly, on many occasions and on a variety of matters, ranging from the highly significant to the relatively trivial. She refused for seventeen years to follow the council's advice to execute the Queen of Scots. And she was notoriously sensitive to interference by council or councillors with anything she regarded as coming within the sphere of her prerogative. Burghley was fully conscious of this, confiding to Sussex that "my doynges have been interpreted as deminutions of hir ma[jes]tie's prerogatyve, which your L[ordship] knoweth, is so gratefull to princes to mayntean, as in no thyng more may a princess displesure be attayned."[40] Francis Knollys, from his privileged position as the husband of the queen's first cousin, had no hesitation in expressing his feeling that when she thus insisted on going her own way against advice, she was being ill served "by sotche affections and passions of your mynde as happen to have domynyon over youe. So yet the resolutions digested by the diliberate consultations of your most faythfull cownsayllors oughte ever to be had in moste pryce."[41] But even Knollys would probably have admitted, when not indulging in his favorite habit of lecturing all who would listen to him, that Elizabeth in

38. BM, Cotton MS. Titus B. ii, f. 361, Walsingham to the Earl of Sussex (?), March 11, 1575.

39. BM, Harleian MS. 6991, f. 64, Walsingham to the Earl of Sussex, March 11, 1575.

40. BM, Cotton MS. Titus B. ii, f. 233, Burghley to the Earl of Sussex, September 27, 1575.

41. Haynes, 498–499, Knollys to the queen, January 1, 1569.

fact usually did heed the advice of her Privy Council. The evidence is heavily in favor of such a view, from the reports of the Spanish Ambassador to the formal, though not therefore meaningless phraseology of Elizabethan public pronouncements. In 1569, de Spes reported to the Duke of Alba that the queen was in complete accord with her council.[42] The following year his successor in London, da Silva, told Philip II that though she herself was often "full of good resolutions, they soon disappear, thanks to the crew she has around her."[43] And virtually every proclamation issued between 1558 and 1603 contains the words "by the advice of our most honourable privy council." It is clear that as a rule Elizabeth was used to accepting and helping to implement her council's advice, and that the occasions when she went against it were so relatively rare as to be noteworthy for that very reason. The Privy Council effectively monopolized the advisory function during the whole of Elizabeth's reign—as it had failed to under Mary—by jealous guardianship of a privileged position, even if it was able to do so in the last resort only because the queen herself wanted things that way.

What Elizabeth wanted was the best advice she could get. Suggestions from individuals were by no means excluded. She put the matter perfectly plainly to Sir William Cecil when she appointed him principal secretary at her first council meeting in the Great Hall at Hatfield. "This judgement I have of you," she said, "that without respect of my private will you will give me that counsel which you think best, and if you shall know anything necessary to be declared to me of secrecy, you shall show it to myself only. And assure yourself that I will not fail to keep taciturnity therein."[44] But this was in a sense merely saying that any one of her councillors was to feel free to put in a minority report whenever he felt sufficiently strongly that the recommendation of the council as a whole was wrong. What Elizabeth wanted above all was group advice, reached after careful scrutiny of all the sides of a problem from the varied viewpoints that a single individual could not command.

In 1566, for example, the Queen of Scots was considering marrying her cousin Lord Darnley, not only a subject of the English queen, but a person having almost as sound a claim to the English throne as had Mary Stuart herself. She, therefore, before being carried away completely by her feelings towards her intended groom, thought it tactful to obtain her

---

42. CSP Spanish, II, no. 160, p. 213, de Spes to the Duke of Alba, December 1, 1569.

43. *Ibid.*, no. 5, p. 4, da Silva to the King of Spain, February 2, 1568.

44. Conyers Read, *Mr. Secretary Cecil and Queen Elizabeth* (New York, 1955), 119.

fellow sovereign's reaction to the scheme. So she wrote a letter, queen to queen. Elizabeth, however

> thought it convenient to communicat this message to hir Privy Counsell and to understand their advises in the same. And to this intent the counsellors whose names be underwritten, were made privye to the message above mentioned. . . . And after sundry conferences, long deliberations, and many arguments amongst themselves, they all with one assent and judgment thought this mariadg . . . to be unmete . . . . The said counsellors . . . did for their partes according to their bounden duties, humbly offer to hir majesty, that whatsoever shuld seme mete to hir majesty . . . the same shuld be allowed with their advises, and furdered with their services.[45]

This passage describes exactly what Queen Elizabeth wanted from her council. She did not aspire to emulate Philip II of Spain, who deliberately chose as his councillors men of such divergent personalities and predilections that they could never agree among themselves, but would regularly propose two or more different courses of action that they felt to be open, leaving the choice between them to the king.[46]

The Queen of England, on the contrary, required to be told in straightforward language what she should do. This meant she had only one decision to make—whether to do it or not—not two, like her former brother-in-law, who had to make up his mind which of his council's various pieces of advice was the right one, then decide whether to implement it, ultimately thereby taking responsibility for the whole process upon himself. Elizabeth demanded an advisory body that would, as a general rule, meet outside her presence and without a formally designated presiding officer usurping her designedly empty place, but be kept from becoming a mere discussion session by the presence of her own personal right-hand man, the agenda-producing principal secretary. She insisted on this assembly making decisions cleanly, at the same time not only accepting responsibility for *them*, but also for any decisions of *hers* she later regretted having made in the first place. In total, she expected a great deal from her Privy Council in its advisory capacity; by careful initial selection of its members and through the constant maintenance of firm, yet reasonable control over its proceedings, that which she expected of it was precisely what she got.

---

45. BM, Harleian MS. 6990, no. 32, f. 68, "a determination of the Pryvy Counsell," May 1, 1565.

46. Garrett Mattingly, *The Armada* (Boston, 1959), 70–71.

Part II
The Executive Function:
Positive Aspects

Chapter V

THE COUNCILLORS
AS EXECUTIVES

 N addition to wanting theoretical advice from a council, Elizabeth required the practical assistance of a governing body to help her actually discharge the extraordinary responsibilities and take care of the everyday chores involved in running her realm of England.

When the occasion was extraordinary enough, Privy Councillors themselves became executives. There were jobs, indeed, that only someone as highly placed as a Privy Councillor could do. One was to act as the guardian of a queen, and it has already been pointed out that the Earl of Shrewsbury's membership of the council was primarily the consequence of his becoming the permanent jailer of Mary Stuart. But even before Shrewsbury took over, from the moment of her flight into England a councillor had been detailed to keep her under his close and personal surveillance. This was Sir Francis Knollys, sent to meet her at Carlisle in 1568. Knollys was an excellent choice for at least two reasons. He was a particularly devout Protestant, for one. It could therefore be taken for granted he would not fall for Mary's notorious, but Catholic charm, and it could at least be imagined he might manage to incline her to what he regarded as the true religion. The assumption was amply justified by his almost amusingly strait-laced conduct towards her and even the hope momentarily seemed not entirely unrealistic. It was nearly two and a half months before he could find a single sympathetic word to say about the woman he consistently referred to as "this queen," and his first kind comment came just over a week after he had reported she was showing signs of becoming converted to Church of England views.[1] Knollys was touched by this, though he remained sensibly skeptical as to her sincerity, as his second personal qualification for the job, his kinship with his own queen, would lead one to expect. While never less than perfectly civil and respectful to the Queen of Scots, his kinship with Elizabeth nonetheless enabled him to treat her on a basis, if not of equality, at least on one of some familiarity from the beginning, when he "fell to comfortyng . . . hyr with a declaration of your hyghnes great affection." He regarded

---

1. BM, Cotton MS. Caligula C. i, f. 134, Knollys to Cecil, July 28; Caligula B. ix, f. 294, Knollys to [the Earl of Leicester], August 6, 1568.

himself primarily as Elizabeth's personal agent, and went on in the same letter to comment that although he thought Cecil should be informed on the progress of his task, "how farr otherwayes [it should] . . . be imparted I referr to your hyghnes pleasure."[2]

The fact that he was kin to the queen and one of her Privy Councillors as well put him in a position which he exploited to the full. The reason he had had to fall to comforting the Queen of Scots at all was that he felt free to speak his mind in the first place. In response to what he called her "railings" against her deposition, he had calmly informed her that, contrary to her own assertions, such action could indeed sometimes be justified, in cases, for example, of lunacy or murder.[3] But this was only a beginning, and he was soon in need of all the authority he could muster when it came to moving her from Carlisle to a site less dangerously close to the Scottish border. Mary at first flatly refused to budge an inch without specific written instructions from Elizabeth personally to herself.[4] Even after their arrival, and in full cognizance of the council's wholehearted support of Elizabeth's decision, she continued to decline to move of her own free will. Knollys, therefore, supported by his associate, Lord Scrope, had to act on his own initiative. "Synce we see hyr styffe and obstinate to remove hence otherwyse than compelled therto," he decided to threaten ". . . to barr hyr from all intelligences owte of Skotland."[5] Even the unsympathetic Knollys was impressed almost to admiration by the result of his own firm action, and reported to Cecil that "after she dyd see that nether hyr stowte thretenyngs, nor hyr exclamations, nor hyr lamentations cowlde disswade us . . . then lyke a very wyse woman" she went about making certain that in return for agreeing to go, her lines of communication with Scotland should after all be permitted to remain open.[6]

On one occasion in particular, Knollys acted with notable flexibility. A proclamation had been issued by Elizabeth that virtually recognized the Earl of Murray as the legitimate ruler of Scotland, and Knollys was instructed to convey its contents to his prisoner. He at once realized not only what an outburst it was likely to provoke, but also the effect it might have on Mary's willingness to cooperate. They were still at this time at Carlisle, and the council was soon showing its displeasure at the length of time it was taking him to persuade her to agree to move to Bolton. Knollys therefore took it upon himself to substitute for the word Regent, which

2. BM, Cotton MS. Caligula C. i, f. 82, Knollys to the queen, May 30, 1568.
3. *Ibid.*
4. BM, Cotton MS. Caligula B. ix, f. 281, Knollys to Cecil, June 27, 1568.
5. BM, Cotton MS. Caligula C. i, f. 117, Knollys to Cecil, July 5, 1568.
6. *Ibid.*, f. 123, Knollys to Cecil, July 14, 1568.

had been applied to Murray in the proclamation, the word Governor, and went to great lengths to explain the difference to the angry Stuart.[7] She was, he admitted, not deceived, but his action mollified her at least to some extent; she eventually agreed to go, and in the event no exception was taken to his tactic. It could, however, very easily have misfired. If it had resulted in Mary's becoming so antagonistic to Knollys that she refused to change her place of residence while he was permitted to play cat and mouse with her, great floods of wrath from above might well have come pouring down upon his head, a risk that no one but a personage of Knollys' standing could take. That he took it goes a long way toward explaining why, in spite of his own passionate assertions to the effect that he was entirely superfluous and that his position could quite adequately be filled by Lord Scrope (who, he insisted, was fully conversant with all his own dealings with their prisoner), he was retained as the guardian of the Queen of Scots until it had been decided to hand her over to the Earl of Shrewsbury.[8]

No one liked looking after the wicked witch of the north. Sir Ralph Sadler was sent to relieve the Earl of Shrewsbury of his wardship over her in 1572, and his appreciation of the honor thereby accorded him was no greater than Knollys' had been four years previously.[9] But Sadler was a natural choice, since he was regarded as being the council's Scottish expert and was also perhaps more personally familiar with the affairs of the northern part of England than most of his colleagues. He had participated directly in the negotiations which had led up to the signing of the Treaty of Edinburgh in 1560. He had on-and-off contacts with the Queen of Scots and her affairs throughout her captivity. His final mission of many was to James VI in 1587—at the age of 79 or 80—to reconcile the Scottish king to his mother's execution.[10] And he also played a vital executive role in the suppression of the rising in the north in 1569.[11]

The northern rebellion was naturally an event of great concern to the council as a whole, a concern which it evinced in two main ways. It undertook, in association with the Queen herself and her secretary Cecil, the supervision of the countrywide measures taken to put it down. And it nominated three of its own members to fill important positions in the

7. *Ibid.*, f. 99, Knollys to Cecil, June 16, 1568.

8. *Ibid.*, f. 90, Knollys to [Cecil], June 11, 1568; f. 220, Knollys to Cecil, November 11, 1568.

9. BM, Cotton MS. Caligula C. iii, f. 125, Sadler to Burghley, January 9, 1572; f. 195, Sadler to Burghley, January 31, 1572.

10. DNB, Sadler, Sadleir, or Sadleyer, Sir Ralph.

11. Wallace MacCaffrey, *The Shaping of the Elizabethan Regime* (Princeton, 1968), 346, speaks succinctly of Sadler being sent "to do his usual efficient job as general nursemaid for administrative and financial matters."

field.[12] The Earl of Bedford was sent immediately westward. As a major objective of the rebels was assumed to be the release of the Queen of Scots, it was at first intended that Sadler should be sent to assist the Earl of Shrewsbury in holding her prisoner.[13] But there was more important work for him to do, and he was actually sent north, not to help guard the Scottish queen, but to join the Earl of Sussex (Lord President of the Council of the North) as treasurer and paymaster of the northern army.[14] Third, the Lord Admiral (still Lord Clinton, later Earl of Lincoln) was placed in joint command, with the soldier Earl of Warwick, of the southern army, which was to be assembled in the midlands and march north to the aid of Sussex.[15]

The rebellion never really came to a fight. But before the insurgents gave up in the face of lack of popular support in the countryside, where they had expected to find it, large numbers of men had been raised all over England by the Lords Lieutenants and their deputies, and some of them had actually been marched from their own localities and merged into a united force which came together under Clinton and Warwick at Leicester.[16] Such an army required both weapons and powder to fight with, and money: at the outset to feed it and latterly, after it had become clear that it was not going to have to do any fighting, to discharge it. It was with these matters that the correspondence of Sadler and Clinton with the queen, with the council and with Cecil was largely taken up. (Since the revolt never got properly under way, the Earl of Bedford was little heard from in the west).

Both Sadler and Clinton enjoyed considerable autonomy, largely because their provincial locations and the uncertainty of the situation made it necessary for them to make on-the-spot decisions without first referring back for definite instructions. Lord Clinton informed the council on November 29, 1569 that he had decided to move from Lincolnshire to Leicestershire on December 3, unless he were commanded otherwise.[17] On December 1 he wrote to Cecil that he was postponing until the last moment his eventual move to Doncaster, where he was to join forces with

---

12. PRO, SP.12/60, no. 35, the Earl of Warwick and Clinton to the council, December 14, 1569.

13. PRO, SP.12/59, no. 23, "memoryall" on the situation in the north, in Cecil's hand, November 19, 1569.

14. BM, Add. MS. 33593, f. 27, Sadler to the queen, November 26, 1569.

15. PRO, SP.12/59, no. 53, Clinton to Cecil, November 29; BM, Add. MS. 33593, f. 25, Cecil to Sadler, November 25 and 26, 1569.

16. Hatfield House, MS. 156, f. 118, the queen to the Lords Lieutenants, November 24, 1569; PRO, SP.12/59, no. 30, the queen to the Earl of Derby, November 24, 1569.

17. Ibid., no. 54, Clinton to the council, November 29, 1569.

the Earl of Warwick, in order not to deplete the local food supplies any earlier than was absolutely necessary.[18] And both he and Warwick, once they and their troops had coalesced, were almost entirely successful in *not* putting into practice what they had repeatedly agreed, on orders from the council, to do in theory: to send some of their best men ahead of their main body to give assistance to Sussex before they arrived themselves.[19] They wanted to be in at the death, not help Sussex snatch all the glory before they got there. And their position at the end of an inefficient postal service gave them considerable room in which to maneuver within the limits imposed by their instructions.

Ralph Sadler, in York, enjoyed a similar latitude in financial affairs. Finding that a private citizen owed £500 to a creditor in London, Sadler persuaded him to pay the debt to him instead, on the assurance, which a Privy Councillor was in a position to give, that he would be repaid by the queen in London.[20] This procedure benefited both parties, since all carriage charges were thereby avoided. Sadler's position as a councillor also made it easier to borrow money from the local merchants on the strength of the royal credit, and eventually even to discharge many of the soldiery "without pay uppon [nothing but] fayre wordes and sure promises to have a full pay . . . wherewith the captaynes and souldiours helde themselfes well satisfied and departed very well contented."[21]

Sadler must have had a silver tongue. He certainly had a persuasive pen and an outstanding character, and both played an important part in the successful conclusion of the northern rising. The tensions were great, and could easily have resulted in quarreling among those in positions of trust in the loyal forces. The Earl of Sussex was already, at the time of the outbreak of the rebellion, suspected by at least some of those in the innermost circles of the Court of unspecified but supposedly disloyal sympathies and dealings. He himself soon became irritated with Clinton and Warwick and their reluctance to send him advance assistance. Later on, he also resented the fact that their undisciplined troops had ravaged the countryside to such an extent that there were few rebel goods left for him to confiscate to the queen's use. Clinton, in his turn, objected to Sussex's aspersions on his conduct, and was in a position to do something about it, since any money sent north from London had to come past him on its way to York. It was Sadler who smoothed out these potential difficulties. As

---

18. PRO, SP.12/60, no. 7, Clinton to Cecil, December 1, 1569.

19. *Ibid.*, no. 11, the Earl of Warwick to the council, December 12, 1569; no. 15, Clinton to Cecil, December 3, 1569.

20. BM, Add. MS. 33593, f. 59, Sadler to the council, December 9(?), 1569.

21. *Ibid.*, f. 67, Sadler to Cecil, December 24, 1569.

soon as he arrived at his destination, he put pen to paper to contradict the stories of Sussex's disaffection. He assured the queen that "I do fynd my . . . lord of Sussex a trew and faithfull servant to your Majestie . . . carefull diligent and circumspect in the execution of his charge," and protested to Cecil, the following month, that "there is no noble man in Englande that . . . could . . . make a more clear . . . accompt of this charge then he is able to do afore indifferent auditors."[22]

With equal tact, Sadler avoided coming into collision with the Lord Admiral over the £10,000 that was eventually sent from London to pay the wages of the northern army. Originally expecting to receive the full amount, he first consented to make do with six, then five, then four— and finally with three, in spite of the fact that "I had lever be out of my lif then be, as I am, cryed and called upon daylie for money."[23] He finally got £1500. But he plainly realized the foolishness of quarreling over the inevitable, and instead of carping at Clinton for taking advantage of a situation that could quite conceivably have been reversed, Sadler set out to work in the closest agreement with him in pressing for more support for them both from London. For notwithstanding the autonomy they both enjoyed in making minor tactical decisions, they were ultimately powerless without money and munitions, and dispatch of these depended on the queen and council. Both Sadler and Clinton wrote to Court continually to ask for both.

There seems to have been no particular reason why either of them chose one day to write to the council and another to Sir William Cecil, which may in itself account for the fact that both the council and the secretary on various occasions complained that they were not being informed of what was going on as fully as they should have been.[24] But there was a tendency, when there was time to write only one letter, to write to Cecil, who was assumed to pass on the information to the council.[25] When something was particularly urgently required, both were written to at the same time. "Albeit I know your care of the Queen's Majestie's affayres to be suche as the same must be the onely furtherer of the same," wrote Sadler to Cecil on December 9, "yet I thought it

---

22. *Ibid.*, f. 27, Sadler to the queen, November 26, 1569; f. 92, Sadler to Cecil, January 2, 1570; f. 90, Sadler to Cecil, January 16, [1570].

23. *Ibid.*, f. 88, Sadler to Clinton, January 1, 1570; f. 105, Sadler to Mildmay, January 9, 1570.

24. PRO, SP.12/60, no. 15, Clinton to Cecil, December 3, 1569; BM, Add. MS. 33593, f. 107, Sadler to Cecil, January 9, 1570.

25. PRO, SP.12/60, no. 7, Clinton to Cecil, December 1, 1569; BM, Add. MS. 33593, f. 105, Sadler to Mildmay, January 9, 1570.

best to write to all the councell [as well]" to help him with money for defraying his mounting expenses.[26] When things became almost impossible, he also wrote to Sir Walter Mildmay for his personal assistance in moving the council to action.[27]

The northern rebellion was a test of the whole Elizabethan system. It provides the opportunity for the observation of four councillors (Cecil, Clinton, Sadler, and now and then Mildmay) and two men (Sussex and Warwick) who would soon join them at the council table, working together under the most trying circumstances. It shows that they could operate in notable harmony in spite of pressures tending to divide them. Sadler's reward for doing so much to achieve this harmony was not, as he had hoped, to be allowed to return either home or to Court as both the Earls of Warwick and Lincoln were permitted to do, but to be sent directly from York to Scotland on yet another mission, this time to assess the situation that had resulted from the assassination of the Regent Murray.[28]

Like, and sometimes along with, several other councillors, Ralph Sadler now and again acted as an interrogator in cases of suspected treason in, or on the fringes of, high political society. Such an occasion occurred with the suspected drift into treason of the Duke of Norfolk. His arrest was entrusted to Sadler, who replied to Cecil on September 4, 1571 that although he had not received his letters until an hour after midnight, he nonetheless immediately left his bed and proceeded to Norfolk's house, placed the Duke in custody, and set out there and then to interrogate him as instructed.[29] Alone, however, he got nowhere. "The Duk denyeth the truth," commented Cecil dogmatically on the back of Sadler's first report.[30] So Sir Thomas Smith and Dr. Wilson, who had already been engaged for some days in questioning Sir Thomas Stanley and two other gentlemen suspected of being involved in the Duke's treasonable activities, were thereupon warranted, by a Signet letter, to join Sadler in the examination of the Duke himself.[31] This first warrant was followed by an-

---

26. *Ibid.*, f. 61, Sadler to Cecil, December 9(?), 1569.
27. *Ibid.*, f. 105, Sadler to Mildmay, January 9, 1570.
28. *Ibid.*, f. 154, the queen to Sadler, January 29, 1570.
29. Hatfield House, MS. 158, f. 6, Sadler to Burghley, September 4, 1571.
30. PRO, SP.12/81, no. 8, Sadler to Burghley, September 5, 1571.
31. Hatfield House, MS. 157, ff. 134–135, Smith, Wilson and William Fleetwood: examination of Francis Rolleston, Sir Thomas Gerrard and Sir Thomas Stanley, July 18, 1571; ff. 136–139, Burghley to Smith, July 18, 1571; PRO, SP.12/81. no. 1, Smith and Wilson to Burghley, September 2, 1571; BM, Cotton MS. Caligula C. iii, f. 258, the queen to Smith and Wilson, September 3, 1571.

other three days later directed specifically to "Sir Raff Sadler, Sir Thomas Smyth as our Counsellors . . . [to] take order that . . . the Duke of Norfolk be conveyed to the Towre."[32] This they did, "I, Sir Raufe Sadler, at the one side and I, Sir Thomas Smyth, on the other side and I, Dr. Wilson, comyng immediately after."[33] The three of them then reported—most fully to the queen, in brief to Cecil—that they had formally presented him with written interrogations, which he was to consider by the morning.[34] The interrogations were evidently Cecil's questions, for Smith wrote him on September 8 to "pardon me, that the articles wer gyven to him as instruccions from the cownsell to us . . . to put hym in the more terror."[35] No authority but the council's, or the queen's, executed by a councillor or councillors in person, was sufficient to overawe a subject as mighty as the head of the house of Howard, and a formal letter from the council soon followed instructing that "the duke be particularly examined uppon suche articles as you shall receyve hereincl[osed]."[36]

In June 1572 Sadler, Smith and Wilson—all "others" rather than "lords" of the council—were sent to examine the Queen of Scots.[37] Both Sadler and Smith also examined lesser persons on occasion, as did Sir Walter Mildmay.[38] But when mass treason in the very highest circles was thought to be afoot, no councillor was too proud for such employment. In 1569 the Earl of Arundel was scheduled for questioning by the Lord Keeper, the Marquess of Northampton, the Lord Admiral, the Lord

---

32. PRO, SP.12/81, no. 9, the queen to Sadler and Smith, September [6], 1571.

33. Hatfield House, MS. 158, f. 12, Sadler, Smith and Wilson to Burghley, September 7, 1571, as quoted in William Murdin, *Collection of State Papers relating to Affairs in the Reign of Queen Elizabeth* (London, 1759), 148.

34. Hatfield House, MS. 6, f. 15, Sadler, Smith and Wilson to the queen, September 7, 1571, as quoted in Murdin, 149.

35. Hatfield House, MS. 158, f. 13, Sadler, Smith and Wilson to Burghley, September 8, 1571, as quoted in Murdin, 150.

36. BM, Cotton MS. Caligula C. iii, f. 256, the council to Smith and Wilson, September 21, 1571.

37. *Ibid.*, f. 311, Hatfield House, MS. 7, f. 39, articles with which Sadler, Wilson, Bromley [and Lord Delaware] were to charge the Queen of Scots, June 11, 1572.

38. BM, Cotton MS. Caligula C. iii, f. 251, Burghley to Smith, October 19, 1571; f. 73, interrogatories put by the council to the Bishop of Ross, May [1571]; Murdin, p. 215, the examination of Thomas Bishop before Sir Ralph Sadler, Gilbert Gerrard, Thomas Bromley and Thomas Wylbraham, May 5, 1572; PRO, SP.12/103, no. 69, Sadler to Burghley, June 29, 1575; BM, Lansdowne MS. 16, f. 44, Smith to Burghley, February 17, 1573; f. 49, Mildmay to Burghley, March 2, 1573.

Chamberlain and Cecil; nine others were to be interrogated by those already mentioned, plus the Earl of Bedford, Walter Mildmay, Mr. Vice-Chamberlain and the ubiquitous Sadler.[39]

The most frequent executive operation, however, in which the members of the council themselves engaged was the conduct of international relations. Sometimes a councillor's diplomatic role was largely ceremonial, or at least apparently so. The Earl of Lincoln went to Paris in August 1572 to represent the Queen of England at the wedding of the King of France's sister, Marguerite de Valois, to the future Henry IV.[40] But even this superficially ritual occasion had profound political undertones.

The bridegroom, heir to the throne, was a Protestant, which Lincoln's presence tacitly not only acknowledged, but approved. And the expedient nuptials provided the setting for one of the most notorious series of events in the entire sixteenth century, the massacre of the Huguenots on St. Bartholomew's Day, a firsthand account of which the English visitor was able to take back with him for the edification of his horrified fellow councillors and coreligionists at home, with serious consequences for the immediate future of Anglo-French amity.[41]

Forays by councillors into diplomacy, however, were usually more actively concerned with the implementation of a particular policy than Lincoln's mission was intended to be. Cecil had personally constructed the settlement which was crowned by the Treaty of Edinburgh, having been sent to Scotland by a council which thought his journey "necessary for the matter and convenient for me." He plainly was not happy about being sent at all, but fully realized why it was necessary for him as a councillor to go. He knew that only "by this means shall be tried that we shall trust unto."[42] It was the abiding reason for the repeated use of Privy Councillors for such purposes. Councillors on such missions were superficially in no different a position from that of less highly placed ambassadors, but in fact they were. Although, like any other diplomat, they could always avoid making binding commitments by pleading the necessity of first consulting with the queen, they possessed an authority both to negotiate and

---

39. Hatfield House, MS. 157, f. 1, a note in Cecil's hand of persons to be examined and by whom, 1569.

40. DNB, Clinton, Edward Fiennes de.

41. Conyers Read, *Mr. Secretary Walsingham and the Policy of Queen Elizabeth* (Oxford, 1925), I, 232–251.

42. Conyers Read, *Mr. Secretary Cecil and Queen Elizabeth* (New York, 1955), 177, quoting from Dr. Forbes, *A Full View of the Public Transactions in the Reign of Queen Elizabeth* (London, 1740), I, 494, Cecil to Sir Nicholas Throgmorton, no date.

to make decisions no ordinary representative could command, for they were (and were known to be) in a position of trust occupied by no one else.

These factors behind a choice of emissaries were again evident in 1570 when Cecil was sent with Walter Mildmay to deal with the Scottish queen at Chatsworth. They took with them proposals for a treaty, the terms of which had been agreed on by the council the previous May. On October 5 they dispatched their first report to Elizabeth. She laid it before the council, and her reply left the Court on October 13. Mary, when it was conveyed to her, conceded on almost every point, and Cecil and Mildmay left for the south on October 15. The dates are revealing, for they indicate that once queen and council had managed to make up their minds what the next step was to be, their highly responsible agents on the spot lost no time and were all but entirely successful in implementing it.[43]

The secretary was the councillor most intimately connected with the business of diplomacy. Except for Cecil, all three secretaries of this period—Sir Thomas Smith, Sir Francis Walsingham and Dr. Thomas Wilson—had had experience overseas before they were appointed to the office, and Smith and Walsingham were again employed abroad after they became members of the council. Smith was sworn on March 5, 1571, and was sent to France early in 1572 to add his prestige as a councillor to the diplomatic finesse of Walsingham, who was there already.[44] He was not happy in his task any more than Cecil had been in his at the time of the Treaty of Edinburgh.[45] But he was more successful than he had been on his previous mission to France, and returned to England only after the Treaty of Blois had been concluded. He was, however, back home by the middle of the year, was sworn secretary in succession to Cecil on July 13 and did not go abroad again during his period of office, which terminated only with his death.[46] Walsingham, on the other hand, was once more made use of as special envoy to France in 1581 (by which time he had been secretary himself eight years), in a situation of such delicacy that it called for the exercise of the greatest tact, the most skillful diplomacy—and something more.

Walsingham had been sent to Paris originally in 1570 to work under Sir Henry Norris for toleration for the Huguenots. He stayed on as ambassador in Sir Henry's place to conduct the negotiations with the

43. Conyers Read, *Lord Burghley and Queen Elizabeth* (New York, 1960), 27–29.

44. APC, VIII, 16, March 5, 1571.

45. BM, Cotton MS. Vespasian F. vi, f. 53, Smith to Burghley (?), April 22, 1572.

46. *Ibid.*, f. 115b, Burghley to Walsingham, July 27, 1572.

French Court which were aimed at the conclusion of a marriage between Queen Elizabeth and the French king's brother, the Duc d'Anjou. The prospects for this match shriveled in the heat of English anger at the massacre which flooded the streets of Paris with Huguenot blood on St. Bartholomew's Day, 1572 and were permanently blighted when Anjou succeeded his brother Charles IX as Henry III, the last, as things turned out, of the Valois. Even so, the possibility of a French marriage for Elizabeth was not lightly abandoned by the successive kings' mother, Catherine de Medici, or, it appeared, by the English queen herself, and in 1581 Elizabeth began once more to show an apparently serious interest in renewing the direct diplomatic negotiations which had died away nearly a decade earlier. The situation by this time, however, had two quite different aspects.

The first was almost farcical. The French prince who now figured as the prospective groom had been only nineteen in 1572, when he had been first put forward as a possible substitute for his elder brother. He had been dangled on a string by the English throughout the later 1570s, and the twenty years which separated him as inescapably as ever from Elizabeth were even more significant in 1581 than they had been previously. At forty-eight, she was, whatever the doctors might say, past the age when childbearing would be safe, even if she were still capable of it. There was surely little here to tempt him into marriage and, since he was pimply-faced and unattractive, not much to attract Elizabeth either. Yet both showed signs of the greatest enthusiasm for the project. This is accounted for by the second aspect of the situation, the circumstances of the current international scene, and these were not even vaguely funny.

Both France and England had long been wary of the risen power of Spain, and were currently particularly anxious about what might happen should Philip be successful, as he seemed on the verge of being, in suppressing the revolt which had been going on in the Netherlands for seventeen years. There were consequently very real reasons for the two countries to seek an alliance more binding and comprehensive than the Treaty of Blois, and it was at least plausible for both sides to suggest that such an alliance would be more firmly cemented by a royal marriage than by mere words on a piece of parchment.[47] Furthermore, if the marriage took place and were virtually guaranteed to be childless, there would be no problem about a possible future succession to the thrones of both France and England by a single person. Thus, in spite of the superficial unlikeli-

---

47. BM, Cotton MS. Titus B. ii, f. 231, Walsingham to the Earl of Sussex, August 5, 1581.

ness of the proposal, there were grave reasons for taking it seriously. Even so, keeping all these political balls in the air at once had long called for the exercise of a fine talent for diplomatic juggling. By 1581 the feat was impossible to maintain except by the personal appearance in the forefront of the act of the only man who could convince the increasingly skeptical French that England's purpose was still serious. That man was principal secretary and Privy Councillor Sir Francis Walsingham, a person the French already knew as an upright and honest diplomat, who now returned to France as one known to play a crucial role in the counsels of the English queen.[48]

Some councillors were used less often than others in such matters for purely practical reasons. Some were old, some unreliable. By 1568 Winchester was already too venerable to undertake anything over and above the duties of his office as Lord Treasurer, and he did not even attend meetings of the council after March 19, 1567.[49] Similarly, the Earl of Pembroke, though younger, had been in poor health since 1564 and made his last appearance at the council table on May 3, 1567.[50] The Marquess of Northampton, on the other hand, attended until very shortly before his death in 1571,[51] but he seems to have been otherwise little employed. The Earl of Arundel was a member of the commission set up to look into the affairs of the Queen of Scots in 1568, but then found himself under house arrest in 1569 for his too-close association with the Duke of Norfolk's plan to marry the lady himself. He was also involved in the plot to overthrow not only Mr. Secretary Cecil and Lord Keeper Bacon, but the queen as well, with the aim of restoring the old religion; and from 1571 until his death he passed much of his time in seclusion as a private person.[52] Even the Duke of Norfolk was a member of the 1568 commission to inquire into Mary Stuart's affairs, but thereafter rapidly drifted, at least in some measure because he felt he was *not* being made use of as he had every right to be, into the treason which resulted in his execution in 1572.[53]

Lord Howard of Effingham, who died the following year, also falls to some extent into this category, but he really belongs to a second group of those not often employed in this fashion, comprising those whose official

48. Read, *Walsingham*, II, 54–55.
49. APC, VII, 336, March 19, 1567.
50. *Ibid.*, 350, May 3, 1567.
51. APC, VIII, 29, June 12, 1571.
52. DNB, Fitzalan, Henry.
53. Neville Williams, *Thomas Howard, Fourth Duke of Norfolk* (New York, 1964), 135.

positions tied them closely to the Court. Both Howard and Sussex had been notably active in earlier life in diplomacy, and Sussex, as we have seen, had also been regularly made use of, prior to being elevated to the council, in successive positions of vice-regal authority. Both were brought to earth by the demanding duties attaching to the office of Lord Chamberlain. Sussex was certainly a member of a commission of gaol delivery in 1573; of another to treat with the Portuguese about commercial relations the same year; of a commission to take steps for the increase of horses in Norfolk, Suffolk, Cambridgeshire and Kent in 1580; and, finally, of a fourth, to treat with the French for the marriage of the queen with the Duc d'Anjou in 1581. But he was at Court much of the time between his appointment as Lord Chamberlain in 1572 and his death ten years later, and, as his office would require, he was often noted as having accompanied the queen on progress.[54] Sir James Croft's position in the Household seems to have been similarly restricting, although he was sent with Lord Cobham, the Earl of Derby and Dr. Dale to treat for peace with Alba in 1558.[55] Nicholas Bacon and Thomas Bromley were both comparatively tied down by their duties at the chancery.

The Earl of Leicester's special relationship with the queen kept him much at Court as well, and it was not until 1584 that he received an assignment of any moment. Indeed, his duties and responsibilities prior to this date were perhaps most typical of any councillor, for he held no office of state, was sent on no missions, and his whole position in the country, and relative to its affairs, though originating in the queen's affections, actually stemmed from his position as a Privy Councillor. He was Lord Lieutenant of a number of counties, just as all his fellows were; sat on the bench as a justice of the peace just as they did; and was named in a variety of specific commissions, like the rest.[56] But, unlike the others, he was not saddled with the dirty work, which, over and above their regular duties as Privy Councillors, was at one time or another visited upon almost everyone else.

---

54. DNB, Radcliffe, Thomas.
55. DNB, Croft, Sir James.
56. DNB, Dudley, Robert, Earl of Leicester (1532(?)–1588).

Chapter VI

SUPERVISION AND MANAGEMENT

HE everyday chores of government, unlike extraordinary undertakings, were never-ending. They involved overseeing the smooth running of the existing legal, financial and military machinery of state and the issuing of instructions, not on the council's own authority, but exercising the prerogative of the Crown to implement plans and programs initiated in principle by acts of parliament, letters patent or proclamations and to take action in circumstances not provided for by law. The range of the council's concern, therefore, was wide. The council did things for the queen, and many of the things it did, it did very well indeed.

The English legal system, on its foundation of common and statute law, was well established by the sixteenth century. The courts, both ancient and more modern—King's Bench, Common Pleas, the Exchequer, Chancery, Star Chamber and Requests—all normally followed their own courses without the necessity or, from the lawyers' point of view, the desirability, of external interference. Yet the council did interfere in legal processes for a variety of reasons.

Although ancient—indeed to a great extent *because* of its antiquity— the common law was notoriously liable to the inefficiency so often consequent upon the triumph of habit over the spirit of initiative in the conduct of human affairs. The legal machinery was decentralized; much business, although formally concluded at Westminster, was actually conducted in the counties. These local proceedings were scandalously liable to local interference. The council, therefore, had constantly to be on guard to see that the ordinary operations of the law actually proceeded at least approximately as they were supposed to. It was to this end that in 1578 Burghley, Lincoln, Knollys, Hatton, Walsingham and Wilson wrote to Bassingbourne Gaudy, a Norfolk gentleman who, typically, served the queen and council in a variety of ways, instructing him to take inventory of the goods of a suspected murderer and to see they were not "embeseled and conveyed away" before his trial. Gaudy was also to see that the "coroners quest . . . for the inquiry thereof be not pact of such persons as shall . . . hinder the dew cours of justice and defraude the queen's majestie of her right in the forfeature of the sayd goods."[1]

---

1. Bodleian Library, MS. Tanner 241, f. 3v, the council to Bassingbourne Gaudy, December 22, 1578.

Back at Westminster, the regular courts, originally distinct in their jurisdictions, had been competing for business for centuries. The invention of legal fictions had long ago made it possible to bring all kinds of cases in virtually all the courts and for separate proceedings to be started in different courts relating to a single issue. Confusion was often the result. Only the council, short of the queen herself, possessed sufficient authority to make a decision when judgments of various courts relating to the same dispute either contradicted or cancelled each other out. John Hippesley and Charles Dudley petitioned in 1578 to be restored to possession of a lead mine in the Mendips. Their contention was that both a verdict at the common law and an order out of the Star Chamber gave them possession of it, but that they were still in fact being kept from occupation by virtue of a commission out of the court of the Exchequer. The delays conducing to the decay of the mine, they asked to "bee restored to their former possession . . . [at the same time undertaking to] abide such further triall for the title as to your honors shall seeme meete."[2]

The court of Star Chamber was unique in several ways. It was the judicial heir of the old, undifferentiated council, just as the Privy Council was the earlier body's deliberative offspring. The continuing close relationship between the two was underlined by the circumstance that the Privy Councillors, along with the Chief Justices, were, *ex officio*, the Star Chamber judges. The court of Star Chamber exercised public functions of considerable importance. "Remember[ing] . . . its origins," it issued ordinances and decrees "in some cases . . . so closely analogous to orders in council that they may not very incorrectly be regarded as such." Lady Neale sees this as coming at least very close to the actual making of law.[3] Nonetheless, as this case of the Mendips lead mine makes clear, where its private jurisdiction was concerned (in its handling of disputes between party and party) Star Chamber had become virtually just another court of the realm.

When Sir William Paulet failed to make his appearance before the council "at a tyme prefixed, to have a matter of controversie betwixt [him and Sir John Young] . . . ordered by their Lordships," he was ordered to pay Young's charges in coming himself, not to leave without license and to "prosecute the matter betwixt them in variaunce in the Starre Chamber."[4] Conversely, the court of Star Chamber occasionally referred a case that was causing it particular difficulty (although not always with

2. PRO, SP.12/127, no. 61, John Hippesley and Charles Dudley to the council, 1578.

3. Cora L. Scofield, *A Study of the Court of Star Chamber* (Chicago, 1900), 49.

4. APC, VIII, 12, February 12 and 13, 1570.

great effect) to the council. On December 3, 1571 the council wrote to the Lord Keeper concerning a matter between John Lacie and the Earl of Sussex and others that had been "by your Lordship and the whole consentes of the lords and others of the courte of Starre Chamber, with thassent also of bothe parties, by the advise of their learned counsell, compromitted unto us . . . . We have . . . assembled sondreye tymes . . . . but in effect our doinges in that behalfe have taken no place . . . . And therefore . . . we doe eftesones retorne them againe with the matter as we founde it to the Starre Chamber."[5] The connection between the council and "its own" court was more intimate than its contacts with other judicial bodies, but in instances such as these the council's attitude toward the court of Star Chamber in particular was identical with its attitude toward the other prerogative and common law courts in general. Indeed, at a point in its dealings with Sir William Paulet and Sir John Young prior to that cited above, the council itself likened Star Chamber to "any other court."[6]

The council was the most obvious institution for people to appeal to who felt that they had been denied, or for some reason or another would not be able to obtain, justice in the ordinary courts. Andrew Maignewe petitioned in 1579 that it give orders to one Innocent Lucatelli for payment of £155. 11.4d, which he claimed the latter owed him but which he could not recover at law. In order to help Lucatelli come to an accommodation with his other creditors, Maignewe had given him a written acquittance for the whole amount of the debt to himself before it had actually been paid off.[7] If the council's willingness to consider such a man's avoidable but nonetheless unfortunate predicament draws attention to its realization that for some injustices the law offered no redress, its attitude on other occasions shows that it was equally conscious that the law could err. In 1578 it could only have been this awareness that prompted the instruction to Lord Burghley to produce for its perusal those letters and papers on the basis of which the indictment of a man named John Prestall, ever since his conviction a prisoner in the Tower, had been drawn up seven years before.[8]

In all these instances the Privy Council, functioning as a sort of supreme court, was acting essentially within the established system, attempting to make it run more effectively and equitably. The council also,

---

5. BM, Add. MS. 32323, f. 117, the council to Bacon, December 3, 1571.
6. Scofield, 37, quoting APC, VII, 405.
7. PRO, SP.12/132, no. 23, Arnold Maignewe to the council, September 1579.
8. PRO, SP.12/126, no. 7, the council to Burghley, October 12, 1578.

however, operated judicially outside the regular system, being willing in certain circumstances to set itself up as a court of first instance.

Sometimes this was because of the social prominence of disputing personages. A complicated situation arose in 1580 out of a series of episcopal translations involving both archdioceses and the see of London. The dissatisfied clerics were apparently bickering over what diocesan expenses should be paid by whom, and the quarrel became sufficiently acrimonious for threats of suits to be exchanged. At the request of the Bishop of London, the council stepped in to prevent such an eventuality and agreed to determine the matter of dilapidations in his diocese, since "it will breede offence that three of the cheef bishops should go to lawe."[9] On other occasions, the council agreed to become involved because of the very lack of position of petitioners and their inability to afford the luxury of regular legal proceedings. Thus it settled "the matter in contrav[ers]ie betwene Lodowick Grevill and the pore men of Glouc[ester]shere" and that concerning a Lancashire resident "so as the pore man may have no cause further to complaine unto us."[10]

A third explanation of the council's willingness to act as a court where legal proceedings could be initiated is to be found in the endemic violence of the age. Nearly a century after Bosworth, some individuals were still locally powerful enough to ignore the due process available to them at the assizes and defy the law, attempting to settle disputes among themselves by force. Such quarrels, almost by definition, involved men holding positions of prestige and authority, the very people the council looked to to keep everyone else in order: people like Richard Denny and Robert Wekes, who were squabbling over the possession of a house in 1574. This particular quarrel threatened to cause fairly widespread disorder in Gloucestershire, not so much on account of its bitterness but because neither party stood alone. Each was able to count on the support of others. In taking order for the disagreement's ending, therefore, the council was careful to add in a final, but important clause the warning that "the peace [was to be] kept . . . and . . . the forces removed on ether side."[11]

The council as a whole was not quite so burdened by judicial business as a casual glance at its register might lead one to suppose. Some cases should never have been submitted in the first place, remedies being quite

9. PRO, SP.12/137, no. 39, the Bishop of London [to the council], April 18, 1580.

10. PRO, SP.12/107, no. 89, the council to certain gentlemen, March 18, 1576; SP.12/108, no. 60, the council to the justices of assize on the northern circuit, July 17, 1576.

11. APC, VIII, 287–289, August 28, 1574.

readily available elsewhere. These were forwarded by the secretary to the appropriate court without coming before the council at all.[12] In many of those disputes it did undertake to deal with, the actual work of hearing the evidence and even determining the outcome was assigned to others, sometimes including councillors and sometimes not. A controversy between Sir George Cavarley and Mr. Dutton first appears in the Privy Council register on May 20, 1574, when Dr. Wilson (as a master of Requests) and the solicitor-general were instructed to examine Dutton "uppon certen articles sent inclosed to be ministered unto him on behalf of Sir George . . . with a *postscript* to returne thexaminacions to their Lordships."[13] On June 19 the secretary made a note to "knowe what order they wyll take in the matter."[14] On July 12th Dutton was permitted to go home, on condition he would reappear next term for the hearings to be resumed. In the meanwhile, he was granted a commission "to examine certain gentilmen as witnesses in his purgacion."[15] The council referred the matter of Richard Dunse's charges against John Tanner, which probably came to their attention in the same way, to Sir William More for his investigation, and they wrote to Sir Thomas Scott, Thomas Wotton, William Crips, William Cromer and the mayor of Sandwich or any three of them, "whereof Mr. Wotton to be one, for the hearing and ending of all matters in contraversie between Haukes . . . and Isham."[16]

There was a great deal of variety among both the tasks delegated and the persons to whom cases were delegated. Some, like those mentioned above, were forwarded to other gentlemen who lived in the same neighborhood as the litigants and who were told to put an end to the matter. In others, the chosen agents were told simply to investigate the matter and report back so that the council could itself decide what further or final action should be taken. Or, instead of referring a case to inexpert local gentry, the council might pass it on to professional lawyers. The case of Richard Knight versus Thomas Blagrave and son was commended to the justices of assize for action "as shall be agreeable to justice," and that of Edward Turner by the queen to the council, and by the council in its turn to Sir Gilbert Gerrard (the master of the rolls) and Sergeant John

---

12. Robert Beale, "A Treatise of the Office of a Councellor and Principall Secretarie to Her Majestie," printed in Conyers Read, *Mr. Secretary Walsingham and the Policy of Queen Elizabeth* (Oxford, 1925), I, 424.

13. APC, VIII, 241, May 20, 1574.

14. PRO, SP.12/97, no. 16, note of council business, June 19, 1574.

15. APC, VIII, 267, July 12, 1574.

16. Surrey Record Office, Loseley MS. 2013, no. 7, June 4, 1567; PRO, SP.12/108, no. 10, April 29, 1576.

Puckering.[17] Sometimes a case would be assigned to a group of councillors, or even a single individual. "Blande's petition" was thus committed
to the Lord Treasurer and Sir Walter Mildmay.[18] A dispute between the
Earl of Hertford and Lord Wentworth was referred by the queen to the
Lord Treasurer alone, as "Lord Wentworth hath beyne at great charge
in the sute, which should as well tend to ower commodyty as to his
owne."[19] Another case where the quarrel was over the possession of land
was referred ultimately to Mr. Secretary Walsingham.[20] There were
almost endless variants on these fairly basic patterns. In the settlement of
John Ashburnham's affairs, the council ordered Lord Hunsdon and Francis Walsingham to write to the gentlemen who were to do the actual
settling and did not itself communicate with them directly at all.[21] If
Gerrard and Puckering were unable to come to any decision with regard
to Edward Turner they were instructed to report back to the council,
and then Lord Burghley and Christopher Hatton would see what they
could do. Lord Wentworth's copyhold suit was committed to Mr. Wylbraham, attorney of the court of Wards, and Mr. Fleetwood, recorder of
London, who were to send it back for the Earl of Sussex, the Earl of
Leicester and Lord Burghley to make some decision if they were unable to
agree between themselves.[22] Councillors and legal officers were sometimes
associated in these committees. Francis Walsingham, Walter Mildmay,
William Cordell (master of the rolls), and Thomas Bromley, while still
solicitor-general, on receipt of the council's letters "for the diligent exami-
nacion of the matters in controversye betwene her majestie's officers of her
Countie Palatine of Chester, and the maior of the cytye of Chester,
towching dyvers contemptes and disorders by him committed against the
jurisdiction of her majestie's coorte of thexchequer there, [reported that]
we have travailed therein accordingly, and thereuppon have sett downe
unto your Lordships by our certificate in writinge."[23] Sir Walter Mildmay

---

17. West Sussex Record Office, letters of the Earl of Winterton at Shillinglee
Park, Sussex, file 1, the council to the master of the rolls and Sergeant Puckering,
June 1589.

18. PRO, SP.12/95, no. 9, note of council business, January 15, 1574.

19. PRO, SP.12/75, no. 28, the queen to the Marquess of Winchester(?),
1570(?).

20. BM, Harleian MS. 6035, Walsingham's letter book, f. 9, 1583.

21. BM, Harleian MS. 703, f. 2, Hunsdon and Walsingham to certain
Sussex gentlemen, November 16, 1583.

22. Hatfield House, MS. 159, f. 34, order by the council in a suit over
copyhold land held from Lord Wentworth, July 5 [1572].

23. PRO, SP.12/95, no. 72, Walsingham, Mildmay, William Cordell and
Thomas Bromley to the council, April 3, 1574.

was frequently employed in such assignments, and the case of Sir Thomas Leighton's dispute over two Guernsey mills, in the investigation of which he was associated with Sir Thomas Egerton, is sufficiently well documented to provide a view of the proceedings virtually from start to finish. Mildmay wrote to Egerton, who had by this time succeeded Sir Thomas Bromley as solicitor-general, from his house on December 30, 1584, telling him what he had done so far in the matter. He then continued "and if yow see noe cause [for] alteracion, I will cause a letter to be drawen, that we may send by the parties to my Lords of the councell. . . . [with] our opinions, leavyng the fynall ordre therof to their Lordships."[24] The two of them together then wrote, enclosing their joint certificate as to what they had done.[25] And on January 6th, William Waad, then clerk of the council, wrote to Sir Thomas Egerton that "their Lordships, having considered the report made by Sir Walter Mildmay and your worship in the cause committed unto your hearinge by their order, did call both the parties before them this present day, who likewise did consent to the order you had taken betwene them. . . . Their Lordships thinke it reason that . . . you see . . . the order performed."[26] The council order would be recorded in the Privy Council register, and the interested parties could then purchase a copy for the standard fee.

In all these phases of its role in the legal life of England, the council can be seen working *ad hoc*, but eminently responsibly, as a supplement to the traditional and relatively rigid inherited judicial system. This way of doing business was equally characteristic of its financial activities and its orientation toward those departments of state and institutions whose whole or partial concern was the raising or disbursing, or both, of money: the exchequer, the treasuries of the Household and the Chamber and parliament. All were long-established; all had their own accepted functions; all went about their own business in their customary ways, virtually running themselves under their own officers. Yet all their individual operations needed both coordination by and cooperation from an outside, directing agency if they were effectively to meet the fiscal requirements of national policy, just as the legal system needed constant adjustment if it were to approach the ideal of providing universal justice.

The outside agency that provided these essential services was Elizabeth's

---

24. Huntington Library, Ellesmere MS. 1901, Mildmay to Sir Thomas Egerton, December 30, 1584.

25. Huntington Library, Ellesmere MS. 1902, Mildmay and Sir Thomas Egerton to the council, January 1, 1585.

26. Huntington Library, Ellesmere MS. 1903, William Waad to Sir Thomas Egerton, January 6, 1584.

Privy Council. Together with the queen, the council kept itself informed as to the exchequer's current financial position, drew up such national accounts as were kept in the sixteenth century and bore the responsibility for making as sure as possible that the royal income was not exceeded by overly lavish royal and governmental expenditure. The State Papers Domestic include small paper books showing all money paid into the court of the exchequer during specified periods.[27] And many of the minutes of council meetings that *have* survived record that some financial matter then came up for consideration. To whom was the money for Ireland to be paid, and how was it to be employed, Francis Walsingham made a note to ask on January 10, 1574.[28] The council, in response, instructed the Lord Treasurer to designate someone to receive it, and ordered it to be spent on victuals and not on the settlement of debts previously incurred. The council occupied, in the matter of finance, a relatively undefined but crucial position between the queen, in whose power it unquestionably lay to decide just how her revenue should be employed, and her financial ministers, the Lord Treasurer and the chancellor of the exchequer, who were responsible for the technical processes of its collection and distribution. Sir Francis Walsingham, in a letter to the Earl of Huntingdon, who by 1581 had succeeded the Earl of Sussex as Lord President of the Council of the North, expressed the situation aptly. The best way to obtain some recompense for expenses which Huntingdon had incurred in the queen's service, Walsingham wrote, "is that your Lordship shoold wryte a letter unto my Lords of the Counsell, prayeng them to have consyderacyon of your charges, uppon which request I wyll devyce some way that your Lordship shall have interteynment without troblyng of her majesty."[29] Next to the queen's, in matters of finance, the council's word was law, and the Marquess of Winchester, knowing it, left instructions with the tellers of the exchequer that when he was out of town at his house in Basing *they* were to do whatever the council, in his official capacity as Lord Treasurer, ordered *him* to do.[30]

---

27. PRO, SP.12/77, no. 15, note of money paid out of the receipt of the exchequer, February 12, 1571; no. 39, list of warrants sent to the exchequer since October 1569, March 1571; SP.12/91, no. 48, the declarations of the tellers of the exchequer of their accounts from Easter to June 15, June 18, 1573.

28. PRO, SP.12/95, nos. 4, 7 and 9, SP.12/97, no. 33 and SP.12/103, no. 43, notes of council business, January 8, 10 and 15 and July 12, 1574 and May 8, 1575.

29. Huntington Library, Hastings MS. 13064, Walsingham to the Earl of Huntingdon, March 18, 1581.

30. PRO, SP.12/47, no. 71, the Marquess of Winchester to the council, September 15, 1568.

Orthodox sixteenth century financial theory maintained that the monarch should "live of his own." Under normal circumstances and with careful management this came remarkably close to being possible. The multifarious ancient revenues to which the Crown was entitled were mostly paid into the various offices of the exchequer, where their reception was overseen by the Lord Treasurer and the chancellor of the exchequer. It was their job to see that the established system brought in as much as it was supposed to, and the council as a rule did not interfere in the incoming process at any point in spite—in a sense because—of the fact that these officers were also councillors. But the council was constantly and essentially concerned in the business of paying money out, both from the exchequer itself and from such disbursing organs as the treasury of the Chamber. Cash was parted with by the clerks of the Chamber only after they had received specific authorization by warrant from the queen or the council, and by the exchequer tellers on receipt of similar instructions, additionally authenticated after 1572 by Burghley in his capacity as Lord Treasurer.[31]

The treasurer of the Chamber received his regular funds directly from the revenues of the duchies of Lancaster and Cornwall and from the profits of the hanaper, for which he accounted directly to the exchequer itself.[32] He paid them out piecemeal, under warrant from either the secretaries, the council, Burghley, Sussex or the vice-chamberlain of the Household, to cover charges related to "letters, commissions, wrytings and other causes by the queen's majestie and her highnes' most honorable Privye Counsell," in recompense for a variety of services extending well beyond the expenses of carrying letters and messages around the country. The Earl of Leicester's men, the Earl of Derby's men and the children of Westminster School were all paid by the treasurer of the Chamber against the council's warrant for plays presented before the queen.[33] Rafe Bowes, master of her majesty's game at the Paris Garden, received £5 for bringing the said game before her majesty when the Court was in residence at Greenwich.[34] For providing flowers and other necessaries for the beautification and upkeep of the council chamber during the previous year, Robert Langham, its keeper, was allowed £10.[35] £26. 13. 4d went to the posts of the towns of Boroughbridge and Ferrybridge for

---

31. PRO, E.403/2721, f. 3, order taken October 10, 1597 by virtue of a dormant Privy Seal dated April 9, 1596 for certain payments to the lieutenant of the tower "allowed by the lordes and others of the Privy Councell accordinge to the tenor of the said Privy Seale . . . . signed W. Burghley."

32. PRO, E.351/541, f. 140v, Sir Thomas Heneage's account as treasurer of the Chamber, September 1572–September 1573.

33. APC, VIII, 177, January 8, 1573; 71, February 29, 1571.

34. *Ibid.*, 257, June 28, 1574.

35. *Ibid.*, 98, April 19, 1573.

"their grete charges . . . in this last troble in the northe."[36] And the clerks of the council were paid £4. 2. 6d for "two seales for their office" on the last day of April 1573.[37]

These were all relatively ordinary expenses. Those which were less so were met by a council warrant directed, not to the treasurer of the Chamber, but to the treasurer and chamberlains of the exchequer. Apart from their extraordinariness, these payments have almost nothing in common. They are not even necessarily larger than payments made out of the Chamber funds. They range from a few marks to thousands of pounds, from trivial grants made to particular persons on the queen's instructions to crucial expenses closely tied to affairs of state. An Irishman, Malachias Roddi, "late a Popishe bishop," who, after being for some time in prison, eventually conformed himself to the established church, was granted twenty marks, at the queen's pleasure but on the council's actual command, because he had no means of support to turn to on his release.[38] The council instructed the exchequer officials, using the usual form of words, to pay out of "soche of her majestie's treasure as remayneth presently in your handes" £30.13.4d to Thomas Randolph, master of the posts; £300 to John Bland for the victualling of an Irish garrison; and £1000 to the Earl of Bedford or his appointee for unspecified expenditures.[39] In January 1570 the council informed Ralph Sadler at York that £600 had been sent to him and went on to tell him what to do with it.[40] Disbursement of the larger sums usually had a double authorization, a Privy Seal warrant being sent first to the exchequer authorizing a total of some thousands of pounds to be paid out in individual installments on a warrant from the council signed by a stipulated number (usually six or seven) councillors.[41] But double authorization was not by any means a necessity. A warrant from the council appears to have been perfectly ac-

---

36. *Ibid.*, 6, January 14, 1570.
37. *Ibid.*, 101, April 30, 1573.
38. *Ibid.*, 92, March 26, 1573.
39. PRO, E.404/230, the council to the officers of the exchequer, no date; E.403/2423, the council to the officers of the exchequer, September 25, 1579; SP.12/97, no. 3, Privy Seal warrant to the treasurer and chamberlains of the exchequer, June 14, 1574.
40. BM, Add. MS. 33593, f. 131, the council to Sadler, January 14, 1570.
41. PRO, E.403/2300, payments by warrant under Privy Seals and under dormant Privy Seals by authority of letters signed by six of the council, no date; 2423 has a letter from the council authorizing exchequer payment to Edwarde Baeshe of "such somes of money . . . as six or more of hir majestie's Privay Counsaile by their owne (?) letters directed to the Lord Treasourer shall require and appointe to be delivered unto hym. By a Privay Seale for hym and John Hawkings, conteyning the somme of fyve thousand powndes," no date. The actual sum involved, however, has been omitted.

ceptable to the exchequer officials even without any further security, and no questions seem to have been asked even if the warrant for a payment under previous authorization exceeded the maximum amount per particular payment stipulated in the original Privy Seal. What the treasurers and chamberlains, and above all the tellers of the exchequer—the men who actually paid out the cash—wanted was the protection of a valid authorization for every penny they disbursed. Along with warrants under the Privy Seal and the Signet and letters from the Lord Treasurer and under treasurer, letters from the Privy Council constituted such valid authorization and were so recorded in the books and rolls kept by each department of the exchequer concerned with payment or with auditing.[42] A letter from the council was in fact the best such authorization even the most timid official could wish for, and when it came to paying out £3000 for military expenses in Ireland, the Lord Treasurer himself wrote to Robert Peter, auditor of the receipt of the exchequer "you shall herwith receave a letter from the lordes of the counsell to me, which letter I pray you kepe, and observe the contentes therof."[43]

Even in normal times, the council's involvement in finance, however, did not stop here. The sheriffs had to settle their accounts at the exchequer only twice a year—at Michaelmas and Easter—and it was a routine matter to have to borrow ahead to have money to spend before anticipated revenue actually came in. As Winchester put it to Cecil in 1570, the queen had in practice to borrow continually in order to remain "clerlie dischargid ageinst all the world."[44] To conduct transactions of this nature, she needed as her business agent an individual rather than a committee, and she found him in a man first introduced to her by William Cecil. This was Sir Thomas Gresham, himself one of the most important figures of the later sixteenth century, since his successful financial operations constituted one of the most crucial props upon which depended the sound and widely envied credit of the English government. Gresham corresponded constantly with Cecil and arranged loans on the queen's behalf in England, mainly from lenders in the city of London, and on the continent in such commercial centers as Antwerp, Hamburg and Cologne.[45]

42. PRO, E.403/2292–2308. *The Deputy Keeper's Report* (London, 1841), II, 246, describes these rolls as *"solutiones per warranta,* etc., or the auditor's accounts of payments upon warrants and orders, being abstracts of all payments out of the exchequer by virtue of writs of Privy Seal, warrants of the Lord Treasurer and undertreasurer and letters of the Privy Council."

43. PRO, E.404/230, Burghley to Robert Peter, the auditor of the receipt, August 18, 1574.

44. BM, Lansdowne MS. 12, no. 25, Winchester to Cecil, January 12, 1570.

45. PRO, SP.12/74, nos. 11, 14, 15 and 19, Sir Thomas Gresham to Cecil,

In order to borrow, a would-be debtor, be he king or commoner, must normally convince potential creditors that they will be repaid on time, in full and at a profit to themselves. The security offered in return for cash must be credible. For Queen Elizabeth raising a loan in London, an ordinary letter patent acknowledging the royal liability, issued out of the chancery under the Great Seal, was usually sufficient.[46] Others looked to for relief of Elizabethan fiscal distress, however, both at home and abroad, demanded something more. Then the promise of repayment might be sealed not only with the Great Seal, but with the seals of London and/or other great cities of the realm as well.[47] Alternatively, the city of London, in a separate document, sometimes guaranteed to repay, if necessary, money lent by third parties to the queen, the queen at the same time undertaking in her own personal letter "to save harmles the cittie of London for their band given."[48] Lastly, on occasion either individual councillors, groups of councillors or the council as a whole would vouch for the value of the royal word. In instances involving smallish amounts, one or more of Elizabeth's advisers might borrow semi-privately for official use. In this manner, the Earl of Leicester and Lord Burghley—the latter in his capacity as Lord Treasurer—in 1581 pledged their own credit to certain aldermen and citizens of London in return for money "for hir majestie's service." They gave both a general undertaking to repay the total sum and specific assurance of reimbursement to each individual lender. One such was John Spencer. He provided £500 and in return received a promissory note signed by both Leicester and Burghley with their seals impressed upon the document immediately below their signatures.[49]

When larger sums were needed, Crown and Privy Council jointly and

---

October 13, 22, 22 and 26, 1570; SP.12/77, nos. 2, 30, 61 and 62, Gresham to Cecil, January 10, March 17, April 28 and 30, [1571]; Hatfield House, MS. 159, f. 64v, Gresham: holograph list of the queen's debts due between February and April, May 1572; John W. Burgon, *The Life and Times of Sir Thomas Gresham*, 2 volumes (London, 1839).

46. PRO, SP.12/78, no. 49, letter patent acknowledging her indebtedness to certain Londoners, signed by the queen, the seal missing, June 1571.

47. BM, Add. MS 32323, ff. 144v–145v, drafts of a series of bonds sent out to be passed under the seals of various cities, 1570–1573; PRO, SP.12/81, no. 36, Sir Thomas Gresham to Burghley, October 5, 1571.

48. BM, Add. MS. 32323, f. 152, the queen's bond to the city of London, no date.

49. BM, Lansdowne MS. 32, nos. 14–22, the Earl of Leicester's promise to several individual persons to repay money borrowed from them for the service of the queen, September 11, 1581; no. 23, the Earl of Leicester and Burghley to the aldermen and citizens of London, September 11, 1581; no. 24, the Earl of Leicester and Burghley to John Spencer, September 11, 1581.

institutionally undertook the obligation to repay them. The basic document was again a letter patent, but an extraordinarily elaborated one. £11,000 was borrowed from the Genoese financier Benedict Spinola in 1573, and the spectacular confession of indebtedness he received in exchange for his money was not only embellished with the pendant Great Seal and graced by the handsome sign manual of Elizabeth herself on its face, but countersigned by Burghley, Lincoln, Sussex, Leicester, Francis Knollys, James Croft and Thomas Smith on the dorse as well.[50] It was all a question of confidence—confidence in the Crown, attested to by the willingness of English financial figures and centers to support it, but enormously bolstered by the prestige and standing of the royal ministers. The council's promise to pay was rated second only to the queen's, probably because her councillors were known to be rich men in their own right. If the treasury were empty and the Crown could not meet its obligations when they became due—it happened in other kingdoms—then the lords of Theobalds and Kenilworth and Wilton and Holdenby and, if necessary, the others of the council, too, with their somewhat less wide but nonetheless still broad acres, could be dunned with some real hope of getting paid. It never happened. There were other methods of raising money for emergencies available to the council short of disposing of its members' feudal tenements and family plate or of asking the queen to part with her pearl earrings and gem-encrusted gowns, of which her councillors knew and her subjects surely guessed the value very well.[51] But in the last resort, the property was there; it could be sold; it had been committed; and its existence and possession by Queen Elizabeth's closest associates must have been ineffably reassuring once those highly respected (because so well-endowed) individuals had signed their impressive names on that precious, legally-binding, figuratively and literally lovely document.

These commercially negotiated loans bore interest, or at least the Crown undertook to pay back more than it originally received. In August 1570, for example, Gresham borrowed £1500 for the queen from Sir

---

50. PRO, SP.12/91, no. 57, bond of the queen for the payment of £11,000 to Benedict Spinola, June 24, 1573.

51. CPR, V, 30–31, commission to Bacon, Knollys, Cecil, Sadler and Mildmay "all councillors, (or three of them) to take account of . . . all jewels, plate and bullion" in the keeping of John Astely, master and treasurer of the jewels and plate, March 29, 1570; BM, Stowe MS. 555, the inventory resulting from this commission, signed on every other page by the last three named in the commission. There is no date on this ms., but since Cecil signed as "W. Burghley," final execution cannot have been earlier than February 25, 1571. Annotations in Burghley's hand (such as "the gold work loose") make it clear the assignment was not perfunctorily performed.

Thomas Offley, and agreed to pay back £1606 on February 1, 1571. This extra £106 consisted of a 1 percent brokerage charge and an effective interest rate over and above this of 12 percent per annum.[52] If the Crown either could not or did not wish to pay at the time the debt became due, then Gresham embarked on a round of fresh negotiations to have the repayment date postponed.[53] When this second due date had come and gone and the sums involved had actually been paid back, Gresham would appear in person before the council, as he did on December 21, 1571 and present the bonds which had by this time been returned to him. These (on this particular day there are fifty-nine recorded in the council register) were thereupon "by their Lordships cancelled, and those which were sealed with the Grete Seale . . . orderid to be sent to the Lord Threasourer to be laid up in the threasourye, and thothers sealed with the seale of the Citie were returned to the Lord Mayor by the said Mr. Gresham."[54] The canceling in the case of the Spinola bond took the form of an endorsement "£11,000 all payd [signed] W. Burghley." In normal times, such businesslike financial management sufficed to keep the Crown's accounts in order.

The times, however, were not always normal, and the moment regularly recurred throughout the reign of Elizabeth when money which would sooner or later have to be paid back would not suffice to supplement her ordinary income. When a major catastrophe occurred—such as the rebellion in the north—not only did the government find itself compelled to borrow quickly to meet its immediate needs, but sooner or later it had to take steps to increase, at least temporarily, the total amount of money coming in in some way that would not require eventual repayment. The obvious, traditional place to turn was parliament. Four parliaments—those of 1571, 1572, 1576, and 1581—met at Westminster between 1568 and 1582. Three of these were summoned with specifically financial purposes in mind, which two Privy Councillors in particular—Sir Nicholas Bacon (the Lord Keeper) and Sir Walter Mildmay (the chancellor of the exchequer)—were directly involved in furthering.

The Lord Keeper, on behalf of the queen, always made the opening oration, outlining the causes for the summoning of the particular parliament. In 1571, after a few brief and ambiguous remarks about religion,

---

52. PRO, SP.12/73, nos. 44 and 45, Sir Thomas Gresham: notes of "soche somes of monny . . . tackyn upe for the quen's majestie in the cite of London," August 1, 1570.

53. PRO, SP.12/80, no. 23, Sir Thomas Gresham to Burghley, August 20, 1571.

54. APC, VIII, 53–60, December 12, 1571.

Sir Nicholas went on at much greater length to praise the queen's economy and good government, then to summarize the recent causes of extraordinary expenditure, and finally to ask for parliament's assistance in meeting them.[55] After spending several weeks discussing other matters, the commons did vote a supply, and at the end of the session it was again Bacon who lengthily expressed the queen's appreciation of "the readiness with which the money had been granted."[56] In 1576 and 1581, the situation was slightly different, though essentially the procedure was much the same. The "parliaments" which sat in both these years were not in fact new parliaments at all, but sessions of the one that had been elected and prorogued for the first time in 1572. There were, therefore, no opening statements by the Lord Keeper, for there was no formal opening. In 1576, indeed, it was not until the third day, February 10th, that a speech was made explaining that this session, in contrast with its precursor in 1572 but like the parliament of 1571, had been summoned primarily for the purpose of granting another aid.[57] The speaker was Sir Walter Mildmay. He concentrated eloquently on the benefits which the reign of Elizabeth had conferred on England, and one subsidy and two fifteenths and tenths were granted almost immediately. Perhaps because of this success Mildmay again stood up in 1581 and made another brilliant and equally effective speech.[58] This time the results were not quite so immediate, but they were no less ultimately satisfying. A grand committee was appointed by the house, and out of this committee came the subsidy bill for which Mildmay had asked.[59]

Now it is notable in all this that, apart from this instance of their all sitting together on the grand committee of 1581, very few Privy Councillors indeed, apart from Bacon and Mildmay, were directly concerned with forwarding the matter of supply in any of these parliaments. Sir Francis Knollys did speak in support of the Lord Keeper's appeal for funds in 1571, but it was totally unnecessary, and his contribution to the business of the day was pointedly described by a contemporary diarist as "a long [and] needless discourse on the subsidy."[60] There was in fact little direct debate in the house of commons on the subject of supply at all. At first this may seem surprising, given the importance of the matter, but it appears less so after further consideration.

---

55. J. E. Neale, *Elizabeth I and her Parliaments 1559–1581* (New York, 1958), 186.
56. *Ibid.*, 238.
57. *Ibid.*, 346.
58. *Ibid.*, 384.
59. *Ibid.*, 385.
60. *Ibid.*, 218.

Although one of the main reasons for summoning into being England's already ancient assembly of representatives of the community of the realm was the need of the Crown for extra money, once it met other factors immediately came into play. Parliament, and particularly the house of commons, had its own ideas about its function as a member of the body politic. It saw itself as much more than a mere tax-voting royal convenience. In its own view, the pressing questions of the hour—now the insufficiently reformed state of Elizabeth's ambivalent church, again the endlessly fascinating, edifyingly horrid intrigues of the Queen of Scots— were as much its concern as the queen's. It intended at worst to have its say, at best to do something about them. Any Elizabethan parliament, therefore, was bound to be a bargaining session. A significant number of members showed themselves determined not to part with either their own money or that of those they represented without something in return from the Crown. That *quid pro quo* was nonfinancial legislation relating to a variety of matters, many of them of greater concern to the commons than to the queen.

The government, too, had its own non-fiscal objectives. In 1571 it wanted a statute to help it deal with the newly dangerous situation resulting from the papal excommunication of the queen, and in 1581 it desired the extension of a sedition law of Mary Tudor's time.[61] Such elaborations on a basically simple theme of hunger for cash, added to the ambitions of the house of commons, plus the fact that the queen, often enough, wanted one thing and her advisers another, inevitably created tensions, which spawned complexity, which seemed destined to lead to confusion. The amazing thing is that the council managed as well as it did in bringing a reasonable degree of order out of such a potentially chaotic situation. It provided practical, though unofficial parliamentary leadership, tactfully guiding both houses through a maze of verbiage towards a compromise outcome that was at least approximately satisfactory to most—and always got the Crown its subsidy in the process.

The formally unrecognized character of the leadership displayed in parliament by Queen Elizabeth's Privy Councillors cannot be overstressed. Theoretically all parliament men stood on an equal footing within their own house, and it was practically impossible for anyone, be he an ordinary member from the county of Somerset, say, or the Lord Chancellor himself (the official enjoying the highest secular precedence in the land outside the royal family) to stand up in either chamber and simply issue instructions. In 1572 Sir Nicholas Bacon, replying to the oration of the newly elected speaker of the commons, Robert Bell, and obviously hoping for

---

61. *Ibid.*, 225 and 393.

a brief session, flatly forbade the introduction of private bills. Almost immediately six were read.[62] It was often no easier to get officially sponsored legislation through the house of commons than it was to prevent the consideration there of private business. In 1571 when the government introduced a treason's bill, Thomas Norton, a private member and a Puritan to boot, promptly produced another. Norton's action brought Sir Francis Knollys to his feet to urge that the two bills be treated separately, but the house decided to join them, in order to get *its* concerns aired as well as the Crown's, and appointed a committee to perform an act of fusion. The committee, which included all the Privy Councillors in the commons, reported back still with two bills rather than one. The house proceeded to join them anyway.[63] In a similar vein, in his opening oration in 1571 Bacon warned the commons against meddling in matters of state unless specifically asked by the queen for their opinions. This prohibition patently included the subject of the Church. Yet William Fleetwood, a lawyer with an unmistakable penchant for controversy, unabashedly proceeded to assert that religious affairs fell quite properly within the purview of the house, his colleagues agreed with him and the Lord Keeper's injunction was completely disregarded.[64] Altogether, the house of commons under Queen Elizabeth was impossible to do without, difficult to live with, and extremely hard for anyone, let alone a Privy Councillor, to order about.

One of the main reasons, in the face of such an apparently uncooperative attitude, for the success of Elizabeth's Privy Councillors in parliament is that they recognized and even supported the elected part of the legislature's claim to be free to run its own affairs and its right not to be dictated to by the hereditary executive. Sir Walter Mildmay, for one, was a staunch defender of the privileges of parliament; in 1581, along with Dr. Wilson, he came out strongly against an attempt of private member Arthur Hall to get himself out of an awkward predicament by attacking them.[65] And Sir Francis Knollys, in response to what he considered unjustified aspersions on his official character, vehemently denied that just because he was a councillor he was in any way preeminent over his fellow parliamentarians. He spoke out, rather, in favor of the idea of his absolute equality amongst them.[66] Faced with the fact of parliamentary independence, the council wasted no time in trying to undermine it or pull it

---

62. *Ibid.*, 248.
63. *Ibid.*, 231.
64. *Ibid.*, 196.
65. *Ibid.*, 340–341, 407.
66. *Ibid.*, 255.

down. It could be got around much more easily and effectively. The knack was in working with rather than against it. The result was that theoretically nonexistent, supposedly unacceptable leadership was not only provided, it actually operated, in subtle, tactful ways, very well indeed.

This does not mean that the councillors in parliament sat silent—far from it. They openly advocated measures they approved of and recommended policies they had themselves evolved. But their advocacy was manifestly intelligent in its presentation and their strategy in debate carefully planned ahead of time. The council included in its ranks several excellent speakers, and they were used to good effect. Walter Mildmay and Christopher Hatton were especially famous for felicity in verbal expression firmly built upon a foundation of sense, and their oratorical talents were exploited to the fullest. In addition to almost automatically being designated to recommend the voting of supply, Mildmay was frequently selected to head delegations of one sort or another to the queen or the house of lords, where concise, convincing speech was called for.[67] Hatton, too, was often cannily employed by the house of commons as its honey-tongued spokesman to the two other persons of the trinity of parliament, and in 1581 he got both government and house out of a procedural impasse by introducing and eloquently and convincingly singing the praises of a new measure specifically designed to meet the difficulty.[68] The smoothness of Hatton's personality was so great that he was the natural choice to deliver the kind of royal reprimand that, coming from someone less generally admired, might well have created undesirable resentment among his parliamentary colleagues.

Those councillors less notably endowed by Calliope made less dramatic forays into the field of Elizabethan parliamentary politics, although this did not necessarily mean they spoke any less. Francis Knollys, purely as an orator, was not in the same class as Mildmay and Hatton. Contemporary comments on his talent for speechifying were not confined to the occasion already mentioned. But it was Knollys who was regarded as the house of commons' unofficial leader. It seems clear that this was not just because he was the senior of the Privy Councillors who sat there; it was also because when he spoke, even if often at wearisome length, he spoke his conscience and was respected for it. Occasionally, doing so got him into embarrassingly paradoxical positions. At the beginning of the 1581 session, Paul Wentworth, in a deliberately provocative gesture, introduced a motion for a public fast "to the end that it might please God to bless us in our

---

67. *Ibid.*, 236, 331, 346 and 358–359.
68. *Ibid.*, 396.

actions . . . and for a sermon to be had every morning." The motion was actually supported by Dr. Wilson, but although Knollys approved it as a Puritan, because it encroached upon the queen's prerogative as the Supreme Governor of the Church of England he felt it his duty to oppose it as a councillor. This time he failed to carry the house with him. The motion carried and the only concession made to the royal feelings was the leaving of it to the council to appoint the preachers.[69] But the integrity of his stand worked in his favor in the long run even if it meant he lost out on occasion. The upright Knollys was not always on the losing side nor was he put down by an occasional—one might say occupational—defeat, and his persistence in suggesting, commenting, criticising, blaming, praising and otherwise participating continually in the business of the commons significantly assisted the progress of the government's programs in the lower house.

The other commoner councillors played roles similar to Knollys', helping to nudge the barge of royal business safely past the parliamentary rapids. Ralph Sadler, Thomas Smith, Francis Walsingham and, as we have seen, Thomas Wilson, all spoke from time to time, although the secretaries had much else to keep them busy during the time of parliament. Only one councillor was well advised when he refrained from taking part in debate at all. James Croft was far from remaining dumb, but his hectoring manner apparently irritated more than it persuaded, and his comparative quietness, at least compared with the verbosity of Knollys, was probably not accidental.[70]

As much as of their speaking, the influence of Elizabeth's councillors in parliament, however, was the consequence of their expert knowledge of parliamentary procedure and political tactics, itself the result of their constant and, for the most part, long experience in dealing with people, both in parliament and out of it. They knew as well as any and better than the average new member how to get things done. The parliament of 1576 provides an excellent example of their acumen and talent for strategical maneuver. The commons of the day, like their predecessors and successors, favored reform of the Church. A bill could have been introduced for the purpose. It had happened that way before. But the queen regarded such a method of proceeding in matters of religion as impertinent. Ecclesiastical alteration was a matter for the head of the Church, its bishops and convocation, not for parliament. A bill would, therefore, almost certainly have been vetoed. Instead of risking royal re-

---

69. *Ibid.*, 378–379.
70. *Ibid.*, 424.

jection, one Tristram Pistor moved that "an humble petition may be made to the queen's majesty," requesting her to make the desired changes. It does not matter whether the motion was his own idea or not, although it would be interesting to find out; it is sufficient to know what further action it gave rise to. A committee was appointed, including all the Privy Councillors sitting in the house of commons. The committee was instructed to draw up the petition, submit it to the commons, confer with the lords and present it to the queen. On March 2nd three noble and three commoner councillors did just that. Elizabeth, in turn, ordered Walter Mildmay to reply graciously on her behalf, promised to do something, and conferred with the bishops and convocation, which, as a result, passed a series of articles to implement most of the commons' recommendations.[71]

We do not know enough to prove that this comparatively uncontroversial course of action and its happy outcome was the product of council leadership, but it is the most logical deduction to make on the basis of the evidence that has survived. Time and again committees were named—to consider how to comply with the Crown's request for supply, to examine Peter Wentworth, to draft a new treason's bill, to devise, at the Crown's behest, legislation relative to the taking of the sacrament of Holy Communion—that included all the councillors in the commons. This procedure was entirely understandable and was not forced on the house. As long as there was no deep-rooted antagonism to the Crown in parliament— and as long as Elizabeth sat on the throne there was not—it made sense to have as many councillors on committees as possible. They had colleagues in the lords; they were the queen's chosen confidants. They could, therefore, be expected to communicate with them and with her better than other people, and as long as both peers and sovereign possessed working vetoes, it made sense to communicate with them as effectively as possible. But it certainly added to the councillors' power in parliament. Once appointed to committees, councillors were obviously in an excellent position to influence directly what went on in them and hence to have indirectly a considerably greater say than they might otherwise have had in what went on in the house itself. The history of the successful career of the petition presented by Mr. Pistor to a parliament possibly not breathlessly excited by such a careful method of proceeding can best be understood if it is seen as providing us with the opportunity to view this influence in operation.

Lastly, it is worth remembering that the most complete accounts of the

---

71. *Ibid.*, 349–353; Patrick Collinson, *The Elizabethan Puritan Movement* (Berkeley, 1967), 161–163.

proceedings in any deliberative assembly—even Hansard and the Congressional Record—retail, and can retail, only a tiny fraction of what actually happened there. Sixteenth century sources are far from being complete, and they certainly do not tell us what conversations and discussions the various councillors had with friends and neighbors momentarily in London to represent their fellow gentlemen and air their views on national, international or regional affairs, or about anything else of either greater or lesser import. Yet we know that many members of the house of commons were related to, otherwise connected with or had been elected through the influence of Burghley and Leicester and Sadler and the rest and can, therefore, surmise that the interchange of information and ideas that went on outside and in the corridors of parliament was constant. Through such informal contacts between members and other members, and members and councillor-patrons, councillor-relatives and councillor-friends, a *modus* more or less *vivendi* between the two non-judicial elements of the Tudor constitution was arrived at.[72] The Lord Keepers, Mildmay's and, perhaps most interesting of all in view of the forthright contemporary reactions they elicited, Croft's and Knollys's speeches, are the fraction of parliamentary proceedings that shows above the depths of unrecorded history. That we know they were made at all, how, when and by whom, gives us an inkling of what else went on beneath the surface of parliamentary formality. In many instances, the recorded acts of the two houses merely, though by no means invaluably, reflect, as they gave official effect to, agreements in practice reached elsewhere. In any event, one way or another parliament was told what the government wanted of it and why, and if it complied with the demands made of it only in its own good time, sometimes incompletely, and almost always after it had had its say on other matters, neither the right of the Crown to ask for money nor even, usually, the amount demanded were themselves at issue.

Just as the spheres of finance and the law had their own institutions, officers and modes of operation, so had the military world. The admiralty ran the navy. There was a master of the ordnance to see that everyone who needed them for official purposes was supplied with weapons and ammunition. And the nation's militia had traditions stretching back for centuries.

In times of peace, the admiralty was reasonably successful in running

---

72. J. E. Neale, *The Elizabethan House of Commons* (New Haven, 1950), especially in his chapter on the quality of the house in which he vividly shows how "the family ties of members almost defy description," underlines "how intimate a society this was," 312 and 316.

the navy under the authority of a Lord Admiral directly responsible to the queen, who had appointed him and his subordinates. There are, in consequence, only occasional entries in the Privy Council registers dating from the 1570s and comparatively few documents in the State Paper and other great manuscript collections relating to council involvement with the details of naval administration. The council was, nonetheless, actively concerned in the making of decisions relative to the actual use of the navy, in keeping down its cost and in ensuring its defense while not in active operation.

Any navy plays its most easily understood role while sailing the seas. Elizabeth's ships were frequently assigned to such police tasks as clearing the English Channel of pirates, keeping unwanted foreigners out of English ports and arresting alien ships suspected of perpetrating outrages on English commerce.[73] They also patrolled the ocean approaches to the British Isles. A few vessels might be sent, for instance, to cruise off Ireland and keep a watchful eye on waterborne armed forces possibly hostile to the queen.[74] Orders for such employment of the navy went out to its officers either in the queen's name or in the council's with about equal frequency, the council playing a part in the process even when the resulting instructions were in the queen's name rather than its own. Cecil, writing to Walsingham in France after the massacre on St. Bartholomew's day, told him that "we . . . meane to send the queen's majestie's navy to the seas with spede."[75] Two years earlier the queen herself had written to thank the Lord Admiral for "putt[ing] our whole navy in redynes." She added not only that she knew he had done so only because she had been told about it by the council, but that "oppon such [further] conference as we have had here with our counsell," it had been decided to try and make it appear that the whole navy had been mobilized, without its actually being so.[76] The council clearly wished to have the navy at sea; the queen was reluctant to pay the bill this would entail. The result was a somewhat bizarre compromise, whereby the illusion of full mobilization was to be attempted by actually putting into service only half the men who had been got together

---

73. BM, Lansdowne MS. 13, no. 45, council instructions to William Winter and John Hawkins, March 1571; PRO, SP.12/108, no. 23, the council's instructions to Henry Palmer, esquire, May 19, 1576; no. 67, the council's instructions to William Holstock, August 1, 1576.

74. PRO, SP.12/114, no. 60, council instructions to George Winter, July 1577; SP.12/134, p. 628, the council to George Winter, March 17, 1580.

75. BM, Cotton MS. Vespasian F. vi, f. 131, Burghley to Walsingham, September 11, 1572.

76. PRO, SP.12/73, no. 7, the queen to Clinton, August 8, 1570.

for the purpose—a notable example of the council at least half-persuading Elizabeth to move in a direction it recommended on an occasion when she did not really want to move at all.

Costs could be kept reasonably low in a variety of ways. Ships' complements were made up of conscripts, which meant that crews could be had at considerably less than their value in a free labor market, and both producing these involuntary sailors and consenting to their eventual discharge was very much the council's concern. It kept itself informed as to the numbers of ships and mariners based on the ports of England and Wales, so that all or some of them could be called into service should the necessity arise.[77] When it did, the impressment could be variously accomplished. The council's authority could be put behind particular persons especially charged to bring forward the required numbers at the appropriate time; this was done in 1574 when three "placards" were dispatched to the justices of the peace in certain of the maritime counties "to be aiding and assisting to the bringers of the said placartes for the spedie providing and sending awaye of marriners and seamen to the quene's shippes to be sent to the seas."[78] Another time the queen herself would write to the Lords Lieutenants "to put certen men in redine[s] for the navy."[79] Or it might be decided, with or without the advice of the Lord Admiral, to order a "stay" of all ships in particular ports, so that their crews could be drafted there and then into the more direct service of their sovereign.[80]

This last proceeding was understandably disrupting to local economies, but it required as high an authority to revoke a stay as it had taken to bring one about in the first place. Even the Earl of Bedford, long-established as a royal adviser by 1570, wrote directly to the council to ask for permission to release the fishermen he had previously kept in port on its instructions before sending them back to their own business of earning a living.[81]

---

77. PRO, SP.12/71, no. 75, "a certyfycate of shippes and maryners in Devonshere," July 1570; SP.12/73, no. 48, a certificate of all men and shipping stayed in Norfolk and Suffolk, Newcastle-upon-Tyne, Devon, Yorkshire, Somerset, Bristol, Dorset, Hampshire, Sussex, Essex, the Isle of Wight and Cornwall, August 1570; SP.12/147, no. 21, certificate of shipping within the area of Portsmouth, January 26, 1581; BM, Harleian MS. 6991, f. 80, Walsingham to Burghley, June 10, 1574.

78. APC, VIII, 265, July 5, 1574.

79. PRO, SP.12/73, no. 33, the queen to the Lords Lieutenants of Suffolk, Essex and Kent, August 27, 1570.

80. PRO, SP.12/95, no. 85, Burghley to Walsingham, May 4, 1574.

81. PRO, SP.12/73, no. 27, the Earl of Bedford to the council, August 24, 1570.

To discharge men required more than the word of a single councillor, even if he were Lord Treasurer, as the Marquess of Winchester had also realized in 1563. "I dare not," he remarked to Cecil after a Mr. Abington had asked him for permission to go home after serving the queen on the seas off Portsmouth, "give him that leave without thassent of any lorde of the counsaill."[82] Here, too, in some instances, action required the consent of the queen herself.[83]

The council, in the interests of economy, kept itself up-to-date on the current costs of outfitting, manning and supplying the navy and could be quite as hard-headed as the queen when it came to getting value for money spent.[84] It had lists drawn up of the number of sailors, soldiers and gunners it took to man each vessel and from these it could find out quickly enough how much each of them was paid, or had to be paid.[85] In 1579 a pinnace belonging to Sir Henry Sackford was sent to join Sir John Perrot's fleet, which was already at sea. Its crew, naturally, needed to be fed, but Perrot's fleet had already been supplied and further expense was not to be contemplated. So it was ordered victualled out of the stores already assembled for eventually replenishing Perrot's ships, and Elizabeth thereby avoided "anie further charges," even if her seagoing subjects went hungry in consequence.[86]

Ancient obligations were exploited, such as those of New Romney, Old Romney and Lydd "for setting owte of a shipp for the queene's service," and the council employed private ships on expeditions when something less than a whole fleet was called for, for which it authorized payments at "inclusive rates."[87] Sir Arthur Champernowne was paid £66.13.4d

---

82. BM, Harleian MS. 6990, no. 9, f. 19, the Marquess of Winchester to Cecil, August 17, 1563.

83. BM, Lansdowne MS. 31, the queen's orders for the discharge of ships and men, August 29, 1581.

84. BM, Add. MS. 32323, f. 67, estimate for furnishing and victualling the queen's ships, February 5, 1580.

85. PRO, SP.12/60, no. 26, "William Wyntar's bill for 5 hoyes as for 4 shippes of warr," December 9, 1569; SP.12/71, no. 70, a list of the names of all the queen's ships, with details of tonnage and crew required by each, July 30, 1570; SP.12/73, no. 38, an estimate of the cost of pressing 400 men for service in the navy, August 30, 1570; no. 40, an estimate of the stores required by ten of the queen's ships, August 30, 1570; Northamptonshire Record Office, F (M) P. 10, a note of the increases in the costs of the navy, ordnance office and wardrobe since 1558, no date.

86. BM, Stowe MS. 150, no. 17, f. 21, the council to Edward Baeshe, August 21, 1579.

87. Kent Record Office, New Romney MSS. (unsorted), Burghley to [the mayor and corporation of New Romney], May 4, 1588.

for his expenses in setting forth a frigate in the service of the queen.[88] Lord Cobham received £27 for putting two ships into manned, armed and victualled readiness to transport one M. le Shastre and his company across the channel.[89] Edward Horsey, captain of the Isle of Wight, sent a bark to sea at the queen's command, and the council repaid him with a warrant for £60.[90] John Vaughan got £66.6.8d for putting the *Emmanuel* to the seas for service between Ushant and the Scillies for seven weeks, manned by twenty-four men and himself.[91] At nine shillings and fourpence per man per month, which was the rate prevailing in 1570, £19.12.0d of this would go to the crew, leaving £46.14.8d to cover Vaughan's own salary, victuals, armaments and "rent" of the ship for seven unprofitable weeks. Even if this were not an especially cheap bargain, the government gained the services of a ship when it needed them, and avoided the necessity of maintaining it when it had nothing for it to do. Occasional reconnaissance was very often carried out by chartered vessels of this kind.

Perhaps the best way of all to keep a navy's expenses relatively low, however, while it continues to fulfill its protective function, is to keep it in port as much as possible, as both the British and the Germans did during the First World War. Elizabeth, as we have seen, was much addicted to this expedient. Her ships spent much of their time lying up, usually at Gillingham at the head of the estuary of the Medway, but occasionally at Gravesend actually on the Thames, where it was moved in times of apparently imminent national danger. At either location it guarded the capital merely by its presence, and to get past such a watchdog required specific permission. It took a letter from the council for a foreign ship to pass quietly up the river to London.[92]

Gillingham became the navy's home port not simply because of its geographical situation in relation to London, but also because it is an excellent anchorage, protected against the hazard of vicious North Sea weather by the eastward mass of the Isle of Sheppey. To be equally safe from the danger of attack by human forces, however, its natural topography needs artificial exploitation and elaboration. The council, therefore,

---

88. PRO, E.403/2421, the council to the officers of the exchequer, December 21, 1571.

89. PRO, E.403/2422, the council to the officers of the exchequer, November 1, 1575.

90. PRO, E.403/2420, the council to the officers of the exchequer, December 21, 1571.

91. PRO, E.403/2421, the council to the officers of the exchequer, September 12, 1574.

92. BM, Harleian MS. 4943, f. 81v, the council to the officers of the navy, no date.

was permanently anxious about the state of the local defenses. This anxiety naturally came to a head in times of crisis, and the Privy Council registers for 1574 contains letter after letter addressed to William Winter, master of the ordnance of the Navy, to William Pelham, Lieutenant of the ordnance proper and deputy to the Earl of Warwick, and sometimes to Lord Cobham as well, instructing them "to joine [together] . . . for the good gard of her majestie's shippes and the fortificacion of the Ile of Sheppey, to manne the porte townes and to place gonners in the fortes."[93] In 1572 one whole volume of the State Papers is devoted to Isle of Sheppey matters.[94] The entrance to the sound was commanded by the fort at Queenborough, and on this point the plan of defense was focused.[95] In 1574, however, Winter and Pelham were instructed to start work on a second fortress at Sheerness, making use of the council's authorizing letters to "take up and provide as well tymber and other necessaries for the same, as also to imprest any artificers or laborers for the accomplishment of that service."[96] It was the council, too, that authorized the payment for the supplying of the forts with powder and ammunition.[97] But even adequately equipped forts alone were not enough, and it was the council that took the requisite steps to back up armament with men. In 1571 it wrote the sheriff of Kent "to give order that out of certeyne hundreds adjoyninge Jellingham the queen's majestie's shippes may be garded upon all occasions."[98] Some years later it wrote to the same official again to the same effect, but this time directly to the justices of the peace of the surrounding hundreds as well, and also to Lord Cobham, informing him of what had been done and instructing him to see its orders to others effectively carried out.[99]

If the navy was England's first line of defense, its coast line was its second. The loss of Calais in 1558 had not only been a blow to English pride, but its falling into French hands, as the Marquess of Winchester was still reminding the queen ten years later, had made the adequate defense of the shore between Dover and Portsmouth much more difficult.[100]

---

93. APC, VIII, 272, July 20, 1574; 274, July 22, 1574; 281, August 5, 1574; 290, September 7, 1574.

94. PRO, SP.12/87, a book listing who owned property on the Isle of Sheppey, May 1572.

95. PRO, SP.12/97, no. 41, Burghley to Walsingham, July 30, 1574.

96. APC, VIII, 273, July 20, 1574.

97. Ibid., 275, July 25, 1574.

98. BM, Add. MS 32323, f. 65, the council to the sheriff of Kent, December 31, 1571.

99. APC, VIII, 190, February 7, 1574.

100. PRO, SP.12/46, no. 38, the Marquess of Winchester to the queen, February 29, 1568.

Winchester seems to have been quite serious in recommending that every effort should be made to get Calais back again. But even as he suggested it, the council's time and interest and the queen's money were instead being devoted to the much more practical task of strengthening the fortified places along the southern littoral.

Each crucial stretch of coast was under the surveillance of a person chosen not only for his trustworthiness and closeness to some member of the council, but for his ability to work smoothly and efficiently with others, for, as Henry Radcliff, fourth Earl of Sussex, put it in 1588 when asking Leicester to support a request for his cousin Edward to be the next captain of Portsmouth, "ther cannot be a more dangerous thinge then contention and disagrement amongst men placed in charge of governement."[101] Lord Cobham, himself eventually a Privy Councillor, controlled the eastern end as Lord Warden of the Cinque Ports. Sir Henry Radcliff, captain of Portsmouth both before and after acceding to his brother's title in 1583, was, as such, responsible not only for Portsmouth itself, but for other neighboring strongholds, such as the castles of St. Andrews and at Southsea.[102] The Earl of Bedford was in charge in the west, where he made periodic tours of inspection of the coastal defenses, reporting to the council on the state of such important strong points as the castle of St. Mawes and St. Michael's Mount.[103] And in the interstices, the local nobility having property in the area, such as Lords Delaware, Buckhurst and Montague and the Marquess of Winchester and the Earl of Sussex (in his "private" capacity) were entrusted with "taking care of the frontiers against sudden invasion."[104] The Isle of Wight was under the command of Edward Horsey, a close friend of the Earls of Leicester and Warwick, and a man well–liked by the queen. And the great fortress of the eastern coast at Berwick was under the governance of Lord Hunsdon. All these places were constantly in need of assistance of one sort or another and of men and money to repair and maintain the fortifications under their command. All turned for help to the council, as Hunsdon did from Berwick in 1569, and Sir Henry Wallop and Sir

---

101. Longleat House, Dudley MS. II, f. 255, the fourth Earl of Sussex to the Earl of Leicester, August 24, 1588.

102. APC, VIII, 97, April 14, 1573.

103. BM, Lansdowne MS. 18, f. 93, the Earl of Bedford to Burghley, August 3, 1574; PRO, SP.12/132, no. 6, the Earl of Bedford to Walsingham, September 15, 1579.

104. BM, Add. MS. 32323, f. 2 and BM, Harleian MS. 4943, f. 32v, the council to Lords Montague, Buckhurst and Delaware, no date; PRO, SP.12/197, f. 13, orders by the Marquess of Winchester and the Earl of Sussex for the defense of Hampshire, January 10, 1587.

William Kingsmill were to do when appointed commissioners to survey the works at Portsmouth in 1571.[105]

It was the council which authorized the payments to the treasurer of Berwick to cover the expenses of "a doer in the fortificacions," and to Richard Popinjay, surveyor of the works at Portsmouth, for undertakings carried out there in 1572, when the Earl of Leicester and Cecil both seem to have taken a personal interest in what was being done.[106] Popinjay carried out more repairs in 1577, but this time not before the council had instructed Radcliff to keep a close eye on how the alloted money was being spent and to make sure that no man was kept on the payroll a moment longer than there was work for him to do.[107] It required a warrant from the queen to raise the large numbers of men who were sometimes needed to carry out the really big repair jobs, but it was the council that wrote the letter accompanying the warrant, stipulating how the levy was to be made.[108]

The council was concerned with the ordnance, supplied to these fortified places and elsewhere, for several reasons, the one underlying all the others being that it wanted to make it as certain as possible that none got into hands which might then turn it upon the government. Tight control was kept, therefore, over its manufacture. In June 1574, after a period when all production had been completely forbidden, the council issued orders for resumption, but on specific conditions. The main one was that manufacturers should enter into bonds that they would sell nothing for export, but deal only with English merchants for guaranteed English use.[109] This was no new regulation. The sheriff and justices of the peace in Devon had been ordered in 1572 to enquire into what ordnance had already been conveyed abroad through western ports and to prevent such

---

105. Hatfield House, MS. 3, ff. 117–118, Hunsdon to the council, February 9, 1569; PRO, SP.12/78, no. 12, Sir Henry Wallop, Sir William Kingsmill and others to the council, May 8, 1571.

106. BM, Add. MS. 32323, f. 44v, the council to the treasurer of Berwick, April 1, 1571; PRO, E.403/2420, the council to the officers of the exchequer, February 15, 1572; SP.12/89, no. 27, note concerning the fortifications of Portsmouth, October 3, 1572.

107. Longleat House, Dudley MS. II, f. 255, the Earl of Sussex to the Earl of Leicester, August 24, 1588.

108. BM, Harleian MS. 703, new f. 11v, the council to Walter Covert, February 9, 1584; new f. 38, the council to Howard of Effingham, August 16, 1585; f. 38, the council to Howard of Effingham, August 26, 1585; PRO, SP.12/78, no. 15, Sir Henry Radcliff to the council, May 21, 1571.

109. APC, VIII, 254, June 19, 1574; PRO, SP.12/97, no. 17, "orders sett downe by her majestie's Privie Counsell concerninge the castinge of iron ordnance," June 19, 1574.

traffic in the future.[110] No one was to manufacture at all without the royal license; and in 1576, in Surrey at least, production was once more completely halted.[111]

Second only to keeping control over production, the council was anxious about the storage and distribution. It wanted to ensure that military hardware could be supplied where and when necessary and at as little cost as possible to the treasury. The main supply depot was at the Tower. But there were others at such area centers as the Isle of Wight, Portsmouth, Shrewsbury (for North Wales), Gloucester (for South Wales), as well as at individual strongholds like the castle of Calshot.[112] The stores at the Tower were personally checked from time to time by members of the council themselves, and those in the outlying arsenals by commissioners appointed by the council and reporting directly to it.[113] The justices of the peace were periodically reminded that it was their responsibility to see that local ordnance was in good working condition, but movement from the supply center to the periphery took place only when the council ordered it.[114] Informed by Lord Cobham of a shortage of munitions in the Cinque Ports in 1574, the council instructed Mr. Pelham to make it good, at the same time promising to procure from the queen a warrant to cover the quantity actually delivered.[115] The "empcions and the charges of the cariages" to which such an order gave rise were usually met by the issuance of a Privy Seal, payable at the exchequer; but when the matter was particularly urgent, as it was at the time of the northern rebellion, the council's own warrant would suffice.[116] In these instances the Crown met

110. BM, Add. MS. 32323, f. 97, the council to the sheriff and justices of the peace of Devon, December 25, 1572.

111. Surrey Record Office, Loseley MS. 2014, no. 23, the council to Sir William More and Sir Thomas Browne, August 28, 1576.

112. PRO, SP.12/75, no. 56, the Marquess of Winchester to Cecil, 1570(?); SP.12/78, no. 12, Sir Henry Wallop, Sir William Kingsmill and others to the council, May 18, 1571; SP.12/133, no. 18, [the Earl of Pembroke] to the council, 1579; SP.12/147, no. 1, note of the ordnance stores necessary for the castle of Calshot, January 3, 1581.

113. PRO, SP.12/75, no. 48, the queen to Howard of Effingham, Knollys and Mildmay, commissioning them to survey the ordnance and armory offices, 1570; SP.12/78, no. 12, Sir Henry Wallop, Sir William Kingsmill and others to the council, May 18, 1571; BM, Lansdowne MS. 30, no. 6, f. 18, instructions to Beale and Fettiplace, 1580.

114. PRO, SP.12/136, no. 11, the council to the justices of the peace of Suffolk, January 1580.

115. BM, Harleian MS. 6991, f. 94, Walsingham to Burghley, July 26, 1574.

116. PRO, SP.12/59, no. 56, "the charges for sending of certen munition to Leicester for which . . . ther was a warrant from the counsell," November

the cost, but it did so only when strictly necessary. The council might see to the provision of the actual guns, but the cities they protected normally had to pay for the munitions that made them effective. The Privy Council registers are full of examples of council letters written to the lieutenant of the ordnance to supply local authorities, such as the town of Rye, with powder and match, but only in return "for redy money" and at her majesty's price.[117] Any signs of reluctance to foot the bill was liable to bring down the council's displeasure on the heads of the offenders.[118]

Fortifications, ordnance, munitions—all these were of enormous importance for the effective protection of the country, but they were none of them of any value without people to make use of them. The council's most pressing defensive concern of all, in consequence, was the mustering of men for military service.

The council drew its authority over the national musters from the commissions issued by the queen under the Great Seal for periodic investigation into the carrying out of laws relating to the maintenance in readiness for national service of men and weapons. Muster commissioners or Lords Lieutenants were named for each county, and ordered henceforth to act on instructions which they would receive from the Privy Council. Furthermore, the Lord Keeper was authorized "to alter or renew our said commissions," which he actually did at the direction of the council.[119] These two provisions put the council in effective control.

Its initial action after the issuance of the original commissions was to send out specific directions for the holding of musters (that is, local reviews of those men legally liable to serve, and their arms) on a particular day. These usually went out at the same time as the original commission, the president of the Council in the Marches of Wales being concurrently instructed to make arrangements for like proceedings within his own area of jurisdiction.[120] The simultaneous dispatch of the queen's

---

1569; SP.12/74, no. 24, "a brief note of all monies received by William Pelham . . . by Privy Seals since January 1," October 30, 1570.

117. APC, VIII, 241, May 20, 1574.

118. BM, Harleian MS. 703, new f. 43, the council to Howard of Effingham, March 31, 1586.

119. PRO, SP.12/49, no. 78, the queen to Bacon, April 12, 1569; BM, Harleian MS. 6991, f. 23, Smith to Burghley, January 10, 1573.

120. BM, Harleian MS. 4943, f. 31, the council to the Vice-president and Council in the Marches of Wales, March 14, 1571; Surrey Record Office, Loseley MS. VI, no. 29, the council to Lord Lumley and the other deputy lieutenants of Surrey, August 18, 1584; BM, Add. MS. 32323, f. 6, [the council] to certain counties, September 8, 1572; PRO, SP.12/49, no. 65, directions for musters, March 16, 1569; BM, Add. MS. 32323, f. 5v, [the council] to the Lord President of Wales, no date.

authorizing letter patent and the council's orders consequent upon it was not essential. Lord Darcy was informed in 1572 that the council's missive alone was quite "sufficiente warrante to muster without commission under the Great Seale," which he had apparently questioned, since "we directe you not, but as we be appointed by her majestie."[121] But Darcy's reaction suggests that it was the more usual—not to say expected—procedure, and it was probably to avoid such possible delays that at times of crisis, orders for which on other occasions council letters would have been "sufficient warrant" were sent out as letters from the queen herself: orders to the Lords Lieutenants to hold musters and levy hundreds of troops as well as letters to individuals to supply a single man and a horse.[122] At such times the council was not less involved in the decision-making process than at any other. The queen "resolvid with our counsell" before instructing the Lord Admiral to send troops to join the Earl of Sussex at the time of the northern rebellion, and it was by her council's advice that, because of the extraordinary press of such business, she authorized Cecil to "sign" letters for her by means of a rubber stamp representing her signature.[123] However they received their orders, the commissioners reported back on what had taken place, and from then on each problem that arose (and there was no shortage of them) was dealt with on the basis of its merits. What was to be done would be discussed at the council table and the decisions reached, often enough, on the basis of the information contained in the lists and books of precedents kept in the council office.[124] Musters were held sometimes as a matter of routine, at others as the direct result of disturbances abroad. The 1572 musters were a direct consequence of "the greate murther in France."[125] Whenever they were held, each county returned a complete listing of horse- and footmen and weapons in each of its hun-

---

121. BM, Add. MS. 32323, f. 3, the council to Lord Darcy and others, September 24, [1572].

122. PRO, SP.12/66, no. 38, the queen to the Lords Lieutenants, February 15, 1570; SP.12/67, no. 12, the queen to the Lords Lieutenants, March 10, 1570; no. 13, the queen to an esquire, March 10, 1570; no. 14, the queen to a knight or gentleman, March 10, 1570.

123. Samuel Haynes, *A Collection of State Papers . . . left by William Cecil, Lord Burghley* (London, 1740), 566, the queen to Clinton, December 1, 1569; Hatfield House, MS. 156, f. 17, the queen to Cecil, March 8, 1570.

124. BM, Harleian MS. 6035, Walsingham's letter book, f. 67, 1583; Bodleian Library, MS. Perrot 3, a precedent book, the entries relating primarily to diplomacy and dating from early in the reign of Elizabeth; PRO, SP.12/67, no. 15, a list of Buckinghamshire gentlemen supplying troops, March 10, 1570; SP.12/78, no. 36, a list of counties, May 1571.

125. BM, Add. MS. 32323, f. 2v, the council to Lord Darcy, Lord Riche and others, September 1572.

dreds. The Surrey returns alone in 1569 constitute a whole volume of the State Papers Domestic.[126]

It was a massive operation and, on several counts, it can be rated a successful one, as Lindsay Boynton has demonstrated in his recent, excellent book on the Elizabethan militia. Devotion to the queen's service was notable among the commissioners and deputy lieutenants who bore the brunt of organization.[127] The musters themselves were serious military inspections.[128] The council's admonitions, when a county failed to produce an adequate number of men, could be almost startlingly effective in increasing the figures.[129] The seventies were a period of continual experiment, of constant jockeying to reach a reasonable accommodation between royal demands for and the country's willingness to provide an adequate defense force and, on the whole, persistent investment of the council's time paid sufficient dividends for Walsingham eventually to be able to assert that "there was reduced into bands and trained . . . 26,000 foot and horsemen: a thing never put into execution in any of her majesty's predecessors' time."[130]

Horsemen, of course, are of no use without horses, but just as statutes obligated Englishmen to fight in the national interest, so there were legal requirements aimed at ensuring the provision of mounts for them to ride in the royal service.[131] Recusants could be usefully exploited to the same end. Forgiveness for their errors was put up for sale: £24 in cash, or one fully furnished horse, plus man, for service in the wars in Ireland.[132] Wherever they came from, the task of checking on the number of available and serviceable animals at a given moment was usually given to commissioners especially appointed for the purpose.[133]

Orders for the deployment of both troops and horses were issued some-

---

126. PRO, SP.12/50, a book entitled "Surrey General Musters," July 23, 1569.

127. Lindsay Boynton, *The Elizabethan Militia 1558–1638* (London, 1967), 16.

128. *Ibid.*, 17.

129. *Ibid.*, 43, 79.

130. *Ibid.*, 124–125.

131. PRO, SP.12/137, nos. 50–53, the council's orders for the breeding and keeping of horses, April 1580.

132. BM, Harleian MS. 703, f. 15, new f. 19, the council to Walter Covert, August 17, 1584; f. 20, the council to the sheriff and justices of the peace of Sussex, August 7, [1585].

133. PRO, SP.12/67, no. 4, the queen to the Marquess of Winchester, March 4, 1570; SP.12/97, no. 18, Burghley to Walsingham, June 21, 1574; SP.12/147, no. 15, Norfolk muster commissioners to the Earl of Sussex, January 23, 1581.

times by the queen and sometimes by the council, the difference once again being that in times of crisis they went out in the queen's name and at others in the council's. In 1569 it was Elizabeth who ordered the Lord Admiral to move north once the Earls of Derby and Shrewsbury arrived to join him with their own contingents.[134] But when, in 1584, Lord Howard was sent instructions for the dispatch of troops for service overseas, they were signed by seven Privy Councillors.[135] It was the council that gave orders for the training of the London trained bands.[136] It was the council that wrote letters to authorize the requisitioning of ships for transporting troops when necessary.[137] It was the council that sanctioned payment of money in prest to the surveyor-general of victualling, under a Privy Seal previously issued for the purpose, to feed them.[138] When the need for their services was over, and sometimes even before, it was the council that oversaw their disbanding. The Lord Admiral reported regularly to the council, not to the queen, on his progress in discharging his troops in January 1570.[139]

One final thing was of crucial importance to the setting in motion of all this defensive machinery should an attempt actually be made to violate England's territorial integrity, as ultimately it was in 1588. This was the national warning system: the network of beacons which passed the news of the Armada from one end of England to the other as fast as the fires could be set alight. The beacons were not permanently maintained, but at times when there appeared to be a particular threat from overseas the council would send out orders for their preparation and for a watch to be kept until it was assured that the danger had passed.[140]

---

134. PRO, SP.12/59, no. 31, the queen to Clinton, November 24, 1569.

135. BM, Harleian MS. 703, f. 37, the council to Howard of Effingham, August 1, 1584.

136. BM, Harleian MS. 168, f. 186, the council to the captains of the London trained bands, 1589; PRO, SP.12/111, no. 44, council instructions for the training of shot in London, March 21, 1577.

137. City of Chester Record Office, MS. M/L/1, no. 42, the council to the mayor of Chester, June 24, 1593.

138. PRO, E.403/2423, the council to the officers of the exchequer, no date.

139. PRO, SP.12/66, nos. 1, 2, 3, 5, 10, 13 and 18, Clinton to the council, January 2, 2, 6, 8, 12 and 19, 1570.

140. BM, Add. MS. 32323, f. 7v, the council to certain gentlemen living near the coasts, December 22, 1571; f. 8v, the council to the Marquess of Winchester and other Hampshire notables, no date; PRO, SP.12/90, no. 9, a series of letter-precedents relating to provisions for defense against "invasion of forraine enemies," December 2, 1572; BM, Harleian MS. 4943, f. 31v, the council to those along the seacoast having authority over beacons, December 2, 1573; Surrey Record Office, Loseley MS. VI, f. 18, the council to Howard of Effing-

All the council's activities we have considered so far were broadly directive. The law, the exchequer, the Household, the Chamber, the admiralty, the ordnance and the horse and muster commissioners all could, and most of the time did, function relatively independently and quite adequately, following long-established routines and working towards rarely changing ends. They did not need constant procedural orders from above, and they did not get them. What they did require, and what they received as occasion demanded, were instructions aimed at ensuring that what they did achieved something more than simply the provision of jobs for hundreds of people who would otherwise have been unemployed. The council decided on legal, financial and military policy; the judges, tellers, clerks, vice-admirals, muster commissioners, surveyors of works and so on, under the council's prodding, implemented it.

---

ham, May 1, 1569; *Papers Relating to Musters, Beacons, Subsidies etc.*, volume III of the publications of the Northamptonshire Record Society, edited by Joan Wake (Kettering, 1926), 7–8.

Chapter VII
MATTERS OF STATE AND MATTERS OF COMMONWEALTH

 HE council did many things that required it to act without the assistance of an established profession or department. There was no foreign service, state department or career diplomatic service, no ministry of labor or pensions, no board of trade or department of local government, no ministries of food or transportation. Although aspects of the national life which would now fall within the purview of such bureaus had been at various times regulated by acts of parliament, the right—indeed the duty— to take action with regard to them, where not specifically prohibited by law, still lay with the Crown. In helping the queen to exercise such prerogative rights, the council played one of its most essential, yet most varied roles in English public, and, on occasion, private life.

The Privy Council played a crucial role in the formulation and high level execution of English foreign policy. The Duke of Alba, for example, wrote to Elizabeth in 1572, complaining that her subjects were fighting with the rebels in the Low Countries in spite of treaties that made their presence impossible to justify. The queen referred the matter to the council, and the council quite deliberately refrained from giving any hasty reply, a perfectly legitimate diplomatic stalling tactic.[1] On the other hand, the council could and did move swiftly enough when the need for rapid action arose. The Spanish ambassador, on one particular occasion, complained bitterly that the locks on his watergate had been changed and that the council was keeping the keys to the new ones. This had been done in retaliation for his permitting a fugitive Italian (unjustifiably, according to the English, claiming asylum in the Spanish embassy) to escape through the back door opening onto the river while the queen's men were waiting for him at the front. The council, as soon as it heard of the Spaniard's pained reaction, wrote immediately to the resident English ambassador in Madrid, Thomas Chaloner, with the truth of the matter, "leste . . . [the Spanish ambassador in London] otherwise advertise the king his master

---

1. PRO, SP.12/89, no. 3, Burghley to the Earl of Leicester, August 10, 1572.

of our plaine deling with him."[2] In a somewhat similar case in 1576, the Lord Keeper, the Lord Treasurer and Sir Walter Mildmay were instructed by the rest of the council to inquire into a violent episode at the Portuguese ambassador's residence. The recorder of London had originally been instructed to search the house, and in the process had laid hands, it was alleged, on the ambassador's wife. The queen and the council wished for a formal enquiry, since otherwise "he might aggravate the matter more than there is cause."[3] In June 1572, the Lord Keeper, the Earls of Sussex and Leicester, the Lord Chamberlain, Lord Burghley, Sir James Croft, Sir Ralph Sadler and Sir Walter Mildmay met in conference with the Duc de Montmorency and Mm. de Foix and la Motte "to finish matters expressed in the treaty."[4] And it was quite naturally to the council that William, count de la Marck, turned in 1572 when he felt it necessary to complain to *some*body in England about the seizure by one of Elizabeth's more prominent young subjects (William Winter the younger) of seven prisoners of war taken, not by him, but by the Prince of Orange, who wanted them back.[5]

High echelon diplomacy, however, even in times of crisis, was an intermittent business compared with the regular round of international contacts and disputes between such ordinary citizens as the London vintners and the wine merchants of Bordeaux, or the English wool exporters and the Flemish manufacturers of cloth, and on this lower level the council was quite as active as on the higher. In June 1571 the mayor of Waterford was politely informed that he was to release a French ship being held in his port, after taking sureties guaranteeing that its owners would answer the claims of certain (presumably local) merchants in the proper court of law.[6] Lord Cobham was told to arrest certain merchandise that the council had been informed had been pirated from a Spanish ship,

---

2. BM, Cotton MS. Vespasian C. vii, f. 258, "a true rehearsall of certaine matters declared by the ambassador of the King of Spaine to the lords of the queen's majestie's counsell, with such answer as was given him by the said lords in her majestie's name," January 7, 1563; f. 267, the council to Thomas Chaloner, January 9, 1563.

3. BM, Lansdowne MS. 23, no. 53, the council to Bacon, Burghley and Mildmay, November 7, 1576.

4. BM, Cotton MS. Caligula C. iii, f. 398, new f. 413, "the summe of the communication with the D[uc] de Monmorency, [MM.] du Foyx and la Mott," June 1572.

5. CSP Foreign, 1572–1574, Elizabeth I, volume 10, p. 31, no. 90, William, count de la Marck, to the council, January 27, 1572.

6. BM, Add. MS. 32323, f. 74v, the council to the mayor of Waterford, June 28, 1571.

and see it kept in safe custody, pending further action.[7] And Sir Arthur Champernowne was ordered to free a ship of St. Jean de Luz he had arrested on Christmas Day.[8] These three instances are typical of the council's role in day-to-day foreign affairs. It was essentially a commercial and a maritime role, reflecting the fact that England's everyday relationships with her overseas neighbors were of a commercial and a maritime nature. They show the council acting as a kind of agency of international justice, an agency which worked on behalf of the foreigner in order to further its own representations abroad on behalf of Englishmen. By the later sixteenth century, the various states of Europe were maintaining resident ambassadors in each other's Courts on a fairly regular basis. When first appointed, and sometimes during the course of their mission, Elizabeth's emissaries were given instructions, either by the queen herself or by the council, outlining the purpose of their particular embassies.[9] An important part of the job of any ambassador, however, was, as da Silva put it to Philip II in 1568, to go to the council there to dispatch his subjects' private business.[10] Francis Walsingham's mission to France in 1571–1572 was not entirely devoted to the delicacies of diplomacy. He was also frequently called upon by both the English council and individual councillors to make representations, sometimes even to the king himself, on behalf of English merchants upon whom outrages, usually in the form of robbery, had been committed by the French.[11] That this was an entirely routine occurrence is emphasized by the fact that the books kept by the clerks of the council containing prototypes of the various types of letter they were most likely to be called upon to write provide numerous variations on this theme. For example, Walsingham, in France, was told to speak up on behalf of one man whose goods had been "wrongfully detained," and of another whose wool had been interfered with by Spanish merchants at Rouen; contrariwise, the Lord Mayor of London was instructed to take

---

7. *Ibid.*, f. 73, the council to Lord Cobham, September 29, 1571.

8. BM, Harleian MS. 4943, f. 82v and f. 81, the council to Sir Arthur Champernowne, January 12 and February 10, 1572.

9. Cambridge University Library (England), Gg. 5. 76, pp. 100–104, "Instructions for our trustye and welbeloved Sir Amyas Poulet, knight, appointed to be our ambassador resident with our good brother the French king," no date; Gg. 5, 36, pp. 96–98, instructions by the lords of the council to Robert Beale, sent to the Prince of Orange, April 9, 1576.

10. CSP Spanish, II, no. 18, f. 26, da Silva to the King of Spain, May 1, 1568.

11. BM, Cotton MS. Vespasian F. vi, f. 105b, the Earl of Leicester to Walsingham, July 15, 1572; f. 171(1), the council to Walsingham, October 26, 1572; f. 171(2), the council to Walsingham, October 1572.

bonds from "TF" to appear before the Duke of Florence to answer charges touching his alleged embezzling from a fellow Florentine.[12]

In return for fair treatment for English subjects, the council could be not only just in taking action itself in furthering the settlement of foreigners' claims, but fast moving as well, once the case had come to its attention. The secretary's minutes of a council meeting held on May 8, 1575 record not only "the Marchauntes of Roan's requeste for the discharge of the two hulkes laden with saulte stayed at Falmouthe," but also the council's order "that the saulte shoold eyther be sowlde at sooche pryces as are presently currant or the hulkes released."[13] That the council had a reputation for taking effective action seems further indicated by the fact that a Frenchman, Nicholas Masselin, felt it worthwhile to submit a petition, in French, for help in obtaining redress for the detention of his cargo, not by Englishmen but by Spaniards.[14]

Not infrequently, the council's top level "diplomatic" and lower level "consular" roles overlapped. The crisis in Anglo-Spanish relations which occurred at the turn of the years 1568–1569 provides an excellent example of this. On January 3, 1569 Lord Cobham, Lord Warden of the Cinque Ports, passed on to Cecil the information that there had been a general arrest of English shipping and goods in Flanders.[15] The following day reports to the same effect began to pour in to the council from local officials all along the southeast coast, and from London as well. The Flemish action was not unprovoked. It resulted from the seizure by the English of the cargo of Genoese bullion, destined by the king of Spain for his troops in Flanders, which had been forced by storms to take refuge in English ports the previous month. The decision to seize the bullion was a political decision, and so was the next step taken by the English, replying to Alba's arrest of English ships in Flemish ports by the arrest of Flemish ships in English ports. But once the original political decisions had actually been made, and a proclamation issued on January 10th, what happened next was essentially an administrative concern. The council was equally involved at both stages of the proceedings.

Letters from southern and western ports addressed to the council began to arrive as early as January 10th, reporting the dutiful arrest of the alien property and asking for instructions as to how restitution should be made, out of the vessels and merchandise seized, to local merchants who

---

12. BM, Add. MS. 32323, f. 52v, the council to Walsingham, June 27, 1571; f. 51, the council to the Lord Mayor [of London], August 21, 1571.

13. PRO, SP.12/103, no. 43, note of council business, May 8, 1575.

14. PRO, SP.12/75, no. 20, Nicholas Masselin to the council, 1570(?).

15. PRO, SP.12/49, no. 5, Lord Cobham to Cecil, January 3, 1569.

had incurred losses as the result of Alba's action.[16] It was a peculiar situation, and it called for a peculiar remedy. There were regular Admiralty court processes available to the individual who had received similar treatment at foreign hands, and in such individual cases the council could often be prevailed upon to supply a letter of assistance in an attempt to make the procedure more rapid and more effective. It communicated directly with one Robert Christmas to instruct him to state what losses he had incurred in a seizure of a ship of his by the Portuguese so that it could order appropriate reprisals.[17] At the same time, it instructed Dr. David Lewes, the judge of the Admiralty court, to issue process to Christmas authorizing the seizure of Portuguese goods up to the value of his loss.[18] Soon after it did almost the same service for Dominic Chester.[19] But in the case of a mass arrest, the problems were too great for the Admiralty court to handle, even with the council's aid, and special proceedings became necessary. In June 1572, for example, after another wholesale seizure of Spanish goods, the queen, since the "whole counsell here attendant upon us . . . [is] daily occupied with divers other affairs . . . thought good to make choice of certain of our said counsell to have particular care of the speciall matters relating to [the] arrest, to whom all number of persons may have recourse for expedition of their sutes thereto perteyning."[20] This group of councillors—the Earls of Lincoln, Sussex and Leicester—oversaw the sale of some of these Spanish goods.[21] The distribution of the rest to those Englishmen who had *their* goods seized by the Spaniards was assigned to a subordinate group of special commissioners, which included Sir Ralph Sadler, Sir Walter Mildmay and Dr. Thomas Wilson.[22]

---

16. For example, PRO, SP.12/49, no. 18, the mayor and corporation of Southampton to the council, January 10, and no. 25, the Lord Mayor of London to Burghley, January 14, 1569.

17. BM, Cotton MS, Nero B. i, f. 177, the council to Robert Christmas, September 25, 1570.

18. PRO, SP.12/73, no. 69, the council to the judge of the Admiralty court, September 25, 1570.

19. BM, Add. MS, 32323, f. 58, the council to the judge of the Admiralty court, May 3, 1571.

20. PRO, SP.12/85, no. 31, the queen to the Marquess of Winchester and other members of the Privy Council, January 1572.

21. PRO, SP.12/86, no. 61, Burghley and the Earls of Lincoln, Sussex and Leicester to the commissioners for the sale of Spanish goods, May 1572; BM, Add. MS. 32323, f. 54v, the council to the commissioners for the sale of Spanish goods, August 28, 1572.

22. PRO, SP.12/86, no. 61, the council to the commissioners appointed to make distribution of confiscated Spanish goods to those Englishmen whose goods had been seized by Spaniards, May [1572].

In this particular situation involving English contacts with the outside world, as in others less cosmopolitan in their implications but nonetheless often having far-reaching effects within the realm, the council reveals itself able and willing to accept the consequences of its own previously taken initiatives. Anyone can issue orders; it takes real leaders, with a firm determination to succeed in what they have set out to do and a natural bent for the hard work necessary to make that success possible, to see them carried through to the sometimes bitter end. The council regularly exhibited such readiness and such capability in all areas of its activity. Its talents are more noticeable in its handling of diplomacy only because the arena in which it acted out its international role was more widely open to view than the stage it trod before domestic audiences.

There was no central intelligence agency in sixteenth century England any more than there was a professional diplomatic corps, so here, too, the council filled the breach. Its aim, in this respect, was the defense of the state against the forces of sedition and the protection of the queen in the face of dangers arising from plots against her life.

The Lord Keeper made an oration in the star chamber on November 28, 1567, "before divers of the counsayle and others," in which he not only expressed the council's never ceasing concern with the defense of the Elizabethan state against its enemies, but revealed a clear consciousness of where the danger lay and a firm conviction as to the nature of the remedy. After informing his auditors that the queen had heard that rumors were being spread quite openly to the derogation of God and the dishonor of herself and her supremacy, he went on that this "can not be thought to be done but by the comforte and ayde or at leaste waye [by being] wyncked at by them whom the quen's majesty hathe placed in autorytye to represse theis insolences. . . . Diversytes of myndes makethe seditions, seditions bringethe in tumultes, tumultes makethe insurrections and rebellyon, insurrections makethe depopulacions and bringes in utter ruyne and destruction of men's bodies, goodes and landes. . . . The quen's majestie . . . doethe require of us all a more diligence in execution of the laws."[23] Sedition, in other words, was suspected in almost any outbreak of violence or disorder; it was regarded primarily as arising from the unbridled taking to thought by particular individuals; and the answer to the whole problem was the more efficient enforcement of existing statutes.

If disloyal activity could be anticipated and nipped in the bud, of course, so much the better, and the council could act quickly when it had grounds for anticipating trouble. When the Duke of Norfolk took fright on

---

23. PRO, SP.12/45, p. 4, the Lord Keeper's oration in the Star Chamber, November 28, 1567.

being summoned to Court in 1569 and fled precipitately to his estate at Kenninghall, the council immediately circularized the Lords Lieutenants with a brief explanation of what had happened and the instructions, remembering "how precious a thing common peace is," to pass the word to the local justices to make sure that seditious rumors did not begin to spread as the story of the duke's flight began to circulate.[24] The following month, probably because its precautions had been unavailing, the council wrote another letter, this time to the sheriff and justices of the peace of Surrey, and probably to those of all other counties as well, instructing them to search for those people who were actually inventing rumors.[25]

The council's concern, reflected in Cecil's notes on the unsettled state of Lancashire and Cheshire in 1571, was generally known, and local officials would often take action over suspected persons without specific prompting.[26] Francis Hastings wrote to Walsingham in 1582 from Leicester that "at our last assises . . . a felow suspiciously wandering about our county was taken. . . . I finde him so suttle that my advise was that the lords of her majestie's Privy Counsel shoulde be advertised . . . so (if it pleased theyr honors) he might be sente up and there be more narrowly sifted then my authority wil reache unto . . . [then] your honor and the rest of the honorable[s] of that place . . . may disperse suche orders in every county . . . as they may loke about them carefully."[27] To encourage regional initiative of this sort, and especially the local punishment of offenders without its being bothered at all, the council was careful to express its appreciation of their actions to those responsible. An undated letter to this effect, addressed to the sheriff and justices of the peace in Devon is included in Edmund Tremayne's precedent book.[28]

The councillors themselves were continually on the alert for danger signals. Sir Walter Mildmay reported to Cecil in 1569, typically in an aside in a letter devoted mainly to personal and family matters, on the state of local opinions and loyalties.[29] In such matters, personal contacts could be especially useful. On August 24, 1573 Sir Ralph Sadler sent the

---

24. Samuel Haynes, *Collection of State Papers . . . left by William Cecil, Lord Burghley* (London, 1740), p. 531, the council to the Lords Lieutenants, September 26, 1569.

25. Surrey Record Office, Loseley MS. XIII, f. 57(1), the council to the sheriff and justices of the peace of Surrey, October 20, 1569.

26. Hatfield House, MS. 159, ff. 15–17, Burghley's notes on the state of Lancashire and Cheshire, 1571.

27. Huntington Library, Hastings MS. 5086, Francis Hastings to Walsingham, April 8, 1582.

28. BM, Harleian MS. 4943, f. 47v, the council to the sheriff and justices of the peace of Devon, no date.

29. PRO, SP.12/58, no. 22, Mildmay to Burghley, September 8, 1569.

Lord Keeper a "false, lewde [and] sedicious" book and some letters which had been delivered the previous week by an unknown man to the keeper of the dean's house at St. Paul's. The keeper handed them over to the dean, the dean took them to Sadler, who was currently his neighbor, and Sadler dispatched them to Bacon "because I know not whether your Lordship or the rest of my lordes of the councell have hard of this boke, or sene it."[30] Bacon sent it on to Burghley (both of them were especially maligned in it) and recommended that as it also attacked the queen's government and true religion, it be brought to the attention of the rest of the council as well.[31]

Open sedition and tumult were comparatively easy to deal with. The Lord Mayor of London could be instructed that a man who had been making ill-advised statements should be given time to regret them at leisure in the pillory, or other local agents simply ordered to investigate the particular circumstances, and then proceed in the matter according to law. Proclamations were issued against the importation of seditious books and the harboring of seditious persons.[32] Acts of violence committed either against or by officials or council agents were regarded with particular disfavor. Certain Essex justices of the peace, for this reason, were instructed to examine the injuries done to the sheriff of Colchester by one Lucas and his servants, the vice-president and Council in the Marches of Wales told to inquire into complaints made against the disorderly conduct of Sir John Perrot when en route through the principality to Ireland, and Sir John himself ordered to answer the charges brought against him.[33] Perrot repeatedly embarrassed his superiors before being made a Privy Councillor. But his behavior, and that of others like him, had to be controlled, for if the government's own agents could be roughly handled with impunity, or those agents themselves, uncontrolled by higher authority, appeared to be able to act in a manner detrimental to the public good, the forces of sedition would receive an unwanted degree of encouragement, and popular support for the existing regime decline accordingly.

What caused really serious worry to the council was not overt acts, but

30. Hatfield House, MS. 159, ff. 107–108, Sadler to Bacon, August 24, 1573.

31. *Ibid.*, ff. 109 and 115, Bacon to Burghley, August 25 and September 4, 1573.

32. PRO, SP.12/71, no. 34, proclamation against the import of seditious books and popish bulls, July 1, 1570; SP.12/74, no. 33, proclamation against the harboring of seditious persons, November 14, 1570.

33. BM, Add. MS. 32323, f. 121, the council to certain Essex justices of the peace, August 17, 1571; Harleian MS. 4943, f. 110 and 110v, the council to the Vice-President and Council in the Marches of Wales and to Sir John Perrot, March 20, 1571.

conspiracy, and suspected conspiracy—a "develish and wicked practise," as Sir Ralph Sadler described it to Burghley in 1572 when writing to congratulate him on having escaped the plots which had been laid against his life by the partisans of the Duke of Norfolk and the Queen of Scots.[34] We have already seen the councillors themselves acting as interrogators in such cases; but in the constant search for contrivers against the state and its great men, the council turned to a variety of trusted agents, both in London and elsewhere, to examine suspected persons. In 1570 one Edward Chester wrote to Cecil that rumors were being circulated about the existence of a device reputedly being engineered by Cecil himself, in association with Bacon, and aimed at the assassination of the Duke of Norfolk. A man by the name of Robert Spencer was thereupon imprisoned in the Fleet for his suspected connection with the spreading of the rumors, and Chester was entrusted with questioning him there.[35] Thomas Norton, the parliament man, examined Sir George Peckham and Lord Henry Howard in 1581.[36] William Herle "talked with Dr. Lopes" in the Tower in 1571.[37] Sir Francis Jobson and Sir Henry Nevell examined Thomas Bates, and John Southcote and Thomas Stanley interrogated John Bulkeley and William Bedo.[38] On different occasions the council made similar use in the counties of Sir William More and Edward Clere, who were prominent in Sussex and Surrey and Norfolk and Suffolk, respectively.[39] And the Bishop of Salisbury, receiving the council's letters late at night, reported that he sent at once for John Pildrim, whom he was commanded to examine, and did not even make use of a clerk in doing so, in order to keep the whole matter as secret as he could.[40]

The difference between traitorous and merely seditious activity was

---

34. BM, Cotton MS. Caligula C. iii, f. 206, Sadler to Burghley, January 14, 1572.

35. PRO, SP.12/67, no. 1, Edward Chester to Cecil, March 3, 1570; no. 5, interrogatories ministered by Edward Chester to Robert Spencer, prisoner in the Fleet, no date.

36. PRO, SP.12/147, no. 4, Thomas Norton to Walsingham, January 10, 1581.

37. BM, Cotton MS. Caligula C. iii, f. 79, notes by William Herle of his conference with Dr. Lopez in the Tower, May 17, 1571.

38. PRO, SP.12/67, no. 21, Francis Jobson and Henry Nevell to the council, March 14, 1570; SP.12/71, no. 63, John Southcote and Thomas Stanley to the council, July 29, 1570.

39. Surrey Record Office, Loseley MS. XIII, f. 6, the council to Sir William More, August 30, 1567; Hatfield House MS. 5 [?—BM, MS. M.485/2 (microfilm)], f. 17, the examination of Edward Clere, October 27, 1569.

40. Hatfield House, MS. 4, f. 150, the Bishop of Salisbury to the council, September 30, 1569.

not always an easy one to define. It was indeed a technicality in many cases, which arose only when the parties the council had investigated or had ordered investigated actually appeared for trial. But plotting against the life of the sovereign was certainly treason, and the council plainly regarded it as being in a class of undesirable behavior entirely by itself. In June 1569, therefore, in a "Treatise on the Dangers of the Time," Cecil, recognizing this perhaps better than anyone, recommended "hir majestie's Privee Counsell shuld secretly conferr amongst them selves with speciall noblemen, bishops, knights and others, head gentlemen in every shire . . . to be accompted . . . devoute subjectes . . . in purpose to withstand any foreyn or domesticall attempt against hir majesty. . . . A certificat [should be brought] to the Privy Counsell from every shire . . . [and] a speciall secret booke be compiled of all the persons . . . conformable . . . [as well as of those that] shall refuse."[41] Those chosen were to be entrusted with the task of propagandizing on the council's behalf in their own districts, and one of them in each shire was to be specially appointed to warn the council in the event of any danger which should arise, either within the counties or from without.

Much of the seditious, traitorous and conspiratorial activity of Elizabeth's reign, it was believed, was instigated by the queen's and the country's enemies abroad. "Men of good judgment," wrote Francis Walsingham to Lord Burghley in 1574, referring to the anticipated arrival of the new Spanish ambassador, Mendoza, "thinke that the cheefe end of his commying is to interteyne us with Spanyshe complymentes to lulle us a sleepe for the tyme, untyll ther secret practyces be growen to ther dewe and full rypenes."[42] It was this consciousness of threat from abroad which underlay the council's preoccupation with the process of entering and leaving the country, with keeping track of those who did succeed in getting away without permission, with finding out who had arrived without official sanction, and with the activities of those already resident who were the most likely people to have undesirable foreign connections, that is, with immigrants and recusants.

According to 5 Richard II, st. 1, cap. 2, no one was permitted to enter or leave the country unless he were a recognized fisherman or merchant, or had a license from the sovereign.[43] The council intended to implement the provisions of this, in its opinion, far from archaic statute exactly. It had no libertarian compunction whatsoever about reminding the queen's

41. PRO, SP.12/51, no. 6, a treatise on the dangers of the time, in a clerkly hand, but much amended in Cecil's own, June 7, 1569.

42. BM, Harleian MS. 6991, f. 92, Walsingham to Burghley, July 13, 1574.

43. *The Statutes of the Realm* (London, 1810), II, 18.

subjects that they were forbidden to go abroad at will and calling for their arrest if they tried to get away anyway. Formal orders to this effect were drafted and issued to the ports in general, as well as to the vice-admirals.[44] The mayor of Chester was ordered to go so far as to seize its sails in order to prevent the departure of any vessel from anywhere in his vicinity having anyone on board for whose integrity he was not personally prepared to vouch.[45] Lord Darcy was told to arrest a ship at Harwich and examine any fugitives it proved to be carrying.[46] The Earl of Bedford arrested "certeyne [persons] suspected to travayle without licence, within the ryver of Falmouth" and wrote asking Walsingham to find out what the council wanted done with them.[47] The answer might well have been that he should send them to appear before it, as Lord Cobham was ordered to do with "certaine persons that intended to passe the seas," but who were arrested at Hastings before they managed to do so.[48]

Lisences to go abroad legally were sparingly issued. They were always for traveling purposes acceptable to the government. Although they took the form of some sort of royal letter addressed to the queen's officers generally, authorizing the bearers to pass through the ports, the persons receiving them were recallable at any time, not only by further letters from the queen, but by those of her ambassadors overseas or from a given number of Privy Councillors, usually six.[49] Thus were Richard and Edward Cecil permitted to go overseas to study, and Sir Francis Englefield, with eight servants, eight horses, 600 ounces of plate, 100 marks, and other "necessaries," to go and "receive cure at the baynes," provided that in doing so he did not venture into enemy territory.[50] Thomas Stapleton, who had originally gone abroad without the required permission, was

---

44. Queen's College Library, Oxford, Sel. b. 228, no. 36, the council's orders for the ports, January 14, 1583; Surrey Record Office, Loseley MSS. Correspondence II (1581–1600), the council to Sir William More, December 23, 1583; BM, Harleian MS. 703, f. 49, the council to [the officers of the ports], March 1, 1593.

45. BM, Lansdowne MS. 13, no. 31, the council to the mayor and corporation of "Westchester," May 17, 1571.

46. BM, Add. MS, 32323, f. 20v, the council to Lord Darcy, February 19, 1572.

47. PRO, SP.12/132, no. 6, the Earl of Bedford to Walsingham, September 15, 1579.

48. APC, VIII, 105, May 22, 1573.

49. PRO, E.157/1, licences to pass beyond the seas, 1572–1578.

50. PRO, E.157/26, the queen to her officers, a Signet letter, no date; Calendar of the Patent Rolls, Elizabeth (London, 1939), I (1588–1560), 54, patent for Sir Francis Englefield to pass overseas, April 12, 1559.

pardoned and permitted to remain there for three further years, in one of the few licenses which passed, probably because of its special nature, under the Great Seal.[51] Such licenses were rare, in spite of the fact that the queen instructed the Lord Keeper in 1570 that they could be granted at the behest of "our attorney or our lerned counsell."[52] Usually the Signet was sufficient for the purpose, and it was a Signet letter which prolonged Thomas Bodley's leave of absence in 1578.[53]

Arrivals in the country were the subject of official control as much as were departures from it. Foreigners were not popular in England. Even the God-fearing Francis Knollys attempted to deprive English-born off-spring of immigrant parents of their right to share his nationality by sup-porting a bill in parliament whch would have declared them aliens.[54] Even so, the advent of the one particular group of people from overseas who produced these debatable children in the greatest numbers was winked at, and as a result, during the reign of Elizabeth, England received a large influx of refugees who had left their own countries because of religious persecution. Most of them came from the Low Countries or from France, and they received, on the whole, a not altogether unfriendly welcome in the Protestant island where they sought asylum. But they *were* foreigners, even if they were anti-Catholic, and as such they con-stituted a potential danger to the national security, if not in themselves, as a camouflage for the agents of subversion from without. They were, therefore, on the council's orders, more or less constantly supervised where-ever they settled down. On October 25, 1571 in reply to a council letter of the previous day (of which there is, incidentally, no mention in the register or indication of any meeting held on that date), the Lord Mayor of London submitted for consideration a series of orders he had drawn up in conference with the city aldermen. All immigrants, he suggested, should be registered "at one instante to be apoynted by your honors;" all landings of strangers, except merchants, were to be prevented, house-holders warned not to receive them and the houses of foreigners searched for armor and weapons.[55] Lord Burghley's marginal comments on this document indicate that he agreed wholeheartedly with the first point, but as a general rule the council as a whole does not seem to have been in-

---

51. *Calendar of the Patent Rolls*, 288, March 22, 1560.
52. PRO, SP.12/74, no. 39, the queen to Bacon, November 21, 1570.
53. PRO, SP.40/1, p. 16, the queen to her officers, [September 1578].
54. J. E. Neale, *Elizabeth I and her Parliaments 1559–1581* (New York, 1958), 412.
55. PRO, SP.12/81, no. 53, the Lord Mayor of London to the council, October 25, 1571.

terested in going much further than this. Letters, for example, were sent into Kent, Sussex, and Hampshire concerning the arrival and reception of Frenchmen in particular, ordering that the council be kept informed "every fourtenth daie or oftener" of their numbers and movements, and lists of their resident "straungers" were submitted from time to time by the ports along the southern and eastern coasts, where they appeared and tended to stay in the greatest numbers.[56] But provided they were "'honeste in conversation . . . well-disposed to the good obedience of the queene's majestie and the realme," and could satisfy the council's expert examiners, among whom Edwin Sandys, Bishop of London, was particularly prominent, that they had indeed come to England for purely religious reasons, they were usually permitted to stay.[57] It was, nevertheless, council policy to move them away from the coastal towns, and to control their movements and their actions generally, wherever they were.[58] Sir Christopher Heydon and Sir William Buttes, in another letter which is included in Tremayne's book of precedents, were instructed to move such people within their jurisdictions inland from Norwich, Yarmouth and other towns.[59] And William Waldegrave, having been asked by foreigners living in Colchester for permission to move to Halsted in Essex, on referring the matter to the council, was told that "we have good likinge of the mocion," but asked to see that the "number of housholdes that shall come thether . . . be sett downe in some certentie . . . that by her majestie's grante they may be established in such good order as other of the like sorte be placed alreddie in Colchester and in some other citties and townes of this realme. . . . Wee shall be gladd to give the same the best furtherance that we may."[60]

Although local authorities were usually left to deal with the situation on the basis of local conditions, wherever they were, there were problems

56. BM, Harleian MS. 6990, no. 20, f. 42, the Marquess of Winchester to Cecil, February 1, 1564; PRO, SP.12/78, nos. 9, 10, 13, 19 and 29, letters to the council concerning foreigners residing in Colchester, Harwich, Yarmouth, Lynn, Dover and Sandwich, May 8, 11, 12, 20, 25 and 27, 1571; SP.12/82, the Lord Mayor and aldermen of London to the council, November 1571; BM, Add. MS. 32323, f. 138v, [the council] to the mayor and corporation of Rye, September 7, 1572.

57. BM, Add. MS. 32323, f. 140, the council "to divers portes and places," October 28, 1571; PRO, SP.12/85, no. 50, the Bishop of London to the council, February 20, 1572.

58. APC, VIII, 306, the council to Lord Cobham, October 26, 1574.

59. BM, Add. MS. 32323, f. 136v, the council to Sir Christopher Heydon and Sir William Buttes, April 27, 1572.

60. PRO, SP.12/108, no. 54, the council to William Waldegrave, July 12, 1576.

involved in fitting immigrants into existing social arrangements. From Newington Green in Lincolnshire, Richard Bertie informed the council in 1570 that the foreigners there were "constreyned to enterteyn diverse hedcraftsmen of their misteries, which they intend to set up, to ther great chardge, without any use of them," and asked the council to do something to alleviate the situation.[61] What they did in this particular instance does not appear. But in 1571, what happened when the city of Norwich called on the council for similar assistance, and in doing so submitted for the council's consideration "the booke of orders for straungers," is clear. Hearing of the matter was committed to Sir Walter Mildmay, Sir Thomas Smith and the master of the rolls, and after these three had conferred and reported back the council sent down their decision in the matter as its own.[62]

On March 25, 1583 Sir Francis Walsingham made a note in his day-book under the heading "Cowncell" which emphasizes the association in the council's collective thinking of all these various problems with one other, that of religious disaffection. As matters for consideration by the council, he listed: "Proclamation on portes" and "A vieu [of] strayngers" along with "Recusantes, Jesuistes [and] . . . divers obstinat blaspheming papistes."[63] The fear of the native Catholic becoming the effective agent of foreign attempts to subvert the English state was a real and potent one.

"I have advertyced Mr. Secretarye Cecil of a Roomyshe practyce I can learne nothing as yet therof in pertyculer," Walsingham wrote to the Earl of Leicester in 1572 from Paris. "Your lordship shall doe well to have an eye to thos that are suspected ther with you."[64] It was in view of the danger of their assisting an invader that the council instructed the Lord Admiral and Lord Buckhurst, as Lords Lieutenants of Sussex, to report the number and types of recusants, to imprison "the most obstinate" and refer those "not soe obstinate to . . . the custodie of some ecclesiasticall persons."[65] This particular letter dates from 1587, but the policy it outlines was still that which had been pursued by the council in the early 1570s, when the potential for disloyalty among Catholics was at least believed to be every bit as great.

In the north the danger was particularly evident. Sir Ralph Sadler told

---

61. PRO, SP.12/71, no. 3, Richard Bertie to the council, June 5, 1570.

62. PRO, SP.12/77, no. 58, the book of orders for the strangers of the city of Norwich, with council letter enclosing it, April 28, 1571.

63. BM, Harleian MS. 6035, Walsingham's letter book, f. 2, 1583.

64. Longleat House, Dudley MS. II, f. 62, Walsingham to the Earl of Leicester, March 5, 1572.

65. BM, Harleian MS. 703, f. 32 (new f. 51), the council to Howard of Effingham and Lord Buckhurst, January 4, 1587.

Cecil in 1569 that "ther be not in all this countrey ten gentlemen that do favor and allowe of her majestie's procedinges in the cause of religion."[66] There was obviously a feeling that things might turn out to be almost as bad elsewhere, even before the northern rebellion actually broke out. In order to make sure that those who were justices of the peace were in fact supporters of the settlement of 1559, they were required by a letter from the council dated November 6, 1569 to subscribe their names to the Act of Uniformity. The certifications to this effect began to come in about ten days later, and by the end of January those from most of the shires of both England and Wales had been received.[67] Those who refused to sign were to be removed from the commission of the peace.[68] Even so, four years later Sir Thomas Smith could still express disquiet as to the loyalty of the local justices when it came to executing orders for the suppression of religious disaffection, seeing many of them, in his opinion, would do the same themselves "yf they durst."[69] He had grounds for his suspicions, for "a fowle knot of papisticall justices of peace" had just been discovered, apparently right in the middle of the country, in the Earl of Shrewsbury's territory.[70] Nonetheless, along with the bishops, the justices, as in so many other matters, remained the main agents of the council's policy in religious matters.

They were required, first of all, to submit lists of the queen's subjects who refused to come to church. The most usual procedure was for the council to communicate its wishes to the bishops, and leave it to them to appoint gentlemen from their dioceses to do the job, but for the gentlemen chosen to report their findings directly to the council. On October 25, 1577 Sir William More and Sir Thomas Browne reported to the council from Guildford in response to a letter which had been directed to the Bishop of Winchester on the 15th, asking not only for the names of those not going to church, but for the details of their lands and goods as well.

---

66. BM, Add. MS. 33953, f. 47, Sadler to Cecil, December 6, 1569.

67. PRO, SP.12/59, nos. 20, 21, 22 and 25, the sheriff and justices of the peace of Nottinghamshire and Middlesex and the justices of the peace of Northamptonshire and Derbyshire to the council, November 16, 18, 18 and 22, 1569; SP.12/66, no. 19, the Vice-President and Council in the Marches of Wales, enclosing the certificates of the Welsh justices of the peace, to the council, January 22, 1570; no. 28, the justices of the peace of Warwickshire to the council, January 26, 1570; SP.12/67, no. 57, the justices of the peace of Cornwall to the council, April 10, 1570.

68. Hertfordshire Record Office, MS. HAT/S.R./4, the council to the sheriff, the *custos rotulorum* and other gentlemen, October 20, 1592.

69. BM, Harleian MS. 6991, f. 29, Smith to Burghley, February 19, 1573.

70. BM, Lansdowne MS. 16, nos. 42 and 43, Smith to Burghley, February 12 and 14, 1573.

In London, however, the bishop, at the council's behest, instructed the ministers of every parish to get the information.[71]

Many of those who refused to attend the parish church claimed, like Lord Henry Howard, to be loyal subjects of the queen, and these were treated with comparative leniency.[72] Even many of those who had hitherto been imprisoned or "interned" were released, after the promulgation of an order in council on May 7, 1581, on relatively easy terms. From this date onwards, the Privy Council registers are full of notations concerning the freeing of recusants, usually in their own recognizances of £100, though the sum exacted depended on the rank of the person involved.[73] The two sons of Sir Robert Tyrwhitt, for example, were assessed as high as £200 and £300 respectively, and Anthony Throckmorton had to put up, over and above his own £200, two additional sureties of £100 apiece.[74] But this large a sum was rarely insisted on. The sheriffs, the *custodes rotulorum* and the justices of the peace were sent lists of those thus set at liberty, and were instructed to see that they kept to the conditions of their bonds. The harshest of these were that they should not move abroad above three miles from home and that they should not consort with others, whether equals or inferiors, who shared their faith.[75]

Many of the more prosperous recusants could obtain complete exemption from the laws against them in return for payment of a lump sum to the queen. In 1585, forty-four gentlemen, esquires, wives and widows were specifically named as being eligible to benefit from this concession in a council letter to the recusancy commissioners in Sussex, and long before this, in 1569, the Suffolk muster commissioners had suggested to the council that those who failed to appear in church, instead of a shilling in the poor box, should perhaps be fined instead the maintenance of a harquebusier.[76] Some, however, were placed in the hands of ecclesiastics in the hope of their being brought to a more acceptable way of thinking,

---

71. PRO, SP.12/116, no. 15, the council to the bishops, October 15; SP.12/117, no. 14, Sir William More and Sir Thomas Browne to the council, October 25; no. 19, Francis Hastings and Mr. Astocke to the council, October 27; nos. 21, 22, 23, 25, 26, 27 and 28, further returns to the council's letters of October 15 (*supra*), October 1577; Northamptonshire Record Office, F (M) P. 50, "articles to be enquired of by ministers of every parish in London," no date.

72. PRO, SP.12/147, no. 6, Lord Henry Howard to Walsingham, January 12, 1581.

73. APC, XIII, 40, May 7, 1581.

74. *Ibid.*, 75, June 13, 1581; 175, August 17, 1581.

75. *Ibid.*, 40, May 7, 1581.

76. BM, Harleian MS. 703, f. 21, the council to the commissioners appointed to disarm recusants in Sussex, February 25, 1585; PRO, SP.12/58, no. 24, the muster commissioners of Suffolk to the council, September 25, 1569.

and the council prescribed the "fourme to be observed by my lords the bishoppes in the orderinge of suche as were committed to their custody for poperie."[77] Others were put, or kept, in jail. Letters were written in July 1580 for the assigning of castles to which recusants of the better sort were to be committed.[78] There, at Barnard Castle, for example, the prisoners lived at their own expense, as they did in the ordinary prisons, and generally speaking, they do not seem to have been over-harshly treated.[79] They were certainly let out on temporary bail for the most humane of reasons. William Shelley, imprisoned in the Fleet, was permitted to go home to visit his sick wife under surety for £1000. When he had been away some time, he was granted a further extension of leave because, he claimed, his mother-in-law was now sick too, and "it doth importe him very muche to be with her untill she have disposed fullie of things." The council apparently not only understood such practical sympathy, but felt secure enough to indulge it.[80]

The council was involved in ecclesiastical affairs other than those involving recusants. A proclamation against "An Admonition to Parliament" instructed anyone possessing the Admonition "to bring in the same . . . to one of her hyghnesse['s] Privie Counsel."[81] Bishop Grindal was ordered to repress conventicles.[82] A new sect having come to the attention of the City authorities, they, with the concurrence of the council, sent forty halberdiers to arrest the people involved, and persons were appointed to convert them.[83] The bishops were instructed to "assemble the speciall noted preachers and other ecclesiasticall persones of good calling within your diocese [and to read the enclosed proclamation to them, telling them not to meddle in matters of state in their preaching, but to] teach the people to be thankfull towards Allmightie God for the great benifittes bothe of libertie of conscience, peace and welth, which they have hitherto

---

77. PRO, SP.12/114, no. 69, the council to the bishops, July 1577; BM, Add. MS. 32323, f. 4, the council to the sheriffs and justices of the peace of Dorset, June 9, 1572.

78. Huntington Library, Ellesmere MS. 2080, an entry relating to a council meeting similar in form to those in the Privy Council registers, July 26, 1580; BM, Add. MS. 32323, f. 135, the council to the bishop of Ely, March 11, 1572.

79. Huntington Library, Hastings MS. 4139, the council to the Earl of Huntingdon, the Archbishop of York and the Bishop of Durham, July 27, 1580; BM, Add. MS. 32323, f. 135v, the council to the Archbishop of Canterbury and the Bishop of London, no date.

80. APC, XIII, 286, December 12, 1581.

81. PRO, SP.12/91, no. 47, proclamation against "An Admonition to Parliament," June 11, 1573.

82. PRO, SP.12/46, no. 44, the council to Bishop Grindal, March 1, 1568.

83. CSP Spanish, II, da Silva to the King of Spain, February 7, 1568.

enjoyed by her majestie's good meanes."[84] The sheriffs and justices of the peace of the counties falling within the diocese of Chester were ordered to assist the Bishop of Carlisle in carrying out his visitation there.[85] The Earl of Sussex was reminded in 1569 that the best way to counteract the rebels' religious purposes was with religious activity of his own. He was, therefore, instructed to see Common Prayer, especially the Litany, said daily, and to obtain preachers from the northern bishops to "move . . . [the people] to serve God accordyng to his commandments, and to be faythfull and trew to the quene's majestie, ther soverayn lady." This was followed by a long exposition of the glories and benefits of the queen's reign, which was likewise to be spread abroad.[86] Sir Hugh Cholemeley was ordered to inquire into the beating of a preacher at Northwich, and Bartholomew Baxter not to interfere with Reginald Metcalf's peaceful enjoyment of his Norfolk benefice.[87] The council even became involved in doctrine. In 1576 it expressed its opinion as to what dispensations from canon law, hitherto virtually for sale at prices fixed by the Church, should be done away with. These included the dispensation to marry without banns, and that permitting appointment to church positions of persons under age. It was also recommended that abolition should be considered in cases of commendams (duality in the holding of benefices) and of the eating of flesh in Lent.[88]

If the council was concerned about who left and who entered the country, whether for religious or other reasons, it was, at least in times of crisis or of danger to the national security, quite as fully occupied in restricting movement within it. People of recognizable quality were exempt from interference in their coming and going. Although a councillor might not leave a post to which he had been previously assigned without specific authorization from the queen (Sir Ralph Sadler wrote to Cecil in 1570 that he dared not "risk" leaving the north without her direct order, and even Hunsdon would not contemplate going to London from Berwick for the St. George's Day Garter celebrations unless his cousin gave him unequivocable instructions to attend), no great personage, nor,

---

84. PRO, SP.12/132, no. 26, the council to a bishop(?), 1579(?).

85. BM, Add. MS. 32323, f. 139v, the council to the sheriffs and justices of the peace of certain counties within the diocese of Chester, May 12, 1572.

86. Hatfield House, MS. 156, f. 132, the council to the Earl of Sussex "from a minute of Secretary Cecill," as quoted in Haynes, 558, no date.

87. BM, Add. MS. 32323, f. 143, the council to Sir Hugh Cholemeley, August 15, 1572; PRO, SP.12/75, no. 55, Reginald Metcalf to the council, 1570(?).

88. BM, Lansdowne MS. 23, no. 61, Harleian MS. 4943, f. 28, "dispensacions to be utterlye abolished as not agreable to Christian religion in the opinyon of the lords of the counsell," June 20, 1576.

indeed, anyone who seemed to be a gentleman, would in practice have any trouble moving from place to place unchallenged in his passage.[89] It was very different for lesser men.

In 1569 the Lords Lieutenants were told to make certain that no one moved out of his own county, except for bona fide merchants, without their leave and knowledge.[90] That such restrictions were not entirely consequent upon temporary local disorder—these came at the time of the northern rebellion—is evident from the council's concern, three years later when things had quieted down again, about the number of persons moving about, apparently on the authority of travel documents issued by Lord Hunsdon. The latter defended himself with typical outspokenness in a letter to Thomas Randolph, asserting that he had "graunted no passport at eny tyme to eny man but [that] I ame well able to stand to the doing therof." He nonetheless in the next breath conceded that his issuance of travel permits was itself valid only if "well allowed of of the counsell."[91] The council's right to limit mobility at any time was unquestioned. Open journeying by the unidentified—and unidentifiable—was consequently often difficult, and such suspect persons knew it well enough.

When Father Gerard landed in England as a newly ordained Jesuit priest and attempted to make his way to London through a part of the country in which he had never previously set foot, without any sort of acceptable credentials, he at first kept off the roads as much as possible. When he eventually took to them, his first concern was to equip himself with a horse, not only in order to move more quickly, but more safely, since "people travelling on foot . . . [were] often taken for vagrants and liable to arrest, even in quiet times. . . . [He] had gone barely two miles when [he] . . . rode straight into a group of watchers at the entrance to a village," and before being allowed to go on, he had to convince the constable and the officer of the watch that he was an "honest fellow," which, luckily for him, he did in fact manage to do.[92] If he had not, he would have been in trouble.

Such "watches" for "licentious persons" were ordered kept at certain

89. BM, Add. MS. 33593, f. 144, Sadler to Cecil, January 18, 1570; f. 148, the queen to Sadler, January 22, 1570; Hatfield House, MS. 155, f. 98, Hunsdon to Cecil, February 17, 1569.

90. PRO, SP.12/60, no. 4, Cecil's notes on dealing with the northern rebellion, December 1, 1569.

91. BM, Lansdowne MS. 15, no. 26, Hunsdon to Thomas Randolph, June 23, 1572.

92. John Gerard, *The Autobiography of a Hunted Priest* (New York, 1955), 37–39.

times and in certain localities just as muster-taking was decreed for particular days and particular places. Commissioners for the Parts of Holland, in Lincolnshire, reported on April 28, 1572, in response to council letters of March 14, that a lookout had been established on April 21 and would be repeated monthly in the future.[93] Those arrested at such times were to be put in the stocks, whipped, and then, if able-bodied, set to work or, if not able, given passports to travel back to their counties and parishes of birth, where charitable provision was to be made for them by the rest of the parishioners, exhorted thereto by the local justices of the peace.[94] What was actually done varied from place to place and at different times in the reign, as circumstances changed and new statutes came into operation. A new house of correction was set up at Acle in Norfolk in 1574, and in 1585 the council instructed the Lord Admiral, as Lord Lieutenant of Sussex and Surrey, to gather together "stout vacebondes and masterlesse men . . . that the country might bee disburthened of such unnecessary members, and they withal imployed to some good use."[95] They were to be sent to Rye for transportation to the Low Countries "wher they shalbee well used."[96] The principle remained constant: those who could not show some authority or valid reason for being away from home were liable to be punished and returned there, where someone could be held responsible for them. This does not mean that there was not much small-scale, hardly noticeable migration of very ordinary folk, from the countryside into the towns, for example. It does indicate that "unusual" movement was regarded with suspicion. Thus even such people as the workmen recruited some miles away to repair the fortifications at Portsmouth, as the council reminded Sir Henry Radcliff in 1577, had to be issued with passports to facilitate their unmolested return to their homes.[97]

Such a policy was clearly antipathetic to individual liberty; only the obviously respectable were relatively unrestricted by it. But the age was a violent one, and it is possible that the national peace could have been kept

---

93. PRO, SP.12/86, no. 12, certain Lincolnshire commissioners to the council, April 28, 1572.

94. Humphrey Dyson, *A Booke Containing all such Proclamations as were Published during the Reign of the late Queene Elizabeth* (London, 1618), f. 317A, printed council orders, April 17, 1593; BM, Cotton MS. Titus B. ii, f. 278, the council to the sheriff of an unidentified county, June 20, 1569.

95. BM, Lansdowne MS. 18, no. 97, an unknown person to Burghley, December 25, 1574.

96. BM, Harleian MS. 703, new f. 40v, the council to Howard of Effingham, September 8, 1585.

97. PRO, SP.12/115, no. 5, the council to Sir Henry Radcliff, August 18, 1577.

in no other way than by the sacrifice of some private freedom in the interest of public security. Rogues and vagabonds were nuisance enough unarmed; with weapons in their hands they became a positive menace to law-abiding folk. In 1561 and 1575 the problem was the same: there were too many "disordred persons . . . bearinge . . . dagges [pistols] and handgonnes, whereby many notable and shamefull murders, burglaryes and robberyes are dayly committed."[98] When some act had been perpetrated that the council regarded as being especially dangerous, it called upon one of its agents to do something about it specifically. Thus Sir William More, as sheriff of Surrey and Sussex in 1580, was ordered to search for those suspected of being concerned in a robbery near the court.[99] Sir John Zouche, in 1572, was told to see "no *bastinado cougelles* be any more borne" by anyone in his locality.[100] For a more general remedy, the sheriffs and justices of the peace were instructed to appoint "some honest [and] dyscrete men (not beinge inkepers or victualers) to note whoe shall passe that waye with any dagge or handgonne."[101]

The reference to innkeepers is typical of the council's attitude towards them: they were not regarded as being either honest or discreet. Inns were, in fact, liable to become centers of disorder, and bonds were regularly taken in an attempt to keep them from degenerating completely into sinks of iniquity, as well as to ensure that they did not serve meat in Lent.[102] From time to time, the council ordered the local justices of the peace to check upon and report the number of taverns, inns and alehouses in the various counties, so that councillors could at least get some ideas of how many such potential nests of disturbance existed and see whether their numbers required they be reduced. In 1584, under the heading "cowncell causes," Sir Francis Walsingham made a note "to have the nomber of ale howses in London abrydged."[103]

---

98. Surrey Record Office, Loseley MS. XII, no. 22, the council to the sheriff and justices of the peace of Surrey, February 28, 1561.

99. Surrey Record Office, Loseley MS. 2014, no. 31, the council to Sir William More, June 8, 1580.

100. BM, Add. MS. 32323, f. 111v, the council to Sir John Zouche and others, August 8, 1572. *Bastinado cougelles* were heavy sticks used for beating people up (*Oxford English Dictionary*).

101. Hatfield House, MS. 8, f. 78, the council to Bacon and Burghley, December 4, 1575; BM, Lansdowne MS. 21, no. 21, Smith to Burghley, December 4, 1575; Surrey Record Office, Loseley MS. XII, no. 22, the council to the sheriff and justices of the peace of Surrey, February 28, 1561.

102. Surrey Record Office, Loseley MS. XII, no. 22, the council to the sheriff and justices of the peace of Surrey, February 28, 1561.

103. BM, Harleian MS. 6035, Walsingham's letter book, f. 62, 1583.

That the system worked can be variously demonstrated. When called upon to report on the state of their localities, some places felt no compunction about replying "that we have no[thing] . . . noew to certifie your honors but that by the due executyon of the lawes . . . we fynde this parte of the shire [to be] so disburthened of those malefactors as redoundeth to the great quietnes of the queen's majestie's good subjectes."[104] The queen herself was not assassinated, in spite of numerous attempts—some famous, some so obscure as to be almost unknown. It has never been convincingly maintained that any councillor died from other than natural causes, notwithstanding such rumors as those of poisoning which circulated after the death of the Earl of Leicester. The Catholics neither overthrew the Church of England nor rose to welcome the Spanish in 1588. Above all, despite the many supposed and a few confirmed attempts to overthrow the government of England forcibly, the state survived, the council throve. It can be held that the testing of a course of action is in its working out, and although the security program of the council was challenged by Mary Queen of Scots, the French, the Spanish and the forces of both domestic and international Catholicism, none succeeded in bringing it to a standstill, let alone engineering its abandonment. The council must, therefore, be judged to have achieved its objective of ensuring the safety of England and its sovereign very effectively indeed.

If there was no central intelligence agency, there was no ministry of national insurance either—no insurance even—no departments of health, education or welfare, no national planning board of any kind. Yet problems arose in sixteenth century England which would later come under the auspices of some such offices, and the council dealt with them as well.

The town of Nantwich in Cheshire was not very big even by the standards of the sixteenth century. In December 1583 it was almost completely destroyed by fire. It immediately became apparent that both queen and council were prepared to come to its assistance. Elizabeth herself contributed "to a good valeue" and letters patent were issued to the town, authorizing it to "gather the devocion and benevolence of her well disposed subjectes."[105] The council wrote, in March 1584, to the bishops and the sheriffs and justices of the peace of all the counties of England and Wales, instructing them to collect money for the town's relief and to send it to Thomas Aldersey and Thomas Brassey, London merchants, who

---

104. PRO, SP.12/81, no. 19, Sir Thomas Chamberlayn and others to the council, September 17, 1571.

105. BM, Harleian MS. 703, new f. 13, the council to the sheriff and justices of the peace of Sussex, March 22, [1584].

were appointed as the official receivers.[106] Between May and October a few contributions began to come in; Aldersey and Brassey eventually handed over what they had received, on the council's instructions, to local commissioners, who were told to "distribute and imploy [it] . . . for the re-edifieng of the towne;" and the council laid down regulations under which reconstruction and reoccupation were to be carried out. Before any money was handed over, a book was to be made up, showing who had lost what, and to what extent each man was able to afford it. Then landlords were to be "perswaded" to contribute towards rebuilding *their* houses, and the tenants were to be installed at the old rent. Where landlords refused to cooperate, they were to receive no assistance from the fund, but tenants were to receive compensation, "to thende they may provide howses for them selves." The poorest owner-occupiers were to have all their rebuilding costs met out of the fund, provided the money would go that far, and others were to receive assistance according to their means, provided they were willing to go in bond to build. Everyone was to receive something towards his losses in goods, "in good dyscression . . . with regarde alwayes to the poorer sorte, to whom the benyfyt of the collection ys cheefly intended." Lastly, a market place, with a meeting room for town officials and dignitaries was to be erected, and any eventual surplus was to go to the maintenance of a resident preacher-cum-schoolmaster.[107]

The council's interest in the restoration of this small town in far-off pastoral Cheshire was stimulated by several considerations. The ruin of Nantwich could not be contemplated with equanimity because its fire had made several hundred poor and comparatively helpless people homeless. But it was also a salt town, and if something were not done to get it on its feet again "the necessary trade of saltinge there, for the great benefyt of our realme [is] lyke to decaye for a long tyme, whereof we wold be right sory."[108] It was not only a salt town; it was also a "thoroughfare lyinge conveniently for the receite of souldiers, carriadges and munition

106. BM, Stowe MS. 150, f. 35, the queen to the city of London, March 9; f. 36, the council to the sheriff and justices of the peace of Essex, March 22; Harleian MS. 703, new f. 13(1), the council to the sheriffs of Sussex, March 22; Huntington Library, Hastings MS. 4141, the council to the sheriff and justices of the peace of Leicestershire, March 31; BM, Harleian MS. 368, f. 126, new f. 105, a sheriff to a justice of the peace, March 27, 1584.

107. PRO, E.101/633, no. 9, the council to "the commyssioners appointed to distribute and imploy the sommes of money collected for the re-edifieng of the towne of Namptwich," no date.

108. BM, Stowe MS. 150, f. 35, the queen to the city of London, March 9, 1584.

to be sent into the realme of Ireland"—in other words, an arsenal.[109] No
wonder the council was concerned: Nantwich's condition mattered to
people living a long way beyond the boundaries of the county in which it
lay, as well as to its own citizens.

The council was involved in the affairs of Dover for a similar reason.
Nantwich suffered from a sudden, sharp disaster; Dover labored under
the permanent, onerous responsibility of being the town which stood behind the main English port for France, through which much of the
continental traffic of the whole nation passed. In August 1579 the special
commissioners who had been appointed to look into the cost and difficulties
of repairing the harbor reported to the council that the bill would come to
£21,000, and thereupon the mayor, jurates and the whole commonalty
of the town appealed for assistance in raising the money.[110] They had
already suggested that a nationwide collection, like that which was later
used to assist Nantwich, should be authorized; the device had, in fact,
been exploited earlier in the same year to raise money for the building
of an altogether new harbor at Hastings.[111] But in the case of Dover,
while taking care to enunciate the principle that since every subject stood
to benefit from the repair of the port every subject should be called upon
to contribute towards the cost, the council nevertheless decided that it had
a better idea. Since alehouses were regarded as being the "causes of much
disorder and inconvenience, so this commen benifit is now thought fitt to
be reaped out of them." Letters were written to the justices of the peace
in this instance, not begging for contributions, but instructing them to levy
a fine of two shillings and sixpence on every new license they issued for
the keeping of alehouses, and that all existing licenses were to lapse on
May 31st unless their holders also agreed to pay the fine.[112]

Projects of this sort did not have to be completely national in scope to
involve the central government, but they did have to be of a nature which
made them impossible, or unjust, for one particular area to have to deal
with on its own. Highways and rivers, for example, run through many
districts and communities, some of which benefit greatly from their

---

109. BM, Harleian MS. 703, new f. 13, the council to the sheriff and justices of the peace of Sussex, March 22, 1584.

110. PRO, SP.12/131, no. 72, the commissioners for the repair of Dover
Haven to the council, August 18, 1579; SP.12/133, no. 54, the mayor, jurates
and whole commonalty of the town and port of Dover to the council, 1579(?).

111. Bodleian Library, MS. Tanner 241, f. 5, the council to the sheriff and
justices of the peace of Norfolk, March 1, 1579.

112. PRO, SP.12/136, no. 85, the council to certain justices of the peace,
March(?) 1580.

passage, some hardly at all, most coming somewhere in between these two extremes. Whatever individual local situations happened to be, they required some outside force to make them work together in such cases for the common good or for the benefit of some place which perhaps could not even continue to exist without the cooperation of others. Thus the justices of the peace in Suffolk were successful in obtaining letters patent appointing and authorizing commissioners to collect money in several hundreds for the purpose of repairing an important county road.[113] The cleansing and scouring of the River Wisbech, in East Anglia, required the collective efforts of several *counties* and in 1576, the council wrote to the sewer commissioners of Huntingdonshire, Cambridgeshire, Northamptonshire, Norfolk and the Parts of Holland in Lincolnshire, instructing them to join together in the enterprise with the inhabitants of the Isle of Ely, for whose benefit it was chiefly necessary that it be undertaken.[114] Similarly, they commended the zeal of the mayor and corporation of Carlisle and the gentlemen of Cumberland and Kendall for taking steps to repair "the breach of the river of Eden. . . ."[115]

Its handling of such matters as these reveals more clearly than anything else the Elizabethan Privy Council's humanity. The council was not sentimental; it showed no concern over the destruction of Nantwich for, say, esthetic or historic reasons. But it was not unfeeling, as is clear from its concern for the poorer sort. It was, rather, immensely, Protestantly, practical. Not only were the fire-bereft of Cheshire to be comforted materially, their physical requirements met by the restoration of their houses, they were to be ministered to spiritually as well, the health of their souls and minds provided for by the appointment of the teacher-minister. Education, even if it were education of that particular sort likely to be dispensed by an instructor who was also a cleric, this Reformation council clearly felt, was not something to be confined to a privileged elite, but a benefit to be partaken of by as many folk as possible.

Its attitude towards alehouses, manifest in its exploitation of them for the benefit of Dover, is all of a piece with its handling of the problems of Nantwich. It did not moralize over them any more than it saw Nantwich's Gomorrah-like fate as divine retribution for the sins of its inhabitants. Alehouses were not fulminated against because they were dens of iniquity,

113. Bodleian Library, MS. Tanner 241, f. 12v, the justices of the peace of Suffolk to the queen, March 4, 1581.

114. PRO, SP.12/108, no. 36, the council to the sewer commissioners of Huntingdonshire, Cambridgeshire, Northamptonshire, Norfolk and the Holland Parts of Lincolnshire, June 3, 1576.

115. APC, VIII, 362, April 5, 1575.

merely taxed in a good cause because of their being inconveniently disorderly. Altogether, the council's involvement in the abnormal affairs of these two in many ways very ordinary communities provides as good a particular example as one could wish for of its general approach to what might be called its service responsibilities. It reacted to unusual situations as they cropped up as though they were nonrecurring, once in a lifetime disasters, which they were only from a local point of view. It did not regard them as mere provincial dislocations, almost certain to occur somewhere or other fairly frequently. In consequence, it did not plan ahead with the idea of preventing as many such problems as possible from arising in the first place and of being prepared to deal with the unavoidable ones when they did. But at least it eventually tried to do something constructive in not uningenious, commonsensical kinds of ways, and many of the queen's subjects responded by clearly regarding the council as being the natural place to turn to for assistance when their own nearby resources failed them.

A similar confidence in the efficacy of empirical improvisation is evident in the council's attitude towards national productivity. In spite of the lack of a Board of Trade, a Ministry of Agriculture and Fisheries and an Industrial Planning Commission, neither commerce, rural occupations nor manufacturing activities escaped the council's controlling hand. Examples of conciliar interference in these matters are legion.

Printing without a special license was banned outright. Two knights of Northamptonshire were, therefore, ordered to commit to prison those unauthorized persons who had been responsible for the putting out of "an aunswer against Whitegifte's booke" in 1573.[116] The tanning of leather was regulated by statute, and steps were taken every so often to make sure that the laws were observed.[117] The planting of hemp and flax was encouraged and the sowing of woad forbidden, both by proclamation and by council letter.[118] The bishops were instructed not to cut down any more trees.[119] Restrictions were imposed on brewing.[120] In 1578, Sir Owen Hopton and Mr. Recorder Fleetwood reported that they had ex-

---

116. *Ibid.*, 93–94, March 31, 1573.

117. Surrey Record Office, Loseley MS. XIII, no. 20, the council to the sheriff and justices of the peace of Surrey, November 7, 1574.

118. BM, Lansdowne MS. 25, no. 99, draft proclamation for the sowing of flax and hemp, with annotations in Burghley's own hand, 1578.

119. BM, Add. MS. 32323, f. 17v, the queen to the bishops, February 1580; Harleian MS. 4943, f. 102, the queen to "sondrie bishops," February 29, 1580.

120. Kent Record Office, Sandwich MS. SaZZB 14, council restrictions on brewing, 1577.

amined certain persons who were suspected of having sold "counterfeit and false wax."[121] In the wool trade, men were appointed to oversee "the byeing and . . . broging of wool in the shires, in accord with the provisions of a proclamation and . . . letter from the council," and another proclamation in February 1579 forbade sheepshearing between Shrove Tuesday and the end of July, on pain of imprisonment until "her majestie's and her most honourable counsel's pleasure be further known."[122] As for the trade in corn, the sheriffs were written to in 1574 "for the observacion of certein orders for restraining of the multitude of badgers in corporate townes," and Sir Thomas Mildmay and John Peter, esquire, were told to see that "forestallers, engrossers and regratours . . . were presented . . . at the next assysses according to the lawes of the realme."[123]

One of the most consistently recurring examples of the council's persistence and purpose in interfering with the internal trade of the country is the enforcement of the regulations governing the observance of fishdays and Lent. Almost every year, sometime in February, the council took steps to forbid the killing and eating of animal flesh during the fast that preceded Easter. From the mid-eighties, this took the form of what Robert Steele calls a council proclamation, although this description is in fact incorrect. Proclamations were always issued in the queen's name, even though they contained the phrase "by the advise of our most honorable Privy Council." What were issued each February were simply "orders conceaved and set downe by the Lords," which were then printed in the form and size of proclamations proper, and distributed and publicly posted just as proclamations were.[124] In the seventies and early eighties, the usual practice seems to have been simply to write directly to the sheriffs and justices of the peace, who were urged, first of all, to set a good example by their own restraint. They were also, however, to take bonds

---

121. PRO, SP.12/132, no. 45, Sir Owen Hopton and Recorder Fleetwood to Knollys and Walsingham, October 10, 1579.

122. PRO, SP.12/115, no. 14, "The names of suche as are appointed in sundrye sheires to have the spetial oversight that the byeing and disorderly broging of wool be reformed, according to a proclamation and letters for that purpose sent them from their Lordships," August 1577; SP.12/129, no. 47, proclamation against pulling or clipping of wool fells between Shrove Tuesday and the end of July, February 28, 1579.

123. APC, VIII, 318, November 22, 1574; 192, February 8, 1573.

124. Public announcement of council instructions in this fashion occurred regularly, as, for example, in the case of "the orders appointed for the government and order of the Eschaunge, that the same may be used and kept accordyng to the lawes and statutes of the realme, which are nowe ordeyned to be observed by the queene's majestie's proclamation," September 27, 1576. Robert Steele, *A Bibliography of Royal Proclamations of the Tudor and Stuart Sovereigns* (Oxford, 1910), no. 707.

from butchers, innkeepers and victualers not to kill or sell meat during the forbidden period. The butchers were divided into two categories: those who were not to kill at all, and those who were permitted to kill and sell, but only to those consumers who were exempt from the restriction either on account of sickness or by license from the queen for some other reason. The justices of the peace were to submit lists every fourteen days to the *custos rotulorum*, showing what meat had been killed and eaten and by whom during the preceding fortnight; the lists were to be forwarded by the *custos* to the council. The bond entered into by the second class of butcher was for £50, and those forfeited were to be handed over periodically to the sheriff, whose job it was to pay them in to the exchequer.[125]

The council fixed prices and pegged wages. On July 8, 1565 the Lord Keeper "was, by their Lordshippes, desired to cause to be imprinted and sente abrode" a schedule of commodities and what was to be charged for them.[126] In 1576 the council wrote to the commissioners "appointed for the taking order for the sale of wynes" and to the Lord Mayor of London to see that the wine merchants about to leave for Bordeaux realized that on their return they must sell their cargoes "at suche pryses as by her majestie . . . [were] sett downe."[127]

Exports were also regulated. The justices of assize in Devon and Cornwall were instructed both in 1571 and 1573 to see that the local justices of the peace with whom they came in contact on their circuit "conferre . . . for the better meting with those that by stealthe do use to convey leather beyond the seas."[128] In 1574 the council caused "inquirie to be made what quantities of butter and chese hath been bought in those counties sithe the first of August last past to be carried out of the shiere, either by sea or land, who were the buyers, who the carriers, for what purpose it was bought, for whom, and as nere as they can, where every thereof hath been bestowed, and presently remayneth, and to certifie with diligence what they shall finde."[129] The most frequent commodity of all to have its trade interfered with was grain. On September 16, 1572 a proclamation was issued by the queen from Woodstock, prohibiting the

125. BM, Harleian MS. 360, f. 83, the council to the justices of the peace, February 19, 1582.

126. APC, VII, 230, July 8, 1565.

127. BM, Lansdowne MS. 25, no. 7, the council to the Lord Mayor of London, October 12, 1577; PRO, SP.12/108, no. 22, the council to the commissioners "appointed for the taking order for the sale of wynes according to the statute," May 19, 1576.

128. APC, VIII, 68, February 17 and 18, 1571; BM, Harleian MS. 4943, f. 99, the council to the justices of assize in Devon and Cornwall, February 18, 1573.

129. APC, VIII, 316, November 22, 1574.

export of grain completely.[130] A proclamation, however, was not always necessary. Each county had its own commissioners for the restraint of grain and victuals—those for Sussex in 1586 included the Viscount Montague, Lords Lumley, Delaware and Buckhurst and the Bishop of Chichester, plus two knights and nine esquires—whom the Lord Keeper was not only empowered to appoint by letters patent under the Great Seal, but whose number he was authorized to increase or decrease at his discretion.[131] The council wrote to these commissioners, telling them when, for the time being, exports of grain should cease. Tremayne's precedent book contains the copy of one such letter, addressed to the commissioners of Suffolk, Surrey, Essex, Lincolnshire, Norfolk, Devon, Cornwall, Kent, Hampshire, Dorset, and Somerset.[132] In June 1576 the council wrote to the commissioners of *all* the shires with seacoasts, insisting that the restraint be "severlie exercised."[133] Sometimes it also wrote to the officers of the ports to the same effect.[134]

The council not only restrained, it also fostered. Established trading companies, whether chartered or not, could expect to be able to call on the government for support and protection. It was to the council that the Merchant Adventurers turned when four of their ships were seized in Flanders in early 1569. The council on this occasion seems initially to have responded unsympathetically, on the theory that, conditions being what they were in Flanders at the time, no ships should have been sent over in the first place. When the merchants, however, replied that, not realizing that the council would object, they had deliberately sent only four ships in anticipation of cutting their losses in the event of just such a calamity, they were compensated out of the goods of the subjects of the King of Spain which were seized in England in reprisal.[135] In 1570, too, their fleet was

130. PRO, SP.12/89, no. 45, BM, Add. MS. 32323, f. 101, proclamation for the restraint of the transportation of grain, September 16, 1572.

131. PRO, SP.12/92, no. 40, the queen to A, B, C etc., draft in Burghley's hand of a commission for the restraint of grain, October 21, 1573; BM, Harleian MS. 703, new f. 22v, the council to the commissioners for the restraint of the transportation of grain in Sussex, March 31, 1586; BM, Add. MS. 32323, f. 158, commission for the Lord Chancellor to direct forth commissions for the restraint of corn and to alter and change them at his discretion, no date.

132. BM, Add. MS. 32323, f. 98v, the commissioners for the restraint of the export of grain in certain counties, no date.

133. PRO, SP.12/108, no. 34, the council to the commissioners for the restraint of the transportation of grain from the maritime counties, June 1, 1576.

134. BM, Add. MS. 32323, f. 100v, the council to customers, controllers and other officers of ports and creeks, no date.

135. PRO, SP.12/49, nos. 14 and 15, the company of Merchant Adventurers to the council, January 7 and 8, 1569.

convoyed to Hamburg by the navy, although they probably had to pay for this service. This is suggested by the fact that a council letter to all ports, later in the reign, ordered that the charges incurred in the performance of a similar protective mission—that of the escort of the Bordeaux wine fleet by two royal ships—should be met by a special levy of five shillings a ton on wines and the other goods brought in at the same time.[136] Above all, the council could be counted on to help in keeping interlopers out of a company's market. The queen wrote to the Merchant Adventurers in 1570 authorizing them to prohibit Thomas Clecher, and anyone else, for that matter, who was not freeman of the company, from meddling in the trade of merchandise with the Low Countries. Anyone taking no notice of the injunction was to be sent before the council to explain himself.[137] In 1579, similarly, the council instructed the messengers of the Chamber to "repaire unto suche places which the . . . president and assistantes of the companie shall from time to time in writinge . . . signifie unto you," and bring up before the council all those who were carrying on trade in the area who yet refused to conform to the orders established by the company of merchants trading to Spain and Portugal.[138]

The degree to which the merchants could rely on official support is perhaps most amply demonstrated by the case of a projected voyage to North Africa in 1573.

> Maie it please your honor, I receaved your letter at the Mercers' feast [wrote Dr. Wilson to the Lord Treasurer at the Court at Knole] the contentes whereof, touchinge the trade to Barbarie I did open to my Lorde Maior, Sir Row-lande Heywarde, the Governor and to some others, who al[l] agreed, that the voyage to Barbarie is so necessarie as it wer better to bee forbydden Portugale, and therefore they desired me to bee an humble meane to your honor, that no soche ac-corde showlde passe, as to hynder them that voyage. I went, after the conference, to the Portugale ambassador, unto whome I did [give] my message, and shewed her majestie's ful resolutyon not to forbydde her subjectes the trade unto Barbarie.[139]

---

136. City of Chester Record Office, MS. M/L/1, no. 33, Burghley to the customers, comptrollers and searchers of Chester, March 28, 1593.

137. PRO, SP.12/75, no. 101, the queen to the Merchant Adventurers' Company, 1570(?).

138. PRO, SP.12/131, no. 24, the council to the messengers of the Chamber, June 14, 1579.

139. BM, Harleian MS. 6991, f. 52, Wilson to Burghley, July 27, 1573.

Four days later the ambassador replied that the issuance by the queen of a prohibition against English trade with Barbary would be not an impediment in practice because the king "wyl wynke at the matter." But this assurance was not acceptable. "I towlde hym," wrote Wilson to Lord Burghley, "that betwixte words and deedes, there was greate difference."[140] De Spes was equally unsuccessful in putting a stop to Hawkin's voyage to the Indies in 1570. "Seven ships," he reported to Philip II on November 28, "are ready here . . . and [although] I . . . obtained a stop from the Admiralty court by order of the council . . . I am afraid some of the ships will go." It was a justifiable fear, since the council had told him to his face that it held it to be "unjust to prevent people from making voyages."[141] This was plain speaking, and it reflects the closeness of the relationship between the political and commercial great men of Elizabethan England. In 1574 the council conferred with the "merchantes tradyng estewarde . . . towching sooche necessary poyntes as are to be consydered of the treatye with the King of Denmarke."[142] It is not surprising, therefore, that Cecil should have made a laconic note on one of his many memoranda to the effect that the trading companies were important factors in public business and the making of national policy.[143]

Particular interests of particular companies occasionally came into conflict with one another, whereupon the council was approached to decide the issue between them. The Merchant Adventurers petitioned to be as free to trade in the Levant as they had been before the Turkey Merchants had been incorporated.[144] Company activities occasionally caused resentments in outsiders that the council was called upon to straighten out. In 1570 the shipowners, masters and mariners of the Thames area asked that the merchants trading to Spain and Portugal should be restricted to bringing in nothing but salt after an outward trip with a cargo of grain. What had apparently been happening was that news had come of a famine in Spain, whereupon west country shipowners had chartered their vessels to the merchants "for less than half the freight that others can lyve on," presumably in the anticipation of very high profits on local wheat.[145] If the merchants were forbidden to bring back a

---

140. *Ibid.*, f. 54, Wilson to Burghley, July 31, 1573.

141. CSP, Spanish, II, no. 226, p. 286, de Spes to the King of Spain, November 28, 1570; no. 238, p. 294, de Spes to the King of Spain, March 2, 1571.

142. PRO, SP.12/98, no. 32, note of council business, October 15, 1574.

143. PRO, SP.12/47, no. 92, Cecil's memorandum of public business, September 1568.

144. Huntington Library, Ellesmere MS. 2384, the company of Merchant Adventurers to the council, no date.

145. PRO, SP.12/75, no. 13, a petition of shipowners, masters and mariners of the Thames to the council, [1570].

profitable cargo, the petitioners agreed that "it may followe . . . that lesse grayne wilbe transported, but [asserted by way of compensation that] more good shippes and mariners [will be] sett on worke and mayneteyned . . . to the generall benefitt of this common welth."

There seems to have been no doctrinaire or even clearly defined purpose behind all this preoccupation with economic activity. The planting of flax and hemp was approved because growing both was commercially advantageous; the sowing of woad was forbidden, not on account of any great fear of modern Englishmen emulating the ancient Britons in their use of it, but because its cultivation interfered both with normal tillage and the activities of the cloth industry.

The council decreed that Anthony Becke and John Carre (who had been granted the privilege of making glass for glazing) should come to "sum agreement" amongst themselves because their inability to get along with each other had been upsetting the whole enterprise and so frustrating "her majestie's intention to have the science of the making of that kynde of glas to remayn here within her realm."[146] The bishops were not to sell timber, since what with owners selling to anyone who would buy and every little local woodworker turning into a broker and selling wood for almost every conceivable purpose, "onlesse spedye remedye be provided in these respectes, there shall not be tymber sufficient to be had within these twelve yeares for her majestie to buylde any shippe."[147]

The queen's interest was to be served first in all things, as the council's concern with the collection of customs duties also shows. Normally it was very little involved; the entries in the APC relative to such matters are comparatively few in number. But when they do occur the council's intent is always clear enough. In settling a private quarrel over the ownership of a trading vessel's cargo, it had been decided that a portion of the disputed merchandise should be sold for the benefit of two of the parties involved. The council quickly realized, however, that it had momentarily forgotten something, and it therefore wrote promptly to the judge of the court of Admiralty "to geve order that such goodes as remaine in . . . Mr. Smithe [the Customer]'s handes maie be indifferentlie praised . . . and solde . . . for th'aunsweringe of . . . custome."[148] Similarly, all those grants of special permission to export grain were made conditional "upon the payment of her majestie's customes."[149] People could and

---

146. Surrey Record Office, Loseley MS. XII, no. 34, the council to Richard Onslow and William More, August 11, 1569.

147. PRO, SP.12/85, no. 67, Christopher Baker to the council(?), March 11, 1572.

148. APC, XIII, 171, August 14, 1581.

149. *Ibid.*, IX, 3, July 1, 1575.

should be helped when help was needed, but the Crown was not to lose thereby.

The timber shortage mentioned above had another result, which also, incidentally, involved the council. Londoners had had to turn, because of it, to burning coal, imported from the north by sea, to heat their homes instead of wood, a change for the worse that Elizabeth disliked intensely because the fumes had an unpleasant habit of drifting into her windows. The Company of Brewers, therefore, having heard of the queen's aversion, and claiming to represent not only themselves but also the dyers, hatters and "the greateste nomber of cittezens," informed the council that they had arranged for two or three houses close to the palace of Westminster to be returned to the burning of wood. They wished this fact to be drawn to the queen's attention—and at the same time to make it clear that this was as far as it was possible to go in the process of turning back the clock.[150]

Restrictions on printing were political in intent: unfanned fires are the soonest doused. Attempts to reduce the number of practitioners of a particular trade aimed at preventing cutthroat competition that might help undermine the social structure. The most important reason behind the insistence upon fisheating during Lent was the maintenance of shipping and mariners, "the chefeest fortresse for the defence of the realme," and the policy was fervently supported by those living along the coasts and making their living by the sea.[151] Other justifications, however, were adduced from time to time. It was especially necessary to enforce the regulations in 1586, the council informed the justices of the peace in Surrey, because of "a generall morrion of shepe and other cattell," which was likely to cause a steep increase in prices; in December of the previous year, the already high price of victuals had been attributed to the non-observance of the appointed days of abstinence.[152]

It was desirable to control both wages and prices in the interests of the poor.[153] And restrictions over the export of grain were intended both to

---

150. PRO, SP.12/127, no. 68, the London brewers' company to the council, 1578.

151. BM, Harleian MS. 286, f. 33, the council to the justices of the peace, February 4, 1578.

152. Surrey Record Office, Loseley MS. XIII, no. 63(1), the council to the sheriff and justices of the peace of Surrey, December 28, 1585(?).

153. *Statutes of the Realm* (London, 1819, reprinted 1963), IV, 414, "An Acte towching dyvers Orders for Artificers, Laborers, Servantes of Husbandrye and Apprentices" has a preamble which says that "wages and allowances . . . are in dyvers places to [o] small and not answerable to this tyme . . . An uniforme order . . . concerning . . . wages . . . should . . . yeelde unto the hired person bothe in the tyme of scarsitee and in the tyme of plentye a convenient proporcion

keep prices down and maintain the food supply.[154] A bad harvest, and particularly a succession of lean years, brought scarcity and high prices, which might affect the whole country or only certain areas. Scarcity might be brought to the attention of the council by local authorities acting on their own initiative, or such information might come from the assize justices, who had been told to investigate local conditions while on circuit. The muster commissioners of Devon reported their military activities in May 1573 and then went on to ask for the export of grain to be prohibited because the price had recently risen excessively in their locality.[155] Chief Justice Catelyn and Sir Gilbert Gerrard reported a similar situation in the eastern counties in August 1572. They also made the same recommendation with regard to exports, though they suggested the requested restrictions need apply only to wheat and rye, and they enclosed certificates from the justices of the peace in the areas concerned, giving the actual local prices, so that the council could feel itself entirely conversant with the situation.[156]

The council supported the trading companies because it believed that in following such a long-established policy it was furthering the nation's overall commercial and financial interests in the best possible manner. The proclamation forbidding sheepshearing between Shrovetide and the end of July 1579 says as much. Now that the Low Countries had become peaceful enough to trade with again, it had been decided that the new habit of exporting wool "wrought by strangers here in England" was not as truly profitable to the realm as the Merchant Adventurers' long-established business and, therefore, the latter was once again to be officially encouraged.[157] One can see why. Before the establishment of that confidence in government which eventually led to establishment of the Bank

---

of wages," and clause XI says that wages are to be ascertained by the justices of the peace, certified into the chancery, approved by the Privy Council and proclaimed by the sheriffs, 5 Eliz. c. 4; III, 438. "The prices of . . . victualles be many tymes inhaunsed . . . to the greate damage and impoverishing of the kyng'is subjectis," 25 Henry VIII, c. 2.

154. *Ibid.*, II, 88. The act empowering the council to control the export of grain dated from the late fourteenth century when "the king . . . granted licence to all his . . . people . . . to ship and carry corn out of the realm," at the same time asserting that "his council may restrain the said passage when they shall think best for the profit of the realm," 17 Richard II, c. 7. This act was not repealed until the reign of James I.

155. PRO, SP.12/91, no. 26, Devon muster commissioners to the council, May 8, 1573.

156. PRO, SP.12/89, no. 1, Robert Catelyn, chief justice of the court of King's Bench and Sir Gilbert Gerrard to the council, August 1, 1572.

157. PRO, SP.12/129, no. 47, proclamation against pulling or clipping wool fells, February 28, 1579.

of England and a funded national debt, the credit of a merchant group, which could be threatened with withdrawal of its privileges if it did not pay for them with cooperation, played a crucial role in the maintenance of the credit of the state.

For much the same reason—usefulness—the council continued to tolerate the merchants of the Hanse. They were harassed on occasion. In 1573 a council decree placed restrictions on their trading privileges, but they were not particularly harsh restraints in practice. As the Merchant Adventurers, always touchy where their own interests were concerned, were quick to point out, there was a loophole to be found in the words, "if there be any inhabitant of Hamburgh that hath used to carie wares to Hamburgh, and shall have needefull cause in this meane tyme to ship any wares thether, thereof shalbe reasonable consideracion had."[158] The Hanse merchants brought in bowstaves, "whereof one Henrick von Muelen of Colen, one of their . . . citties, had gotten the hole or chiefest trade into his owne handes," so the concession was probably deliberate.[159] In any event, the Merchant Adventurers' campaign against the Germans got nowhere in the seventies; they were permitted to remain and were not expelled until 1598 when the emperor forbade the English to trade with Germany.

All in all, the council's motives for interfering in the national economic life were mixed and arose out of the particular situation in which it found itself involved at any given moment. It appears to have had no overall plan other than to further a national interest that varied according to circumstances and to have made no attempt to integrate the various business efforts of individual or cooperating groups of Englishmen into a coherent, coordinated whole. It was essentially content to work towards preserving the *status quo* there as elsewhere, simply taking action where and when demanded to help things go along as smoothly and as generally advantageously as possible. The council itself expressed its objectives succinctly enough as early as 1561 in a letter to "all viceadmiralles within the realme." It proceeded to instruct them as to how they should proceed "for the preservation of . . . quiet trade."[160] In this particular instance, the "quiet trade" was the quiet trade of merchants and fishermen. Others, however, were expected to conduct their commercial activities with equal discretion and decorum, and the official emphasis in economic matters was firmly placed on the carrying on of business in traditional patterns.

---

158. PRO, SP.12/131, no. 28, the Merchant Adventurers company to the council, June 22, 1579.

159. APC, VIII, 187–190, February 5, 1573.

160. Dyson, f. 38, printed council orders, 1561.

Nonetheless, the council did at least momentarily think about, and even investigate, the possibility of creating some new ones. It wrote on one occasion to the Merchant Adventurers to consider a scheme reputed to be likely to benefit the Crown and at the same time hurt no one else.[161] More specifically, it considered attempting to draw away the business of Antwerp to a new entrepot in England, to be located at Ipswich. The idea was much in the air in the late sixties and early seventies. A discourse on the staple, endorsed "29 Junii 1569" in Cecil's hand, suggests that "the Portingales may easelye be perswaded uppon reasonable condicions to plante themselves here," and that once English and Portuguese trade is thus removed from Antwerp, the Italian merchants will automatically follow.[162] Three years later, in 1572, John Johnson and Christopher Goodwyn addressed a similar argument directly to the council.[163]

It is at least possible, too, that something may have developed from the attempts to work the ore which Martin Frobisher had brought back from his expedition to the new world. This voyage had been sponsored in the first place by "diverse of us" of the council, along with a group of other investors, who included Sir Henry Wallop, William Pelham (the lieutenant of the ordnance) and Sir Thomas Gresham; and on Frobisher's return, the council appointed Michael Lock special treasurer to collect the money these people had promised to put up, in order to pay off Frobisher's crew and "for building furnaces and bringing me[n] from Germany to refine and try [the] ore."[164]

The scheme, however, came to nothing in the end—the ore was worthless—and its failure, along with that of private initiatives like it and the impracticability of turning Ipswich into New Antwerp, seems to have confirmed an already apparent tendency. The council remained determined to keep the national economic boat on an even keel by continuing to rely on its medieval sails for propulsion rather than by attempting to equip it with novel engines of doubtful value. It was an understandable, if unadventurous decision, and it epitomized the council's attitude towards its state responsibilities. No more than Walpole was the Elizabethan Privy Council much interested in awakening sleeping dogs which, if aroused, might well have leaped up and out of its control. It was, indeed, only too content to let them lie.

---

161. BM, Add. MS. 32323, f. 46, the council to the company of Merchant Adventurers, no date.

162. PRO, SP.12/51, no. 18, June 29, 1569.

163. PRO, SP.12/88, no. 22, John Johnson and Christopher Goodwyn to the council, June 20, 1572.

164. PRO, SP.12/122, no. 10, the council to Michael Lock, January 19, 1578; SP.12/126, no. 20, the council to Michael Lock, October 29, 1578.

Chapter VIII

THE WORKING PROCESS

LL the activities of the council, whether involving the supervision and coordination of the operations of departments of state, the implementing of the principles outlined in acts of parliament and proclamations or the exercising of the general powers inherent in the royal prerogative, required organization. For the system to work smoothly there had to be some person, or persons, to bring to the attention of the council matters calling for settlement and then to see that the council's decisions, once made, were disseminated and its orders carried out. It needed a staff, in other words, and that staff had to be maintained.

The council's chief official was one of its own members: the principal secretary. The role of the principal secretary is a particularly fascinating one, for the power potential in the office itself was enormous, yet its successful exploitation depended, throughout the reign of Elizabeth, on fundamentally personal factors. Nicholas Faunt, who was Walsingham's own secretary from 1580 onwards and wrote a short description of the office, put it in a nutshell. The principal secretary, he said, "is the mouth of the councell of state." He might have pointed out that the secretary was the council's ear as well. Thus Sir Thomas Smith told the Earl of Shrewsbury in 1573 that "the paines . . . you . . . [have] taken to seeke owt the conjurors and masmongers is very well accepted of my lords of the counsell, and they willed me to give your Lordship therfor their most harty thanks."[1] The Earl of Bedford, in 1579, informed the council itself that "some other matters of the state of this countrey I have imparted to Mr. Secretarie Walsingham, wherwith I was unwilling to trowble your Lordships, therby to lett you from your more waightie affayres. And yf the same be of any value, I know he will declare them to your Lordships."[2] Faunt, however, did go on to add that the secretary's position vis-à-vis the council, like his personal standing with the sovereign, was "somewhat accidentary, and alwaies followinge the good conceipt and opinion had of the personne in whome this creditt and trust is to be reposed."[3]

---

1. Edmund Lodge, *Illustrations of British History*, II (London, 1791), 89, Smith to the Earl of Shrewsbury, February 17, 1573.

2. PRO, SP.12/131, no. 65, the Earl of Bedford to the council, August 12, 1579.

3. Nicholas Faunt, "Discourse Touchinge the Office of Principall Secretarie of Estate etc., Aprill 1592," *EHR*, XX, April 1905, 499.

There is no question as to the "good conceipt and opinion" held of the four men who held the secretaryship between 1568 and 1582. Yet the written evidence all of them have left indicates that each filled the office in his own individual way, and that this was owing to the differing effects of their talents and personalities, particularly on the queen. Sir William Cecil, Elizabeth's first, and for fourteen years her only working secretary, was perhaps in a class by himself.[4] He was certainly a great deal more than just a sort of superior civil servant. None of the other secretaries has left the long memoranda on the state of the realm that Cecil periodically drew up in his own distinctive handwriting. None of them was at any time quite so authoritative as Cecil already was in the early 1560s, giving the Earl of Bedford, as governor of Berwick, his advice on "how he shall keepe the queene's favoure and maintaine his honour."[5] Cecil was at least a "policy-suggester," if not necessarily a "policy-maker," and his influential position on the council was not the consequence of his tenure of the principal secretaryship or even of the office of Lord Treasurer. It was the direct result of the fact that both Elizabeth and the rest of the council respected his advice and judgment as a man to the extent that frequently they would make no decision until they had had the opportunity to consult him. Sir Thomas Smith wrote to him from Windsor in October 1572 that the queen was not disposed to sign anything until he arrived at the castle.[6] And in December 1574 the council ordered Smith to forward a particular supplication to Burghley, asking for his advice before taking further action in the matter.[7] These are far from being isolated instances of the deference paid by the highly placed to Burghley's opinions.

Sir Thomas Smith, his immediate successor in the office of principle secretary, filled it very differently, as his personality might well lead one to expect. As secretary he had trouble continually about getting the queen to sign things, let alone consult him as to whether or not she should do so at all. His advice was not only rarely asked, outside the council, but still less frequently acted upon. He ended up, apparently owing to the somewhat pedagogical turn of his nature, as a sort of high class messenger boy who was constantly running back and forth, figuratively if not quite literally, between Elizabeth, the council, and, when he was absent from the Court, the indispensable Lord Treasurer. "I nether can get thother letters signed, nor the letters alredy signed . . . permitted to be sent away,

---

4. Sir William Petre acted as secretary in 1560 and 1561, remaining titular holder of the office until 1566. F. G. Emmison, *Tudor Secretary* (Cambridge, Mass., 1961), 231–234, 262.

5. BM, Harleian MS. 6990, f. 1, Cecil to the Earl of Bedford, no date.

6. BM, Harleian MS. 6991, f. 15, Smith to Burghley, October 15, 1572.

7. BM, Lansdowne MS. 19, no. 44, Smith to Burghley, December 6, 1574.

but day by day and hower by hower deferred till anon. . . . I wold som other man occupied my rowme, who had more credite to get thynges resolved [and] signed," he wrote to Burghley on March 6, 1575.[8] The following day he was denied access to the queen completely. "So it is now as shut up cleane. I thynk hir majestie doth suppose that I will chide (as I dare), lament and compleyne . . . . I wait whiles I nether have eyes to se, nor legs to stand upon."[9]

Dr. Wilson appears to have been more placid than Smith, whom he succeeded in 1577—Elizabeth, at least, does not appear to have kept him waiting quite so long—but he was equally uninvolved in the formulation of policy, other than as a member of the council. Wilson, indeed, sounds remarkably like the perfect civil servant. "Now the lords are like to tarie," he wrote to the Earl of Leicester in 1578, "I doe thynke they shal have good leasure after the Irishe matters ended, to deale with the ryot at Drayton Basset, whiche is prepared and abridged for the[ir] Lordships to heare at al tymes with greate facilitie."[10] He not only handled the council with tact and efficiency, but the queen with calmness and common sense. When Elizabeth was so offended, both by the behavior of Grindal and by the council's "daringes for dealinge with hym so at large" that she wanted to deprive him of his primacy forthwith, it was Wilson who answered in the voice of responsibility "that a deprivation of an archbysshoppe can not bee done so sone, and if that course bee taken, he wyl aske the benefite of the lawe, and praye cownsel for his assistance, wherby the matter wyl growe longer before it bee decyded."[11] But Wilson was secretary for only four short years, and, in any case, both he and Smith, except during the first few months of Smith's tenure of the office, were always "second secretaries," in fact if not in name, playing second fiddle to the man who really counted—Francis Walsingham. As principal secretary Walsingham preceded, accompanied, and survived Dr. Wilson, and left the greatest number of documentary traces of his secretarial proceedings. Although on his death "all his papers and bookes both publicke and private weare seazed and carried away," we can still make out in considerable detail, with the help of Faunt and an invaluable little book by Robert Beale, the working procedures followed in his office.[12]

8. BM, Harleian MS. 6991, f. 124, Smith to Burghley, March 6, 1575.

9. *Ibid.*, f. 126, Smith to Burghley, March 7, 1575.

10. BM, Harleian MS. 286, f. 37, Wilson to the Earl of Leicester, November 13, 1578.

11. PRO, SP.12/122, no. 15, Wilson to Burghley, January 23, 1578.

12. Conyers Read, *Mr. Secretary Walsingham and the Policy of Queen Elizabeth* (New York, 1955–1960), I, 431.

Robert Beale was clerk of the Privy Council from 1572 until the last years of Elizabeth's reign. He was not only Walsingham's brother-in-law, but a man who more than once stepped temporarily into Walsingham's official shoes when Walsingham was away on diplomatic missions. He described the duties of the secretaryhip on the basis of the way Walsingham had filled it in *A Treatise of the Office of a Councellor and Principall Secretarie to her Majestie*, which he drew up in 1592 for the benefit of Sir Edward Wootton, a man who hoped to be made secretary himself, but who never was.[13] Beale describes a personage who was the council's chairman, its mentor, and, if he failed to take adequate precautions, its scapegoat into the bargain. "When the councell meeteth, have a care that the time be not spent in matters of small moment, but to dispatch such thinges as shalbe propounded unto them. . . . Favour not secrett or cabinett councells, which doe cause jealousie and envie. . . . When ther shalbe anie unpleasant matter to be imparted to her majestie . . . let not the burden be layed on you alone, but let the rest joyne with you."[14] Of both Cecil's and Walsingham's tenures of the office of secretary this is a fair and accurate summation. During Elizabeth's reign the office of Lord President of the council was in suspension. In practice its functions were exercised by the secretary; when there were two secretaries, by the more important, notwithstanding the fact that, as Mrs. F.M.G. Higham points out, the secretary's formal standing relative to the rest of the council was no higher, merely by virtue of his office, than that of the treasurer, the comptroller or the vice-chamberlain of the Household.[15] Indeed it was even lower, for in the lists of those attending meetings, his name almost always comes last, his precedence putting him ahead only of Sir Walter Mildmay.

Walsingham, presumably throughout his years as secretary, kept a day-book, although only the volume covering 1583 and a few months of the preceding and following years survives.[16] In this he made a note to remind himself of things he had to bring to the council's attention the next time it met. He made notes of letters he had to write, of instructions to be drawn up and of proclamations to be engrossed. As the council did not usually meet every day, he would put down the heading "counsell causes," and then leave a gap below it to be filled in as things arose that were to be brought up whenever the council did next meet. On Tuesday March 26,

---

13. *Ibid.*, 421.

14. *Ibid.*, 424–425.

15. F. M. G. Higham, *The Principal Secretary of State: A Survey of the Office from 1558 to 1680* (London, 1923), 5.

16. BM, Harleian MS. 6035.

1583 the entries "The warden of Wynchester; the minut Irelande; the lybell; Owtred; Bishop of Chester letters" filled only half the space allotted for council business by the time the meeting took place. Before it did, however, he would translate these cryptic notes into intelligible questions, list them on the lefthand inside page of a piece of ordinary foolscap paper folded down the middle, and then take this with him into the council chamber.[17] The subjects listed, or at least some of them, would then be "propounded," in the order set down, and when the matter had been discussed and a decision taken, Walsingham would write it down on the same sheet of paper on which he had noted the original question, opposite to it and to the right of the center fold. In addition to his day book, Walsingham also kept a diary, in a similarly abbreviated form, and in this he would note what he had actually done and what had actually taken place. "I had ordre," he recorded on the day he was sworn principal Secretary, "from the counsell for the answering of the deputie's letters."[18] There he also set down what letters he had received and written, what audiences had been given to whom, and, on one particular occasion, that he had been sent by the council to the queen, and then by the queen to the Lord Treasurer.[19] The other secretaries probably had a somewhat similar system; Cecil has left numerous scraps of paper scribbled all over with the kind of thing Walsingham put in his daybook, for the job they had to do necessitated some sort of personal arrangement on these lines.[20]

All of them, if they were to be in a position to know what should go before the council and what should not and to give informed and reasoned guidance to the councillors once this initial decision had been made, must have at hand, so Beale advised Wootton, complete data relative to the state of England at any given moment. This meant maps of the whole country and of Ireland, annotated to show who resided where; complete listings of all recusants; copies of the commissions and instructions of the Councils of the North and in the Marches of Wales and of the wardens of the marches; notes of all coastal forts and their state of preservation; the names of the queen's ships, with the requisite informa-

---

17. PRO, SP.12/97, no. 10, just one example of a series of such notes of things to be propounded "in cownsayl" now preserved in this and the following volume of the State Papers, June 13, 1574.

18. PRO, 30/5/5, "Journal of Sir Francis Walsingham from December 1570 to April 1583," printed in *The Camden Miscellany* (London, 1871), VI, 13.

19. *Ibid.*, 13, December 26, 1573.

20. CSP Foreign, 1577–1578, Elizabeth I, volume 12, p. 557, no. 727, notes in Burghley's hand of things the council had to talk about in relation to the Low Countries, March 22, 1578.

tion as to their complements and necessary furniture; "a collecion of the late musters in everie sheire for some few yeares;" a statement from the ordnance office of the realm's supplies of powder and shot; details of subsidies and loans; texts of England's treaties with foreign powers; and a file of documents relating to the privileges of Jersey and Guernsey.[21] All these were to be collected together into books, a number of which, in spite of the spiriting away of Walsingham's papers after his death, some still uniformly bound in plain parchment and secured with a "crossgartered" leather strap and metal clasp, are still to be found scattered in the various great manuscript depositories of England. In Walsingham's day they were kept in the "councill chest," along with other papers and minutes relating to council business.[22] However, even this was far from all that the secretary should know. Not only was he to make sure he received annual lists from the clerk of the Crown of the justices of the peace throughout England (the *libri pacis*) of the details of all special commissions, and of the names of all judges and "principall gentlemen able for service, either civill or martiall," but he should go out of his way to acquaint himself personally with as many of these people as possible. He was to be familiar with mint and money matters, understand the workings of the royal household, keep track of the number of foreigners now living in the country, and "be so sufficiently instructed in the points of the Christian religion which the Churche of Englande professith as to be able to maintaine the same and answer all traitors and other adversaries that he shall have to deal with."[23]

It was a formidable task, but to help him with the paper work the handling of his own and the council's affairs entailed, the secretary had the staff of two offices, two lesser secretaries and a personal clerical staff, which varied in size according to the whim of the incumbent. Walsingham had too many "clercks and servants," according to Beale, and certainly his daybook is crowded with the names of such men who have no other historical existence: Cyprian, Wilford, Cave, Salter, Bayley, Lewes —only Francis Myls and Nicholas Faunt are not quite such shadowy figures. At least twenty-eight such names appear in Walsingham's book to bear out Beale's assertion. Cecil, on the other hand, had only two or three such personal clerks, and Beale thought this quite sufficient, since it was easier to make sure "that they which be about you be no advertisers of anie matters but wher and when and to whom you shall appoint."[24] The

21. Read, *Walsingham*, I, 428–429.
22. BM, Harleian MS. 6035, Walsingham's letter book, f. 4v, 1583.
23. Read, *Walsingham*, I, 430.
24. *Ibid.*, 427.

secretaries of the Latin and French tongues were used as and when their specialized services were required, and when the matter in hand was important enough the secretary himself wrote and sealed his own or the queen's letters, without permitting anyone else to see their contents.[25] But the secretary's main clerical assistants in helping him discharge his dual functions as the right-hand man of both queen and council were the staffs of the Signet and council offices respectively.

The Signet was the most personal of the official royal seals and remained in the secretaries' custody for sealing not only royal warrants directed to the Privy Seal and the chancery, but those of the queen's letters which went direct from her to individuals, covering a wide range of business and approximately paralleling the Privy Council's letters in purpose. There were four clerks of the Signet, and it seems likely that, while their primary concern was with the writing of Signet letters, they were enrolled to help write council letters too when pressure of business in the one department was heavier than that in the other.[26] But the clerks of the council, and the council office, were the functionaries and the office of which the council naturally made the greatest use.

Sir Julius Caesar was not a member of the Privy Council until the reign of James I, but he had been a master of requests and very closely involved in the highest public business long before the death of Elizabeth, and therefore the description which he wrote in 1625 of the council's physical location and its bureaucratic organization, such as it was, can be taken as relevant to the situation as it existed in the 1570s and 1580s. "The Privie Counsell have had allwayes, and so nowe, a faire chambre in every standinge howse, where the king's majestie's abode is, where they kepe the counsell table, with a littele roome thereto adjoyninge, where the clerkes of the said counsell and theire servauntes sitt and wright. The Privie Counsell is attended on by three or more ordinary clearkes to enact theire orders, and wright such letters, or answears as theire Lordshipps shall command them." Much of what they wrote they wrote either in or copied into the "greate faire paperbookes" which, Caesar laments, perished, along with much of the material described by Beale in his Treatise, "in the time of Kinge James . . . by occasion of the sudden fire which consumed the banquetinge howse at Whitthall" where they were kept.[27] However, while the fire destroyed many documents which would be interesting for their content, enough evidence remains, primarily in

25. CSP Spanish, II, no. 1, p. 1, da Silva to the King of Spain, January 3, 1568.

26. Higham, 6.

27. PRO, SP.16/8, no. 77, Sir Julius Caesar's notes on the Privy Council, October 31, 1625.

the form of the Privy Council registers themselves and of letters from the council scattered in archives and attics all over England, for us to be able to get a clear picture of how, in practice, the bureaucratic system worked.

There were normally, at any given time, four clerks of the Privy Council. For most of the period between 1568 and 1582, they were Edmund Tremayne (sworn May 3, 1571), Robert Beale (sworn July 8, 1572), Thomas Wilkes and Henry Cheke (both sworn July 18, 1576).[28] The clerks were all men of ability, experienced, particularly in foreign affairs, long before they were attached to the council in an official capacity, and in social standing at least on a par with the secretaries themselves; also, each had a personal connection of some sort with one or more members of the council which they served.

Edmund Tremayne, the senior clerk during most of our period, came of a family that had been established in Devon since 1366. He had begun his career in the household of Edward Courtenay and, like Sir James Croft, had been imprisoned in the Tower at the same time as Elizabeth, on suspicion of being involved in Wyatt's rebellion, during Mary Tudor's reign. He had refused to implicate either Elizabeth or Courtenay, however, even under torture, and he was eventually released. He thereupon proceeded to join his patron in Italy, where Courtenay died in 1556. Tremayne then managed to attach himself to the Earl of Bedford, who was at the time in Venice; and back in England during the early years of Elizabeth's reign he also succeeded in commending himself to Cecil, who first made use of him by sending him to Ireland to investigate the situation for Cecil's private information. His visit was the beginning of a continuing interest on Tremayne's part in Ireland and its affairs, which continued throughout his tenure of a clerkship of the council. Although he had seen fit to absent himself from England during most of Mary's reign, and in spite of the facility with which he succeeded in attaching himself to one useful patron after the other, Tremayne seems to have been neither a fanatically religious man nor an obsequious, fawning sort of person. He was, in fact, rather like Dr. Wilson in being something very close to the perfect civil servant, and it was his cool capability which commended him more than anything else to one influential person after another.[29]

Robert Beale was a Suffolk man and a much more contentious personality. He, too, found it expedient to leave the country while Mary oc-

---

28. A. F. Pollard, "Council, Star Chamber and Privy Council," *EHR*, XXXVIII, January 1923, 42.
29. DNB, Tremayne, Edmund.

cupied the throne, but his was a flight primarily from an intolerable religious situation, for Beale was an ardent and a learned Protestant. Later
in Elizabeth's reign he engaged in a prolonged and acrimonious theological
dispute with Archbishop Whitgift over the role and authority of the
bishops in the Church that had been established by the settlement of 1559.
His militant protestantism was closely akin to that professed by Walsingham, who found him working in some unspecified capacity in the English
embassy in Paris in 1564 and thereupon made him his secretary. The
close relationship which the two enjoyed in the years that followed—
Beale acted as secretary of state in Walsingham's absences from England
in 1578, 1581, and 1583—was sealed by Beale's marriage to the sister of
Walsingham's wife, and their association remained intimate and apparently untroubled until Walsingham's death in 1590. Beale, like Tremayne, was a highly efficient functionary, but, unlike Tremayne, he had
a knack of offending rather than placating people, and in 1592 he was
even banished from the Court for a short time because of an injudicious
speech in the house of commons against the bishops.[30]

Thomas Wilkes had traveled extensively on the Continent during his
young manhood, obtained his B. A. at Oxford in 1573 and then became
secretary to Dr. Valentine Dale. Dale, D. C. L. from the University of
Orleans, ambassador, member of parliament, dean of Wells and altogether a man of deep learning, catholic interests and wide acquaintance,
was close to Burghley and would be consulted regularly by Hatton during
the latter's tenure of the Lord Chancellorship.[31] Working for a man
himself so close to the highly-placed provided Wilkes with the opportunity
to make an impression on people who held the power to make or break
him. He used it to advantage. His particular patron on the council was the
Earl of Leicester (although Leicester's approbation turned to uncon-
cealed dislike after Wilkes openly criticized his conduct in the Low
Countries in the eighties) and Wilkes proved his worth, prior to being
made clerk, by his tactful handling of the delicate negotiations with France
with which he was entrusted in 1574. Long-lived like Beale, by the latter
part of his life he was well and widely versed in the ways of government
and governors, and eventually set down what his experiences had taught
him in "a briefe and summary tractate, shewing what apperteineth to the
place, dignity and office of a councellour of estate in a monarchy or other
commonwealth."[32] Wilkes was no less competent a person than either

30. *Ibid.*, Beale, Robert.
31. *Ibid.*, Dale, Valentine.
32. BM, Stowe MS. 287, as cited in DNB under Wilkes, Thomas.

Tremayne or Beale, and his services were as widely made use of as theirs, but he was personally not as close to any of the members of the council as both of them were, and as clerk he seems to have been overshadowed, particularly by Beale.

Henry Cheke presents a less distinct figure than any of the others. Even the dates of his birth and death are uncertain. He apparently owed his advancement to his family connections. His first wife was Frances Radcliff, the sister of the Earl of Sussex. But this connection was much less to his ultimate advantage than the fact that, by marriage, he was Cecil's nephew, Cecil's first wife, Mary Cheke, having been the sister of Henry's father. The State Papers contain numerous letters from the young Cheke to his important uncle, reminding the latter of his existence and of his need for remunerative employment. The clerkship of the council was the ultimate, though delayed, reward for his perseverance.[33]

Like the non-noble members of the council, its clerks were all, at one time or another, members of parliament—Beale, at various times, for Totnes, Dorchester and Lostwithiel, Cheke for Bedford and Borough-bridge (in Yorkshire), Tremayne for Plymouth and Wilkes for Downton and Southampton. They were also frequently assigned to much the same kind of extra-routine tasks as the Privy Councillors themselves, and on occasion councillors even asked for their advice. Tremayne was an experienced interrogator, and assisted Sir Thomas Smith, Dr. Wilson and Sir Ralph Sadler in questioning the Duke of Norfolk's men in 1571. He was also closely associated with the examination of Mary Queen of Scots in 1572, when he wrote and signed, along with Lord Burghley, the articles with which Sadler, Wilson and Thomas Bromley were instructed to charge her.[34] Beale was even more closely associated with the affairs of the Queen of Scots than Tremayne. He negotiated with her at Sheffield between 1581 and 1584, took the news to Fotheringay in 1586 that she had been condemned to death, and the following year was the messenger who conveyed the warrant for her execution, at which he was present and later described in detail. But Beale was primarily useful, over and above his duties as clerk of the council, as a diplomat. In April 1576, for example, he was sent with instructions from the council on a mission into Flanders. This was only one of many such journeys which both he and Thomas Wilkes undertook in the course of their years in office. In 1580, Beale was assigned to enquire into the state of the queen's stores in the

---

33. DNB, Cheke, Henry.
34. Hatfield House, MS. 7, f. 39, Sadler, Wilson and Bromley to the Queen of Scots, June 11, 1572.

Tower.[35] The following year he was one of the commissioners who examined Edmund Campion. And in 1589, along with Daniel Rogers, who had been appointed clerk of the council himself in 1587, he received orders from the council as one of the English commissioners appointed to examine complaints concerning piracy that had reputedly been committed by English subjects on the Danes. The membership of this commission is particularly interesting, for it includes, in addition to Beale and Rogers, Valentine Dale and Julius Caesar.[36] Just as the council turned to Dr. Lewes, the judge of the Admiralty court, for advice and assistance in the settlement of disputes involving the nationals of other countries because issues of this nature brought up questions of international law, so it used other experts in the civil law when any matter that had come before it was outside the competence of any of its members. Civilians—Caesar, like Dale and Lewes, was a Doctor of the Civil Law—were in fact frequently employed on council business.[37]

The association of its clerks with the council and its affairs was intimate. Therefore the oath which the new clerk took on entering his office was remarkably similar to that taken by the councillors themselves, its essence being the promises he made to observe the secrecy of the council chamber and to uphold the authority of the queen.[38] At any given time, two of the clerks were always on duty, and in 1579 they arranged a schedule, formally approved by the council itself, which ostensibly rotated them, giving them each six months on full-time duty and six months off.[39] However, it is evident from the fact that their hands occasionally occur in the Privy Council register during times when they should not, according to the timetable, have been in waiting at all, that the two senior clerks, Tremayne and Beale, did not always adhere to the schedule very rigidly. Beale, for example, was scheduled to wait from March through June 1579, and his handwriting appears regularly at these times. But it also appears in July, when he was not supposed to be on duty.[40]

The Privy Council register, to which we have already had occasion to refer so often, is made up of a series of Julius Caesar's "greate faire . . . bookes . . . where all the actes of that counsell should be written, and copies

---

35. BM, Add. MS. 48116, the council to Robert Beale, April 17, 1576; Lansdowne MS. 30, no. 6, f. 18, instructions to Beale and Fettiplace, 1580.
36. BM, Cotton MS. Nero B. iii, f. 374, the council to the English commissioners, August 20, 1589.
37. DNB, Caesar, Sir Julius (1558–1636); Dale, Valentine.
38. APC, VIII, 78, July 8 and 9, 1572.
39. APC, XI, 5, January 3, 1579.
40. PRO, PC.2/12, 529, July 9, 1579.

of letters, and whatsoever that table should ordaine."[41] This is a good description, except that it does not mention that those which have survived were not in fact always so "faire." What happened was that the clerk of the council himself attended council meetings wherever they happened to be held and made a note of the date, the place, the names of those attending, and of the business of the meeting on an isolated piece of paper. These rough notes were later gathered together and copied out into the "greate" books by the clerks' own clerks. These sub-clerks were in fact the work horses of the whole system, and the rough copies of the council register that have survived for part of our period show that even the note taken at the meeting was at least in part taken down by one of them. On a number of occasions the clerk himself wrote down only the date, place and attendance details and then left the rest of the details to be filled in by his assistant.[42] Much the same thing seems to have occurred when it came to writing the council letters authorized at the meetings. Sometimes they would be written by the clerk himself, but much more often they would be written by sub-clerks. The clerks of the council themselves were, in fact, a sort of superior office manager, overseeing a group of scribes who wrote such tidily similar hands that they are impossible to identify as individuals, and taking the blame for clerical errors actually perpetrated by their subordinates.[43]

The letters these sub-clerks wrote on the council's behalf were standardized in format. A sheet of foolscap was folded in half to form a four-page "book." The letter itself began on page one with the words "After our most harty commendations," went on to pages two and three if necessary, and closed with the formal phrase "Your loving friends," immediately preceded by the date and place of origin. The council's letters, notwithstanding the great variety in their content, were standardized to a certain degree even in the intervening text. The entries in the register— these become much fuller and more detailed during the latter part of the reign—were at this time relatively brief. On November 2, 1573, for example, it was noted tersely that divers letters were to be written to the commissioners for victuals in divers shires on behalf of certain Londoners, who were to be provided with grain.[44] To find out in what form such letters should actually be written, however, the clerk, or one of his assis-

---

41. PRO, SP.16/8, no. 77, Caesar's notes on the council, October 31, 1625.

42. PRO, PC.2/12, 382, the place, date and presence in Tremayne's hand, January 27, 1578; 403, the whole of the first part of the entry in Tremayne's hand, February 19, 1578.

43. PRO, SP.12/97, no. 18, Burghley to Walsingham, June 21, 1574.

44. APC, VIII, 140, November 2, 1573.

tants, had only to turn to one of the precedent books in which he had previously made a note of a wide variety of letters, and find a similar, earlier one to serve as his model. Robert Beale had at least two books of this sort, and there are two others, initially identical with each other, now in the British Museum, which were almost certainly drawn up by Edmund Tremayne.[45] Beale's first, largely in his own hand, dates from 1572, when he first became clerk of the council, and the second, much larger and mostly in a clerkly hand, has a fly page holograph notation which reads: "This booke of presidents and letters was gathered in the yeare of our Lord God 1575." In these books it is possible to find a prototype for virtually every kind of letter the clerks of the council were called upon to write.

When the letter had been written, a space would very often be left for the date to be filled in later on. In this state it was submitted by the principal secretary, or a clerk, to the councillors for signature. Usually a letter was signed by at least six of them, and they always signed in strict order of rank, their names being inscribed in four invariable rows. Thus the top row may sometimes contain two signatures, the second none, the third four, with two secretaries and Sir Walter Mildmay all signing at the bottom. The fact that the date was temporarily left blank suggests that usually it was not until a day or so after it had been authorized that a letter was actually ready for signature, by which time those councillors who had been at the original meeting may well have left the Court. Usually, however, there were enough of them available to subscribe sufficient names, even if some of them had not been at the original meeting, and in most cases the signatures all appear to have been added at the same time, and using the same ink. But occasionally different inks appear to have been used by different councillors, and this seems to indicate that the letter had to be carried around the Court from councillor to councillor until enough had been approached for the letter to be dispatched.[46] Sometimes it would even be necessary, owing to the complete departure of most of the councillors from the Court, for a letter to be sent after them, usually to London, in order to obtain enough signatures for a particular letter to be sent out.[47]

---

45. BM, Add. MS. 48150, Add. MS. 48018, Add. MS. 32323, Harleian MS. 4943.

46. West Sussex Record Office, letters of the Earl Winterton at Shillinglee Park, Sussex, file 2, "Instruccions given by her majestie's commaundement to Capten Turnor for certaine services to be don in the countie of Suffolke," December 27, 1587; PRO, SP.12/98, no. 31, note of council business, October 12, 1574.

47. BM, Harleian MS. 6991, f. 29, Smith to Burghley, February 19, 1573.

Once signed, the letter was folded again, in a variety of ways, but always leaving the still-clean page four facing outward, on which the addressee's name would be inscribed. The final phase of this stage of the proceedings was the application of the seal. This, unlike the Signet, which was sometimes applied *en placard* as a wafer, was always used as a sealing seal, and was applied by, or at the direction of the clerks of the council, in whose custody it normally remained. During the early part of Elizabeth's reign it was a very simple affair, in the form of a loosely knotted rope between the initials "E" and "R," and circumscribed by the maxim PULCHRUM PRO PATRIA PATI. But in 1573 this early seal gave way to the more elaborate one, whose central motif was the Tudor rose, supported by a lion and a dragon and inscribed more prosaically SIG CON PRI, which has remained essentially unchanged until the present day.[48] Very occasionally a letter, ostensibly a letter from the whole council, would go out bearing the seal of one of the councillors who signed it, or a letter bearing the council seal would be sent out signed by no more than two council members—who tended to be Leicester and Cecil—but both variants were rare.[49]

Letters, once signed and sealed, were delivered to their destinations as a rule by ordinary and extraordinary messengers of the Chamber, but they were also carried by gentlemen, by at least one man specifically designated as a courier, by pursuivants, pages, footmen, ushers, messengers of the chancery, and even by embroiderers attached to the Court, musicians of the lute and officers of the queen's "gardrobe of beddes."[50] Messengers signed for letters when they received them, frequently travelled to their destinations by post horse and then had the addressees sign for them as well. Council directions were very often then copied out verbatim and sent on further to addressees' own subordinates. This practice was followed almost always in areas under such inferior jurisdictions as that of the Councils of the North and in the Marches of Wales and within liberties like the Cinque Ports.

---

48. L. W. Labarree and R. E. Moody, "The Seal of the Privy Council," *EHR*, XLIII, April 1928, 196–197.

49. BM, Cotton MS. Titus B. ii, f. 288, Burghley and the Earls of Sussex and Leicester to Lord Norrys, February 17, 1578; Cotton MS. Titus F. iii, f. 115, the council to the Earl of Sussex, July 13, 1569; Kent Record Office, Sandwich MS. Sa ZB2/27, f. 38, the council to the mayor and corporation of Sandwich, 1573.

50. City of Chester Record Office, MS. M/L/5, no. 33, the sheriff of Chester to the council by the hand of Richard Holland, esq., December 23, 1581; PRO, E.351/541, f. 140v, Sir Thomas Heneage's account as treasurer of the Chamber, September 1572–September 1573.

The council meetings which gave rise to all this activity are the stuff of the Privy Council registers.[51] Although not all the members of the council were equally often consulted by the queen, they did all attend council meetings at one time or another. This relatively simple statement must be almost immediately qualified, for they did not all attend with anything like the same assiduity, and the "regularly held" meetings themselves did not by any means fall into an immutable schedule. Nonetheless, a careful study of the data in the Privy Council registers, comprising the dates of meetings, a note of the place where each was held, the names of those who attended and the amount of business transacted, reveals certain definite patterns. The period selected for detailed analysis extends from May 24, 1570 to June 29, 1575, during which time a total of 412 meetings took place. There are three gaps in the register during this period. Two of them are small: there are no entries for April 1572 or for August 1573. One is somewhat bigger, extending over several months, from August 1572 to January 1573 inclusive. But these lacunae are all small compared with those which precede and follow the period selected for study. There are no meetings at all recorded between 1568 and 1570 and June 1575 and 1578. This six year period is in fact the first consecutive period of years during the reign of Queen Elizabeth for which the register appears to be reasonably complete. Even so, it seems clear that all the meetings actually held were not recorded. Several months are so "thin" that only four meetings were held, if the register is to be believed, which, as we shall see in a moment, it is not on many occasions, at least in this respect. Yet there is every reason to think that it does provide a fair cross section of the meetings which *were* held—there seems little ground for supposing, for example, that the clerks failed to enter more of those meetings which took place on Mondays than of those which were held on Thursdays—and as such it yields statistics that are just as significant as they would be if one felt more certain about the registers' completeness.

First, the information relating to these 412 meetings shows us where council meetings took place. They were held, most often, wherever the queen happened to be, whether she was at one of her own palaces or staying at one of the greater or lesser houses of her subjects in the course of her progresses round the countryside. Far and away the greatest number of meetings during the period under consideration were held at Greenwich, Hampton Court and Westminster, in that order. One hundred one meetings took place at Greenwich, eighty-one at Hampton Court, and

---

51. The section which follows is based on the information relative to the meetings of the council contained in APC, VIII, 1571–1575.

sixty-seven at Westminster. There is then a sharp drop to twenty-seven held at Richmond, seventeen at Windsor and seventeen at the star chamber. When the Court was on progress, there was frequently only one meeting at each place where the queen stopped. When, however, she was staying with one of her councillors—with the Earl of Bedford at Chenies, for example, where five meetings were held in the summer of 1570, or with Burghley at Theobalds, where there were eight in 1575—she was inclined to stay longer, and more business was transacted.

When the Court was in residence at one of the suburban palaces, such as Hampton Court, Richmond, Oatlands or Greenwich, odd meetings were held at the star chamber. No meetings seem to have been held there when the queen was at Westminster. These star chamber meetings took place in term-time or very shortly after the term was over. This indicates that when the Court was in residence at Westminster, in Whitehall Palace, the council, *as* the council, met in the council chamber there, as it did at Elizabeth's other houses. When the Court was elsewhere, the palace would be shut up. Then the star chamber, certainly during term-time since the councillors would be sitting there anyway as the court of Star Chamber, would naturally become the site of council meetings that, for one reason or another, it was found necessary to hold away from the Court. The star chamber, however, was not the only possible Westminster meeting place outside the palace of Whitehall. On at least one occasion when the Court was away from Westminster the council met in exchequer chamber as an alternative to the star chamber.

Not only were the greatest number of meetings held there, but the average rate of attendance was also the highest at the same three principal residences of the queen. At Westminster it was 8.9 per meeting, at Greenwich 7.7 and at Hampton Court 7.4. These figures are exceeded or paralleled by those relating to a few extraordinary meetings (at Leicester House, the Lord Keeper's house and at Bristol when Elizabeth was on progress in 1574) where the averaged attendance reaches 9, 9, and 8.3. But these are isolated instances. The largest meetings of all, those attended by ten, eleven and sometimes even twelve councillors, took place almost without exception at Westminster, Hampton Court or Greenwich. The average attendance at Westminster, for example, between January 12, 1572 and March 31 of the same year was 10.1.

Council meetings, both large and small, were attended by some councillors considerably more often than by others. Altogether, council meetings were attended by sixteen members during the period under consideration. Sir Francis Knollys attended more often than any other single councillor, appearing at 372 meetings out of a possible 412, and Sir Ralph Sadler less frequently than anyone else.[52] He appeared only thirty-eight times in all. The other sixteen fall into two general groupings: those who attended more often than the others, and those who appeared less often. Into the first category fall Knollys, Smith, Howard of Effingham, Leicester, Cecil, Sussex, Croft, Northampton, Walsingham and Lincoln; into the latter Bedford and Warwick, Bacon, Arundel, Mildmay and Sadler, in descending order of frequency of attendance. The fact that Mr. Secretary Walsingham comes relatively low on the list is misleading. He, in fact, attended regularly from the time of his appointment to the council, and his record is marred, not by frequent absences but by a long period from December 24, 1574 to April 17, 1575 when he did not appear at all. There was indeed, almost without exception, always at least one principal secretary present at every meeting. Until he was succeeded in the office of secretary by Sir Thomas Smith in 1571, Cecil himself missed only five, and possibly not even that many.[53] During the period when there were two secretaries, they were usually both present. Their attendance record, however, is not significantly higher than that of Leicester, Sussex and Croft, who attended 329, 319 and 308 meetings respectively, as compared with Sir Thomas Smith's 356, Cecil's 324 and Walsingham's 283. It is impossible to make many hard and fast statements about the habits of attendance of those who attend most often as compared with those who appear comparatively rarely. But one tendency does show up which is worth noting. Those who appear frequently tend to appear wherever meetings were held, whether the queen was at Greenwich, Westminster or on progress, while those who appear least often tend to appear only when the Court is least peripatetic. To cite the extreme cases, the Earl of Leicester appears at *some* meetings at *all* the places at which they were held during this period. But Sir Walter Mildmay never seems to have gone on progress at

---

52. In order for us to be able to compare attendance figures meaningfully, the figures relating to those who died or ceased attending council meetings during the period under consideration and to those who were not appointed until after its beginning have been prorated on the basis of the number of meetings they actually attended and expressed as a percentage of those at which they *could* have been present.

53. At four of the meetings from which Cecil was apparently absent, the presence is recorded merely as "thapparaunces as before." But this has proved on other occasions to be an unreliable guide to the actual attendance. For example, on February 16, 1572, the entry reads "thapparaunces as before, being absent Sir Walter Mildmay and Sir Rafe Sadler," APC, VIII, 68. The only trouble here is that neither of these men had been recorded as being present on the previous occasion (APC, VIII, 63, an unspecified date in January, 1572) when the full attendance had been written out.

all, and the only meeting he attended that was not held at one of the queen's larger palaces was at Reading.

The average attendance varied from month to month, from week to week and from day to day. It reached its highest points either during or just after the end of the law terms. Averaged out over the whole period, the highest monthly attendance rate comes in February and October, the lowest in the summer months (July through September) and in December. The relevant figures for particular years confirm this overall pattern. In 1574, for example, the high points come at the same periods, except that the May peak is slightly exceeded in June, when a high average attendance of nine per meeting is reached. The council met, over the whole period, on an average of 6.6 times per month. However, the actual monthly figures which these averages conceal range from only two recorded meetings in several widely scattered months to as many as eleven, twelve and thirteen in others. At first sight there appears to be no pattern in this, and indeed, in a sense, there is none. But the figures are not without meaning all the same, for they suggest that the number of meetings held varied according to the amount of business which had built up in a given period of time. If this were so, one would expect to find that the amount of business transacted at each meeting remained fairly constant, as is in fact the case. The average number of items dealt with per meeting which lead to the writing of council letters or the drafting of a council order is 4.1. This ranges only from a high of 5.3 in July down to a low of 2.9 in January.

There is, however, a clear and definite difference between the amounts of business dealt with on different days of the week, a difference which is reflected in both the daily attendance averages, and in the number of meetings held on particular days. The council met on the average only 1.5 times a week, though, like the monthly figures, this conceals a considerable degree of variation, from one meeting per week to five, as in the week of February 11 to February 17, 1571. The day of the week on which the council met most often, and on which attendance reached its peak, was Sunday, followed, although not particularly closely, by Monday. On this first day of the week—which it clearly was, rather than a day of rest— eighty-seven meetings took place, or more than twice as many as were held on Thursdays, on which only forty-three, the least number of any day of the week, were held. On Mondays there were seventy. On Sundays the average number of councillors attending was 8.5 and on Mondays it was only down as far as 8.1. On Mondays the average number of items of business dealt with was 6.1 and on Sundays it was 4.8. The low point in each category—number of meetings, average attendance per meeting and amount of business transacted—comes towards the end of the week in each case, rising again (except in the case of the last, business transacted) on Saturday toward Sunday's peak.

All this indicates, not that some councillors worked harder than others —Sir Walter Mildmay, although he may have attended few council meetings, devoted a great deal of his time to the exchequer, of which he was the principal working officer—but that, throughout the early seventies, eight men consistently carried the burden of the council's administrative duties. The council which met from day to day consisted essentially of the treasurer of the Household (Knollys), the comptroller of the Household (Croft), the two principal secretaries, the Lord Chamberlain, the Lord Admiral, Cecil and the Earl of Leicester. The rest attended as their other duties and responsibilities permitted.

The council was a body of men working hard and regularly at the business of the state in an essentially professional manner. There are no signs of dilettantism in purpose even if there is occasional evidence of amateurism in execution. If the amount of business noted as having been got through at any particular meeting seems less than one might expect it is well to remember that all the business actually handled at any particular meeting did not give rise to the writing of a letter or the setting down of an order, the things most commonly recorded in the register. The minutes which have survived in the State Papers, few as they are, here provide an invaluable counterweight to the evidence the register seems to give. They show not only that whole meetings have escaped being recorded in the registers at all, but also that the discussion of many items resulted in purely verbal instructions being given to the secretary as to how the items should be dealt with or to whom they should be referred for further investigation. They reveal an institution which may have met more often on Mondays and Sundays than on Fridays and Thursdays, but which nevertheless met some time during every week of the year, month in and month out, year in and year out, meeting on the day before Christmas and the day after as a matter of course and, in 1571, even on the holy natal day itself.

It should not be assumed from all this that the life of a Privy Councillor was all work and no play—far from it. But these dull figures, lifeless until interpreted, do show that the work of a Privy Councillor to Queen Elizabeth was something to which he was expected to devote *some* of his time *all* of the time. There were no extended vacations. There were no shifts: three months on and three months off. The council worked continually, it worked as a whole, and on the whole it worked rather well. It retained either copies or notes of its own correspondence and kept the communications it received from others for future reference. Its most trusted employees produced minor treatises on its theory of operation and drew up guides to its practice and, overall, in its comparatively sophisticated office management and methods of government is to be found the present English administration in embryo. Modern bureaucracy was still undreamed of, but its procedures in a basic, simple form, were already in existence and it is as meaningful to assert that twentieth century departmental practices are the children of sixteenth century conciliar ways of doing things as it is to say that the cabinet of the Prime Minister is the direct descendant of the Privy Council of the sovereign. What we have been looking at in the England of the reign of Queen Elizabeth I is the genesis of those bureaucratic forms we are so universally familiar with today. The Privy Council was their parent, and they were the most significant for the future of all its various offspring.

Nobody, of course, worked for nothing. The organization of the council and its proto-bureaucratic structure did not exist in some sort of vacuum where the people involved did not need to feed, clothe and shelter themselves, let alone accumulate fortunes to leave to their posterity, and none of this machinery would have worked without financial lubrication of some sort. Somehow or other, everyone concerned received his hire, even if not always to the extent expected or wished for. The councillors themselves received no formal salary, but they continually pressed their suits, and each other's, on the queen, for grants of land or fee-producing office, which they claimed as due to them for services rendered to herself and to the state. Knollys obtained the manor of Battayle and Bluberie in 1573; James Croft pleaded his cause through his wife; and even rich Ralph Sadler insisted on his inability to go on devoting his life to public service without some further augmentation of income.[54] The noble councillors were hardly less importunate. A thorough study of the economic situations of all Elizabeth's advisers would be unlikely to show that they did not receive adequate reward. Some of them held salaried posts, of course, and these brought in fees as well. The best example of this is the principal secretary. He got £100 a year, plus a proportion of the receipts of the Signet.[55] The State Papers Domestic contain a document listing the payments made to the secretary and "every clerke" from the petty bag and the hanaper of fees which were actually due to the Signet office. As this dates from 1571, it seems likely that it was drawn up by Cecil, the retiring secretary, for the benefit of his successor.[56]

The clerks, too, drew salaries. Robert Beale, as clerk of the council,

54. Hatfield House, MS. 202, f. 107, Knollys to Burghley and Mildmay, April 27, 1573; Conyers Read, *Mr. Secretary Cecil and Queen Elizabeth* (New York, 1955), 152.

55. Higham, 352, quoting BM, Sloane MS. 1520, f. 28, *temp. Jac. I.*

56. PRO, SP.12/83, "accompte of the Signet," 1571.

drew £50 a year which, like the secretary, he received in quarterly installments on the authority of a warrant out of the chancery under the
Great Seal.[57] Beale was also paid as clerk of the Council of the North.
This function he never executed in person, employing a deputy to do it
for him. He was expected to work himself for his fee as clerk of the
council, however, and when he was too old and sick to carry out his duties
the queen, to his outspoken regret, relieved him of it.[58] He and his fellow
clerks, like the secretary, paid their assistants out of their own pockets. But
such expenses did not all have to come out of the £200 which was all
even their joint pay amounted to, for they received for each service they
performed in carrying on the council's business a further fee assessed
according to a scale of charges to which the council gave its assent on
April 4, 1575. "Upon humble peticions heretofore sunderie tymes made
unto the lords of her majestie's most honorable Previe Counsall" by the
clerks, complaining that their income was insufficient to match their expenditure, the council on this date apparently agreed to authorize the
following charges which they were to be permitted thereafter to

> take for their writinges and paines of private persons. What-
> soever person being of abilitie called before their Lordships
> for anie contempte or other notoriouse misdemeanor provid
> against him shall paie unto the clerkes for the tyme attending
> ten shillings. Whoesoever shall have any order entered in the
> counsell booke by the apointment of their Lordships, the parties
> to whose behoof it is entred shall paie for thentry thereof six
> shillings and eight pence.

For copies of entries they were to pay as much as a pound; for recording of appearances, five shillings; for recognizances and bonds and
discharge of same, six shillings and eight pence; for warrants "for en-
largementes of prisoners, being of abilitie," ten shillings; for placards for
post horses and for private letters, not related to the queen's or council
business, five shillings; and for private passports, when not on the queen's
or council business, two shillings.

> For the farther benefitt of the saide clerkes, their Lordships
> do order, as a matter which they are informed hathe ben
> acoustomed heretofore, that whoesoever hereafter shalbe

57. PRO, C.66/1090, membrane 25, Robert Beale's patent as one of the
clerks of the council.

58. BM, Lansdowne MS. 72, no. 73, f. 197, Robert Beale to Burghley,
October 16, 1572; DNB, Beale, Robert.

sworn one of her majestie's Previe Counsell shall paie for thentry of his othe by waie of rewarde to the clerkes of the counsell two pounds. And finally, to thentent nothing maie passe from their Lordships indirectlie as from the borde, but that whereof a note shalbe kepte by the said clerkes in the counsell booke, their Lordships, perceaving that diverse thinges have passed heretofore after that sorte, wherewith either the clerkes were never made acquainted, or ells onlie at soche tyme as it hathe ben broughte to them to be sealed, which they cold not well deney, have nowe, for the avoidinge of like inconveniences hereafter, ordered that from hensforth the clerke of the counsall that shall write anie letter to be signed by their Lordships, shall subscribe his name in the uttermost margent belowe, as the clerkes of the Signet doe in instrumentes to be signed by her majesti, and that they shall not seale any that be not so subscribed and entred in the counsale books accordinglie. All which orders their Lordships' pleasure is shalbe entred into the booke of her majestie's Previe Counsall, there to remaine as a perpetuall recorde of soche allowances as before expressed.[59]

The council's provincial agents, the justices of the peace and other gentry were, strictly speaking, like the councillors themselves unpaid. But if they or their servants performed a particular service on the council's behalf they were entitled, just as were the council's professional messengers and the councillors themselves, to repayment of their expenses. The Earl of Sussex, the Lord Admiral and the Earl of Warwick all got special "entertainment" allowances while serving in the north in 1569 and 1570.[60] The Admiral was allotted £6 a day for subsistence when on his embassy to France.[61] Jeffrey Hall, keeper of the jail at Sandwich received £6. 13. 4d for charges in sending up letters and prisoners to the council.[62] Nicholas Stalleng, gentleman, was awarded £65 for bringing letters from Monsieur at Bordeaux and Edward Denye, also "gent," £30 for his and his man's costs in coming from Dartmouth to Richmond

---

59. This "agreement" is to be found in BM, Add. MS. 48018, Robert Beale's precedent book of 1575, f. 670. There is no mention of it in the surviving Privy Council register, and the practice of the clerks' subscribing letters does not appear to have been followed during the period under consideration in these pages.

60. PRO, SP.12/66, no. 6, BM, Add. MS. 33593, f. 98, the queen to Sadler, January 6, 1570; f. 141, Cecil to Sadler, January 18, 1570.

61. BM, Harleian MS. 6991, f. 19, Smith to Burghley, January 7, 1573.

62. APC, VIII, 89, March 13, 1572.

"with news from the Lord Deputye of the takinge of the forte in Irelande."[63]

All in all, the council's remuneration system worked reasonably well, if not with spectacular effectiveness and thus appropriately brings us to the end of our consideration of the Elizabethan Privy Council's more positive achievements.

---

63. PRO, E.351/542/13, Sir Thomas Heneage's account as treasurer of the Chamber, including allowances "by the sayde accomptaunte . . . to diverse and sondrye . . . by vertue of the queen's majestie and her honorable counsell's severall warrants," September 1580–September 1581.

Part III
The Executive Function:
Negative Aspects

Chapter IX

INTERFERENCE
WITH THE LAW

HE council, in the light of those of its activities so far considered, was an extraordinary institution, its authority in
its own time widespread, its influence upon the future to
be enormous. But there is another side to the coin. The
council's success was a qualified one. As a governing body
it had its drawbacks, and in many ways the limits of both its imagination
and its power were soon reached. It is to a consideration of this other,
less positive side of the council's achievements, therefore, that we must
now turn in order to be able to reach a balanced judgment on its stature,
both in its own time and when viewed from the standpoint of the later
twentieth century.

To begin with, the council's connection with the law calls for further
examination. That the most trusted executives—ministers—of the Crown,
which was itself the fountain of justice in England, should act together
as umpire when the judgments of the regular royal courts came into
collision seems eminently reasonable. Their attempts to prevent the de-
meaning of ruling class dignity—so potentially subversive of social order
—by adjudicating disputes between prominent people is understandable.
Their care to provide a free tribunal for those who could afford to go
to law nowhere else is admirable. But whether quite the same adjectives
can be applied to all their other incursions into the legal sphere is another
matter.

The council was more frequently involved in the settlement of private
disputes than is explicable on the grounds already mentioned. In many
instances, only names have come down to us with little or no indication of
the nature of the quarrels the council was attempting to bring to an end,
but these are sufficient to give us an idea of the amount of time the council
devoted to this kind of thing. On April 29, 1576, of thirteen items "to
be propounded in counsell," four are concerned with private disputes, including "Southwell's complaint against Christmas [and] the matter between Mr. Chrymes and his wief."[1] It does not seem any more obviously
necessary that the council should interest itself in these particular clashes

---

1. PRO, SP.12/108, no. 11, memorandum of business for the council's consideration, the last seven notations in Walsingham's own hand, April 29, 1576.

than that it should consider the assertion of Richard Knight, already referred to in a somewhat different context, that Thomas Blagrave and son
John had stolen his corn and cattle fodder.[2] Yet it did, and it also listened
to Richard Dunse's charges against John Tanner, adjudicated the disagreements between Mr. Hawkes, Captain of Walmer Castle, and John
Isham, gentleman, and set in order the affairs of John Ashburnham, of
Ashburnham in Sussex.[3]

Now it may be that some of these disputes did involve personalities and
issues that, allowed to sputter on unchecked, could have caused an unnecessary amount of trouble and upset in the longer run. But we do know
that many of them were indeed relatively petty or, at least, not sufficiently
threatening to justify the council's giving them as much attention as it did.
There is, however, one explanation, and a contemporary one at that, which
goes at least some of the way toward clarifying things. It is Robert Beale's,
expressed in his treatise on the office of the secretary. Beale starts out by
saying that the secretary, in order "to avoide the number and trouble of
manie unnecessarie suites," should have a thorough knowledge of the
"jurisdiccions of the particular courtes of this realme," to which he was
to refer as many requests for the council's judgment as possible. Yet, he
goes on, "I would not have her majestie's councell wholie abridged of
the prerogative, for in times past they did deale in such causes, as appeareth
by the first book or register of the court of Requests and many other
presidents of great moment."[4] What this amounts to is justifying the
council's wasting its time in adjudicating private disputes or simply in
referring them to others for settlement, because it always had, because it
was traditional, and *not* because of any pressing reasons of state, efficiency
or other necessity. The pressure of precedent was simply accepted and no
serious attempt made to throw it off or change things for the better. As
we shall see, this was characteristic of much other conciliar activity as well.

The council's relationship with the justices of assize is a case in point.
The judges of the common law courts and the legal officers of the Crown

---

2. PRO, SP.12/45, p. 9, the council to the justices of assize, March 12, 1579.

3. Surrey Record Office, Loseley MS. 2013, no. 7, the council to William
More and others, June 4, 1567; PRO, SP.12/108, no. 10, the council to Sir
Thomas Scott, Thomas Wotton, William Crips, William Cromer and the mayor
of Sandwich, or any three of them provided Mr. Wotton be one, April 29, 1576;
BM, Harleian MS. 703, f. 2, Hunsdon and Walsingham to certain gentlemen
of Sussex, November 16, 1583; PRO, SP.12/97, no. 16, note of council business, June 19, 1574.

4. Robert Beale, "A Treatise of the Office of a Councellor and Principall
Secretarie to Her Majestie," printed in Conyers Read's *Mr. Secretary Walsingham
and the Policy of Queen Elizabeth* (Oxford, 1925), I, 424.

in their capacity as assize justices were the institutional descendants of the old justices in eyre. The latter, from the earliest times, had been almost as much royal administrators as magistrates. The justices of assize had retained, to some extent, this dual function and had been performing executive services for Crown and council long before it had become established practice, as it had by the 1570s, for the Lord Chancellor to harangue them in the star chamber before they left Westminster to ride their circuits. Their social and professional standing was one of great authority in the country as a whole. Their regular circulation through the shires of England were progresses accompanied by ample pomp and circumstance. Their arrival in the county towns where the assizes were to be held was both the great public spectacle of the year and the beginning of a local social season that drew the people of importance in the county into one place as nothing else was able to do. The justices, therefore, were admirably suited to act as the council's representatives in checking on how the council's local agents were in practice carrying out council orders, and in exhorting them to greater diligence in the future. Conversely, they were in as good a position to collect information as they were to pass on the council's messages.

When things came up after the justices had left London, the council would write them a letter conveying its wishes. Sergeant Jeffreys received such a communication at Dorchester in July 1572. This instructed him to inform those gentlemen whom he met in the course of his travels through the counties "of the true entencion of the statute consernynge lybertye for transportacion of grayne. And uppon conference with them to understand the plentye and prices of the same in the severall contreyes." In replying three weeks later, Jeffreys enclosed the reports which local gentlemen and justices of the peace had made to him, except for those relative to Hampshire and Wiltshire, which counties he had already left by the time he received the council's orders.[5] We can see the process in action even more clearly in the pages of a letter book kept by Bassingbourne Gaudy, who was sheriff of Norfolk in 1578. The justices of the Norfolk circuit, Sir Christopher Wray, chief justice of the court of King's Bench, and Attorney-General Gilbert Gerrard were ordered to remind the sheriffs of the counties through which *their* circuit took them, of the penalties to be levied on defaulting juries at *nisi prius*, the said levies not having shown up recently on the estreats into the exchequer to the extent expected.[6] Gaudy's letter book contains copies not only of the

---

5. PRO, SP.12/88, no. 52, Sergeant Jeffreys to the council, July 27, 1572.
6. Bodleian Library, MS. Tanner 241, f. 4, Burghley and Mildmay to Sir Christopher Wray and Mr. Gerrard, February 21, 1578.

original letter to the justices, but of their letter to him, his letter to the local justices of the peace, and of the replies of the latter. Gaudy's book is also interesting in that it shows how little official contact a local officer such as a sheriff could expect to have with the central government in the course of a particular period of time, whether through the agency of such people as the assize justices or more directly. During his tenure of office, Gaudy was directly ordered only to receive certain prisoners from the sheriff of Suffolk and sent a copy of the queen's lisence under the Great Seal to Hastings, authorizing the town to raise money throughout the realm for a new harbor, which Elizabeth "especialy comanded us by thes our letters most effectually to recomend . . . unto you."[7]

The use of judges in what really amounts to an extralegal capacity is certainly understandable and even comparatively easy to justify: there were no other officials who could do the job as well. As long as a fairly clear distinction was made, and kept, between the assize justices' independent, judicial activities, such as the delivery of the jails, and the administrative responsibilities delegated to them by the council for doing things like reminding local Shallows of the real meaning of the grain transportation statutes, a conflict of interest between their two roles was not, in theory, inevitable. But one cannot help wondering if in fact overlapping was always avoided in practice. On occasion, the council was in the habit of making its views known openly even where the operation of due process was involved. Sergeant Weston and Justice Harpur had seen fit in 1563 to report "that, whereas at our now being at Salisburye, at the assises, there was presented unto us, by ten justices of the peace . . . certayne examynacions concerning most odious and faulse slaunderous tales against the quene's majestie, the copie whereof you shall receyve here enclosed. We wish, therefore, to understande your pleasures, whether the same develishe persons shalbe openly detected, indicted, and arraigned . . . or elles otherwise by discreacion punyshed, without such open or particuler rehersall of the faulte."[8] There seems no reason to think things had changed by the seventies. It is difficult not to conclude that the council had little hesitation about interfering with the ordinary course of justice if it felt the situation warranted it.

This is not to say that the law could simply be set aside. Robert Catelyn, an earlier chief justice of the court of King's Bench, wrote Cecil in 1571

---

7. *Ibid.*, f. 4v, the council to the sheriff of Norfolk, February 23, 1579; f. 6, the Bishop of Norwich to the sheriff of Norfolk, April 1, 1579; f. 5, the council to the sheriff and justices of the peace of Norfolk, March 1, 1579.

8. BM, Harleian MS. 6990, no. 24, f. 49, Richard Weston and Richard Harpur to the council, July 10, 1563.

that he had been asked by Christopher Hatton, on behalf of the queen, to change the form of the entry of a judgment in the King's Bench in favor of the Earl of Leicester. He said he could not do it because it would mean interfering with the procedure of the court. Leicester, he pointed out, had received the judgment he would have received if all the judges of the kingdom had sat on the case. The only thing he could suggest was that he would order a further search to be made for precedents that would enable him to comply.[9]

But if the law itself was difficult to trample on and ignore, at least without the judges' cooperation, it could be sidestepped, for legal *proceedings* could be, and were, manipulated without much trouble. The council ordered, in 1573, postponement of the hearing of a suit brought by one Robert Hitchcock against Thomas Moyle and William Alcock.[10] The Earl of Bedford, with apparently complete confidence that he would be listened to, asked Burghley to see if he could not ensure that a case affecting himself, the queen and the city of Exeter should be heard the following term, in spite of Exeter's attempt to put it off again.[11] In the middle of 1569 there was a riot in Cumberland, and the council immediately made known its views to the Earl of Sussex, the current President of the Council of the North. The punishment was to fit the crime. If "the offendors shall be founde to have taken the matter in hand of malice, frowardnes, or any other evill intencion, without coullor of wrong or injustice offered unto them, then is theyr caase to be ordred and they to be punisshed with the more severitie, to the terror and example of others. But if it shall fall owt that they have byn, by inordinat and straight dealing towardes them, provoked thereunto, then is there good reason why they ought the rather to bee in sume degree the more favorablie delt withall."[12] When it had become clear that the riot was not in fact a rebellion, the council proceeded to say what should in fact be "farther doon." As many as possible were to be dealt with as felons, but none executed except where absolutely necessary to make an example. Fines were to be "meete and agreable with theyr habilities." Five months later, Cecil remarked to Ralph Sadler, in a letter addressed to him at York after the outbreak of the

---

9. PRO, SP.12/80, no. 2, Robert Catelyn, chief justice of the court of King's Bench to Burghley, July 5, 1571.

10. BM, Add. MS. 32323, f. 114v, the council to the chief justice of the court of Common Pleas, February 1, 1573.

11. BM, Lansdowne MS. 28, no. 61, the Earl of Bedford to Burghley, June 18, 1579.

12. BM, Cotton MS. Titus F. iii, f. 123, the council to the Earl of Sussex, July 11, 1569.

northern rebellion, that the policy remained the same, notwithstanding the greater danger. "Some of those rascalls . . . [should be] hanged by martiall lawe," he conceded, "but . . . the rycher . . . taken and attaynted, for otherwise it is doubtfull how the queen's majestie shall have any forfeture of ther landes and goodes, and herof I pray you thynk, and tell my Lord Lieutenant therof."[13] The law, in other words, sometimes seems to have been what the council said it was and to have been administered the way the council, sometimes even individual councillors, said it should be administered. In 1572 Leicester passed on a message from the queen to Burghley. Henry Percy was about to come up for trial and the trial he received, Elizabeth insisted, was to be a fair one. She did not mean, however, what she seems to have been saying: that Percy should be convicted only if the evidence proved him guilty. Her concern, rather, Leicester went on to explain, was that he should not be acquitted by a jury under the impression it was doing what Burghley wanted; and that she should have come right out and said so bluntly, without any beating around the bush, is testimony in itself to existence of two home truths accepted without thinking by all three.[14] They assumed that juries *could* be tampered with and took it for granted that such interference was legitimate when the interests of policy demanded it.

That the council felt no qualms whatsoever about behaving in such an essentially cavalier manner was widely known and, at least among the governing class itself, apparently accepted without question. This is made quite clear by the action of the Lord Mayor and the Recorder of London in 1571. They informed Cecil that one Thomas Bates had allegedly been asserting in public that the queen was Leicester's mistress, that the Earl of Bedford was a heretic and that the Lord Keeper, the Earl of Warwick, Cecil himself in particular and the bishops in general were men of wicked governance. The allegation that the man had resorted to such intemperate language was ample justification for a case to be brought against him. Looking at the situation from the viewpoint of the accused and supposing him innocent, we can see that resort to the law was probably the only way to clear his name. Yet the Lord Mayor and the Recorder, so they said, meant to proceed against him according to law only "if from your Lordeshipe we receave not contrarie commaundement."[15] At least

---

13. BM, Add. MS. 33593, f. 65, Cecil to Sadler, December 20, 1569.

14. Hatfield House, MS. 7, f. 556, the Earl of Leicester to Burghley, November 1, 1572, as quoted in William Murdin, *Collection of State Papers relating to Affairs in the Reign of Queen Elizabeth* (London, 1759), 228.

15. PRO, SP.12/80, no. 9, the Lord Mayor and Recorder of London to Burghley, July 26, 1571.

to a degree, whether or not resort to law could be had rested in the control of Queen Elizabeth's Privy Council. It would be untrue to suggest that it was lacking in respect for the legal institutions of the country over which, with Queen Elizabeth, it ruled. But it was nonetheless willing, indeed eager, to use them whenever possible to help it to maintain the peace of England, if not at any cost, at least at the price of regarding the law as the bastion of domestic peace and quiet rather than as the protector of the rights of the individual against the incursions of a paternalistic state.

Chapter X

FINANCIAL FAILINGS

N the matter of finance, the council's failings were of a rather different order. Although the borrowing activities carried on by Sir Thomas Gresham were famously effective and in spite of the fact that as a consequence of them Elizabeth's credit was among the best in Europe, the amounts raised in this manner were both expensive and often not sufficient to meet the Crown's short-term needs. Under such circumstances, another supposedly cheaper and certainly long established method of raising money was resorted to: cash was obtained by mean of forced loans. About the only charges the Crown incurred were those of transporting the money collected in the shires to London.[1] Such expedients had been resorted to by all the earlier Tudors and many of their predecessors. Beale's precedent book contains a letter for a "benevolence" dating from the reign of Henry VIII.[2] So, once the decision had been made to go ahead, the levying process was perfectly straightforward.

There were, however, two major things wrong with forced loans as a means of raising money. They were extremely unpopular, for one thing, not only because they were demanded at all, but because they carried no interest.[3] In consequence, the excuses put forward for not paying them were legion. Claims of being too poor to pay came by way of those appointed to collect the loan, through local notabilities presumably felt to have more influence with the council than the petitioner, and from those who felt aggrieved themselves. Sir William Sneyde, the Staffordshire collector, asked that John Bowes be excused from lending £50 because of expenses he had already incurred in the queen's service and because his corn, barns and other buildings had recently been consumed by fire.[4] Lord Delaware wrote on behalf of Dame Margery Henly, whose inability to lend he put down to the "great debtes . . . her latte husband . . . left her in," and the Earl of Huntingdon forwarded without further comment

---

1. These were met by the principal secretary, acting under the authority of a letter from the council, PRO, SP.12/74, no. 38, the council to Cecil, November 17, 1570.

2. BM, Add. MS. 48018, f. 145, "instruction for the benevolence," no date.

3. BM, Stowe MS. 150, f. 71, instructions by the council to the loan collector of Norfolk for the repayment of Privy Seal loans, February 7, 1590.

4. PRO, SP.12/71, no. 9, Sir William Sneyde to the council, June 9, 1570.

Anthony Colby's "allegacions" concerning his own incapacity to pay.[5] Mrs. Julyan Holocrest spoke up for herself, citing "my charges of howse, my sewtes in law, my costes this last voyage into the northe, my expences other wayes" as the cause of her poverty of resource.[6] But it was not only individuals who so clamorously demanded relief. Whole sections of the country claimed exemption from the obligation to contribute. Making use of the services of Sergeant Manwood, the Cinque Ports in July 1570 put forward their charter which, they stated, specifically excepted them from having to bear such impositions.[7] The entire Cornish gentry was too impoverished to contribute, so they said, and by June had, in fact, produced only £400 between them towards the 1570 loan, the fifth lowest amount of all the counties of England which had then been heard from.[8]

Some communications of this type were addressed to the principal secretary, but quite as many came directly to the council, for it was obviously widely known that the council was not completely immune to blandishment if aptly put. Mrs. Holocrest knew this, for one. "I beseche your honors," she had written, "that by your good meanes I may be discharged . . . for you have shewed this honorable favor to all other gentellwomen that have their daughters attendinge upon her highness."[9] And the council might have had to consider the complaints of many more had not the loan collectors often acted on their own initiative. As Sir Christopher Heydon and Sir William Buttes put it, "had we written so often as we wer ernestlye required, your Lordship[s] shoulde have bene troubled with tenne tymes as manie of our letters as now you are."[10]

The second thing wrong with forced loans was that the way in which they were levied was disorganized in the extreme. Royal letters bearing the Privy Seal were despatched to persons of supposedly known wealth whose names and status were recorded in the loan book kept by the principal secretary. Addressees were required to lend the queen such and such a

---

5. PRO, SP.12/73, no. 70, Lord Delaware and others to Cecil, September 26, 1570; no. 13, the Earl of Huntingdon and others to the council, August 12, 1570.

6. PRO, SP.12/71, no. 73, Mrs. Julyan Holocrest to the council, July 1570.

7. Ibid., no. 49, Sergeant Manwood to [the council], July 15, [1570].

8. PRO, SP.12/67, nos. 62 and 63, Mr. Edgecumbe to the council, April 17, 1570; SP.12/71, no. 29, "a note of such sommes of money as hath ben paid of the lone" to the treasurer of the Chamber, June 29, 1570.

9. Ibid., no. 73, Mrs. Julyan Holocrest to the council, July 1570.

10. PRO, SP.12/68, no. 16, Sir Christopher Heydon and Sir William Buttes to the council, May 10, 1570.

sum of money, usually £50 or £100 which, it was promised, would be repaid at the receipt of the exchequer in six months time.[11] Local collectors and a receiver-general—in 1570 Sir Thomas Heneage, not yet a Privy Councillor, but already treasurer of the Chamber—were appointed.[12] The former were told to report their proceedings to the council and the latter instructed by the queen that he was not to pay out any of the money brought to him except "by warraunte signed with our hande and with our Signet or els by the warraunte of sixe of our Privie Councell, whereof our secretarie . . . be one, so as the saide warraunte from our councill excede not at anie one tyme the somme of foure hundred poundes."[13] There would appear to be little for the council to do but authorize the spending of the money once it had been raised. But the very opposite was in fact the case, for the decision to raise a compulsory loan, as de Spes reported to Philip II in April 1570, caused such "excitement and annoyance" amongst the gentry that once the Privy Seals had actually been received, the council was bombarded, as we have seen, with a barrage of special pleading from both collectors and individuals alike.[14]

The major trouble was that much of the information "owte of the lone boke" was both out of date and ill considered in the first place.[15] In consequence, Privy Seals were sent to the deceased and the departed, as well as to those still living in the collectors' counties who were either unable or unwilling (it was hard to draw the line between them) to pay what was demanded of them. Sir Thomas Stanhope reported from Nottinghamshire that only one man could pay the £100 asked of him, and that many of the others "be ded long sens."[16] Not only was money demanded of the defunct, often enough it was *not* asked for from those who were in the best position, at least financially speaking, to contribute. Mr. Edgecumbe—he who had reported the impoverishment of the gentlemen of Cornwall—went on to add that "ther are diverse of meaner callinge who have greate welthe and maie spare verie well by reason of their greate usurie [as well as] diverse Papistes of greate welthe whose moneyes will

---

11. BM, Harleian MS. 4943, ff. 148v and 149v, a Privy Seal letter for a loan and instructions for the collection of such a loan, no dates.

12. PRO, A.O.1/1535, the queen to Thomas Heneage, April 21, 1570.

13. *Ibid.*

14. CSP Spanish, II, no. 186, p. 242, de Spes to the King of Spain, April 19, 1570.

15. PRO, SP.12/78, no. 53, lists of gentlemen living in Derbyshire, Staffordshire, Leicestershire and Nottinghamshire, June 1571.

16. PRO, SP.12/67, no. 46, Thomas Stanhope to Cecil, April 8, 1570.

better serve the quene's majestie then theire hollowe hartes."[17] The result of all these circumstances was that Privy Seals never brought in as much as had been anticipated.

Not only did forced loans fail to deliver the required sums; once in, the money that had been forthcoming disappeared with frightening rapidity. In September 1570 Sir Thomas Heneage reported to the council that he had received £31,233, of which only £4,244 remained in his hands.[18] Elizabeth and the council were evidently appalled at the speed at which so much had dwindled to so little. When Heneage, on being asked for more money, replied that he had almost none, "her majesty was not well pleased." She was, indeed, sufficiently upset to order Cecil to write directly to the loan collectors to check whether Heneage had actually accounted for all he had received from them. It appears he had.[19] It is therefore not surprising, the money all gone, and parliament not having met and voted supply until April, that on May 15, 1571 the queen was writing Signet letters to these same collectors to instruct them to persuade lenders to forbear demanding the promised repayment until the end of the coming Michaelmas term.[20]

In November, however, the process of reimbursement was set in motion. The queen addressed a warrant under the Privy Seal to the treasurer and chamberlains of the exchequer to pay, out of the subsidy money, "such persons as our said four counsellers or three of them shall by their writing name unto you."[21] The four councillors—the Lord Keeper, the Earl of Leicester, Sir William Cecil and Sir Walter Mildmay—were named in a further warrant addressed to them and dated the same day, ordering them to instruct the treasurer and chamberlains regarding the actual repayment procedure to be followed.[22] A "booke of the confessions of such as

---

17. *Ibid.*, no. 63, P. Edgecumbe to the council, April 17, 1570.

18. PRO, SP.12/73, no. 54, Thomas Heneage to the council, September 5, 1570.

19. Hatfield House, MS. 157, f. 61, Thomas Heneage to Cecil, September 4, 1570.

20. William Murdin, *Collection of State Papers relating to Affairs in the Reign of Queen Elizabeth* (London, 1759), the queen to the collectors of the loan, May 18, 1571; Northamptonshire Record Office, W: B2, P XII, no. 1/D5, the queen to Mildmay, May 17, 1571; Hatfield House, MS. 6, f. 6, the queen to [the loan collectors], no date.

21. PRO, SP.12/83, no. 17, the queen to the treasurer and chamberlains of the exchequer, November 23, 1571.

22. Hatfield House, MS. 158, f. 135, the queen to Bacon, the Earl of Leicester, Burghley and Mildmay, November 23, 1571.

receyve money . . . uppon repayment" was kept in the exchequer, signed by the receiving individuals, who testified there that they had received the full amount due to them "without anything paying to any personne for the same."[23] The council's dubious work on the loan was done.

The long-term financial problems of the Crown were handled little more imaginatively than the short term. Parliamentary subsidies sufficed during the seventies mainly because neither asking for them nor the process of collecting them caused great difficulty, owing to the fortuitous circumstance that the country was still at peace.

The very lack of evidence in the debates in parliament of any great attention to taxation is, in this regard, extremely significant. Parliament, notwithstanding all Elizabeth's frustration with it on occasion, was *too* cooperative with the Crown, and this attitude, agreeable in the short term, surely sprang, at least in part, from the fact that subsidies were a thoroughly inefficient means of raising money, since they actually brought in much less than, on paper, they were supposed to. It was routine for the queen's commission naming collectors to be sent down to the counties accompanied by a written admonition from the whole council urging those appointed to use diligence in carrying out their assignment. "You shall take speciall care, and use your uttermost indevors that the taxacion of the person chargeable maie be made indifferentlie . . . . The good example of the just taxacion of your selfes sha[l] be doubtles the best meanes to induce others to be rated in such reasonable sorte as is convenient."[24] In other letters it was felt necessary to adjure "that men may not be soe lowe taxed as before they had byn."[25] But the problem was an intransigent one, exacerbated by the frustrating, but understandable circumstance that those "so lowe taxed" were not themselves complaining very loudly about the situation, either in parliament or outside. No one, indeed, among those who paid the subsidy, wanted to do much talking about it and thereby risk the possibility of something more effective, from the government's point of view, being invented to take its place. As things turned out, nothing was; instead, in order to ensure that the collections at least brought in as much as possible, councillors simply permitted their names to be included in subsidy commissions and themselves took part in

---

23. PRO, E.404, no. 519, "a booke of the confessions of such as receyve money owt of the receipts of teschequire uppon the repayment of the lone money borowed by Privay Seales," no date.

24. PRO, SP.12/107, no. 97, the council to the subsidy commissioners, March 31, 1576.

25. BM, Add. MS. 32323, f. 146, the council to the subsidy commissioners, no date.

the implementation procedure, which could be held up without their presence. Sir Ralph Sadler, in September 1571, requested that he be relieved from interrogating the Duke of Norfolk "to attend the execucion of the commision for the subsidie in my countrey, which will stay in my division till my retorn."[26] Here one comes face to face with conscientiousness unallied with creativity, and the consequence of following that line of least resistance was that when the coming of open war with Spain increased the royal expenditure inordinately, no more efficient source of extra income than the subsidy had been evolved to meet what turned out to be a prolonged emergency.

---

26. Hatfield House, MS. 158, f. 6, Sadler to Burghley, September 4, 1571. Elizabeth herself, however, both on this occasion as on others, did not automatically put money and its collection first on her list of priorities. She refused Sadler's request on the grounds that "she had rather lese hir subsydy in Hertfordshyre tha[n] not to have by your presence and wisdom that from my lord of Norfolk that wer mete to understand truthe," BM, Cotton MS. Caligula C. iii, f. 254, Burghley to Smith, September 9, 1571.

Chapter XI

PLAYING WITH
PIRACY

s far as the affairs of the maritime world were concerned, in spite of its overall success in maintaining and managing the navy—a feat advertised to the world in 1588 by the fending-off of the Armada—there the council failed in some ways as notably as it did in finance. The English Channel was unsafe. Both some of the uses to which the navy was put in peacetime and much of the activity of English diplomats sent to lie abroad for their country positively publicizes the fact. The Lord Admiral, to cite a single example, was ordered to send a ship (the *Bonaventure*, the *Philip and Mary* or the *Lion*) to escort the Merchant Adventurers' fleet to Hamburg in 1570. In any given period, many of the representations made by official English spokesmen in foreign countries and by alien ambassadors at the Court of Elizabeth were concerned with the failure of someone or other to escape the hazards of voyaging, which the navy was supposed to be a protection against, but on the whole was not.[1] Altogether, one of the most persistent problems governments were faced with in the sixteenth century was that of deciding how to deal with piracy on the high seas.

Piracy in all its aspects, like jurisdiction in private suits, took up a good deal more of the English council's time than should, on the face of it, have been necessary. Stringent laws were on the statute books, and there was no shortage of courts in which those who infringed them could be brought to trial and decrees obtained ordering redress to be made to those who had suffered loss. Criminal actions involving piracy had always been heard by common law. Civil suits, prior to the middle of the fourteenth century, had fallen within the jurisdiction of the Lord Chancellor. Then, between 1340 and 1357, the Admiralty court had been instituted both to deal with the difficulties hitherto experienced in handling piracy claims made against Englishmen by foreigners, often with support of their sovereigns, and for the purpose of seeing the king's peace kept on the sea as it was on land.[2]

---

1. PRO, SP.12/67, no. 32, the queen to Clinton, March 23, 1570; SP.12/66, no. 23, the queen to the officers of the navy "for setting furth" an English vessel to protect an Aragonian ship at Venetian expense, January 24, 1570.

2. Reginald G. Marsden, *Select Pleas in the Court of Admiralty* (London, 1894 and 1897), I, xvi and xiv.

By the middle of the sixteenth century, however, the Admiralty court was proving markedly unsuccessful in carrying out either of these tasks—so unsuccessful that in 1582 the queen went so far as to suspend its jurisdiction in all towns for the space of the ensuing three years.[3] The failure of the Admiralty court threw the problem squarely on the shoulders of the council, and the Marquess of Winchester put the matter in a nutshell in 1563, insisting that the council should consider taking steps to prevent English ships from committing acts of piracy on the queen's own subjects and on friendly shipping generally, "seing the narrowe seas be wholie in hir grace's government."[4] The council tried hard to prevent lawlessness at sea in a great variety of ways, choosing two general methods of approach: first, enforcing the laws against piracy; second, attempting to see that they were not broken in the first place.

On the council's advice, the queen issued proclamations calling on her subjects to observe the statutes: five having some relation to piracy were issued between 1568 and 1582. The first, in April 1569, attempted to isolate the culprits by forbidding anyone to receive, aid or deal with them, and by making port officers who permitted pirates to go to sea equally responsible for whatever spoils they should thereafter perpetrate.[5] To try to discourage port officers from acting in collusion with pirates was a favorite line of approach to the problem, and the council tried it again in 1579, when it issued orders for avoiding the committing of depredations by such as go to sea for the discovery of new trades. This general order stipulated that particular letters were to be directed from the lords of the council to vice-admirals and commissioners for matters of piracy at the various ports, instructing them "to take annual bonds of £500 from principal port officers to observe [the law]." Customs officers were to be similarly bound, and in places where there were no officers at all "honest, discreet, and trusty persons" in the locality and "the lord or lordes of the soyle where . . . creekes are" were to be held responsible in like manner. No one, it was reiterated, other than recognized merchants and fishermen, was to go to sea without specific warrant from the queen, "or from the lords of the councell, or from six of them at the least," and these warrants were to be granted only on the condition of bonds being placed with the Admiralty court for good behavior. Proof of the existence of such bond

3. *Ibid.*, II, xvii and xvi.

4. BM, Harleian MS. 6990, no. 10, f. 21, the Marquess of Winchester to Cecil, August 31, 1563; no. 11, f. 23, the Marquess of Winchester to the queen, September 3, 1563.

5. Robert Steele, *A Bibliography of Royal Proclamations of the Tudor and Stuart Sovereigns* (Oxford, 1910), no. 638, April 27, 1569.

was to be shown to port officers "under the great seall of the highe court of the Admiraltie uppon warrant given to the purpose to the Lord Admiral . . . from her majestie or the counsell subscribed with eight of their handes, which bondes yt is thought meet shoold be certefyed every quarter into the eschequier."[6] The exchequer had been previously enlisted in the struggle in 1576, when the Lord Treasurer had been instructed by eight of his colleagues on the council to "forthwithe give order throughout your office to make staie of all shippes, barkes and other vessels belonging to any of them of the towne of Flusshing" who had then recently been involved in numerous piracies upon English subjects.[7]

The proclamation of August 3, 1569 forbade the purchase of imported goods which had not passed the customs, on pain of prosecution for piracy, and informers on conniving officials were to have their places.[8] In June the following year such officials were further threatened with imprisonment and guilty corporations with loss of their charters.[9] But the August proclamation reluctantly admitted that these approaches to the problem had not been "entirely" successful—though they were matched by energetic efforts by the council to cure what it seemed unable to prevent.

Its main curative policy was to support the judge of Admiralty. Thus in 1571 the council wrote to all mayors and other local officers to assist the bearer of its letter to obtain delivery of certain goods belonging to the Merchants of the Steelyard which had been taken from a ship called the *Salvator* and brought into Portsmouth. The Admiralty court had already issued its own process, which, it turned out, could "in no wise . . . be accomplished."[10] Similarly, after he had obtained "good proofe out of her majestie's highe courte of Admyraltie," one Julian Maignare was issued with a letter of assistance signed by seven members of the council and addressed to vice-admirals, mayors, sheriffs, justices of the peace, bailiffs, constables, controllers, searchers, headboroughs, and other of Queen Elizabeth's officers, instructing them to assist him in recovering his ship, the *Golden Falcon* of Flushing, taken by English pirates into English ports.[11] When even such assistance proved ineffectual, the council was

6. PRO, SP. 12/131, no. 45, orders for avoiding depredations at sea by such as go to sea under pretence to discover new trades, July 26, 1579.

7. Hatfield House, MS. 160, f. 34, the council to Burghley, March 5, 1576.

8. Steele, no. 640, "a proclamation agaynst the maintenaunce of pirates," August 3, 1569.

9. *Ibid.*, no. 653, "a proclamation to proclaym and put in execution a proclamacion made the last year against pyrates," June 6, 1570.

10. APC, VIII, 27; BM, Add. MS. 32323, f. 125 and Harleian MS. 4943, f. 125, the council to the queen's officers, May 12, 1571.

11. City of Chester Record Office, MS. M/L/5, no. 52, the council to the queen's officers, March 16, 1586.

still acting on the recommendation of the Admiralty judge when it awarded letters of marque (which authorized the wronged person to go out and seek his own redress by force) as "the onlie remedie, althoughe it be extreme and rare, provided in law in cases where justice is either denied or overmuche delayed."[12]

Either at the instigation of private persons who petitioned it or on its own initiative, the council tried a number of less drastic methods of keeping the scourge of piracy at least within bounds.[13] It commissioned local notables to seek out pirates in general and present them for trial, and it instructed individuals, ranging from the Lord Admiral himself down to minor local gentlemen, to apprehend particular suspects. Certain gentlemen in Devon were so commissioned in 1570, and a Mr. Borking told to use "either . . . pollicie or . . . force" in catching one especially wanted man.[14] The State Papers Domestic for 1578 are full of reports to the council from piracy commissioners in virtually all the maritime counties, the council having instructed them to certify the value of the lands and goods of offenders.[15] In 1589 the council appointed commissioners to examine complaints about piracy committed on English subjects by the Danes.[16] Individuals were commissioned to go to sea and catch pirates, and local officials, notwithstanding previous orders to the contrary, specifically instructed to let these amateur coast guards pass.[17] Corporations were ordered to arrest the owners of vessels which were suspected of having committed acts of piracy.[18] And commissions, instructions and orders were

12. PRO, SP.12/49, no. 26, Dr. Lewes to Cecil, January 16, 1569.

13. PRO, SP.12/97, no. 25, petition of John Langrake to the council, after June 1574; SP.12/47, no. 92, memorandum of public business by Cecil, September 1568; SP.12/131, no. 5, petition of William Knight and Peter Hall to the council, May 10, 1579.

14. BM, Harleian MS. 4943, f. 219v, commission to certain gentlemen of Devon, July 18, 1571; f. 57v, the council to Lord Chandos and others, January 12, 1573, f. 57, the council to Mr. Borking, June 23, 1572; PRO, SP.12/134, no. 397, the council to William Holstock, August 6, 1576; SP.12/107, no. 52, the council to the Earl of Lincoln, March 5, 1576.

15. PRO, SP.12/122, 127 and 129 contain numerous letters of the council to piracy commissioners in the various counties of England and Wales, together with their replies, during 1578 and the early part of 1579.

16. BM, Cotton MS. Nero B. iii, f. 374, the council to the English commissioners appointed to examine complaints about piracy committed by English subjects on the Danes, August 20, 1589.

17. PRO, SP.12/85, no. 57, the queen to her officers, February 29, 1572; SP.12/109, no. 3, the council to the captain of the Isle of Wight, September 6, 1576; BM, Lansdowne MS. 16, f. 5, the council to the queen's officers, February 25, 1572.

18. Kent Record Office, Sandwich MS. ZBZ/27, the council to the mayor and corporation of Sandwich, 1573.

all often followed by directions for their "better and more spydye execution."[19] Cases brought to the attention of the council which had occurred in the north or in Ireland, or in which residents of those areas were involved, were referred to the Lord President of the Council of the North and the Lord Deputy respectively.[20] Yet when the Council in the Marches of Wales had had the temerity to deal with a case which did not belong to it, the Privy Council had no hesitation in ordering its transference to the proper place for it: the court of Admiralty.[21]

At least two books were kept in the council office, containing information likely to be useful to the council in dealing with these piratical matters. In them were listed all the ports, creeks and landing places in England and Wales, and the names of those who had been aiders and abettors of pirates, as well as of the commissioners appointed to seek out such people and to take bonds for their future good behavior. All these commissions, letters, and instructions did result in the capture of some pirates and the relief of some owners of stolen property. But the very fact that they form a never-ending series parading through the folios of the State Papers, the Privy Council registers and nearly all the other large manuscript collections indicates the magnitude of the problem. It was simply never solved and piracy continued to flourish virtually unchecked throughout the reign.

It is fairly easy to see why. For one thing, piracy was closely associated with foreign relations. Sometimes it was politic to put down a particular pirate, at others not. In 1576 Henry Palmer was sent to sea to arrest as many of these maritime thieves as possible, both English and foreign; but he was also quite explicitly informed that "yt is not meant that you deale with any of those that shall appeare unto you to apperteyne unto the Prince of Orange."[22] Similar political considerations moved Francis Walsingham to an exactly opposite course of action in regard to relations with Scotland. It would, he thought, be a good idea to put down a particular pirate the Scots had been complaining about. It would only cost a couple of hundred pounds, and it would be money well spent, since, as he put it to Lord Burghley, it would not be a very good idea to alienate Scot-

---

19. PRO, SP.12/114, no. 68, "a dyrectorye for the better and more spydye execution of the commission for the ponyshment of thayders of pyrates," July 1577.

20. APC, VIII, 275, July 25, 1574.

21. PRO, SP12/111, no. 7, the council to the Vice-President and Council in the Marches of Wales, January 21, 1577.

22. PRO, SP.12/108, no. 23, the council's instructions to Henry Palmer, esquire, May 19, 1576.

land just at the time when England's enemies were increasing and her friends standing at the brink of destruction.[23]

Now and again the council's shortsightedness in dealing with the business of buccaneering even took on a slightly humorous air, although this was probably unintentional. The notoriously lawless Sir John Perrot (that perennial problem child who may or may not have been Queen Elizabeth's half-brother, the son of her father Henry VIII, whom he so markedly resembled) was ordered to "chase and capture any pirates, of whatever nationality"; any pirates at all—with certain exceptions, that is. For the council's letter went on to say "in case you shall happen to meet ... Mr. Courtney, who is said heretofore to have committed some disorder uppon the seas, you maie assure him uppon our honors, that her majestie, being advertised of his bolde enterprise attempted uppon the rebells' shippes, is well pleased and contented to bestow her gratious pardon upon him, in hope that he will behave himself more dutifullie heerafter, and therfore youe maie use his service in this exploit as you shall see cause."[24] Setting a pirate to catch a pirate sounds like a fine theatrical idea and has a sharply Shavian ring to it, but that the council should actually find it a useful tactic in its war on depredation at sea can only be regarded in the final analysis as sad and even more depressing than its other methods of dealing with piracy.

The council too often condoned private vengeance. International law was rudimentary and doing so may, in consequence, have been difficult to avoid. But such tolerance certainly tended to create the kind of atmosphere in which lawlessness was most at home. In 1568 the council was informed that the Danes had suddenly, without warning and for no very obvious reason, arrested every English ship they could lay their hands on. For an explanation of this unexpected development, the council turned to Dr. Lewes, the judge of the Admiralty court. Dr. Lewes, after making due enquiries, discovered that the Danish action was a reprisal for the arrest made in England of some Danish ships. This arrest, in its turn, had been made by one William Martyn under the authorization of a perfectly legal commission permitting him to seize Danish goods in order to recoup himself for losses he had received earlier at Danish hands. Lewes's suggested way out of the labyrinth into which Anglo-Danish relations had wandered as a result of this one small, and originally private, incident,

---

23. BM, Cotton MS. Caligula C. iii, f. 486, Walsingham to [Burghley], July 24, 1577.
24. PRO, SP.12/131, no. 74, the council to Sir John Perrot, August 19, 1577.

sums up the council's perpetual dilemma in dealing with piracy. He recommended that the council should deal directly with Martyn, so that "sum way may be devised by bothe the princes to understand his matter rightlye."[25] There *was* no other way of dealing with such individual incidents without a radically revised, and expensive, approach to the whole broad problem.

Even such policy as it had, the council was often halfhearted and partial in carrying out. In 1577 the Lord Keeper, the Lord Treasurer, the Lord Admiral, the Lord Chamberlain, the Earl of Leicester, Sir Francis Walsingham, the attorney-general, Dr. Dale and Dr. Lewes, "having taken uppon them the execucion of the commission for the punishment of the aiders of pirattes, called before them Sir Richard Rogers"—only to decide to move the queen to pardon him—on payment of a £100 fine and his entering into bonds to satisfy the parties aggrieved.[26] A few days later, the same commission treated six other gentlemen in much the same way.[27] And on November 16 they had before them Francis Rogers, charged with receiving John Calles (whom the council pursued intermittently for years) and with supplying the same people with the victuals which enabled them to stay at sea. Rogers was not exactly severely punished. He was actually freed from the Marshalsea prison and dismissed from the presence of the commissioners, simply on bail for his good behavior for one year, "in consideration of his povertie, and lack of habilitie."[28]

Lastly, but most important of all, the council failed to deal with piracy effectively because it failed to attack it at its roots. This would have entailed making it too dangerous a pastime to indulge in with comfort and too uncertain a trade to attract personal involvement of any kind at any level. The Earl of Sussex's brother, Sir Henry Radcliff, in a letter to the council in 1581 about the problems arising out of the presence in local waters of the Prince of Orange's "flie botes"—so called because they made a habit of preying especially on certain islands off the coast of Flanders "called the flie and the tassell"—clearly explained the situation.[29] Piracy was relatively safe and extraordinarily profitable, not only to the owners and captains of the vessels which engaged in it, but to the ordinary seamen who manned them as well. Why should a man slave at a job on

---

25. PRO, SP.12/47, no. 81, Dr. Lewes to the council, September 25, 1568.

26. PRO, SP.12/118, no. 26, proceedings of the piracy commissioners, October 29, 1577.

27. *Ibid.*, November 3, 1577.

28. *Ibid.*, November 16, 1577.

29. PRO, SP.12/78, no. 15, Sir Henry Radcliff to the council, May 21, 1571.

land that paid him only forty shillings for a whole year's labor, when a voyage on a pirate ship might well bring him four or five pounds in a single week? Sir Henry had already found that such inducements were upsetting to the labor market in his locality and now discovered for certain, in the rounding up of idle persons on the council's orders, that many such had in fact been living for long periods on the profits of such tantalizingly rewarding ventures. The only real remedies were restraint from indulgence in international irresponsibility of the type to be so famously demonstrated by the queen's favorable and widely known reaction to Drake's unquestionably piratical activities during his voyage of circumnavigation, the creation of an efficient, professional, constantly-operating maritime police force—a full-time navy—and either the institution of social programs or the encouragement of economic advance, or both, aimed at reducing the greedy unconcern for anyone but themselves and theirs of the well-to-do and raising the standard of living of the lower orders. The council did not seriously attempt any of these things—the first two of which *were* forthcoming in the following century—and all in all, therefore, its policies toward piracy have to be put down as total failures.

Chapter XII

THE MUSTER MESS

 N exercising its authority over the national musters, the council permitted itself to experience some of the same difficulties that plagued it in financial matters. It found that although it was easy enough to issue orders, it was too much to hope that they would thereupon be put into effect without further ado. Qualifications were made and exceptional circumstances pleaded, all of which came before the council for further action. A hundred men were available in the Isle of Wight; however, Sir Henry Radcliff, a maverick among the commissioners, who as a group reported their roundup without explanatory comment, felt obliged to make it clear in a personal letter that "they wer the barest and meanest servisable that I have seene."[1] Boroughs refused to be mustered with the county, insisting on their charter rights to do the job themselves. The Surrey commissioners questioned whether they were to muster servants from the queen's, Privy Councillors' and noble households. Complaints of being overburdened were routine, and rose to a crescendo when extraordinary demands were made: the muster commissioners in Kent, for example, quite understood that royal office holders and "everie ecclesiasticall person" should be charged with the maintenance of arquebusiers, but echoed most of their fellows in other counties in being deeply shocked at the idea that they themselves should be so put upon.[2] Requests to postpone muster day were frequent. The commission and the council's letters, it was alleged, were late in arriving in Sussex. It was harvest time in Oxfordshire. The clerk of the peace was absent in Middlesex. There was plague in Norfolk.[3] The Dorset commissioners asked to be excused from being called on to assist the neighboring county, Devon, if Devon should be attacked: the very opposite obligation was the correct one, so they claimed—not only Devon, but also Somerset and Wiltshire should, if necessary, be prepared

---

1. PRO, SP.12/78, no. 15, Sir Henry Radcliff to the council, May 21, 1571.

2. PRO, SP. 12/59, no. 1, the muster commissioners of Kent to the council, October 1, 1569.

3. PRO, SP.12/147, no. 13, Lord Cobham to the council, January 17, 1581; SP.12/137, no. 8, Lord Wentworth to the council, April 3, 1580; SP.12/58, no. 5, Oxford muster commissioners to Knollys, August 5, 1569; SP.12/137, no. 41, Norfolk justices of the peace and muster commissioners to the council, April 21, 1580.

to come to Dorset's rescue.[4] And the Lord Keeper had to be told to make up the gaps in the Hereford commission; otherwise the council's orders could not be carried out for lack of men to do it.[5]

Not all, but many of these complaints were listened to with sympathy and the council's original instructions modified in the light of them. Many of the entries in the Privy Council registers that have to do with musters are of letters specifically recognizing borough privileges: Norwich, Lynn and Yarmouth prepared their own returns after their rights had been conceded in 1580.[6] The Surrey commissioners were told to go ahead and muster royal, councillors' and noble servants in 1569, although for that occasion only.[7] And, another time, the commissioners of Norfolk and Suffolk were informed, after an initial rebuke had been administered to them, that the queen had "graciously" reduced her demands from four thousand to two thousand men.[8] The only people who really got into trouble were those who simply did nothing and did not even offer an excuse. In 1584 the commissioners for Leicester made this mistake, which prompted the earl their Lord Lieutenant to threaten that unless their certificates were received "presentlie . . . your defaults herein must be known to her majestie whom how it will please to like thereof . . . I leave to your own considerations."[9]

Such adjustments were not only concessions to reality, made in the name of greater military effectiveness and the hope of improving quality by reducing, where necessary, the originally asked for quantity—better 2000 troops than a 4000-man rabble—they sometimes also seem to have constituted a practical, if crafty, way by which the council could achieve unpopular ends without actually seeming to. Following this line of reasoning, Lindsay Boynton suggests that it was a positive advantage to recognize municipal pretensions. Although in theory two plus two always equals four, in practice the total arrived at often depends on who does the

---

4. *Ibid.*, no. 3, Dorset muster commissioners to the council, April 1, 1580.

5. *Ibid.*, no. 32, the sheriff and justices of the peace of Herefordshire to the council, April 16, 1580.

6. *Ibid.*, no. 58, Norfolk muster commissioners to the council, April, 1580.

7. Surrey Record Office, Loseley MS. XII, no. 33, the council to Howard of Effingham and other Surrey muster commissioners, May 1, 1569.

8. BM, Harleian MS. 703, ff. 14 and 15, the council to the sheriff and commissioners for musters of Sussex, May 21, 1584; Bodleian Library, MS. Tanner 241, f. 21, the council to the sheriff and muster commissioners of Norfolk, May 21, 1584.

9. Huntington Library, Hastings MS. 2378, the Earl of Leicester to the muster commissioners of Leicestershire, March 29, 1584.

adding, and the council may well have got more men from boroughs and counties mustering separately than it would have if towns' military obligations had been merged with those of their surrounding shires.[10] Such open-minded, pragmatic attitudes are quite respectable in one sense. They show us a ruling group sufficiently secure and confident of its position to be capable of making allowances (graciously, like the queen) when such understanding was required, of withdrawing unruffled from untenable positions and of turning potentially awkward situations to advantage. But it also reveals a degree of conciliar inefficiency, "woolly thinking" and reluctance to tackle problems at their sources that may be explicable, but is hardly admirable.[11]

It was little less than insulting that the Isle of Wight's contingent should have been so sorry a crew. The council could, and therefore should, have known which boroughs were exempt from parading their soldiers with the county's. It would have made much more sense to have had a definite and permanent policy on the military service owed by such special segments of the population as royal employees. And the council could have found out ahead of time as easily—and less humiliatingly—than it did *after* the musters had been held that East Anglia could only produce half as many militiamen as expected. It should, too, have been capable of working out a better system of estimating individuals' obligations to contribute to the national defense. A man's rating was based on his wealth as recorded in the subsidy book and this, as we have already suggested, often enough had little to do with his actual degree of prosperity. Frequently, too, many people of substance were omitted altogether.[12]

The list of the council's military failures makes particularly dismal reading because many of them could have been easily prevented. The florid language of some of its orders, which apparently sometimes made implementation difficult, was not, after all, characteristic of all its letters. The "scant notice" too often complained of was obviously not always avoidable —frights such as that arising out of the St. Bartholomew's Day massacre in France could scarcely be anticipated—but no more was it usually necessary. Surely important correspondence did not *have* to get lost, as it did occasionally. The printed forms that greatly facilitated the mustering process, when used, could have been sent out regularly, rather than simply now and then. The optimism the council exhibited with regard to captains

10. Lindsay Boynton, *The Elizabethan Militia 1558–1638* (London, 1967), 40.

11. *Ibid.*, 92.

12. *Ibid.*, 71–72.

of companies verges on the absurd: it expected them to contribute to the maintenance of the troops under their command, which hit their pocket-books; and it tried to reduce the size of their contingents, which touched their pride, to such an extent was status still associated with the number of one's subordinates. To appoint as a deputy commissioner for the enforce-ment of the horse statutes the same man who had repeatedly and success-fully objected to his own rating in the past was asking for trouble. And in 1588 the bows sent to Tilbury at the council's command were thrown aside as useless, which might have been expected, since the queen's advisers had previously been just as much in the habit of disdaining as of com-mending the practice of archery.[13]

In military matters in general, as in financial, things were still being done, in other words, in much the same old, too often unthinking and ineffective ways. Take the case of armor. The queen sold it, although her loving subjects did not always appreciate its cost or quality. In April 1570 during the careful period which followed the northern crisis, the council seems to have written a letter (the register is missing for these particular months) to the justices of the peace throughout the realm, asking for contributions to be collected to make possible the replenishment of local stocks, which the rebellion had revealed to be somewhat less than ade-quate.[14] A follow-up letter went out on July 10 with instructions that such money as had been collected be sent up to the council which would then buy both armor and shot on behalf of its local agents "owte of the queene's majestie's store."[15]

Sir Henry Wallop and Sir William Kingsmill, two of the recipients of this letter in Hampshire, did not object to the procedure—although they admitted to having difficulty in obtaining many voluntary contributions—but they did have serious reservations about the goods the queen was likely to supply. They had bought from her before, with unsatisfactory results, and now therefore asked permission to purchase a better and cheaper arti-cle from a Hamburg merchant who, they had heard, was currently in London with a far superior German product. The council's reply to this hardheaded proposal has not survived. It might not have been flatly negative, since purchases from private suppliers were by no means un-known. They were not encouraged, however, and the whole proceeding

---

13. *Ibid.*, 42, 43, 44, 102, 84 and 63.
14. PRO, SP.12/68, no. 25, the justices of the peace of Worcestershire to the council, May 12; no. 27, Lord Chandos to the council, May 13, 1570.
15. PRO, SP.12/71, no. 53, Sir Henry Wallop and Sir William Kingsmill to Cecil, July 21, 1570.

was typical of the improvised nature of the council's approach to such problems, its patent aim being to kill as many birds as possible with a single stone. In this case it would not only increase provincial supplies of armor by strictly legal means, but make a profit for the Crown at the same time. In 1588 it was to take a similar attitude towards the disarming of recusants. Their weapons were to be sequestered and sold and the money paid to the original owners. In this way potential dissidents would be rendered relatively harmless with a minimum of resentment caused among them, and at the same time many presumably loyal subjects would be armed.[16] That the military hardware thus acquired or redistributed might very likely be of neither good quality nor modern design was evidently not important.

As Boynton repeatedly points out, for most of its setbacks in the military sphere, the council had only itself to blame, was, in many ways, its own worst enemy and, when it did try something different, tended not to go about it in a convincing or imaginative manner.[17] In 1569 it came up with a plan to raise a corps of expert marksmen. This was not in itself a foolish notion, but the council's hope that such a body would be voluntarily maintained, without the pressure of statutory obligation, by specified royal officials, including the justices of the peace, was naive, to say the least. The opposition was immediate, shrill and could not be ignored. The scheme was dropped.[18]

Overall, the council was not much interested in newness, whether in materials or methods. Suggestions were submitted to it. John Kynde proposed marking all the weapons in the country with the owner's name in order to avoid "borrowing" at muster time, a service he was prepared to offer at a penny per footman and tuppence for a man on horseback.[19] It might not have proved a very good suggestion, but at least Mr. Kynde had it and tried to do something with it. The council's own military ideas were few and there is little evidence it ever managed to do very much in the way of successfully implementing those it had. The militia did improve from the early 1580s onwards. The council no longer had to retreat quite

---

16. Huntington Library, Ellesmere MS. 2084, minute of letters to the council for the selling of weapons sequestered from rescusants, April 12, 1588; Bodleian Library, MS. Tanner 241, f. 23v, the council to Lord Crumwell, Sir Arthur Heveningham, Sir Edward Clere, Sir William Heydon, Bassingbourne Gaudy, Nathaniel Bacon, William Bleconhasset and John Peyton, April 4, 1585.

17. Boynton, 103 and 107.

18. *Ibid.*, 60–62.

19. Huntington Library, Ellesmere MS. 1274, John Kynde to the council, no date.

so regularly from its initial demands for men at muster time as it had in the past. But this was primarily the result of increasing national consciousness of a threat from Spain. The council exploited the situation effectively enough, but it was following a trend, not blazing a trail. Its military policy, to the extent it can be said to have had one, can therefore be rated, at best, only a qualified success.

Chapter XIII

ENFORCEMENT

F, in overseeing the functioning of the established departments, the council's most obvious characteristic was a strong tendency to try and keep things as undeviatingly as possible trundling along the same old tracks, a similar lack of either willingness or ability to branch out in new directions can be seen in its exercise of the royal prerogative. The council, as we have seen, was deeply involved in diplomacy. It was preoccupied by sedition and conspiracy. It tried to police the ports of access to and lines of communication within the country. It befriended both people and places. It made forays into the affairs of the Church and concerned itself with commercial, industrial and agricultural affairs. But, whatever else it was doing, the council was also almost always reacting to stimuli arising out of conditions it did not create, rather than trying out policies and ideas it had evolved as the result of unprompted, imaginative evaluation of the state of English society in the later sixteenth century. Perhaps the overriding—certainly a major—reason for this is to be found in the difficulties the council ran into getting its orders obeyed even when they were not particularly controversial, which they certainly would have become if they had been aimed at implementing schemes for bringing about really drastic change. The council, in short, found it extremely difficult to get things—anything—done.

The plan drawn up for the rebuilding of Nantwich, for example, was admirable in theory; it simply did not work in practice. Even after those to whom the council had originally written had "ben daylye sent and sued unto for the space of towe yeres and a quarter," the money really forthcoming was hardly enough to cover even the most basic reconstruction expenses, let alone put up a new market and support a preacher. Eleven bishoprics, twenty-seven English counties and all the Welsh ones contributed nothing at all, and those sums which did come in did not amount to very much.[1] The Bishop of Hereford, reporting that his clergy had mainly reacted "contempteouslie," came up with £28.18.0d, thinking it "better to . . . [send] somethinge than nothinge."[2] And even the money the commissioners did eventually receive seems to have been misused. Mrs. Bridgitt

---

1. PRO, E.101/633, no. 9, [the council] to "the commyssioners appointed to distribute an imploy the sommes of money collected for the re-edifieng of the towne of Namptwich," no date.

2. PRO, SP.12/171, no. 64, the Bishop of Hereford to the council, June 28, 1584.

Furvill, still, in July 1586, living "with other poore folkes . . . in the churche porche . . . . [threatened that] yf . . . the commyssioneres do not deal better with poore men than hitherto the[y] have done, there wilbe another maner of complaynte putt up to the queene's majestie's handes before it be longe."[3] The patience of the poor may have been no greater than the council's concern, but it was definitely a necessary virtue.

Three years after the council had given orders for the cleaning up of the River Wisbech, a Mr. Carleton drew its attention to the unpalatable truth that the work was either not yet done or had never been completed satisfactorily.[4] Similarly, the fact had to be faced that "the gentleman of Lowe Westmerland . . . absolutely refuse[d] to contribute anything at all" to repair the break in the River Eden's banks.[5] As for upholding ecclesiastical discipline, the bishops were not nearly as successful as the council expected them to be. They were, of course, responsible for maintaining the religious orthodoxy of their own dioceses, but they proved incapable of stamping out dissent, as the laws required of them. The Mass continued to be said in England—Father Gerard managed to celebrate it in prison even after his first set of altar plate had been found and confiscated—and Roman practices to be followed—in public, no less—in remote districts.[6] Whole "nests of papists," in the words of Sir Thomas Smith, came to light from time to time.[7] Sir Henry Wallop, Sir William Kingsmill and other Hampshire gentlemen were ordered in 1576 "to make searche in the howse of one Alexander Gearinge for vestimentes and other massing tooeles belonging to papistrie."[8] The Bishop of Bangor had to be told to investigate an "unlawfull and superstitious disorder" which had taken place at a recent burial. Thus woken to his duty, the possibly good, although certainly either not very well informed or something less than conscientious cleric took steps to make sure that "the curates [involved] . . . shuld openly before the whole paraeche recant in writing," but he should not have needed prompting in the first place.[9] At Cirencester the laxity of the clergy assumed scandalous proportions. In 1576 the people of the town had to complain to the council that their common sergeant, a justice of the

---

3. PRO, E.101/632, no. 27, Bridgitt Furvill to Alexander King, July 4, 1586.

4. PRO, SP.12/131, no. 48, Mr. Carleton to the council, July 1579.

5. APC, VIII, 362, April 5, 1575.

6. John Gerard, *The Autobiography of a Hunted Priest*, (New York, 1955), 31.

7. BM, Lansdowne MS. 16, f. 42, Smith to Burghley, February 12, 1573.

8. PRO, SP.12/108, no. 40, the council to Sir Henry Wallop and Sir William Kingsmill, June 9, 1576.

9. PRO, SP.12/69, no. 14, the Bishop of Bangor to the council, May 24, 1570.

peace, the clerk of the peace and the lesser adherents of all three, being papists, were keeping their fellow citizens in fear of confiscation of goods, imprisonment and even death. "It wilbe your Lordships' good pleasures," they asserted confidently, "clerelie to remove and weede out the said persones, from havinge eny aucthoritie, or to lyve emongest Christian people."[10] The Bishop of St. David's, with worldly perspicacity, claimed that the cure for all such problems of spiritual disorder was to spend more money and therefore requested the council to help him obtain sufficient livings for incumbents in his diocese.[11] But the council had other views. "Nothinge is required," the bishops in general were reminded in 1573, "but that godly and seemly orders allowed by the quene's majestie and the hole realme be kepte. The which excepte you did winke at and dissemble, there neded not this new proclamacions . . . which sholde be greate pleasure to her majesti and comforte to us."[12] Thus the council fell back on exhortation to compliance with its and Queen Elizabeth's orders.

Such a policy was cheap; it was not necessarily effectual. That often resoundingly sanctimonious exhortations were composed, as the wording of this one demonstrates, at the same time as the original decree was sent out, is alone enough to make one suspect that widespread heeding of orders not thus buttressed was not even expected. Sheriffs were regularly written to for such routine purposes as the execution of council decisions in private disputes and the attachment of persons in the queen's disfavor. In 1568 Elizabeth wrote to the Earl of Derby and the Bishop of Chester to the effect that understanding "by commen reporte, but specially by your own letter sent unto our counsell what secret and disordered practises ther be in Lancashire . . . under the coulor of religion. . . , we do presently send our letters heerwith to the sherif of Lancashire commaunding him straitly to attache from tyme to tyme all suche persons as you shall by your letters . . . prescribe."[13] But sheriffs—and even such an eminent personage as the Lord President of the Council in the Marches of Wales—had also to be used to finish jobs others were supposed to have done, but had not, had not managed, or could not be expected to conclude successfully. To this end the Lord President was instructed to see that two gentlemen residing within the area of his jurisdiction actually carried out a council order set-

10. PRO, SP.12/71, no. 30, petition of Cirencester to the council, June 1570.

11. PRO, SP.12/66, no. 26, the Bishop of St. David's to the council, January 25, 1570.

12. BM, Add. MS. 48035, f. 177, the council to the bishops, November 2, 1573.

13. PRO, SP.12/46, no. 19, the queen to the Earl of Derby, the Bishop of Chester and others, February 3, 1568.

tling a dispute between them and the sheriff of Kent told to deliver a collector's letters to those who had refused to accept them from him, thereby avoiding, thus far, contributing to the Crown's financial needs.[14]

Loan collectors altogether were a troublesome lot. As Sir Thomas Smith pointed out in July 1570, while it was imperative to make use of local men in this capacity for the simple reason that they were the ones who knew where the wealth of the counties actually lay, it was dangerous as well, since they were likely to cheat the distant queen for nearby friendship's sake.[15] Sir Nicholas Arnold of Gloucestershire twice fell under such suspicion, and was summoned to go over his accounts in person.[16] But collectors, and indeed, others, could be a problem for quite opposite reasons. Not only did they tend not to do things which they ought to have done; they did things which they ought not to have done as well, which meant that, from the council's point of view, there was no health in them. Sir Edward Clere had to be examined on suspicion of having threatened with Privy Seals, for his own gain, persons to whom they had not been addressed in the first place.[17] And one unidentified individual, whose purposes remain titillatingly obscure (could he perhaps have been planning to make private war upon the Tsar?) was ordered sent before the council to explain his odd behavior in unlawfully calling to arms within the confines of the City certain of the queen's subjects, presumably too poor and ignorant to recognize a genuine muster commissioner when they saw one.[18]

Council agents of all sorts, not to mention the actual objects of its orders, often had to be contacted repeatedly and sometimes in a variety of ways prior to the successful conclusion of a single item of business, "uppon occasion of the little regarde had to the former letters," first letters relative to a particular subject sometimes being ignored completely.[19] They fre-

---

14. BM, Harleian MS. 4943, f. 114v, the council to the Lord President, no date; f. 156v and f. 160, the council to the sheriff of Kent, March 27, 1571.

15. PRO, SP.12/71, no. 42, Smith to the council, July 9, 1570.

16. BM, Harleian MS. 4943, f. 143v and f. 156, "certain of the council to Sir Nicholas Arnold," December 9, 1572.

17. BM, Add. MS. 32323, f. 127v, Harleian MS. 4943, f. 129, APC, VIII, 71, the council to Sir Christopher Heydon and Sir William Buttes, March 1, 1572.

18. BM, Add. MS. 32323, f. 4v, the council to the Lord Mayor, May 22, 1572.

19. *Ibid.*, f. 146v, the council to the subsidy commissioners, no date. BM, Harleian MS. 286, f. 42, the council to the muster commissioners of Suffolk to "procede to the full execucion" of an April royal commission and council letters, "which you may not fayle to doe without any farther delay, as you will answere the good opinion heretofore conceived of your readines in the furthering of her majestie's service," August 28, 1580.

quently failed to do as they were told even then, like the Northamptonshire commissioners who omitted to include the names and addresses of "our best accompted gentilmen" in the report of their muster proceedings.[20] Viscount Bindon and the other justices of Dorset supplied too few officers for the troops they raised.[21] The defendant whom Walter Mildmay had found to be in the wrong in a dispute over a parsonage refused to accept the adverse decision, which prompted the disregarded chancellor of the exchequer to appeal to Burghley to exercise *his* authority to put the plaintiff—"this pore man"—in possession.[22] And Sir John Perrot had to be required to explain why he had taken men with him to Ireland who were too old for service, there or anywhere else.[23] It is hardly any wonder that the council sometimes decided it was necessary to go as far as appointing special deputies to check on the effectiveness of its ordinary ones. It happened regularly in respect to military matters and not infrequently in others. Such individuals were sent into particular counties after the musters there were over to make sure they had been well conducted.[24] In Norfolk a man known to be ill-affected to the true religion had been elected to local office at Thetford despite a series of council letters and orders forbidding it. Six gentlemen were therefore assigned to enquire further into the situation.[25] "Notwithstanding . . . our particuler letters many tymes written . . . fleshe is continuallye eaten in those dayes forbidden" and occasionally, therefore, persons were specially appointed and equipped with "a letter patent or placard" addressed to the queen's officers generally for their assistance "for searche and inquirie for thobservacion of fishdays" which, since an act of the parliament of 1563, had included Wednesdays as well as Fridays throughout the period of the year outside of Lent itself.[26]

---

20. PRO, SP.12/59, no. 9, Northamptonshire muster commissioners to the council, October 15, 1567.

21. BM, Add. MS. 32323, f. 5, [the council] to the justices of the peace of Dorset, no date.

22. BM, Lansdowne MS. 21, no. 9, Mildmay to Burghley, August 15, 1575.

23. BM, Add. MS. 32323, f. 129v, the council to Sir John Perrot, September 9, [1571].

24. PRO, SP.12/124, no. 15, "instruccions geven by the lords and others of the quene's majestie's most honourable Privie Coun[sell] unto AB appointed by order from her majestie to repeire into the counties E, D and F to take a viewe of the number of able men and armor certified by the commissioners upon the late musters taken," May 1578.

25. Bodleian Library, MS. Tanner 241, f. 14, the council to Sir Robert Jermyn, Sir William Spring, Sir John Highem, Robert Ashfeilde, Bassingbourne Gaudy and Thomas Pooley or any five or four of them, August 27, 1582.

26. BM, Harleian MS. 4943, f. 97, Add. MS. 32323, f. 93, the council to

That such repeated action should have been necessary may seem astonishing, for the council had several tactics at its disposal, the employment of which at first sight would seem to have been more than sufficient to ensure that its slightest whim would be instantly obeyed. Simply the threat of being summoned to appear before the council in person to answer for his actions was alone sometimes enough to exact a man's obedience, and it was regularly used. Such a threat had real meaning because it entailed the expenditure of a considerable amount of time, money, and physical effort, even if the person so summoned was eventually dismissed with no more than an admonition to behave himself more circumspectly in the future. As George Puttenham put it to Sir John Throckmorton in 1578, "they be all bente apon you, thinking to werrye you with expences and with attendaunces and with checkes before their Lordships."[27] Throckmorton was summoned directly by letter addressed to himself; sometimes people were summoned by name by messengers of the Chamber on specific instructions from the council to go and bring them in; but more generally, the messengers, or certain justices of the peace, or other local gentlemen, or the officers of trading companies were instructed to send up whoever had failed to comply with particular instructions the council was currently especially interested in having carried out effectively.[28] Anyone, for example, wrote the queen to the Merchant Adventurers, not being free of the company, yet persisting in meddling with the trade of the Low Countries, was to be commanded "in our name to appere before our Pryvie Councell."[29] If the person concerned was *not* brought in by someone, then he was to enter into a recognizance to make his appearance on a day specified or to be specified in the future.[30] Thus Richard Evans, clerk of the

---

the Lord Mayor, no date; Harleian MS. 4943, f. 98, Add. MS. 32323, f. 95, a "placard," no date. There is ample other evidence of the council's difficulties in enforcing this political fast. In Loseley MS. XIII, f. 24, for example, the council issues orders to the sheriff and justices of the peace of Surrey for the strict keeping of Lent, February 4, 1578, and in BM, Harleian MS. 286, f. 33, the justices of the peace in general are required "very earnestlie to devise by all good meanes howe the same maie be best observed," same date.

27. PRO, SP.12/126, no. 65, George Puttenham to Sir John Throckmorton, 1578.

28. *Ibid.*, no. 51, the council to Sir John Throckmorton, November 6, 1578; SP.12/95, no. 61, "the names of all those as were warned to appere before the quene's majestie's most honorable Privie Counsell at the Courte by Robert Pedley, one of the messengers of her majestie's Chamber," February 1574; SP.12/132, no. 61, Sir Henry Radcliff to the council, November 16(?), 1579.

29. PRO, SP.12/75, no. 101, the queen to the Merchant Adventurers' company, 1570(?).

30. BM, Harleian MS. 703, f. 15v, the council to Walter Covert, sheriff of

parish of Hoseley in Suffolk, entered into an obligation of £40 to the queen's use to appear before the council "within tenne daies warning to him to be given" to answer accusations against him of having had dealings with pirates.[31] John Christmas entered into an obligation for a similar sum before Lord Darcy of Chiche and four other gentlemen, who had been appointed commissioners for the purpose by virtue of a special letter from the lords of the council themselves.[32]

Once in London, the summoned person was likely to experience a protracted and expensive delay before his case actually came before the council. "May it please your good honors in respect of the chargable attendaunce of your poore orator . . . to hasten your most honorable resolutions," Dr. Beacon, chancellor of the diocese of Norwich requested in 1578.[33] It was a familiar cry. The person arrived at Court, or at the council office at Whitehall, paid his fee to the clerk for recording the fact that he had made his appearance at the time appointed, and then, as likely as not, was instructed to remain in attendance at their Lordships' pleasure. "Robert Wilde, gentleman," for example, "made his apparaunce and was willed by us, the clerkes of her majestie's Privy Counsell, to make his attendaunce before their Lordships untill sume . . . order were by them taken" in his case.[34] It could be months. John and Nicholas Harpesfield were instructed on August 19, 1574 "to make their appearance before . . . their Lordships . . . the first day . . . after the feast of All Saintes next coming." They appeared accordingly on November 12, 1574, and were then "appointed to appere . . . againe this day fortnight . . . and so from tyme to tyme as their Lordships shall [require] . . . untill . . . [they] obtaine furder licence." They thereafter appeared, and were likewise remanded, on November 26, December 1, February 11, 1575, on April 29 and May 6, when the Privy Council register notes succinctly that "the two Harpesfildes . . . made their apparaunces this day, according to their recognisaunces."[35] The Harpesfields perhaps did not have too much to complain about; they were free men, even if they were tied to regular appearances

Sussex and Surrey, December 16, 1583; PRO, SP.12/132, no. 2, Sir Robert Wingfield to the council, September 12, 1579; SP.12/131, no. 24, the council to the messengers of the Chamber, June 14, 1579.

31. PRO, SP.12/132, no. 8, bond of Richard Evans to appear before the council for piratical dealings, September 16, 1579.

32. PRO, SP.12/131, no. 1, May 2, 1579.

33. PRO, SP.12/127, no. 2, Dr. Beacon to the council, December [1], 1578.

34. APC, VIII, 231, April 28, 1574.

35. Ibid., 284, 312, 318, 320, 339, 371 and 373, August 19, November 12 and 26 and December 1, 1574 and February 11, April 29 and May 6, 1575.

at the council office, and they had previously been prisoners in the Fleet for religious disaffection. But being summoned before the council was, it is clear, a dubious honor. Though a few positively sought it out, having been misrepresented, in order to "purge ourselves . . . before your Lordships," most went out of their way to avoid a summons, even going to the extent of attempting to bribe the messenger who brought the bad news, if such a course of action appeared to have any chance of achieving its objective.[36] Such a course could have almost comical results. The mayor of New Romney paid a messenger by the name of Robert Brown forty shillings to get him out of having to make an unwelcome appearance—then promptly complained to Francis Walsingham when he found out that he had not been summoned at all, but that Brown was as corrupt as he, and had simply used the threat to extort the money.[37] This was, in fact, a kind of sharp practice which persisted throughout Elizabeth's reign, and in 1596 she had to issue a proclamation warning the public to be on its guard against people who, falsely claiming to be messengers of the Chamber, were armed with counterfeit warrants from the council for appearances before it, and had been relieving credulous recipients of the supposed obligation—in return, of course, for a substantial fee.[38]

If the timid summonee did not somehow manage to avoid an appearance, he was likely to be intimidated once he found himself in the council's presence. Those comparatively few descriptions which have come down to us—set-pieces, mostly, by representatives of foreign courts—present a striking picture of how imposing this group of extremely prominent people looked to the outsider. In 1569 a Spanish envoy informed the Duke of Alba that he had been received by the English councillors sitting in solemn state along one side of a broad, shallow table, he and his party being placed along the other.[39] This is an arrangement often seen in contemporary paintings of both the council and other similar gatherings, and the impression conveyed was aptly expressed by the newly appointed representative from the republic of Venice writing to his government with an account of an interview he had been accorded in 1603.[40] "These lords of the

36. PRO, SP.12/112, no. 29, Thomas Palmer, Richarde Erneley and Thomas Leoknor to the council, April 26, 1577.

37. PRO, SP.12/127, no. 59, John Mynge to Walsingham, 1578.

38. Humphrey Dyson, *A Booke Containing all such Proclamations as were Published during the Reign of the late Queene Elizabeth* (London, 1618), 334, Robert Steele, *A Bibliography of Royal Proclamations of the Tudor and Stuart Sovereigns* (Oxford, 1910), no. 882, May 3, 1596.

39. CSP Spanish, II, no. 167, p. 218, Chapin Vitelli to the Duke of Alba, December 19, 1569.

40. The picture in the National Portrait Gallery in London of the Anglo-

council," he reported, "behave like so many kings."[41] The use of the last noun in the singular would have been even more apposite, for the council when it spoke, whether advising the queen, being polite to an ambassador or reproving an erring loan collector, spoke as one man. The prospect of having to face such a tribunal was an unnerving one, as a comment of 1581 expressly indicates. In reply to a letter they had previously received from the council, a group of gentlemen made the suggestion that "your good Lordships . . . resume this matter into your handes and . . . call Mr. Hoe with his agents before you into her majestie's courte of Starre Chamber where your praesence and savere censure, procaeding from you, mighte strike a farre graeter terror not only into themselves, but ther associates and others of like inclination."[42]

Should a thick-skinned culprit decline to be over-awed by showmanship alone, he could hardly have helped remembering the council had two powers at its disposal, the thought of the exercise of either one of which was enough to inspire fear and trembling in all but the stoutest-hearted. Probably the more dreaded was the power of arbitrary imprisonment.

Even if such imprisonment were merely the prelude to a fair trial in an appropriate court, as in the case of John Love, whom the Knight Marshal was ordered to "take into his custodie, and to kepe close prisoner . . . prior to bringing him to be examined before the officers of the Admiraltie," the power to order it was a horrifying one.[43] Elizabethan prisons were unpleasant places, where it was perfectly possible to starve to death, something which the Earl of Leicester had to take urgent steps to prevent happening in Chester in 1578.[44] And one never knew, once commitment had taken place, how long it would be before one's case either came up for trial or one would obtain the council's pardon and be released. It took courage and a peculiar obstinacy to trust to the processes of the law for rescue. The best way out was to repent one's error and petition for forgiveness, emphasizing one's own humbleness and appealing to the council's clemency. Then if one were lucky, like Thomas Hillis of Chichester, originally imprisoned for lewd speeches uttered against Lord Burghley, absolution and

---

Spanish peace negotiations of 1604, although the number of persons shown is smaller than would have been present at an important gathering of the council, gives one some idea of the scene.

41. CSP Venetian, IX, no. 1171, p. 566, Giovanni Carlo Scaramelli to the doge and senate, April 7, 1603.

42. Bodleian Library, MS. Tanner 241, Robert Wingfeilde, Robert Jermin, Nicholas Bacon, Richard Wingfield, Bassingbourne Gaudy and John Ryvett to the council, August 12, 1571.

43. APC, VIII, 180, January 19, 1573.

44. City of Chester Record Office, MS. M/L/5, no. 24, the Earl of Leicester to the justices of the peace of Cheshire, June 28, 1578.

release would follow.[45] To bring about such a happy outcome, it helped to have someone working for one from outside, and whenever it imprisoned someone, the council, and individual councillors, were soon deluged with petitions from his friends and relations for his release, which are themselves indications of a general recognition of the council's virtually absolute power to shut away and liberate at will.[46] Prisoners, too, were liable to forgotten, at least as individuals. In 1583 the secretary had "to write to the severall prysons to certifie how manie have ben comitted by order from their Lordships since the last certificate retourned."[47] So the threat of Newgate and the Marshalsea, the Fleet, the Counter and the Tower loomed large behind the council's exhortations to its unpaid agents, and the experience of the high as of the low—of the Duke of Norfolk and plain John Love—constituted effective warnings of the fate of those who failed in prudence. The summons to appear before the council in person to explain one's actions was, therefore, especially feared because of the possibility that the highway to London might well prove to be the road to jail.[48]

Torture, that other grim instrument of established power's ascendancy, may well have been less feared than imprisonment, since the council's own attitude towards it was ambivalent. It *was* used. When they judged the matter at issue to be of sufficient importance, both the queen and her advisers authorized the resort to physical mistreatment in order to extract desired information. If Charles Bailly, being interrogated by Edmund Tremayne, continued to refuse to talk, the lieutenant of the Tower was told in 1571 to "putt him upon the racke, and . . . with some payne of the sayd torture, procure him to confesse the truth."[49] Walsingham, the zealot assigned with the solicitor-general and Thomas Randolph to examine a man by the name of Corkin in 1575, remarked to Burghley that "without torture I knowe we shall not prevayle" and three days later, having so far got precisely nowhere without it, he made it clear that, in his opinion, the mere threat, which Burghley appears to have suggested trying, would be little help.[50] Elizabeth, even though "always of our owne nature inclyned to mercie," at least occasionally leaned towards Walsing-

---

45. Hertfordshire Record Office, Gorhambury MS. XII, B. 2, the council to Burghley, September 5, 1576.

46. PRO, SP.12/131, no. 50, Annies Acton to the council, July 1579.

47. BM, Harleian MS. 6035, Walsingham's letter book, f. 63v.

48. PRO, SP.12/126, no. 65, George Puttenham to Sir John Throckmorton, 1578.

49. Hatfield House, MS. 157, f. 114, the council to the lieutenant of the Tower, April 26, 1571.

50. BM, Harleian MS. 6991, ff. 114 and 116, Walsingham to Burghley, February 2 and 5, 1575.

ham's view.[51] "Hir majesty," he told Thomas Smith in 1571, "wold have you use some extremyte with Barker, to confesse more truth . . . and . . . will have you putt hym in feare of torture if he will not."[52] But there was no general agreement on its efficacy. Smith and Wilson, unlike Walsingham and, occasionally, Elizabeth, were "Burghley men" on this issue. They complained of the "unpleasant and panefull toile" involved in examining followers of the Duke of Norfolk during the latter's time of troubles and reported that "tomorrow do we intend to bryng a couple of them to the rack, not in eny hope to get eny thyng worthy the payne or feare, but because it is so earnestly commanded unto us."[53] Physical force, as a result of this division of opinion, was normally resorted to with reluctance, and probably only then applied to those suspected of involvement in ideological conspiracy. The council, ordering Lord Scrope in 1565 "to use some kinde of torture unto" a particular suspect, immediately qualified the instruction with the proviso that it was to be done "without any grete bodely hurte."[54] The lieutenant of the Tower, the solicitor-general, Thomas Randolph, Henry Knollys and Thomas Norton were actually ordered to bring Humphrey Needham to the rack "without stretching his body" at all.[55] There are, altogether, only eleven entries relating to the subject in the *Acts of the Privy Council* during the first seventeen years of the reign of Queen Elizabeth. Moreover, the council was careful to see that, comparatively little use as it made of torture itself, no one else did so without its specific permission. In the instance of a murder in Somerset, for example, it was made clear to Sir Hugh Paulet and others, who had been instructed by the council to investigate the matter, that they were not to use torture without first certifying the names of those to whom it was to be applied and then waiting to receive a warrant from the council authorizing them to go ahead.[56]

The erring subject, once it had him in its clutches, and conscious of what it then could do to him, had no alternative but to repent his sins of the past, make amends for his present failings and promise to do better in

51. Samuel Haynes, *Collection of State Papers . . . left by William Cecil, Lord Burghley* (London, 1740), the queen to the Earl of Sussex, November 18, 1569.

52. BM, Cotton MS. Caligula C. iii, f. 254, Burghley to Smith, September 9, 1571.

53. Hatfield House, MS. 158, f. 28, Smith and Wilson to Burghley, September 17, 1571, as quoted in William Murdin, *Collection of State Papers relating to Affairs in the Reign of Queen Elizabeth* (London, 1759), 95.

54. APC, VII, 222, June 22, 1565.

55. APC, VIII, 319, November 29, 1574.

56. BM, Add. MS. 32323, f. 128, APC, VIII, 67, the council to Sir Hugh Paulet, February 14, 1572.

the future. When the council was satisfied with his submission, it sent him away—but only after it had taken steps to prevent him, once out of its august presence, from reverting to his former state of irreverence for its authority. It could, and frequently did, take bonds to ensure its orders were carried out.

This was a common procedure throughout the English governmental and administrative system. The Earl of Sussex was instructed that "the Dacres . . . [were to] be bound either to the good abearing, or to the peace at the least" in 1569.[57] The Archbishop of Canterbury was ordered to take bonds from a Dr. Drury for good behavior in his prerogative court.[58] Robert Wingfelde gave William Fitzwilliam a £200 bond to guarantee that he would abide by Sir Walter Mildmay's arbitration in a dispute between them.[59] The sheriff of Somerset was instructed to make an inventory of the goods of a Mr. Stowel and to take sureties that they would be forthcoming "to such uses as hereafter shalbe by lawe ordeined.[60] "Such as have any grant of forfeitures upon penal statute," the council instructed the justices of assize, were to be bound by recognizance not to vex the subjects of the queen for wrongful causes.[61] The Knight Marshal was ordered to deliver a prisoner in his charge "upon bandes to be deliverid at Sandwich to aunswer to justice."[62] And Thomas Digges and Reynald Higate "acknowledged before the Lord Chancellor . . . to stand bound unto the queen's majestie in the some of £2000 to give their attendance from tyme to tyme uppon their Lordships, and not to depart without their Lordships' speciall licence."[63]

Yet the letters exhorting obedience to the council's own orders went on; council instructions continued to be disregarded; countless ordinary Englishmen declined to be overawed by the fear of a council summons and some even failed to be intimidated, at least immediately, by imprisonment. Robert Brett and William Broke, both tanners, "for their unsemely and malapert speches when before their Lordships for their not execution of the statute for the tanninge, were committed to the Mar-

---

57. BM, Cotton MS. Titus F. iii, f. 124, the council to the Earl of Sussex, August 2, 1569.

58. APC, VIII, 37, August 2, 1571.

59. Northamptonshire Record Office, F (M) P. 29, bond in the sum of £200 of Robert Wingfelde to William Fitzwilliam to abide by Mildmay's arbitration in a dispute in which he is involved, October 19, 1575.

60. APC, VIII, 82, February 9, 1572.

61. BM, Harleian MS. 169, f. 207v, and f. 206, the council to the justices of assize, May 31, 1573.

62. APC, VIII, 180, January 19, 1573.

63. Huntington Library, Ellesmere MS. 5839, order set down by the council in a dispute between Thomas Digges and Reynald Higate, January 23, 1584.

shalsey" in June 1574, and it was two full weeks before they made the
"humble submission" which ultimately got them out.[64] In 1584 the Lord
Admiral, in his capacity as a Lord Lieutenant, was instructed "to appoint
some discreete and well chosen persones" to check on the effectiveness of
the commissioners already appointed to see "that no manner of grain be
transported."[65] The council found itself obliged to write regularly to the
justices of the peace to order them to take action against speculators who
engaged in "the craftie inhaunzing of the prices of graine."[66] These people tried to keep prices high by buying in quantity, anywhere they could,
regulations notwithstanding, biding their time and then selling when
demand was greatest. The wrath of the council was apparently well worth
risking when the possibility of profit was in the offing.

It also found its instructions being ignored when following them would
result in loss. The council's faith in Martin Frobisher's ore from across
the Atlantic proved unfounded. Some of its fellow "adventurers" in what
had only too soon turned out to be an abortive speculation were unwilling
from the first to pay their share, and the council wrote in October 1578,
ordering the Lord Mayor of London and Sir William Cordell to send
those who ignored their further reminders to appear before it and account
for their reluctance.[67] The reaction appears to have been precisely nil,
and on December 7 the council wrote another letter, this time to the Earl
of Pembroke, with the information that the queen "hath . . . geven us
expresse commaundement to require you . . . to geve order for the payment . . . within ten dayes after the receipt hereof."[68] Still the effect
seems to have been slight, for on January 13, 1579 Pembroke was approached "once againe to praye [you] to geve present order for the payment." And this was a toning down of the phrasing, which had originally
been intended "once again to require [you] to have more regard unto" the
council's orders.[69] Later the same year, the council sent Edward Fenton,

---

64. APC, VIII, 251, June (?) 1574 and 256, June 20, 1574.

65. BM, Harleian MS. 703, new f. 41, the council to Howard of Effingham,
August 31, 1585. This letter to himself is signed by Lord Admiral Howard, along
with Hunsdon, Knollys, Hatton and Walsingham.

66. APC, VIII, 111, June 7, 1573; Surrey Record Office, Loseley MSS.,
Correspondence II (1581–1600), the council to an unspecified person, October
24, 1600; PRO, SP.12/95, no. 86, note of council business, May 9, 1574.

67. PRO, SP.12/126, no. 21, the council to the Lord Mayor and Sir William
Cordell, October 29, 1578.

68. PRO, SP.12/127, no. 8, the council to the Earl of Pembroke, December
7, 1578.

69. PRO, SP.12/129, no. 4, the council to the Earl of Pembroke and others
[January 13, 1579].

a west country gentleman, a commission from the queen, supplemented by its own instructions, directing him to locate a certain native ore which the council had heard existed in that part of England and which might help in working Frobisher's. For some time Fenton got nowhere at all.[70] Eventually he managed to track down something which might or might not have been what the council had been thinking of.[71] In any case, Frobisher's enigmatic cargo was still lying at Dartford, after being moved from the Tower, where, on the council's orders, it had originally been stored in 1581 when negotiations were carried on with Michael Lock with the object of *his* trying his hand at doing something constructive with it.[72] Altogether the council was not particularly successful in the exploitation of minerals, either in the national interest or its own. Sir Thomas Smith, Cecil and the Earl of Leicester were all taken in by a Mr. Medley, who sold them completely on his plan "for the transformation of rawe iron into copper."[73] The iron mines were worked by private owners, with whom the council interfered only when there was some private dispute threatening to disrupt the industry; and the only approximately successful venture in the mineral field was the bringing over of Germans to work the copper deposits in Cumberland in the 1580s.

The problem of putting the council's policies into effect persisted everywhere. Wage control was simply not feasible in practice. The regulations "imprinted and sente abrode" by the Lord Keeper were based directly, as the 1563 act directed, upon reports which the justices of the peace were required to send into the chancery before July 12 each year, certifying where, in their opinion, rates should be pegged for the coming year.[74] The market, either in goods or labor, could not be ignored. Wages were fixed at a level at which, with luck, they *could* be kept, not where the council thought they *ought* to be. It was the same with prices. "My lords' intent," wrote Sir Thomas Smith to Lord Burghley on December 6th, 1574, "is that *if the vynteneres do agree* [my italics] to those prices, bonds be taken of them not to sell above those prices."[75] The wine merchants were to be bound, in other words, simply not to change their

---

70. *Ibid.*, no. 2, Edward Fenton to the council, January 2, 1579.

71. *Ibid.*, no. 6, Edward Fenton to the council, January 13, 1579.

72. PRO, SP.12/116, no. 25, the council to the officers of the mint, October 16, 1577; SP.12/147, no. 69, Michael Lock to [the council], February 1581.

73. BM, Lansdowne MS. 19, no. 45, Smith to Burghley and the Earl of Leicester, December 16, 1574; Harleian MS. 6991, f. 112, Smith to Burghley, January 28, 1575.

74. APC, VII, 230, July 8, 1565.

75. BM, Lansdowne MS. 19, no. 44, Smith to Burghley, December 6, 1574.

minds, once made up, and go back on an understanding once one had been reached among themselves; they were not being forced to charge what the council thought was fair and equitable. The council's policy with regard to living costs can, accordingly, be more realistically described as one of attempted price stabilization rather than one of price control.

Although particular individuals could be imprisoned and tortured and otherwise coerced into doing the council's bidding—in absolute terms, quite a number—nonetheless, when faced with a general reluctance to obey their orders, Queen Elizabeth's Privy Councillors were impotent and knew it. Their position is exactly described in those "instructions for a benevolence," dating from Henry VIII's time, but still entered in Robert Beale's precedent book in 1575, to which we referred earlier. A benevolence was to be asked of county residents whom those chosen as collectors thought rich enough to pay. But as a benevolence, or voluntary contribution to the expenses of the sovereign, had no legal standing, its collection called for the exercise of considerable tact. The collectors were to deal with each man separately in order to reduce the possibility of the rapid spread of any uncooperative attitude from a recalcitrant individual to all the rest. There follows a whole page of specific instructions as to how to speak softly and winningly of the royal necessity, with pathetic references to the defenselessness of the kingdom in the face of its enemies. But there was no iron hand inside this velvet glove, and the council knew it. If this gentle tactic failed to impress, the collector had no other to fall back on, and he was therefore instructed in the last resort simply to command the stubborn non-contributor "to retorne into his howse, and so passe him over in such a silence as he be no impeechment or evill example to the reste, who wilbe more tractable, and frame them selves to the consideration of thinges as appertainethe."[76]

Whether or not it was this particular piece of advice inherited from an earlier day that provided the precedent for the council's practice is hard to tell, but the principle expressed in it was nonetheless evoked when the circumstances seemed appropriate. In 1573 a series of interrogatories was presented to Edward Derynge, including the question, did he think that the *Book of Common Prayer* was permitted to be used in churches by God's word, or no? Derynge was a preacher and held the post of the reader of the divinity lecture at St. Paul's, so was worthy of the council's careful attention. He was the rotting apple which would quickly spread its decay to all the others in the barrel if not either thrown out

76. BM, Add. MS. 48018, f. 145, "instruction for the benevolence," no date.

altogether or the badness cut out of him in time. As the Bishop of London put it to Lord Burghley, "yf this man be somwhat spared and yet well scoled, the other[s], beyng manifest offendors, maye be delt withal according to ther desertys."[77] But if he refused to be "scoled," if he did *not* go along with the use of the Prayer Book, and if too many others of the clergy began to follow his example, then the council was going to be hard put to make them.

There were a good many reasons for the council's predicament. Some of them were its own fault. It was not in day-to-day practice actually as efficient as the praise showered earlier on its advanced techniques of office organization and management would lead one to expect. The council chest, into which so many things were put and from which documents were regularly taken by order of their conscientious Lordships was no rival of the modern filing cabinet. Consignment to it—and probably "it" was actually several pieces of furniture—took place without any great regard being paid to ease of retrieval. When some important piece of information was needed at short notice, finding it could be a long enough job for Walsingham to have to remind himself to cause a search for it to be made instead of simply telling one of his assistants to go and get it out.[78] Partly owing to this lack of system, revealed also by the very marked difference between the numbers of Walsingham's and Cecil's personal clerical assistants, the council was not as well-informed as it might have been and because its knowledge of local conditions was out of date or inaccurate or both, it constantly found itself bombarded with protests about the wishful quality of its orders and the excessiveness of its demands. The choruses of complaint aroused intermittently by the levying of forced loans and regularly by the holding of musters were typical, but not unique. Lady Wallop asserted in 1579 that she should be allowed to go ahead and export grain as usual, in spite of a current restraint, by virtue of a warrant which the queen had granted to her husband six or seven years before.[79] Lord Cobham simply asked Cecil in 1568 to "graynt me your letter to my Lord Tresorer for the straynsporting of soom quantetye of corne upon they other syde. And yf you maye not doo yt alone, I hoppe my Lord Stuard [the Earl of Pembroke], with others, wyll seatt the[ir] hayndes to they[r] letter."[80] Minutes of the council meeting held on

77. APC, VIII, 133, July 22, 1573; Hatfield House, MS. 159, f. 99, the Bishop of London to Burghley, June 3, 1573, as quoted in Murdin, 255–256.

78. BM, Harleian MS. 6035, Walsingham's letter book, f. 4v, 1583.

79. BM, Lansdowne MS. 28, no. 66, Walsingham to Burghley, December 6, 1579.

80. PRO, SP.12/46, no. 73, Lord Cobham to Cecil, June 6, 1568.

May 8, 1575 record the request of the justices of the peace of Cornwall for permission to transport corn in order to bring back salt.[81] On December 27 of the same year George Hyggins, a Bristol merchant, made a similar request.[82] The commissioners for the repair of Dover harbor requested approval for their plans to raise a further sum of money necessary for the work by borrowing £1000 in London and by exporting 1000 tons of beer and an unspecified quantity of malt and barley.[83] Colchester appealed for understanding with regard to its obligation to keep horses for use in the royal service, the town fathers hopefully asserting that the land requisite for such purposes was not available.[84] But at least they offered a *quid pro quo* in return for consideration of their plight. They volunteered to supply arms and armor instead of animals.

We do not know what action the council took in regard to some of these and numerous other special pleadings made to it over the years, but in many cases requests for exemption from some obligation or another were acceded to. The Lord Mayor was instructed that, notwithstanding the queen's own letters fixing wine prices—which he would have only just received—certain persons nominated by Mr. Horsey, to whom "authorytie is graunted . . . to lycense three persons to by and sell wynes in grosse or by retaile at what prise or pryces whatsoever," should be exempt from the regulations.[85] George Hyggins, "uppon understanding that some of his losses have grown in her majestie's service and he being accounted a verie upright and substancil occupier for the benefit of his country," was given permission to export his grain, and the council wrote specially to the commissioners in Norfolk, Gloucestershire and Somerset, instructing them to allow him to proceed with the transportation unmolested.[86] A Signet letter of 1576 instructed Burghley to permit M. de Mauvissiere, a protege of the French ambassador, to export ordnance, planks and wheat in limited quantities.[87] An order in council of January 1571 confirmed the legality of the Cinque Ports' contention that they

---

81. PRO, SP.12/103, no. 43, notes of council business, May 8, 1575.

82. PRO, SP.12/105, no. 92, note of business "to be propownded in cownsayl," December 27, 1575.

83. PRO, SP.12/147, nos. 36 and 37, the commissioners for the repair of Dover harbor to the council, January 1581.

84. *Ibid.*, no. 26, Colchester to the Earl of Sussex, January 31, 1581.

85. BM, Lansdowne MS. 25, no. 8, the council to the Lord Mayor, November 30, 1577.

86. PRO, SP.12/105, no. 92, note of business "to be propownded in cownsayl," December 27, 1575; no. 94, the council to the commissioners for the restraint of the transportation of grain in Norfolk, Gloucestershire and Somerset, December 29, 1575.

87. PRO, SP.12/110, no. 33, the queen to Burghley, 1576.

were exempt by the terms of their charter from the obligation to contribute to a compulsory loan and, indeed, most of the entries in the Privy Council register relating to such matters are of letters excusing individuals from paying "the sommes of money that was required of them by Privy Seal."[88]

Many of the council's exceptions to its own orders and policies were made for seemingly perfectly sound and sensible reasons. In its own immediate—that is, narrow—context, it is entirely logical that "friendly" foreign pirates should not have been interfered with in the pursuit of activities that were regarded by the council as nefarious when engaged in by the queen's own subjects and enemy (or potentially enemy) aliens.[89] It is understandable that foreign victuallers should have been given permission to buy herring for sale outside the country during a period when exports in general were prohibited: without it they would not have been able to spend their English earnings.[90] The maintenance of peace and tranquillity between England and her allies (or potential allies), quite adequately explains such otherwise incongruously discriminatory attitudes, and equally convincing, yet essentially specious justifications are easy enough to find for the host of similar grants of special permission to do something or other normally forbidden that crop up repeatedly throughout the council's records.

Woad could be grown, the sheriff of Sussex was informed, to achieve the "setteing on woorke of the poore." The sheriff sent copies of this letter to all the justices of the peace of the county, asking them to let him know how best this permission could be taken advantage of, and suggesting that they in turn request the local constables to let them have *their* opinions.[91] Thomas Fenner of Shoreham had 500 quarters of wheat he desired to ship to Ireland at a time when grain was badly needed there. The council ordained that he be granted the privilege he desired, provided bonds were taken from him that he would ship his cargo only according to the orders of the Lord Treasurer.[92] Sir Thomas Gresham, notwithstanding the prohibition against the private manufacture of ordnance, was permitted to make a specified number of pieces to satisfy an order from the King of Denmark whom, presumably, it would have been diplomatically ill-

---

88. PRO, SP.12/77, no. 9, order in council, January 31, 1571.

89. PRO, SP.12/108, no. 23, the council to Henry Palmer, May 19, 1576.

90. PRO, SP.12/48, no. 40, the Marquess of Winchester to Cecil, November 12, 1568.

91. BM, Harleian MS. 703, f. 20v, the council to the sheriff of Sussex, February 22, 1585.

92. BM, Lansdowne MS. 28, no. 34, the council to Burghley, December 8, 1579.

advised to offend by denying.[93] And in 1574, a year in which Elizabeth took a particularly long time to make up her mind about whether to put the navy on a war footing or not—eventually deciding against it—the council wrote seven letters "for provision of grain and victuals to be made by Edward Basshe, esquier [the general surveyor of the victuals for the seas] for the furniture of a staple of vittels appointed to be at Portesmowthe for her majestie's navie, according to the minute and rates remayning in the chest."[94] The grain commissioners themselves were instructed that specific exceptions to its earlier general prohibition of grain exports were to be made in favor of the bearers of such letters.

The council was clearly determined to prevent unauthorized comings and goings to and from the country. It aimed at doing so by upholding in principle the existing and virtually complete legal restrictions over entry and exit, while often retreating from the rigid implementation of such a policy in practice. The result was confusion. Special orders, and frequent exceptions to ordinary ones, made it difficult for subordinate officials to sort out those whom the council really wanted prevented from leaving the country from those whose unofficial departures it was in fact abetting. Some orders were simply not intended to be obeyed at all, as the Spanish ambassador, da Silva, told Philip II in July 1568. In spite of a proclamation expressly forbidding armed men leaving from English ports to aid the rebels in the Low Countries, such people were still going over, supported by "private intimations to the officers of the ports."[95] Until February 1572 the circumstance that the ships and men of the Count de la Marck were permitted to come and go at will provided an additional complicating factor.[96] The whole business got so complex that particular exemptions from general council orders themselves sometimes came into conflict and exceptions ended up having to be made to exceptions. John Hendrie was given a letter in May 1574 to the commissioners for the restraint of grain and victuals in Cornwall, telling them to permit him to export 200 quarters of wheat to London, as long as "the provision of her majestie's shippes be served notwithstanding."[97] Altogether the fact that it made exceptions to its own instructions (never mind exceptions to ex-

93. PRO, SP.12/95, no. 62, obligation by Sir Thomas Gresham to make certain pieces of ordnance for the King of Denmark, March 21, 1574.

94. APC, VIII, 232, May 1, 1574.

95. CSP Spanish, II, no. 38, p. 52, da Silva to the queen, July 14, 1568; no. 39, p. 54 and no. 41, p. 59, da Silva to the King of Spain, July 17 and 19, 1568.

96. Hatfield House, MS. 157, f. 104, the queen to the mayor and corporation of Dover, February 21, 1572, as quoted in Murdin, 210–211.

97. APC, VIII, 232, May 1, 1574.

ceptions, even for apparently good and sufficient reason) must have helped to undermine respect for the council's wishes and encouraged people to take its commands at least a little less seriously than they might have otherwise. In any case, the cycle of disregard went on.

Another reason for its continuance stemmed from the difficulties involved in conveyance—the conveyance of anything anywhere in the sixteenth century. Communications were terrible. The only way the council's orders could be transmitted was physically, by messengers carrying instructions to be delivered either by word of mouth or in the form of a letter. Couriers could travel either by road or water. Both were agonizingly slow, and the council did nothing to speed up either. Boats drifted downstream little faster than they could be rowed or sailed up. There were no canals. The roads were dirt and crooked and the only way they could be traveled faster than on foot was on horseback. Pursuivants, pages, footmen, ushers, messengers of the Chamber and chancery and all the other amateur errand-boys the council made use of traveled across England by post horse, and both queen and council repeatedly issued orders aimed at keeping the posts working with some degree of efficiency. It was impossible, as Francis Knollys, complaining from the north in 1568 of the "slowe spede" of the mails, clearly realized.[98] The use of the posts was supposed to be restricted to official business, yet some people had been managing to make use of them for private purposes.[99] Queen and council therefore insisted that "no poste shall deliver anie horse to anie man that ridethe in poste, except he firste shewe his commission signed either by the queen's majestie, three of the lordes of her majestie's councell, the Erle Mareschall . . . the Lord President or . . . Vicepresident of the northe, the three wardens . . . and . . . their deputies, and the masters of her majestie's postes."[100] But they were not willing to pay the price which such a monopoly commanded. The queen herself, at one point, instructed Thomas Randolph that the posts were to be discharged unless they were willing to serve for half their normal wages.[101] The result of such a policy was inefficiency in service and petitions to the council from the people of towns that were on the postal

---

98. BM, Cotton MS. Caligula C. i, f. 107 and 216, Knollys to Cecil, June 21 and October 29, 1568.

99. "So lucrative were . . . receipts from private letters that many applicants were willing to pay for appointment as deputy postmasters." John, Lord Stanhope, appointed Postmaster-General in 1590, and his son Charles, who succeeded him, both profited greatly from their tenure of the office. Joseph C. Hemmeon, *The History of the British Post Office* (Cambridge, Mass., 1912), 8–9.

100. PRO, SP.12/96, f. 193, the queen's orders for the posts, no date.

101. PRO, SP.12/46, no. 22, the queen to Thomas Randolph, February 4, 1568.

routes, who claimed that they were "not able to abide yt, we are so overchardged."[102]

Weeks sometimes went by between the council's ordering of a letter to be written and receipt of a reply. In 1577 a shire by shire survey of the number of alehouses, taverns, inns and victualling places of the realm was decided on. There is no note of this in the register, but instructions to that effect must have been sent out because the State Papers Domestic contain reports referring to them, the first of which, that of the muster commissioners of Staffordshire, is dated October 3.[103] From then on, other responses trickled in over the next few months. The justices of the peace of Devon, however, stated flatly on October 4 that they had not even started on the job and were not going to be able to until after Christmas.[104] The certificate demanded of them was not ultimately produced until just before the middle of January the following year.[105] Misunderstanding or a mistake in the form of communications received could be pleaded. The piracy commissioners of Lincolnshire were not able to draw up the review of the state of maritime security in their area they had been asked for because their deputies had not been properly authorized, they said, to administer oaths. The commission appointing them had reputedly been at fault.[106]

Intermediaries, such as slow, unofficial letter-carriers, confusion of one sort or another and the Dogberry-like characters who were, often enough, the ultimate executors of council orders, could all be blamed for ineffective implementation of the council's policies. Lord Cobham, excusing himself for the unsatisfactory Sussex musters of late 1580, claimed "your letters of the xxth of December last . . . cam to my handes the xth of this present moneth of Januarie" and because of this and various other delays—none of which, he is careful to assert, were the council's fault—he asked "your good Lordshippes to graunte some resonable time for the better doeing therof."[107] There was nothing they could do but accede to his request. The whole business of the transmission of council orders could become *very*

---

102. PRO, SP.12/127, no. 65, the people of Grantham to the council, 1578.

103. PRO, SP.12/116, no. 3, the Staffordshire muster commissioners to the council, October 3, 1577.

104. *Ibid.*, no. 4, Devon justices of the peace to the council, October 4, 1577.

105. PRO, SP.12/122, no. 5, Devon muster commissioners to the council, January 11, 1578.

106. *Ibid.*, no. 20, Lincolnshire piracy commissioners to the council, January 27, 1578.

107. PRO, SP.12/147, no. 13, Lord Cobham to the council, January 17, 1581.

mixed up. Sir John Gilbert "verie hoatly" demanded of John Weston "howe I durste keepe the counsell's letters from him, which were sente to him, and by what authoritie I keapte them, to whome I saide that I kepte none from hym." Gilbert, however, claimed to have had recent letters from the council asking why he had not answered earlier ones. Weston, in refuting Gilbert's charges, admitted that he *had* had *some* letters from both the Lord Admiral and the council—not, apparently, addressed to Gilbert—but then seemed to feel it necessary to excuse himself for having confessed even this much, which "a duetifull officer unto your honors mighte happely have otherwise keapte unto himself secreate," even if he had not gone so far as to say what was in the letters.[108] In 1580 the Bishop of Chichester made a not-unprecedentedly ineffectual gesture towards doing the council's bidding. He wrote directly to the minister and constable of each parish in his diocese to obtain the information the council required of him. That this was quite regular is shown by the number of occasions on which people as low down on the scale of command as parish constables not only were used in this manner, but also reported directly to the council after the receipt of such relayed instructions.[109] But it was not a very reliable proceeding. The certificates the bishop got back were most imperfect. The names and addresses of those refusing to go to church were too often just plain wrong, and many people capable of proving their conformity had been included. The hapless prelate was therefore instructed to do the job again and this time to call in Sir Thomas Shirley, George Goringe and Richard Shelley to assist him.[110]

There was rarely any need for outright defiance of the council's authority. Its purposes could be frustrated, unintentionally by laziness or incompetence or, more deliberately, by default. Insufficiently precise wording of laws and statutes and orders and proclamations made locally convenient interpretation easy. Ministerial good nature was not hard to trade on. The council was not long in discovering, for example, that its kindness towards that William Shelley whom it had let out of the Fleet prison to go home to visit a sick wife and a failing mother-in-law, had been

---

108. Hatfield House, MS. 160, f. 43, John Weston to the Lord Admiral, May 9, 1575.

109. PRO, SP.12/81, nos. 15, 16, 17, 20, 40, 42 and 43, certificates of rogues and vagabonds taken and punished "accordinge unto the precept unto us directed for the purpose from the quene's majestie's justices of the peace in the" county of Oxford by the constables of the hundreds of Chadlington, Ploughley, Billingeton, Bampton, Bullington, Dorchester and Pirton, 1571.

110. West Sussex Record Office, Episcopal Archives, Episc 1/37/1, October 1580.

misguided. The overly trusted recusant, it learned, was planning a "solemne and extraordinary Christmas, a thing very inconvenient for him, standing in suche termes of disobedience to her majestie and her lawes." Sir George Bromley, therefore, was instructed to take "bondes of him on the sodaine" (by materializing from behind an arras perhaps?) to appear before the council on St. Stephen's day and to check up on who attended the ill-starred party, should the Shelley womenfolk decide to hold it anyway.[111]

As Lord Cobham reported in 1570, in spite of their being against the law and notwithstanding the council's admonitions to the officers of the queen's ports to prevent them, the comings and goings of "merchants" who were not merchants at all were virtually constant, a fact hardly to be wondered at.[112] The most detailed investigation, whether by councillor or constable, of the credentials of every passenger on every ship or smack seeking to depart from every English port or creek, harbor or haven, and the establishment of the identity, financial standing and business qualifications of each would-be traveler could still leave it uncertain in many cases who was and who was not a bona fide merchant or fisherman within the meaning of the applicable statute; but even cursory examination of this sort was impossible most of the time, and there was little the council could do about it. There was no police. There was virtually no army, since the queen's guard could not safely be taken off the duty of protecting Elizabeth's person and used for other purposes. There was no one and no body that the council could send out to force, if necessary, obedience to its commands. Much of the time, therefore, there was no alternative to exhortation. And so, often enough, the council's commands were simply ignored.

The justices of the peace in Berkshire had been ordered to take bonds from everyone refusing to go to church to make their appearance in person before the council and explain themselves. They found, however, that some people who were undoubtedly guilty flatly refused either to pay or to appear. They therefore wrote to the council, completely at a loss as to how to act under such circumstances, to ask for further instructions.[113] The town fathers of distant Chester were equally independent. Francis Walsingham had recommended a servant of his, Peter Proby, to the city for the reversion of the clerkship of the Pentice there. Proby, felt the mayor and aldermen, was not qualified for the job and they told

---

111. APC, XIII, 286, December 12, 1581.

112. PRO, SP.12/73, no. 23, Lord Cobham to Cecil, August 18, 1570.

113. PRO, SP.12/59, no. 36, the justices of the peace of Berkshire to the council, November 25, 1569.

Walsingham so in no uncertain terms. What is more, they told his colleagues too, maintaining their position even in the face of the council's reiterated support of Proby's suit.[114]

In spite of all their admitted busyness, Queen Elizabeth's councillors scarcely attempted to do anything really positive to change the basic situation in which they found themselves. They might have made the effort and, even if they had failed, as they may well have done, gone down with colors flying, which would at least have commanded respect. They did not.

Indeed at least one of the methods of enforcement they attempted to make use of testifies implicitly to the weakness of the system as a whole. By taking bonds from people in hopes of thereby making it worth their while to be obedient, the council was really setting a price for breaking the law. This was tantamount to admitting it had no truly effective coercive system at all.

Similarly, ordering the Lord Warden of the Cinque Ports to obtain as much information as he could about those "knowne to be proceeded in [to] Fraunce," the use of approved travelers to report on the overseas doings of the *un*approved—Robert Barrett, in 1581, wrote four discourses on his foreign journeyings, including in them a list of all the expatriate English Catholics he had met—and the resulting compilations of the names of those known to have left the country without permission are all further evidence of conciliar impotence.[115] The council disapproved of such people. It disapproved of those who sent them money enabling them to stay overseas.[116] And it also objected to their coming home, since when they came back of their own accord, it was not usually to beg for forgiveness, but with quite another purpose in mind, and they were liable to do "great micheyf."[117] So the gentlemen living along the coasts were instructed to keep such people out, and the deputy-lieutenants, in a sort of

---

114. City of Chester Record Office, MS. M/L/5, no. 203, the council to the mayor, recorder and aldermen of Chester, June 27, 1589. Nos. 176–217 of this volume are all concerned with the case of Peter Proby and his suit for the clerkship of the Pentice.

115. Kent Record Office, New Romney MSS. (unsorted), the council to Lord Cobham, August 2, 1564; PRO, SP.12/83, no. 63, the names of rebels now overseas, 1571; BM, Lansdowne MS. 19, no. 29, Smith to Burghley, May 3, 1574; PRO, SP.12/147, nos. 38–41, four discourses on his foreign travels by Robert Barrett, January 1581.

116. PRO, SP.12/47, no. 7, submission of William Roper before the council for having sent money to persons who had left the realm without the queen's licence, 1568(?); CSP Spanish, II, no. 37, p. 50, da Silva to the King of Spain, July 10, 1568.

117. Kent Record Office, New Romney MSS. (unsorted), the council to Lord Cobham, February 3, 1577.

backstop arrangement, to examine those who succeeded in slipping through this first line of defense.[118] In 1580 there was an added problem: English soldiers were deserting from service in the Low Countries and then attempting to get home without, naturally enough, a passport from their generals. The Lord High Admiral, as Lord Lieutenant of Surrey and Sussex, was ordered to prevent such entries continuing.[119]

This particular problem affected only the southern coast of England. But, although the commissioners of ports and havens reported in 1578 that there were no landing places in Denbighshire for the council to worry about, the west coast constituted an area of concern in its own right, owing to its proximity to Ireland, which provided an ideally located base for infiltrators bent on illegal entry.[120] The mayor and corporation of Chester were, we know, warned later in the century to make sure that seditious persons did not succeed in getting through in the guise of legitimate traders, and their intercepted correspondence showed that Agnes Mordaunt and Richard Sefton, both recusants, carried on a seditious interchange of letters with people in Ireland through the port of Chester. There is no reason to suppose that the phenomenon was a new one.[121] Illicit intercourse with foreign parts continued unabated.

The council was merely coping with existing conditions, and not very systematically or effectively at that. An incident that could well stand as the original inspiration for a sentimental episode in a romantic novel about the glorious reign of Good Queen Bess drives the point home. Writing to a Mr. Barton, when its letter is read with this contention in mind, the council gives evidence against itself.

> The queen's majestie removinge yesterdaie from Ewelme to this towne, to avoide thextremitye of a showre chaunced to come into a ten[emen]te called Smithes, belonginge to the lordship of Stoke, which, as hir majestie is enformed, you doe holde in fe fearme of the colledge of Christchurche in Oxforde. And as hir majestie was by reason of the foule shower

---

118. BM, Harleian MS. 703, f. 46, the council to the deputy-lieutenants of Sussex, February 16, 1593; f. 47, the council to certain gentlemen, no date.

119. *Ibid.*, new f. 41v, the council to Howard of Effingham, September 30, 1585.

120. PRO, SP.12/124, no. 11, the commissioners of ports and havens to the council, May 20, 1578.

121. City of Chester Record Office, MS. M/L/1, no. 56, the council to the mayor and corporation of Chester, February 22, 1594; MS. M/L/5, nos, 128–243, various papers relating to the allegedly seditious activities of Agnes Mordaunt and Richard Sefton, 1594.

abiding in the bearne of the pore tenn[an]tes, hir highnes chanced to question with an aged woman dwellinge in the same copie holde, to understande howe longe she had dwelte therein, and what intereste she had for contynewance. Wheareuppon it did appeare unto hir majestie that she had tearme only for herself and one sonne, whoe is also of good yeres, and hathe sondrye children livinge, whoe, after theire father's lief, are to have nothinge lefte for their releife. And findinge by the saide olde wooman and hir sonne that they have noe hope to obteyne any further intereste after the presente state expired, she tooke great compassion upon them, and of hir majestie's only grace and mere goodnes, hathe comaunded us to wryte theise our earneste letters unto you to move you to have charitable consideracion towardes the saide ten[an]tes, that they may have further state in theire coppie for other lives to some of his children upon a reasonable fine. . . . [The queen has heard that Barton has been making a practice of taking over copyholds as they fall in] wheareby not only houses be dispeopled, but hir subjectes undone and begered, which manner of dealinge hir highnes takethe to be very harde and extreame.[122]

The words which are important here are "of hir majestie's only grace and mere goodnes," for in using them the council accepts, on its own behalf and on Elizabeth's, full responsibility for its view of its task, and the way in which it carried that task out. It was well aware of the horrors and terrors of vagrancy, and its states plainly in this letter that if Mr. Barton's poor tenants are evicted they are likely to be "undone and begered." Yet respect for the system, for the *status quo* and for the laws and customs of England, as they happened to exist on the day when Mary Tudor was alive and dead, was so strong and so taken for granted that the possibility of doing anything except appealing to a greedy landlord's clearly nonexistent sense of feudal obligation does not appear to have crossed their minds.

Admittedly, even the queen was bound by the laws of the land—that is, was herself subject to certain specific restrictions. As the same letter implies, although she and her council could vary the enforcement and influence the interpretation of the law, they could go clean against it only when doing so was sufficiently uncontroversial as to be unlikely to arouse widespread opposition. Here the law pretty clearly backed the holder of

122. BM, Add. MS. 32323, f. 128v, the council to Mr. Barton, September 21, 1572.

the lordship of Stoke, and trying to set it aside would have given rise to the same kind of stubborn resistance from the legal profession (to which Barton would have resorted for support) that the Earl of Leicester encountered in the chief justice of the court of King's Bench in 1571.

Elizabeth and her advisers were victims of circumstances in general. It would have almost certainly been impossible to attempt a policy of great innovation—to try and do something about this kind of injustice—early in the reign. The experience of trouble resulting from too much change, pushed too fast, under Edward and Mary militated against it, and there were in any case powerful and comparatively constant forces rigidly opposed to altering society in any but the most personally profitable ways. The system of clientage, brilliantly described by Wallace MacCaffrey and Sir John Neale, was firmly entrenched because it provided the remuneration for services rendered that the Crown was unable to pay directly out of its limited financial resources.[123] The law, so often slow and ineffectual in dispensing justice, provided a lucrative livelihood for its hordes of practitioners, most of them, therefore, being only too happy to leave things as they were. The councillors themselves were not notably sympathetic to adventure; Burghley, as Lawrence Stone has shown, identified so little with youthful tendencies towards rebellion against established authority that his aristocratic wards, once they escaped his tutelage, tended to run riot in reaction to the dour restraint he had formerly imposed upon them.[124] It could certainly be argued with a degree of plausibility that "the times were not ripe" for even the mildest of revolutions.

Yet surely none of this means that caution *had* to be the watchword of the entire last half of the sixteenth century, at least to the extent it was. There is a time to retreat and retrench in all things; but equally, there is a time to emerge from cover and take the offensive, to consider the possibility that those who allow their own lives (and careers) to remain conditioned by their environment indefinitely are liable to end up the creators of crisis for others, especially those who come after them. The kind of argument which suggests that lack of innovation is not surprising because no one can be expected to have seen the long-range need for it is untenable, just as the contention that the English council must be praised simply because it did a better job than its French and Spanish counterparts

123. W. T. MacCaffrey, "Place and Patronage in Elizabethan Politics," printed in *Elizabethan Government and Society*, essays presented to Sir John Neale, edited by S. T. Bindoff and others, (London, 1961), 95–126; J. E. Neale, *Essays in Elizabethan History* (London, 1958), 59–84, "The Elizabethan Political Scene."

124. Lawrence Stone, *The Crisis of the Aristocracy, 1558–1641* (Oxford, 1965), 582.

is irrelevant. Both have been put forward. Certainly one should not blame the dead because they did not do things we think they might have done or take action we consider they ought to have taken, and it would be equally foolish to judge either persons or institutions of the past without viewing them in the context of their own times. But their achievement should not, therefore, be spared from criticism that aims at evaluating it in the light of those sufficiently unchanging criteria as can legitimately be used to gauge the accomplishments of any groups or individuals operating in similar situations, no matter when they happen to have lived and worked. States need sound finance, just laws, easily accessible courts, means of maintaining their security and effective methods of sampling the currents of significant opinion; governments exist to provide such things. Their reputation stands or falls according to how well they do so.

The later sixteenth century was a time of great intellectual sophistication among thinking people, among whom the Privy Councillors must obviously be numbered. The subject of human possibilities was not only common in such circles but was one whose ramifications were examined from almost every possible point of view. The works of Shakespeare alone make this amply clear, although they are not unique in this respect; other writers were concerning themselves similarly with the lot and potential of humanity, and the output of many of them was being read by and performed before audiences perhaps not as knowledgeable but quite as involved in the issues being talked about as the authors themselves. Shakespeare, however, more effectively than anyone else both showed men what they might aspire to and depicted them as they were. On the one hand Hamlet, regarding his kind as patricians of the intellect, raising themselves almost to divinity through the use of their rational faculty, implies there is almost nothing they cannot do. "Noble in reason, in form and moving ... like a god," man's potential is infinite.[125] On the other hand Gloucester, seeing around him only superstitious plebians, denies responsibility for anything. "These late eclipses of the sun and moon portend no good to us," he laments; "we have seen the best of our time." It is left for Edmund to speak for the majority. "We make guilty of our disasters," he retorts, "the sun, the moon and the stars, as if we were fools by heavenly compulsion."[126] Men, then as now, whether Privy Councillors or private citizens, tend to blame circumstances for their lack of accomplishment, in order to avoid acknowledging, even to themselves, that they have not done all that—they *know*—they might have, to make the world a better place.

Although the council was exhorted, figuratively speaking, by Hamlet,

---

125. William Shakespeare, *Hamlet*, II, ii.
126. Shakespeare, *King Lear*, I, ii.

Edmund gave it an excuse for not trumpeting abroad its own shortcomings. Later generations, too, have tended to keep quiet about them, tending to blame everything but the chief instrument of Elizabethan royal government—the Stuarts and all their works especially—for the post-Tudor difficulties of the English state, difficulties that were to overwhelm and almost completely destroy it in the 1640s, difficulties we admit even Elizabeth herself would have had more and more trouble coping with, had she lived. The queen was dead, and her councillors along with her, by the time things got completely out of hand, and so the council has been exonerated from responsibility, at least by implication. It should not have been, at least not so totally and automatically. Events cast their shadows before them, to be perceived by those who have eyes that look out on the world with a critical understanding. Institutional and social pollution is as easily seen, and *fore*seen, as dangers to the environment and its ecological balance. Responsibility for knowing that something is wrong, yet doing little or nothing about it is always heavy. The council could, at worst, have done more than it did to avert the ultimate disaster.

Under the leadership of someone as capable as, say, Thomas Cromwell, the council could, indeed, have accomplished a great deal. Prodded by a more driving spirit, Walter Mildmay was eminently capable, professionally, of working out a scheme of fiscal reorganization as sound as Robert Cecil's Great Contract; but nobody pushed him. Complaints about the inadequacy of official salaries were constant, shrill and obviously sincere; even so, no plan was envisaged for increasing them as part of a general financial and bureaucratic overhaul, which Mildmay, Burghley and Walsingham who, most of the time, worked comfortably enough together, could have put into effect as well as anyone. Similarly, no one suggested law reform, although the men were readily available who could have carried it out. Lord Keeper Bacon was probably too set in the old ways to have been easily moved to take the lead, but Lord Chancellor Bromley was the kind of man who could have done it, shown the necessity, and his successor, Hatton, had exactly the right personality to still the fluttering among the legal dovecotes that drastic alterations in the judiciary would certainly have aroused. What a matchless team, too, the Privy Council of the seventies could have mounted to take on parliament, whose cooperation would have been as necessary (but surely no more impossible to obtain) for the reform of almost anything as it had been in the days of Henry VIII. Walsingham and Mildmay could have handled the Puritan vote, Knollys and Bacon rallied the conservatives while Hatton appealed to the uncommitted.

Naval affairs did not go badly as it was. Could it have been because the navy was presided over for so long by a capable individual (Lincoln) who *was* encouraged in providing dynamic leadership, by a queen and council that *did* see, in this one instance, a need for modernity so pressing it could hardly have been overlooked under any circumstances? The idea is worth considering, especially since less effective adjustment to altered, and altering, conditions in the military sphere can probably be attributed to the council's, and Elizabeth's, lack of conviction that a real army was something they and England needed. In this instance they may well have been right; in any event, the militia, which they did value, was in better shape by the end of the reign than it had been at the beginning, thanks to conciliar persistence. But on the whole the council merely muddled through, and this is still accepted as being an achievement in itself. If it is, it is a limited one, overrated because pragmatism has come to be a supposedly English virtue so widely admired and taken for granted that those of us who have grown up and now thrive in an Anglo-Saxon environment tend to assume that anything that looks like an example of it occurring in times past is a good thing. It is not always so, by any means. In the latter part of the sixteenth century the council's tendency to let things be, unless taking an initiative were forced upon it, was at the very least regrettable. A reasonably convincing start on dealing with just one of the problems already mentioned would have not only made its own eventual solution that much more likely, it would have set the pace for tackling others. That start was not made.

In 1641 the still essentially Tudor state collapsed. The following year, for the first time in over a century and a half—and for the last time up to the present—civil war, that most vivid testimony of all to failure, both personal and institutional, rent the English nation. To blame its coming on the Elizabethan Privy Council would be absurd. There were many times after the death of Elizabeth when the rot, which ultimately resulted in the actual dissolution of so many of the basic components of the national organism, could have been stopped. Yet the war came, and, at the very least, the Privy Council could have helped prevent it. A state whose institutions had been adequately adapted to changed and changing conditions could have survived even Charles I. Earlier abolition of archaic, feudal ways of raising money would have made the royal financial expedients that underpinned the Personal Rule impossible, for one thing. But such adaptation, on the whole, was neither advocated nor implemented early enough, and for that the Privy Council must share some of the responsibility. Mr. Barton had obviously reached the stage where he was not conducting his affairs along the lines of old-fashioned theory. Perhaps the Queen of England and her closest associates need not have been doing so either. As it was, they never did decide that the time had come to take the offensive, or prove capable of the effort of mind that would have been required to take the fullest advantage of the splendid opportunity they had conjured up for themselves to exercise great leadership in the implementation of great ideas.

The 1570s came closest to being the perfect time. The settling-in period of the reign was over. The council was experienced. The international crises that so catch the attention of later observers of the sixteenth century scene were continuing, but not continuous. To contemporaries they even appeared the exception rather than the rule, the recorder of Warwick going so far as to speak of the queen's realm having "not been touched with any troublous season, the rude blast of one insurrection except.[127] . . . There was a buoyancy in the whole economy and society of mid-Elizabethan England. . . . About 1575 . . . the tide of prosperity really turned . . . . , economic activity was at a higher level than for some years past; and, for a time, the queen governed a smiling land."[128] The time was ripe for change, then if ever, but the kind of changes we have been considering did not occur. The councillors were already too set in their ways; perhaps that is why. In any event, by the eighties, if it was not too late—and it could never have been too late, the way things turned out —at least the immediate situation had deteriorated so markedly as to make the possibility of long-range planning much less likely. Room to maneuver had been restricted, by English involvement in the Netherlands before 1588, by outright war with Spain thereafter; the moment was lost.

The age of Elizabeth was one of great achievement in many areas, especially those of essentially private activity, but in the last resort the overriding characteristic of its public life was unoriginality and lack of imagination. The history of the Privy Council in the 1570s makes this sadly clear.

---

127. Joel Hurstfield, *Elizabeth I and the Unity of England* (New York, 1960), 85.
128. *Ibid.*, 106–107.

Part IV
The Council's Achievement

Chapter XIV

CONCLUSION

 VER and over again in the history of the West, times of revolution have been followed by reaction, periods of rapid change by a comparative slowing down in the process of social, political or economic development and ages of confidence in the superiority of the present by eras which looked nostalgically back to some relatively distant, supposedly better past. The Napoleonic monarchy rose from the ruins of the republic and Bourbon restoration followed Bonapartist reforms. The New Economic Policy succeeded the first flush of communization after the Bolshevik take-over in Russia, just as marriage has come back into fashion there after being for a while in disrepute. Romanticism's gushing idealization of the Middle Ages was an entirely understandable, if depressing response to the cool pride of the Enlightenment in modern civilization's own achievements. Woodrow Wilson's lunge into international involvement presaged Franklin Roosevelt's and Harry Truman's extension of American influence in world affairs, but it soon lost momentum when the United States withdrew into the isolationism of Harding, just as much of the spirit of the New Deal petered out under Eisenhower in the socially unconcerned fifties. Advance has almost always been followed by retrenchment, or even retreat, and many, even among those who believe most passionately in the idea of progress, would maintain that such cycles of ebb and flow in human affairs are essential if an overall forward movement is to be indefinitely kept up. The tide comes in and goes out, but the alluvium rises inexorably out of the sea and, in driving back the drowning element, serves the cause of man even at high water.

The disparagement of the Elizabethan Privy Council essayed in the preceding pages, in other words, does not necessarily mean that its sins of omission totally outweigh the virtues of its accomplishments. Criticism can be complimentary. Only of those who have already done great things is it realistic to hope for greater, and negative comment on the council's achievement was made only after the premise had been established that its lords and others were competent, hardworking and responsible patriots who aimed at the consolidation of a financially respectable, just and popular monarchy. It may be regrettable that not one member of the council, once appointed, grew in mental stature sufficiently thereafter to put forward radical new ideas, or demonstrated willpower strong enough to override the cautious queen and get them implemented. Cecil, in a long series of memoranda, admittedly proposed numerous practical reforms, of great value as far as they went; some of them, such as the 1560 recoinage, were actually carried out. But no one suggested permitting parliament to play a larger role in policy making, say, in return for the establishment of some kind of realistic taxation system that would have ended, or at least eased, the Crown's chronic financial difficulties. Nor was there any concerted attempt, which might well have been made, to play upon the queen's well-known distaste for bishops by way of opening up a path towards further ecclesiastical reorganization, possibly extending even to the ultimate abolition of the episcopate itself. Had such a prophet—a man of vision dynamic enough to carry his fellows along with him, thus, in effect, using the council's overwhelming masculinity as the potent weapon it could have been for the overawing of a single woman—arisen within the ruling circle, she might conceivably have listened to him—have *had* to listen—with less antagonism than she reacted, for example, to what she regarded as the insolent preaching at her, from outside, of such a man of principle as Archbishop Grindal. But the times and circumstances produced only gentlemen. To suggest, therefore, that Elizabeth's Privy Councillors could have done more than they did to reach goals they did not even aim for, is to judge them by ideal rather than realistic standards, and to assert that they failed to do all they might have done is to make no denial of their actual achievement.

Moreover, particularly if we accept the fact that another Thomas Cromwell did not—could hardly have been expected to—appear *ex machina* or from the head of Gloriana to provide the drive whose absence we can nevertheless regret, many of the strictures that can be made against the council of the later sixteenth century seem actually unfair. Its members were all selected for their compatibility with her, as well as for their ability, by a queen who was herself not much interested in innovation. Unlike Henry VIII, Elizabeth, as Water Mildmay boasted in parliament in 1576 when praising her parsimony, was not a great or dedicated builder.[1] She was quite content to live in other people's houses.[2] Her councillors were not, but they shared the queen's conservatism even so.

Their new edifices were hardly monuments of originality and they themselves scarcely pioneers in any field of endeavor. Almost all half-educated at best at universities where the curricula were classical and at law schools amongst the most tradition-oriented anywhere; living at a

---

1. J. E. Neale, *Elizabeth I and her Parliaments, 1559–1581* (New York, 1958), 348.
2. Ian Dunlop, *Palaces and Progresses of Elizabeth I* (London, 1962).

time when the highest accomplishment—that of the Tudor dynasty, hosannaed by Holinshed and sung by Shakespeare—was considered to be restoration of stability and resurrection of the glories of a mythical past stretching back at least to Arthur; deeply indoctrinated with the belief in a universe of which the fundamental characteristic was established order; middle-aged, sober and respectable as they almost all were by the time they were finally admitted to the seats of power, it is scarcely surprising that Elizabeth's councillors did not blaze new trails through the social, political and economic jungles of sixteenth century England.

This inherently conservative council, presided over by a determinedly unprogressive queen, inherited an intrinsically extremely difficult general situation. The periphery of England is an eccentric one, crinkled with creeks, honeycombed with harbors and bordered with beaches, lonely even now, perfectly suited for clandestine embarkations and arrivals. Father Gerard landed easily enough on one near Happisburgh, between Great Yarmouth and Cromer, in 1588 and such people as "one Nippevyle," whom the council directed the queen's officers in general to prevent escaping to France in 1577, stood a good chance of getting away from somewhere or other along the cooperative coast.[3] It was not the queen's and the council's fault the royal income was insufficient. English roads had been disgraceful since the departure of the Romans. The untitled, rural English aristocracy had been used to having its own way at the local level and to the monarch's accepting the situation since at least the time of Edward I. Enjoying liberties granted them by previous sovereigns, boroughs and corporations could often quite legally go their own sweet ways without the council being able to do a thing about it. It had been Henry VIII and the ministers of his last years, not Elizabeth I and William Cecil who had permitted the confiscated lands of the Church to enrich the gentry in the long run rather than the Crown, thus strengthening provincial independent-mindedness rather than aiding the process of centralization. The dice were already heavily loaded against further enhancement of the power of the royal government even at the beginning of Elizabeth's reign. This political fact of life was to a great extent disguised by the council's very success in making the existing system work as well as it did, but it was not changed and it did not conveniently go away.

Even supposing that the council had wished to strike out in novel and constructive, not to say revolutionary directions, it simply was not free to

---

3. John Gerard, *The Autobiography of a Hunted Priest* (New York, 1955), 35; Kent Record Office, New Romney MSS (unsorted), the council to the queen's officers, July 5, 1577.

hew an independent line. In practice, as well as in theory, the queen's wishes were paramount. In 1580 Lord Hunsdon, in Berwick, confided to the Earl of Huntingdon, the Lord President of the Council of the North that "apon consultacyon amonge the lords [of the council] by hyr majestie's commandment, they thought ytt fytt to have sent 1000 men more hyther. . . . But when ytt came too hyr majestie's consent, she wolde none of ytt."[4] She "wolde none" of the French ambassador visiting Mary Queen of Scots either, however angry he got at permission being continually refused.[5] If she were absolutely determined not to "arme by sea" no amount of pressure could persuade Queen Elizabeth to do so.[6] And when in 1573 the Lord Keeper agreed with Lord Burghley as to the necessity of calling a parliament, he was under no illusions as to who would make the final decision as to whether it should actually be summoned or not.[7] "Nothyng [is] resolvid," wailed Sir Thomas Smith to the absent Lord Treasurer, in spite of his "daily attendyng, for the most part three or four tymes in the day. . . . And therfor . . . hir majestie's mynisters lie still in suspence."[8] Sir Francis Walsingham, whose daybook is fuller of "queen's memorialls" than of "counsel causes," in his lugubriously apocalyptic way, could only lament the queen's orders to Lord Hunsdon for a wholesale discharge of men in 1581 "by which accompt I see that Scotland is clene lost, and a greate gate opened thereby for the losse of Ireland. My lords here have carefully and faithfully discharged their deuties in sikinge to staye this dangerous course, but God hath thoght good to dispose otherwise of thinges, in whose handes the heartes of all princes are."[9] Even the melodramatic de Spes, although he reported to Philip II on one occasion, apparently entirely on hearsay evidence, that she had been overruled by a unanimous council, was usually fully conscious of Elizabeth's key position. "They cannot," he told Philip in February 1570, "persuade the queen to call parliament together."[10] But it was Robert Naunton, writing when

4. Huntington Library, Hastings MS. 1214, Hunsdon to the Earl of Huntingdon, April 14, 1580.

5. Hatfield House, MS. 8, f. 81, Smith to Burghley, September 10, 1575, as quoted in William Murdin, *Collection of State Papers relating to Affairs in the Reign of Queen Elizabeth* (London, 1759), 288.

6. BM, Harleian MS. 6991, f. 84, Walsingham to Burghley, July 8, 1574; *ibid.*, f. 90, Walsingham to Burghley, July 13, 1574.

7. Hatfield House, MS. 159, f. 115, Bacon to Burghley, September 4, 1573.

8. BM, Harleian MS. 6991, f. 124, Smith to Burghley, March 6, 1575.

9. BM, Harleian MS. 6035, Walsingham's letter book, f. 63, 1583; Huntington Library, Hastings MS 13067, Walsingham to the Earl of Huntingdon, April 5, 1581.

10. CSP Spanish, II, no. 181, p. 237, de Spes to the King of Spain, February 27, 1570.

Queen Elizabeth was still very much a recent and a living memory in England, who summed up the situation most succinctly. "She was," he said, "though very capable of counsel, absolute enough in her own resolutions."[11]

This assertion of the queen's personal importance is not one whit disturbed by the fact that Sir William Cecil, whether as principal secretary or as Lord Treasurer Burghley, was openly regarded by his contemporaries and colleagues as the first minister of the state, or the circumstance that her advisors sometimes sought to guide her action by censoring the information she received. Edmund Tremayne described Cecil as "he that sitteth at the helm in the ship of government of this common weale."[12] He did not call him the captain. The queen and the council depended on Cecil's judgment, and he certainly occcupied the position of the queen's most trusted lieutenant. He was in no sense the equivalent of a modern premier. If he did not have the trouble in actually getting to see Elizabeth that Sir Thomas Smith had as secretary, he was nonetheless equally dependent on her living habits. "The queen's majesty . . . is not styrring," he told Sir Ralph Sadler on one occasion, "and therefore can I wryte nothyng at this tyme."[13] "The queen's majesty had a disposition to have my Lord Kepar and me, with Sir Ralph Sadler, to abyde at London," he remarked to the Earl of Sussex on another occasion. "I know not yet why, [but] I shall do as I am commanded."[14] Nor did he by any means always exert an irresistible influence over appointments. "I have a desyre to have Sir William Pykeryng vic[e] chamberlayn," he confided to Sadler in 1570. "But others they saye lyke better of an other that lately was here in custody. God send hir majesty a faythfull counseller."[15] He did—but not Sir William.

The limitations on Cecil's power with and over Elizabeth are reflected in his relationship with the Earl of Leicester and Leicester's relationship with the queen. Cecil could, and did, draw up a document headed "Certen matters wherin the queen's majestie's forbearing and delayes hath produced, not only inconveniences and incress of expences, but also dangers."[16] He could not always count on Elizabeth's paying much attention to it. However, Leicester's privileged position as a royal intimate gave him a freedom

---

11. Robert Naunton, *Fragmenta Regalia* (London, 1824), 10.

12. PRO, SP.12/132, no. 5, Edmund Tremayne to Burghley, September 14, 1579.

13. BM, Cotton MS. Caligula C. iii, f. 227, Burghley to Sadler, September 8, 1571.

14. BM, Cotton MS. Titus B. ii, f. 298, Burghley to the Earl of Sussex, July 15, 1574.

15. BM, Add. MS. 33593, f. 141, Cecil to Sadler, January 18, 1570. Sir William Pyckeryng.

16. BM, Cotton MS. Caligula C. iii, f. 425, in Burghley's hand, April 1572.

of access to the queen's attention, as well as to her presence, which was available to no one else, at least until Christopher Hatton's rise to favor. It was to this that Leicester chiefly owed his political importance. "My Lord Lecester is very muche with her majestie, and she sheweth the same great good affection to him that she was wonte," Gilbert Talbot informed his father, the Earl of Shrewsbury, in 1573.[17] It was Leicester who sat up with her until two o'clock in the morning when she had the toothache.[18] So it was Leicester who acted as an often necessary intermediary between Elizabeth and her other important councillors, particularly Cecil and Walsingham, in both public and private affairs. "Lest you shuld think I were negligent in moving her majesty in these thinges," he wrote to Walsingham in 1577, ". . . I thought good to let you knowe . . . her further pleasure."[19]

> For your owne matter [he told Burghley in 1573] I assure you I found her majestie as well dysposed as ever at any tyme . . . and so I trust hit shall alway contynew. God be thanked, her blastes be not the stormes of other princes, though they be very sharp some tymes to those she loves best. Every man must render to her ther dew, and the most bounden most of all. You and I cumme in that ranck, and I am wytnesse hetherto [to] your honest zeal to performe as much as man can. And hit cannott be but yt wyll work satysfactyon, which shalbe a recompense to your toyling boddy, and a great quyeting of your carefull mynd, even in the most trowblesome end of your days. I know your old princypells. Hold them [and] you can never fayll.[20]

But even Leicester was unable to exercise much influence over Elizabeth's actual decisions, and frequently enough, even he could not persuade her to make them at all. "I . . . dealt with her . . . for the removing of the Queen of Scots from Bolton," he wrote to Cecil in 1568," . . . [but] she did not fully resolve [the matter] with me . . . albeyt I se she ys ernest inough."[21]

---

17. Edmund Lodge, *Illustrations of British History*, II (London, 1791), Gilbert Talbot to the Earl of Shrewsbury, May 11, 1573.

18. PRO, SP. 12/126, no. 10, the Earl of Leicester to Burghley, October 17, 1578.

19. PRO, SP.12/75, no. 3, "instructions for the obteyning of a lease for the office of the butlerage, for termes of yeres, at such reasonable rent as the same (by my Lord Treasurer) shalbe thought meete," 1570.

20. BM, Harleian MS. 6991, f. 27, the Earl of Leicester to Burghley, February 12, 1573.

21. BM, Harleian MS. 6990, no. 37, f. 78, the Earl of Leicester to Burghley, October 17, 1568.

Indecision of this sort Walsingham was inclined to attempt to forestall by the judicious editing of the information that actually reached the queen. If a particular matter could be prevented from coming to her attention at all, then the danger of shilly-shallying, or of her coming to a decision of which her council disapproved, was avoided, or at least postponed. The Earl of Huntingdon had written to him in 1581 with what Walsingham regarded as an overly sanguine view of the loyalty of the northern part of the country. He therefore replied, "I must needs tell your Lordship I am not alltogether of your mynd in this matter, but feare a great number of those which make nowe a good shewe of good likying of the present state wowld be fownd verie dangerouse and doubtfull in the obedience to hir majestie, uppon anie suche occasion to bee offred them as the obstinate papists expect of forayne ayde. . . . Therefore I do wyshe in this case hir majestie styl to doubt the worst, and the worst accordingly by hir . . . to bee provided for."²² Sometimes he even took the risk of giving orders without consulting her. He had already advised Huntingdon in an earlier letter the same year to try to form a queen's party among the Scottish borderers without talking to her about it first, "being acquainted with her disposicion in like cases."²³ Burghley evidently got quite used to saying one thing, while Elizabeth did, or talked about doing, another. Scottish affairs, as he remarked to Walsingham with resignation, "keep a tolerable course more by our private fair overtures than by good matter, which, without her majesty's royal assent, we cannot deliver to them."²⁴

These examples of her closest advisers' relationships with Elizabeth reveal the existence of a considerable degree of flexibility and personal, practical autonomy in the system, but at the same time they testify to nothing so strongly as they do to the overriding authority of the queen herself. Walsingham summed up the situation in a letter to Lord Hunsdon in 1584 when he explained that whatever he did was done at the queen's behest, even when she had no apparent hand in the matter. Sometimes he was deliberately made to appear the instigator of a particular policy, the queen being moved "to use the credite of the [secretary's] . . . place in the directing of some speciall services without the use of her owne warrant."²⁵

---

22. Huntington Library, Hastings MS. 13065, Walsingham to the Earl of Huntingdon, March 21, 1581.
23. Huntington Library, Hastings MS. 13055, Walsingham to the Earl of Huntingdon, January 24, 1581.
24. CSP Foreign, 1578–1579, Elizabeth I, volume 13, pp. 163–164, no. 208, Burghley to Walsingham, August 31, 1578.
25. BM, Cotton MS. Julius F. vi, f. 148, Walsingham to Hunsdon, November 7, 1584.

The council was planted firmly in the middle, between a potent monarch on the one hand and an independence-loving gentry on the other, neither of which could be coerced but had to be cajoled. It is surely at best a little surprising (and becomes more so if one can forget, or at least disregard, the comforting legend of Anglo-Saxons having the inherited, almost mystical, ability to make even theoretically impossible political systems work in practice) that the council got anything done at all.

The Privy Council, it appears, was a paradoxical political animal. It was grand, respected and even feared. It had a pedigree as long as that of the monarchy itself. Elizabeth was childless; the Tudor dynasty was therefore doomed to expire with her, and it even seemed for a moment as though the council, rather than any other person or institution, would inherit her sovereign power in the state. A bill was introduced into the house of commons aimed at preventing the anarchy it was long and widely feared would follow the death of the queen if there were no recognized and generally acceptable heir. Had it passed both houses and been given the royal assent, it would have enacted that "the Lord Chauncellor, the Lord Tresurer and all other officers spiritual and temporall whatsoever at the decease of her majesty beinge in authoritye may still remayne in, and continue the exsquution of their saide offices and authority, till the . . . courtes of parliament shall resolve of the rightes and titles offered, and that a newe prince be thereby established and crowned . . . . Till the said parliament shalbe assembled, it shalbe lawful for any fower of her majestie's councell . . . to constitute and ordeyne orders."[26] Passage of such an act would have exalted the council to heights it never in fact reached and could, just possibly, have profoundly affected English constitutional development in the succeeding centuries. The roles of monarch and council would have been reversed, certainly temporarily and possibly even permanently, for the new prince would have been the nominee of a corporate institution that had been publicly and legally empowered "to constitute and ordeyne orders" for which it had to answer to no one. But the bill came to nothing. At least one councillor himself spoke against it— in doing so, incidentally, emphasizing once again the extent to which Elizabeth's ministers were good parliament men as well as loyal servants of the queen—and the monarchy remained the keystone of English public life.[27]

---

26. Northamptonshire Record Office, F (M) P. 4, a speech by Mildmay against an act for declaring an heir to the queen.

27. There is no date on this document, but it seems most likely to have been drawn up for the parliament of 1584, and that in fact Mildmay's speech was never made because Elizabeth's own lack of enthusiasm for the project nipped the proceedings in the bud.

As a defined and formalized institution, the Elizabethan Privy Council was not only a relatively recent creation, it had no long standing tradition of success behind it and none at all of independence. It built up the former; it never achieved the latter. It began its institutional life as an instrument of royal authority with little or no responsibility of its own and, notwithstanding all its apparent grandeur and authority, it remained at the end of Elizabeth's reign almost exactly what it had been at the beginning. A long and brilliant period in English history, dominated by a personality who happened to be a strong as well as a female ruler and who chose to use the council constantly and confidently merely disguised the fact. The council still existed only because the prince wished it to exist. It was the prince's creature. Although it impressed its own time with its dignity and importance, we can see that it never really matured beyond that point. Its later decline stems more from this than anything else. That is why it failed to step into the power vacuum created when the kingship itself eventually broke down. It explains the circumstance that when the monarchy came at last to share and ultimately to abdicate its sovereign authority over Englishmen, the Crown first admitted to participation in the exercise of power and later abandoned its prerogative virtually completely, not to the Privy Council, but to the house of commons. That the house of commons was, in a sense, an earlier council come of age—as a branch of parliament which had itself originally evolved out of the *curia regis*—is perhaps some consolation; it does not change the situation: by 1603 the Privy Council was up a blind alley, and it never thereafter found its way out.

Yet as long as Elizabeth lived and reigned it fulfilled a unique and absolutely necessary function. Monarchy had itself failed in the turbulent middle years of the sixteenth century. From November 17, 1558 on, it not only rallied, it got up off its bed and strode confidently down the corridors of power. It was the existence and effectiveness of the council, coupled with the accident of Elizabeth Tudor's character and personality that made such a spectacular recovery possible, that enabled the still-medieval and, as the following century was to reveal to all the world, essentially archaic institution of royalty to work once more so remarkably effectively.

Sixteenth century Englishmen in general still accepted as valid much ancient propaganda justifying existence of a hierarchical social system.[28] "The heavens themselves, the planets and this centre observe degree, priority and place, insisture, course, proportion, season, form, office and

---

28. E. M. W. Tillyard, *The Elizabethan World Picture* (New York, no date).

custom, all in line of order."[29] Earthly societies, modelling themselves upon the graduations of the cosmos, formed a stratified pyramid, narrowing upwards from the broad mass of the common people at its base to the lone figure of the monarch at its pinnacle. In such an artificially ordered environment, political theory intended for public dissemination could hardly be expected to be devoted to the propagation of the unvarnished truth. It was not. The monarch, where his power was not specifically limited by statutes assented to by him or his predecessors, was supposedly absolute. It was a cardinal principle of English law that the king could do no wrong.[30] He was "the glorious planet Sol in noble eminence enthroned and sphered amidst the other; whose med'cinable eye corrects the ill aspects of planets evil."[31] The body politic was comparable with the human body. The sovereign gave orders to his subjects as assuredly as his own head controlled the movements of his body's members, and a king issuing commands which were not for his people's good was no more conceivable than his brain instructing his hand to plunge a dagger through his heart. Such colorful—one might even say entertaining, certainly instructive—analogies were current throughout the reign of Elizabeth.[32]

The trouble with metaphors, however, is that, although meaningful and useful, they are not exact. Often enough the people who devoted themselves most wholeheartedly to the upholding of the theory of immutable social distinction, according to which each individual had a fixed place and a specific function in life, were those who themselves, or whose immediate ancestors, had disproved its validity in practice, some of Elizabeth's Privy Councillors prominent among them. William Cecil, Lord Burghley, whose sure knowledge of his ancestry extended no further than his great-grandfather, took a positive delight in "frolic[ing] around the facts" in the process of fabricating a pedigree that would seem to locate him by hereditary (the only theoretically acceptable) right as a member of the ruling class.[33]

Personal prominence could actually be achieved by merit; the proprieties

---

29. William Shakespeare, *Troilus and Cressida*, I, iii.

30. William S. Holdsworth, *A History of English Law*, 3rd edn., IX (London, 1944), 4–5; Edward Jenks, *The Book of English Law* (Boston and New York, 1924), 171–172.

31. Shakespeare, *Troilus*, I, iii.

32. One of the principal secretaries himself informs us, for example, that "the prince is the life, the head, and the authoritie of all thinges that be doone in the realme of England." Thomas Smith, *De Republica Anglorum* (London 1583), 47.

33. A. L. Rowse, "Alltyrynys and the Cecils," *EHR*, LXXV, January 1960, 54 *et seq.*

still demanded it be attributed to descent. Similarly, supposedly at least *semi*-divine kings—and certainly queens—were actually human. They were obviously *not* absolute, other than in the sense of their being free from papal or any other superior authority and its being generally acknowledged that they possessed the sensibly "absolute" right to perform such practical services as issuing coinage. In the last resort they could not, alone, force anyone physically stronger than themselves to do what *they* wished rather than what *he* wanted. And they were inescapably fallible, as Mary Tudor had so tragically proved.

It is extremely hard to tell to what extent people like Cecil admitted, even to themselves, these inconsistencies between social and political mirages and reality. Fortunately, at least in this context, private convictions do not matter much. What is relevant is how such people behaved; and they behaved as though the maintenance of the regal supremacy they helped to exercise depended upon the perpetuation of a pyramidal, Crown-capped social system and the continued widespread acceptance of the myth of royal inability to err. It follows that the existing social system had somehow or another to be kept in order and some means found of explaining away situations in which it appeared that the wearer of the Crown had made mistakes. Potentially unconvincing social and political theory had to be buttressed by effective and generally respected regal practice. The feat was accomplished and it was the council that made it possible.

We have already seen how the council went about keeping society at least outwardly unchanged, although the fact was not particularly stressed at the time. It did it primarily by deciding who should be justices of the peace, sheriffs, vice-admirals and so on. The process of selection, as much for social as political reasons, required careful consideration. Cecil, in 1569, expressed anxiety about the increasing "poverty" of the nobility and "almost all gentillmen of service, the wealth being in the meaner sort, which are unmete for service."[34] He was not the only one who worried about such things. The same fear that the social sky was falling can as easily be seen in the Earl of Leicester's almost hysterical appeals to Francis Walsingham for assistance in getting back a young man who had fled from his household to take refuge in France with the Cardinal de Bourbon as in the otherwise incomprehensible amount of attention the council showed itself willing to devote to such apparently trivial matters as the protection of the family pride of a certain Mr. William Huberson.[35] In the first

34. Samuel Haynes, *Collection of State Papers . . . left by William Cecill, Lord Burghley* (London, 1740), "A Short Memoryall," 1569.

35. BM, Cotton MS. Vespasian F. vi, f. 57, the Earl of Leicester to Walsingham, April 23, 1572; APC, VIII, 215, March 22, 1573.

instance Leicester wanted the boy back, not because he was of any particular use, but "to make him an example unto other our servantes not to presume hereafter to abuse their masters." So when Walsingham told him that the lad now wanted to return, Leicester declined to take him on such a voluntary basis, but suggested Walsingham let sleeping dogs lie for a while, then have the culprit suddenly apprehended.[36] In the second case, precedent was again the underlying issue. Thomas Dunye, a mere yeoman and his servant, had "sought privily to contract him self with Mr. William Huberson's daughter." If one lady of such quality could so forget herself as to contemplate marrying beneath her father's dignity, she might not only live to regret her folly—about which fate the council was presumably not much concerned, other than, perhaps, to rejoice at it—but also to set a fashion that would lead to the population of the English countryside with over-ambitious, therefore "unserviceable" and possibly even dangerous nobodies of Dunye's ilk. For the upstart Elizabethan great, it cannot have been a pleasant prospect.

Fortunately for them the system was saved, and served, by enough adequately gentle folk turning up in practice to meet the royal requirements for service, notwithstanding Cecil's lamentations. Throughout Elizabeth's reign the competition among those anxious to work for the Crown was almost literally cutthroat. Lord Delaware, for example, protested vigorously against too great a use of two rival Hampshire notabilities in particular. "The worste of us," he wrote to Leicester, "ys as well able to serve you . . . as ether [Sir Edward] Horse[y] or [Sir Henry] Wallope."[37] In fact, all three of them were occasionally employed, along with most of their social equals in the country and it was not until the 1630s, when Elizabeth had long been dead, that a real problem in finding enough sufficiently well born provincial magistrates and administrators began to bother the central government seriously.[38]

It was in providing a way in which the Crown's errors could be credibly accounted for without the queen's having to take the blame for them, however, that the council played its most important role in English life in the sixteenth century. Elizabeth did almost nothing without taking care to make it appear that what she was doing she did on the council's advice, even if, or, indeed, especially when this was not in fact the case. She was unwilling to let her signature stand alone. "My good lord," wrote Sir

---

36. BM, Cotton MS. Vespasian F. vi, f. 79(2), the Earl of Leicester to Walsingham, May 26, 1572.

37. Longleat House, Dudley MSS., II, f. 113, Lord Delaware to the Earl of Leicester, June 24 [no year given].

38. Thomas Garden Barnes, *Somerset 1625–1640* (Cambridge, Massachusetts, 1961), 303.

Thomas Smith to Lord Burghley from Windsor in 1572, "to this commission of the Cownsel in the North, altho I said it cam from you, I
cannot get her majestie's hand. After all other excuses, she said she was
not wont to sygne such thynges except some bodie's hand wer to it that
all was well conceived, and as it was wont."[39] Only after having conferred
"with our counsell and having advisedly consideryd with them the whole
circumstance" of the answers of the Queen of Scots to the articles that
they had been instructed to charge her with did Elizabeth inform Lord
Burghley and Sir Walter Mildmay that "we have thought meete to express [our decision] hereby at some length unto you."[40] Four closely written pages follow. Burghley wrote to Walsingham after the massacre in
France on St. Bartholomew's Day that "of the queen's majestie's answer to
this ambassador I have at good length comprised the same in a wrytyng
which cometh now to you signed by the counsell."[41] "By the generall
letter from my lords of the counsell to your Lordship," Walsingham informed the Earl of Huntingdon in 1581, "and by the coppie of her
majestie's to the Lord Generall, which I send you herewith, youe may
perceave what resolucion hath ben taken here oppon recipt of yours of the
26th of this present."[42] Instructions to ambassadors, as we have already
seen, were sometimes made out in the queen's name and sometimes in the
council's with no apparently significant reason for their being drawn up
now one way and now the other. What *is* noteworthy is that when they are
in the queen's name they cite the advice of the council and when in the
council's they refer to the pleasure of the queen. The wording of proclamations—"by the advice of our Privy Council"—is merely the most
public expression of the royal determination never to act in isolation if it
could possibly be avoided.

But there is even more to this aspect of the council's role than that. If the
council was invaluable for the queen to have to accuse of having given her
bad advice in the event of her having done something seriously unpopular
—as Burghley expressed it, to assume the responsibility for something that
turned out badly and thus save "the honour of the highest"—it was quite
as useful to her subjects for much the same reason.[43] If royal instructions
were misunderstood or something done of which the queen did not ap-

---

39. BM, Harleian MS. 6991, f. 15, Smith to Burghley, October 15, 1572.
40. BM, Cotton MS. Caligula C. ii, f. 46, the queen to Burghley and
Mildmay, October 13, 1570.
41. BM, Cotton MS. Vespasian F. vi, f. 131, Burghley to Walsingham,
September 11, 1572.
42. Huntington Library, Hastings MS. 13057, Walsingham to the Earl of
Huntingdon, January 31, 1581.
43. Neale, 311.

prove, Tudor fury could be overwhelming. But if those in high authority could somehow be associated with the disprized activity, at least the blame could be shared. In 1570 Lord Cobham was asked for an opinion on the state of the defenses in his liberty of the Cinque Ports. He replied as requested, but, in doing so, left it up to the council to make the final decision as to the actual military furnishings which were to be supplied to Dover Castle, "least yn asking that were necessarye, they chargyes myght seeme to great, and yn requyerynge a smayll forneture, I myght herafter be blamyd."[44]

The council was thus the queen's scapegoat, a responsible buffer between her and public opinion, and her subjects' shield, as sure a guarantor as could be had against the dangers of regal disapproval. The council's operations made possible the functioning of the entire traditional governmental and social system. Without it the two poles, ruler and ruled, would have come into far too close contact for either safety or comfort; the necessary distance between power and those it played on would have become much too narrow, as it did the following century, when the council shrank in stature. The mystery of monarchy might have vanished much earlier than it has. "Neglection of degree" could well have appeared in England at a time of considerable actual mobility in society, with who knows what profound consequences for the future.[45] But the end of domestic tranquillity might easily have turned out to be the immediately painful result, and this was a price for loosening up the social structure few were prepared to pay.

It has become something of a cliché to assert that one of the secrets of Queen Elizabeth's extraordinary popularity in her own time was her knack for keeping her finger on the national pulse, for somehow knowing how her people felt and acting always on the basis of her instinctive understanding of their hopes and fears, both remarkably similar to her own. This was certainly an impression she strove herself to create. "Grante me," she prayed God, "that I may render up and present the same again unto Thee a peaceable, quiet and well-ordered state and kingdome."[46] "If any look for eloquence," she told the parliamentary session of 1576 with carefully calculated self-deprecation, "I shall deceive their hope. . . . I cannot satisfy their longing thirst that watch for those delights. . . . If I should say the sweetest speech with the eloquentest tongue that ever was in man, I were not able to express that restless care which I have ever bent

---

44. PRO, SP.12/73, no. 23, Lord Cobham to Cecil, August 18, 1570.
45. Shakespeare, *Troilus*, I, iii.
46. PRO, SP.12/113, no. 14, instructions for Mr. Martin Furbisher, on the dorse of which is inscribed this prayer of the queen's, May 1577.

to govern for the greatest wealth."[47] Peace, quiet, order, wealth—these
were the words that touched the hearts and minds of sixteenth century
Englishmen. Elizabeth knew it, worked towards achieving a society
characterized by them and rarely missed an opportunity to inform her
subjects of how large a part her own "restless care" for their interests had
played in turning their dreams into reality.

She had not done it alone. The council helped enormously and was able
to, in large part, because its aims were the same as hers. It both strove to
deal justly in all its various concerns and, perhaps even more important,
was believed to be more effective in doing so than some other executives
of the royal prerogative. When Edward Clere, forced loan collector,
appeared before the council accused of presenting people to whom they
had not been addressed with Privy Seals, he denied the charge. This created
an awkward situation. Further evidence was needed, but complainants
were not sent for. The expenses to which they would have been thereby
put would have been exorbitant, and it was not fair, therefore, to ask them
to come all the way to Court to speak against a man they had denounced
for robbing them in the first place. The case was referred back to Clere's
locality for further investigation in his own neighborhood prior to final
council action.[48] The same year, after a vessel belonging to one Thomas
Standley had been shipwrecked, its cargo was simply walked off with by a
local population obviously confident that it could get away with lawless
behavior. William Heydon, assistant to the vice-admiral of the county
in which the incident took place, did his best to help Standley get his property back, but without success, so he recommended going to London to
"gett out of her majestie's court of Admiraltie a comission to searche out
all suche goodes." Standley did so, but seems to have had little real confidence that alone would do him any good. He therefore stayed on to
petition the council for its support as well, asking for "your Lordships'
honorable letter of assistance for the better execution . . . of the said commission, to thend . . . your pore suppliant may attayne to sum parte more
of the said goodes."[49]

The council worked, above all, for "the preservation of . . . good
subjectes [in] quytnes amonge themselves."[50] It was kind even to foreigners in trouble, from time to time taking action, for example, to help

---

47. Neale, 364.
48. BM, Add. MS. 32323, f. 127v; BM, Harleian MS. 4943, f. 129; APC,
VIII, 71, the council to Sir Christopher Heydon and Sir William Buttes, March
1, 1572.
49. PRO, SP.12/131, no. 44, Thomas Standley to the council, July 26, 1579.
50. BM, Harleian MS. 703, f. 10(2), the council to the sheriff and
justices of the peace of Sussex, September 8 [no year given].

out the Hanse merchants when "heynous murders and spoiles [had been] committed against greate nombers of their agentes, factours and servantes upon the seas" by pirates and freebooters, or to see that they were paid the money due to them by their English debtors.[51]

Peace, quiet, order and the wealth that seemed to come in their train were ends in themselves for Queen Elizabeth and her advisers. Maybe these alone should be considered to constitute too low a mark for a society, most of all for its leaders, to strive towards. If it is not, however; if achieving a degree of public safety and satisfaction with the government within the realm of England that contrasted, or seemed to contrast favorably with the disturbed conditions of the fifteenth century, is worthy of respect in its own right, then it would be difficult to maintain that Queen Elizabeth and her Privy Councillors were unsuccessful. At the very least, one could hardly say that the suffering, which the motto of the council committed them to undergo *pro patria*, was entirely vain.

---

51. PRO, SP.12/108, no. 61, Walsingham to Sidney, July 20, 1576; APC, VIII, 341, February 12, 1574.

Bibliography and Index

Bibliography

ANY attempt to describe the sources for the history of the Elizabethan Privy Council must begin with a lament: so many key elements are missing. All those who have ever attended faculty or similar committee meetings know how dangerously misleading and infuriatingly uninformative minutes can be; it so often happens that such phrases as "after discussion" are used prior to the bald recital of a decision taken, with the deliberate intention of drawing a discreetly impenetrable veil over that most interesting aspect of the proceedings of any advisory or executive body: the debate that precedes action. He who has plowed through reams of sometimes scintillating, often irrelevant and almost always either consciously or unconsciously distorted memoirs in search of a particular aspect of "the truth" realizes how frustrating the task can be. Even private diaries and letters never intended for the public eye can be traps for the unwary soul who fails to read or sees too much between the lines. And yet how one longs for the challenge of working such priceless ore when trying to deal with sixteenth century men and institutions. Unfortunately it simply does not exist.

Even so, there *are* materials for the history of the council in the sixteenth century; they can be grouped into two broad categories; and the little which falls into the first—that comprising documents containing direct references to the council's deliberative undertakings—does provide some slight, but usable evidence relating to the council's decision-making processes; that is, it can tell us at least something about what went on at meetings. There are reports from foreign ambassadors and envoys resident in England writing home to their sovereigns and making frequent allusion to the English Privy Council and its activities. These must be used with caution, since they are often based on guesswork, deliberately leaked information or hearsay, but they are nonetheless worth having. More reliable are the scattered accounts of council meetings or decisions to be found here and there in various collections of sixteenth century public and private papers. And the State Papers Domestic contain those few of the secretary's notes of business he intended to bring up at council meetings— sometimes complete with the decision that the council reached—that have survived. However, taken together, the amount of this kind of thing that has survived is small. One must settle for the kind of material that falls into the second category: the documents which the council created in executing its role in English life. These include the letters and orders sent out once the council had conferred and made decisions, and the correspondence it received.

The prime source for the letters that the council sent out is the Privy Council register, published verbatim as the *Acts of the Privy Council*. Some volumes of the register are fair copies, others rough; the latter contain rather more detail than the former, which are often drastically condensed in form. None of them, apparently, contains notes of all the letters the council ordered written. This becomes apparent on finding an actual council letter of which the register makes no mention. These letters turn up all over England, and it is rare to visit a county record office and find that it has none at all. They are to be found in private collections, such as Major More-Molyneux's from Loseley House in Surrey, which has remained in the possession of the same family since Sir William More entertained Elizabeth there in the latter years of her reign. The Hastings manuscripts, now the property of the Huntington Library in San Marino, California, which include the papers of the first Earl of Huntingdon, President of the Council of the North during much of the last quarter of the sixteenth century and, as such, one of the council's chief agents in the country, comprise many letters from the council, from the secretaries of state and from other councillors. Most of the family collections listed in the following pages are included because of the council letters they contain. Council letters, however, appear also in city archives such as those of Chester. As the council frequently made use of bishops in a variety of capacities, letters are to be found among episcopal records and, since the council gave orders to the exchequer for the payment of a wide variety of expenses, many council letters and warrants are also included in its *fonds*.

The council precedent books and other paraphernalia of the office from which the council's own correspondence originated (those not consumed in the disastrous early 17th century Whitehall fire) are also widely scattered. Books containing "information" of various kinds are now to be found in places as far apart as the British Museum, the Perrott manuscripts in the Bodleian Library, Oxford, and the Ellesmere manuscripts in the Huntington Library. The most notable set of documents of this sort, however, is located among the papers of clerk of the council Robert Beale. These descended to Beale's daughter Mary and are now known as the Yelverton Papers (British Museum, Additional Manuscripts 48018–48167).

Communications *to* the council are to be found in three main places, the most noteworthy of which is the Public Record office, which now houses the corpus of documents from the State Paper Office known as the State Papers, Domestic Series. As Professor Thomas G. Barnes has pointed out, whereas the Privy Council register constitutes the council's "out" file, the State Papers Domestic are essentially its "in" equivalent. But the State Papers Domestic are both more and less than this, for they are made up of the remains of a much larger, never properly separated collection of documents addressed to the secretaries of state, the Lord Treasurer and the queen as well as to the council, its individual members and such unexpected personalities as the Duchess of Suffolk. There being no clear dividing line between the secretary's papers and the council's, between public and private and official and unofficial records, when a secretary or a clerk of the council vacated his office or died, "his" papers were likely to go with him, as happened in the case of Burghley, or to be otherwise "spirited away," as happened at the demise of Walsingham. Under such circumstances it is perhaps surprising that as much remains in public archives as it does. This is in no small measure owing to the public spirit of Sir Joseph Williamson who, in the later seventeenth century, collected together much of what had been previously dispersed and thus formed the nucleus of the State Paper Office.

Much of what was never returned, either then or later, is today to be found in two separate repositories: Hatfield House, where Lord Burghley's papers form the earlier sections of the Salisbury Manuscripts; and the British Museum, where other Burghley Papers comprise the important first division of the Lansdowne Manuscripts. Although the documents in both these locations tend in large part to be addressed to Burghley himself, they are nonetheless essentially public papers in that they are largely concerned with official business and therefore complement the State Papers proper. It is meaningless to consider them as three separate entities. The Cotton and Harleian Manuscripts also contain great quantities of later sixteenth century material that falls into basically the same category, and in gathering together everything he could lay his hands on, Sir Robert Cotton in fact managed to reassemble at least some of the dispersed Walsingham collection.

The State Papers Foreign are, of course, also packed with intrinsically fascinating information. Little of it, however, proved directly relevant to this study. Although the council was involved in virtually everything that had to do with England's overseas relations and so, in a sense, stands behind every document that concerns the subject, there are, in this collection, few letters addressed to the council specifically, few emanating from it, and the council is very rarely referred to even in passing.

As far as personal papers are concerned, what has survived has been a matter of luck, and finding them is often to be credited to the work of the National Register of Archives. The tortuous descent of the Burghley Papers (appropriated on Burghley's death by his secretary Michael Hicks, they remained in his family for generations before eventually appearing on the market and passing into the possession of that Earl of Shelburne who later became Marquess of Lansdowne) is perhaps the classic example of how the richest finds can be made in the most unlikely places. The private papers of a great eighteenth century aristocrat would not be the first and most natural place to look for sixteenth century official documents, but in many instances such documents have often been found in just such unexpected locations. The Earl of Leicester's papers passed, via his wife Lettice Knollys and her grand-daughter Frances, who married a Duke of Somerset, to the Seymours, then to the Finches and eventually to the Thynnes, with the result that they are now neatly bound and well looked-after in the Marquess of Bath's muniment room at Longleat. They are disappointingly thin. The fact that so many of them remain for the month of August 1588 alone indicates what a treasure trove has disappeared. Yet, rich or disappointing, it is in such places as these that one must seek the history of the Privy Council. In the following bibliography the manuscripts have been listed alphabetically by location, then by categories therein, and the printed works, both secondary and primary, alphabetically together at the end.

Manuscripts

BODLEIAN LIBRARY, OXFORD
Mss Perrot

3   Letters and papers relating to France, mainly precedents for instructions to ambassadors, 1559–1567.

Mss Tanner

78   Letters and papers, 1581–1586
241   Letter book of Bassingbourne Gaudy, sheriff of Norfolk, 1578–1579.

BRITISH MUSEUM, LONDON
Additional Mss

32323   Copybook of letters of the Privy Council, with other letters and documents on state affairs, 1571–1581, many of them stated to have been penned by Edmund Tremayne, clerk of the council. This is a council clerk's precedent book.

33271   Copies of letters and speeches, 1545–1579.
33591–33594   Sadler papers: the correspondence of Sir Ralph Sadler, 1559–1560, 1569–1572 and 1584–85.

34216   Letters and papers, Elizabeth I – Charles I.
48018–48167   Yelverton papers:

48018   Precedent book compiled by Robert Beale, signed by him and partly in his own hand, although mostly in a clerkly one, commenced in 1575.

48035   Letters and papers of Robert Beale, *temp.*
48049   Elizabeth.
48063
48065
48085
48150   Robert Beale's precedent book, largely in his own hand, compiled on his appointment to the clerkship of the council, 1572.

48158–48162   Letters and papers of Robert Beale, *temp.* Elizabeth.

48167   Another book of precedents for council letters, the examples quoted dating mainly from the later fifteen eighties.

Cotton Mss

Caligula	B. viii	Letters and papers, 1528–1584
	B. ix	1556–1570
	C. i	1567–1570
	C. ii	1570–1572
	C. iii	1571–1580
	C. iv	1572–1575
	C. v	1575–1579
	C. vi.	1580–1581
	C. vii	1582–1583
Julius	F. vi	Letters and papers, *temp.* Elizabeth and James I.
Nero	B. i	Papers connected with England's relations with Portugal, mainly sixteenth century.
	B. iii	Papers connected with England's relations with Denmark, mainly sixteenth century.
	B. ix	Papers connected with England's relations with the Empire, mainly sixteenth century.
Titus	B. ii	Letters and papers, Edward VI through Elizabeth.
	F. iii	Letters and papers, Henry VIII through James I.
Vespasian	C. vii	Papers connected with England's relations with the Emperor Charles V and Philip II of Spain.
	C. xiv	Letters and papers, Elizabeth and James I.
	C. xvi	Papers connected with England's relations with Scotland, a few dating from the reign of Elizabeth.
	F. iii	Papers connected with England's relations with Portugal, Scotland and the Empire, a few dating from the reign of Elizabeth.

F. iv   no. 5, grant by the queen of the manor of Sul-
thay to Sir Walter Mildmay, August 3, 1571.

F. ix   Miscellaneous documents, a few dating from the
reign of Elizabeth.

F. xii   Papers relating to Irish affairs between about
1557 and 1605.

Egerton Mss

3048   Clerk of the council Antony Asheley's precedent book,
containing letters dated 1540–1590.

Harleian Mss

38   A "book of collections," Edward VI through James I

168–169   "Small tracts and papers of state matter" written by
Ralph Starkey, 1574–1599 and 1574–1606.

285   Letters and papers relating particularly to England's
relations with the United Provinces, 1564–1586.

286   Miscellaneous documents, 1560–1648, but mainly
Elizabethan.

368   Miscellaneous documents, 1580s and 1590s, some
undated.

703   A book compiled at the direction of Sir Walter Covert,
sometime sheriff, justice of the peace and deputy lieutenant of Sussex, containing copies of orders and letters
received by him from the Privy Council and others
relating to public business, 1583–1627.

4943   "Orders of the Privy Council," 1570–1580. This is
another precedent book of a clerk of the council.

6035   Sir Francis Walsingham's letter book, 1583.

6990   Letters to and from Privy Councillors and others,
1560–1570.

6991   A similar volume, 1571–1574.

Lansdowne Mss (Burghley Papers)

6, 37   Letters and papers, 1563–1583.

68   Letters and papers, 1591.

155   Miscellaneous documents, mainly instructions to English ambassadors abroad, various dates.

238   Miscellaneous documents, various dates.

Stowe Mss

150   Letters and papers, 1526–1623.

160   A clerk of the council's precedent book, late 1570s and
early 1580s.

493–496   Copies of the Privy Council register, 1581–1591.

555   Book of "the quen'is majestie's juelles," each leaf signed by Burghley, Sadler and Mildmay, 1574.

570   Parts I and II of a reference book, originally among the papers of Robert Beale, including such details as the names of vice-admirals, the number of churches in each shire and the names of the forts and castles along the coast, *temp.* Elizabeth.

CAMBRIDGE UNIVERSITY LIBRARY

Ms Ee. 2. 34   Includes a few letters to and from the Earl of Leicester, 1572.

Ms Gg. 5. 36   Letters and papers, mainly instructions to ambassadors, all copies in a seventeenth century hand, *temp.* Mary I and Elizabeth.

Ms Mm. 5. 7   Instructions by the Privy Council to the commissioners for musters in Norfolk, no date.

CITY OF CHESTER RECORD OFFICE

Ms M/L/1   "Great Letter Book," 1541–1598.

Ms M/L/5   Letters and papers, *temp.* Elizabeth.

HATFIELD HOUSE

Salisbury Mss

3–8, 58, 138, 154–161,   Letters and papers, *temp.* Elizabeth.
179, 198 and 202.

HERTFORDSHIRE RECORD OFFICE

Gorhambury Mss

VII, XII   Letters and papers of Lord Keeper Bacon, *temp.* Elizabeth.

Deeds

82, 267   Letters and orders from the Privy Council, 1593–1596.

Ms HAT/S. R./4

Letters from the council to the sheriff and *custos rotulorum* and others, October 20, 1592.

HUNTINGTON LIBRARY, SAN MARINO

Ellesmere Mss

1183, 1187–1190, 1198,   Letters and papers, including letters to
1205, 1256, 1258, 1271,   and from the queen, the council and
1274, 1299–1307, 1553,   individual councillors, entries similar
1701, 1874, 1901–1904,   to those in the Privy Council register
2079–2080, 2327, 2380,   and reference books (1198 and
2384, 2390, 2583–2584,   6206B) probably at one time in the
2653, 2660, 5839, 6030   council office, fifteen seventies and
and 6206B.   eighties.

Hastings Mss

1210–1214, 1302–1303, 2377–2378, 2535, 2537–2538, 4138–4142, 5086, 5350, 5356, 5358, 5362, 13054–13055, 13057–13059, 13062, 13064–13067, 13069–13070	Letters to the Earl of Huntingdon from the queen, Walsingham, Hunsdon, Burghley, Leicester and the council, with a few replies from Huntingdon to Walsingham, 1569–1570, 1581–1582, 1584.

KENT RECORD OFFICE, MAIDSTONE

New Romney Mss

Unsorted	Mainly letters from the council to Lord Cobham, Lord Warden of the Cinque Ports, and of Burghley to the town of New Romney, 1564, 1577, 1588 and 1592.

Sandwich Mss

Sa. ZB2	Letters and orders from the Privy Council to the town of Sandwich and to the Lord Warden of the Cinque Ports, 1570–1579.

LONGLEAT HOUSE, WARMINSTER

Dudley Mss

I, II and III	Letters and papers of the Earl of Leicester, *temp.* Elizabeth.

NORTHAMPTONSHIRE RECORD OFFICE

Fitzwilliam Mss (Mildmay Papers)

F (M) P	Letters and papers of Sir Walter Mildmay, *temp.* Elizabeth

Westmoreland Mss

W: B2, PXII	Letters of the queen to Sir Walter Mildmay, 1570.

PUBLIC RECORD OFFICE, LONDON

Chancery

C.66	Patent Rolls
C.82	Warrants for the Great Seal, Series II.
C.227	Petty Bag Office, sheriff's rolls.

Exchequer

E.101	King's Remembrancer, accounts, various.
E.157/1	King's Remembrancer, licences to pass beyond the seas, 1572–1578.
E.159	King's Remembrancer, memoranda rolls.
E.351/541–568	Lord Treasurer's Remembrancer, declared accounts (pipe office), accounts of the treasurers of the Chamber from 1557.

E.403/2420–   Exchequer of Receipt, payments book for the Privy
2429   Purse, Wardrobe, Household etc., including details of
"paymentes to diverse personnes uppon extraordinarie
warrauntes," among them warrants of the Privy
Council.

E.403/2721–   Order books (pells); the substance of orders by the
2801   Lord Treasurer directing payments.

E.404/229–   Exchequer of Receipt, Treasury orders and warrants
250   to the tellers of the exchequer for payments, 1547–
1794.

E.405/2–182   Exchequer of Receipt, tellers' rolls, Henry IV to
Charles I.

Privy Council Office

PC.2/10–13   Privy Council registers, 1570–1582.

Privy Seal Office

PSO.2   Warrants for the Privy Seal, Series II.

State Paper Office

SP.12/1–157   State Papers, Domestic Series, 1558–1582.

SP.16   State Papers, Domestic Series, Charles I.

SP.40   Signet Warrants, 1558–1625

QUEEN'S COLLEGE, OXFORD

Ms Sel. b. 230   Elizabethan draft proclamations and drafts of printed
council orders.

SURREY RECORD OFFICE, GUILDFORD

Loseley Mss

V, VI, VIII,   Letters from the Privy Council and other communica-
IX, XI, XII,   tions received and sent by Sir William More, some-
XIII, 2013,   time sheriff, justice of the peace and deputy lieutenant
2014 and   in the counties of Surrey and Sussex, *temp.* Elizabeth
Correspon-
dence II.

WEST SUSSEX RECORD OFFICE, CHICHESTER

The letters of the Earl Winterton of Shillinglee Park, Sussex, and
the Episcopal Archives of the diocese of Chichester contain a number of letters from the Privy Council.

Printed Works

Acts of the Privy Council of England, The, new series, edited by J. R.
Dasent, vols. VII to XIII, 1570–1582 (London, 1893–1896).

Adair, E. R., "The Privy Council Registers," *EHR,* XXX, October
1915, 698.

————, "Rough Copies of the Privy Council Register," *EHR*, XXX-VIII, July 1923, 410.

————, *The Sources for the History of the Council in the Sixteenth and Seventeenth Centuries* (London, 1924).

Alumni Cantabrigiensis (to 1751), 4 vols., edited by J. and J. A. Venn, (Cambridge, 1922).

Alumni Oxoniensis (1500–1714), 4 vols., edited by J. Foster (Oxford, 1891–1892).

Ashton, Robert, *The Crown and the Money Market, 1603–1640* (Oxford, 1960).

Baldwin, J. F., *The King's Council in England during the Middle Ages* (Oxford, 1913).

Barnes, Thomas G., *Somerset 1625–1640, A County's Government during the "Personal Rule"* (Cambridge, Massachusetts, 1961).

———— and A. Hassell Smith, "Justices of the Peace from 1558 to 1688: A Revised List of Sources," *Bulletin of the Institute of Historical Research*, XXXII, November 1959, 221.

Beale, Robert, *A Treatise on the Office of Councellor and Principal Secretary*, printed in Conyers Read's *Mr. Secretary Walsingham and the Policy of Queen Elizabeth*, I (Oxford, 1925).

Beckingsale, B. W., *Burghley. Tudor Statesman, 1520–1598* (London, 1967).

————, *Elizabeth I* (New York, 1963).

Bentwich, Norman, *The Practice of the Privy Council in Judicial Matters* (London, 1912).

Bibliography of Royal Proclamations of the Tudor and Stuart Sovereigns, 1485–1714, 2 vols., edited by R. R. Steele (Oxford, 1910).

Birch, Thomas, *Memoirs of the Reign of Queen Elizabeth from the Year 1581 till her Death*, 2 vols. (London, 1754).

Birch, W. de G., *Catalogue of Seals in the Department of Manuscripts in the British Museum* (London, 1894).

Black, J. B., *The Reign of Elizabeth* (Oxford, 1936).

Boynton, Lindsay, *The Elizabethan Militia* (London, 1967).

Burgon, John W., *The Life and Times of Sir Thomas Gresham* (London, 1839).

Burke's Peerage, Baronetage and Knightage, edited by L. G. Pine (London, 1949).

Cabala Sive Scrinia. Mysteries of State and Government in Letters of Illustrious Persons and Great Ministers of State (London, 1691).

Calendar of Letters and Papers Relating to English Affairs Preserved

Principally in the Archives of Simancas, Elizabeth, vols. I–IV, edited by Martin A. S. Hume (London, 1892–1899).

Calendar of the Manuscripts of the Marquis of Salisbury, Parts I and II, Historical Manuscripts Commission (London, 1883).

Calendar of the State Papers, Domestic Series, 1547–1590, 2 vols., edited by R. Lemon (London, 1856–1865).

Calendar of State Papers, Foreign, 1566–1577 edited by A. J. Crosby, *1577–1583* edited by A. J. Butler (London, 1871–1913).

Calendar of State Papers, Ireland, vols. I–IV, 1509–1596, edited by H. C. Hamilton (London, 1893–1905).

Calendar of State Papers relating to Scotland and Mary, Queen of Scots, 1547–1603, 12 vols. (Edinburgh and Glasgow, 1898–1952).

Calendar of State Papers and Manuscripts relating to English Affairs existing in the Archives and Collections of Venice, and in other Libraries of Northern Italy, VII edited by Rawdon Brown and G. Cavendish Bentinck and VIII and IX edited by Horatio Brown (London, 1890–1897).

Camden, William, *Britannia*, 2 vols., edited by Edmund Gibson (London, 1722).

——, *The History of the Most Renowned and Victorious Princess Elizabeth, late Queen of England* (London, 1688).

——, *Reges, Reginae, Nobiles et alij in Ecclesia Collegiata B. Petri Westmonasterij sepulti, usque ad annum . . . 1600.*

Cecil, R., *The State and Dignity of a Secretary of State's Place*, edited by T. Park, printed in *The Harleian Miscellany*, II (London, 1809), 281.

Chambers, E. K., *The Elizabethan Stage*, I (Oxford, 1923).

Cheyney, E. P., "The Court of Star Chamber," *AHR*, XVIII, July 1913, 727.

——, *A History of England from the Defeat of the Armada to the Death of Elizabeth*, 2 vols. (New York, 1914–1926).

Collection of State Papers . . . Left by William Cecil, Lord Burghley, edited by Samuel Haynes (London, 1740).

Collection of State Papers relating to Affairs in the Reign of Queen Elizabeth from the Year 1571 to 1596. Transcribed from Original Papers . . . at Hatfield House, edited by William Murdin (London, 1759).

Collinson, Patrick, *The Elizabethan Puritan Movement* (Berkeley, 1967).

Complete Peerage, The, 12 vols., edited by G. E. Cokayne, Vicary Gibbs and others (London, 1910–1953).

Correspondence Diplomatique de Bertrand de Salignac de la Mothe Fenelon, Ambassadeur de France en Angleterre de 1568 a 1575, 7 vols., edited by A. Teulet (Paris and London, 1838).

Croft, O. G. S., *The House of Croft of Croft Castle* (Hereford, 1949).

Cross, Claire, *The Puritan Earl* (London, 1966).

Cruikshank, C. G., *Elizabeth's Army* (London, 1946).

Dewar, Mary, *Sir Thomas Smith. A Tudor Intellectual in Office* (London, 1965).

Dicey, A. A., *The Privy Council* (London, 1887).

Dictionary of National Biography, 22 vols., edited by Leslie Stephen and Sidney Lee (New York, 1908–1909).

Dietz, F. C., *English Government Finance 1485–1558*, 2nd edn. (New York, 1964).

———, *English Public Finance 1558–1641*, 2nd edn. (New York, 1964).

Digges, Dudley, *The Compleat Ambassador* (London, 1655).

Dunham, W. H., "Henry VIII's Whole Council and Its Parts," *HLQ*, VII, March 1943, 7.

———, "The Members of Henry VIII's Whole Council, 1509–1527," *EHR*, LIX, January 1944, 187.

———, "Wolsey's Rule of the King's Whole Council," *AHR*, XLIX, July 1944, 644.

Dunlop, Ian, *Palaces and Progresses of Elizabeth I* (London, 1962).

Dyson, Humphrey, *A Booke Containing All Such Proclamations As Were Published during the Reign of the Late Queene Elizabeth* (London, 1618).

Ellis, Henry, *Original Letters, Illustrative of English History* (London, 1825).

Elton, G. R., *England Under the Tudors* (London, 1955).

———, "The Problems and Significance of Administrative History in the Tudor Period," *The Journal of British Studies*, IV, no. 2, May 1965, 18–28.

———, *Star Chamber Stories* (London, 1958).

———, *The Tudor Constitution* (Cambridge, 1960).

———, *The Tudor Revolution in Government* (Cambridge, 1959).

———, "Why the History of the Early-Tudor Council Remains Unwritten," *Annali della fondazione italiana per la storia amministrativa*, I, 1964, 268–296.

Emmison, F. G., *Tudor Secretary: Sir William Petre at Court and Home* (Cambridge, 1961).

Faunt, Nicholas, *Discourse*, edited by Charles Hughes, *EHR*, XX, July 1905, 499.

Foedera, Conventiones, Literae etc., VI and VII, edited by George Homes (London, 1741–1742).

Forbes, Dr., *A Full View of the Public Transactions in the Reign of Queen Elizabeth*, 2 vols. (London, 1740).

Gerard, John, *The Autobiography of a Hunted Priest* (New York, 1955).

Gladish, Dorothy M., *The Tudor Privy Council* (Retford, 1915).

Guide to the Contents of the Public Record Office, 2 vols. (London, 1963).

Harleian Miscellany, The, 10 vols., edited by W. Oldys (London, 1810–1813).

Hemmeon, Joseph C., *The History of the British Post Office* (Cambridge, Mass., 1912).

Herbert, J., *The Duties of a Secretary*, printed in Sir George Prothero's *Select Statutes and Other Constitutional Documents* (Oxford, 1898).

Higham, F. M. G., *The Principal Secretary of State* (London, 1923).

Historical Geography of England before 1800, An, edited by H. C. Darby (Cambridge, 1951).

Holdsworth, W. S., *The History of English Law*, 12 vols. (Boston, 1922–1938).

Jenkins, E., *Elizabeth and Leicester* (New York, 1962).

Jones, W. J., *The Elizabethan Court of Chancery* (Oxford, 1967).

Keir, D. L., *The Constitutional History of England, 1485–1951*, 5th edn. (London, 1953).

Kempe, Alfred J., *The Loseley Manuscripts* (London, 1835).

Labarree, L. W., and Moody, R. E., "The Seal of the Privy Council," *EHR*, XLIII, July 1928, 190.

Lambarde, William, *Eirenarcha, or the Office of the Justices of Peace* (London, 1619).

Lehmberg, Stamford E., *Sir Walter Mildmay and Tudor Government* (Austin, 1964).

Lipson, Ephraim, *The Economic History of England*, II, 5th edn. (London, 1948).

Lodge, Edmund, *Illustrations of British History, Biography and Manners*. . . . (London, 1791).

MacCaffrey, Wallace, *The Shaping of the Elizabethan Regime* (Princeton, 1968).

Naunton, Robert, *Fragmenta Regalia* (London, 1824).

Neale, John E., *Elizabeth I and Her Parliaments*, 2 vols. (London, 1953–1957).

———, *The Elizabethan House of Commons* (London, 1949).

————, *Essays in Elizabethan History* (London, 1958).

————, *Queen Elizabeth I* (London, 1952).

Newton, A. P., "The King's Chamber under the Early Tudors," *EHR*, XXXII, July 1917, 349.

————, "Tudor Reforms in the Royal Household," in *Tudor Studies*, edited by R. W. Seton-Watson (London, 1924).

Nicolas, Nicholas H., *The Life of William Davidson* (London, 1823).

————, *Memoirs of the Life and Times of Sir Christopher Hatton* (London, 1847).

————, *Observations on the Office of Secretary of State*, printed in the introduction to volume six of the *Proceedings and Ordinances of the Privy Council of England 1386–1542*, 7 vols. (London, 1834–1837).

Oppenheim, M., *A History of the Administration of the Royal Navy*, I (London, 1896).

Otway-Ruthven, Jocelyn, *The King's Secretary and the Signet Office in the Fifteenth Century* (Cambridge, 1939).

Palgrave, Francis, *An Essay on the Original Authority of the King's Council* (London, 1834).

Peck, Francis, *Desiderata Curiosa; or A Collection of Divers Scarce and Curious Pieces Relating Chiefly to Matters of English History* (London, 1732).

Percy of Newcastle, Eustace Percy, *The Privy Council and the Tudors* (Oxford, 1907).

Pickthorn, K., *Early Tudor Government: Henry VII; Henry VIII* (Cambridge, 1934).

Pollard, A. F., "Council, Star Chamber and Privy Council," *EHR*, XXXVII, July 1922, 337.

————, *The Evolution of Parliament* (London, 1920).

————, "The House of Lords Journal and the Privy Council Register," *EHR*, XXX, April 1915, 304.

Ponko, Vincent, "The Privy Council and the Spirit of Elizabethan Economic Management, 1558–1603," printed in the *Transactions of the American Philosophical Society*, New Series, volume 58, part 4, 1968.

Putnam, Bertha H., "Justices of the Peace from 1558 to 1688," *Bulletin of the Institute of Historical Research*, IV, 1927, 144.

Read, Conyers, "Factions in the English Privy Council under Elizabeth," printed in the *American Historical Association Annual Report for the Year 1911* (Washington, 1913), 109.

————, *Lord Burghley and Queen Elizabeth* (New York, 1960).

————, *Mr. Secretary Cecil and Queen Elizabeth* (New York, 1955).

————, *Mr. Secretary Walsingham and the Policy of Queen Elizabeth*, 3 vols. (Oxford, 1925).

————, "Walsingham and Burghley in Queen Elizabeth's Privy Council," *EHR*, XXVIII, January 1913, 34.

Reid, R. R., *The King's Council in the North* (London, 1921).

Richardson, W. C., *Tudor Chamber Administration* (Baton Rouge, 1952).

Round, J. H., *Studies in Peerage and Family History* (New York, 1901).

Rowse, A. L., "Alltyrynys and the Cecils," *EHR*, LXXV, January 1960, 54.

————, *The England of Elizabeth* (New York, 1961).

St. John Brooks, Eric, *Sir Christopher Hatton* (London, 1947).

Sawyer, Edmund, *Memorials of Affairs of States in the Reigns of Queen Elizabeth and King James I, collected (chiefly) from the Original Papers of the Rt. Hon. Sir Ralph Winwood*, 3 vols. (London, 1725).

Scarisbrick, J. J., *Henry VIII* (Berkeley, 1968).

Scofield, Cora L., *A Study of the Court of Star Chamber* (Chicago, 1900).

"Select Cases in the Council of Henry VII," edited by C. G. Bayne and W. H. Dunham, *Selden Society Publications*, number 75 (London, 1958).

"Select Pleas in the Court of Admiralty," edited by Reginald G. Marsden, *Selden Society Publications*, vol. VI, no. XI (London, 1894–1897).

Sharp, C., *Memorialls of the Rebellion of 1569* (London, 1840).

Slavin, A. J., *Politics and Profit, a Study of Sir Ralph Sadler, 1507–1547* (Cambridge, 1966).

Smith, Alan G. R., *The Government of Elizabethan England* (London, 1967).

Somerville, R., "Henry VII's 'Council Learned in the Law'," *EHR*, LIV, July 1939, 427.

State Papers and Letters of Sir Ralph Sadler, The, 3 vols., edited by Arthur Clifford (Edinburgh, 1809).

Statutes of the Realm, The, 9 vols. (London, 1810–1822).

Stone, Lawrence, *The Crisis of the Aristocracy, 1558–1641* (Oxford, 1965).

————, *An Elizabethan: Sir Horatio Palavicino* (Oxford, 1956).

Tanner, Joseph R., *Tudor Constitutional Documents* (Cambridge, 1930).

Thomson, Gladys S., *Lords Lieutenants in the Sixteenth Century* (London, 1923).

——, *Two Centuries of Family History: A Study in Social Development* (London, 1930).

Trimble, William R., *The Catholic Laity in Elizabethan England, 1558–1603* (Cambridge, Massachusetts, 1964).

Turner, E. R., *The Cabinet Council of England in the Seventeenth and Eighteenth Centuries, 1622–1784*, 2 vols. (Baltimore, 1930–1932).

——, *The Privy Council of England in the Seventeenth and Eighteenth Centuries, 1603–1784*, 2 vols. (Baltimore, 1927–1928).

Ward, B. M., "Queen Elizabeth and William Davidson," *EHR*, XLIV, January 1929, 105.

Wernham, R. B., "The Disgrace of William Davidson," *EHR*, XLVI, October 1931, 633.

White, E. F., "The Privy Council and Private Suitors in 1603," *EHR*, XXXIV, October 1919, 589.

Williams, Neville, *Elizabeth, Queen of England* (London, 1967).

——, *Thomas Howard, Fourth Duke of Norfolk* (New York, 1964).

Willson, D. H., *The Privy Councillors in the House of Commons, 1604–1629* (Minneapolis, 1940).

Wilson, Jean, "'Sheriffs' Rolls of the Sixteenth and Seventeenth Centuries," *EHR*, XLVII, January 1932, 31.

Wright, Thomas, *Queen Elizabeth and her Times: A Series of Original Letters* (London, 1838).

Index

Abington, Mr., 103
Acle, Norfolk, 133
Admiral, Lord, 34, 36, 101, 188, 190, 191, 197, 226; as Lord Lieutenant, 214
Admiralty, 31, 160; court, 118, 144, 145, 188–189, 190, 192, 193, 210, 249; judge of, 190
Admonition to Parliament, 130
Africa, North, 143
Alba, Duke of, 62, 79, 114, 117–118, 209
Alcock, William, 179
Aldersey, Thomas, 135
Alehouses, 134, 137, 138
Ambassadors, instructions to, 116, 247
Anglo-Spanish bullion crisis of 1569, 4, 117, 142
Anjou, Duke of, 33, 77, 79
Antiquaries, Society of, 19
Antwerp, 90, 149
Arches, court of, 34
Armada, Spanish, 188
Armor, purchase of, 199
Arnold, Sir Nicholas, 205
Arundel, Earl of. See Fitzalan, Henry
Ashburnham, John, 85, 176
Assize justices. See Justices of Assize
Assizes, 177

Bacon, Sir Nicholas, 17, 19, 20, 31, 40–48 passim, 56, 59, 74–82 passim, 93–96 passim, 100, 109, 115, 119, 121, 125, 142, 165, 166, 180, 185, 194, 197, 215, 230, 238, 239; death of, 32; early career of, 18; not made Lord Chancellor, 32
Baeshe, Edward, 220
Bailly, Charles, 211
Bangor, Bishop of, 203
Bank of England, 147–148
Barbary, 143–144
Barnard Castle, 130
Barrett, Robert, 225
Barton, Mr., 226, 227, 231
Bates Thomas, 122, 180
Beacons, as signals, 112
Beale, Robert, 4, 154, 157, 160; income of, 170; precedent books of, 162, 182, 216; treatise on secretaryship, 152–153, 176
Beaufort, Lady Margaret, 12
Becke, Anthony, 145

Bedford, Earl of. See Russell, Francis
Bedo, William, 122
Bell, Robert, 95
Benevolences, 182, 216
Berkshire, 224
Bertie, Richard, 127
Berwick on Tweed, 23, 30, 35, 38, 106, 107, 131, 238
Bindon, Viscount, 206
Blagrave, Thomas, 84, 176
Bland, John, 89
Blois, Treaty of, 33, 76, 77
Blount, Elizabeth, 24
Bodley, Thomas, 125
Boleyn, Anne, 29, 40
Boleyn, Mary, 29, 37, 40
Bolton, 55, 240
Bonds, taking of, 213
Bordeaux, 141
Boroughbridge, 88
Bosworth, battle of, 83
Bourbon, Cardinal de, 245
Bowes, John, 182
Bowes, Rafe, 88
Brassey, Thomas, 135
Bray, Reginald, 11
Brewers, Company of, 146
Bristol, 218
Bromley, Sir George, 224
Bromley, Sir Thomas, 17, 20, 31, 40, 45, 47, 85, 159, 230; made Lord Chancellor, 32; as man of the world, 32
Browne, Sir Thomas, 128
Buckhurst, Lord, 106, 127, 142
Bulkeley, John, 122
Bullion crisis of 1569. See Anglo-Spanish bullion crisis of 1569.
Burghley, Lord. See Cecil, Sir William
Buttes, Sir William, 126, 183

Caesar, Sir Julius, 156, 160
Calais, 105, 106
Calles, John, 194
Calshot, castle of, 108
Cambridgeshire, 138
Campion, Edmund, 160
Canterbury, Archbishop of, 57, 213; consulted by queen, 53
Carey, Catherine, 37
Carey, Henry, 1st Baron Hunsdon, 17, 20, 28–31 passim, 38, 42–47 passim,

50, 54, 55, 85, 106, 131, 132, 238, 241
Carlisle, 67, 68, 138
Carlisle, Bishop of, 131
Catelyn, Robert, CJKB, 147, 178
Catherine de Medici (Queen), 77
Catholics. See Recusants.
Cavarley, Sir George, 84
Cecil, Edward, 124
Cecil, Richard, 124
Cecil, Robert, 230
Cecil, Sir William, 1st Baron Burghley, 4, 17, 20, 28–32 passim, 36, 39–62 passim, 68–93 passim, 100, 101, 103, 107, 111, 115, 120, 122, 125, 128, 131, 143, 149, 151–159 passim, 166, 168, 169, 179, 180, 185, 192, 194, 206, 210, 211, 215, 217, 218, 228, 230, 235–241 passim, 244–247 passim; 1569 plot against, 46; as chief minister, 21, 30, 58, 73, 74, 151, 239; as council coordinator, 57; and Mary, Queen of Scots, 247; has Sir Thomas Smith appointed to council, 32; moves to Treasury, 32; primacy in council, 46; and queen, 240; "saves the honor of the highest," 247
Chaloner, Thomas, ambassador, 114
Chamber, 143; messengers of the, 163, 207, 209; treasurer of the, 89; treasury of the, 86, 88
Chamberlain, Lord, 79, 115, 194; as ex officio member of council, 36; functions of, 34, 36
Champernowne, Sir Arthur, 103, 116
Chancellor, Lord, 19, 21, 95, 177, 213, 230, 242; as ex officio member of council, 36; Christopher Hatton as, 37; sits in Star Chamber, 13. See also Bromley, Sir Thomas
Chancery, 18, 31, 80, 91, 215; and council, 9; at Westminster, 9; vacancy at, 32
Charles, Archduke of Austria, 26
Charles I, King of England, 231
Charles IX, King of France, 77
Cheke, Henry, clerk of the council, 157, 159
Chenies, 165
Cheshire, 85, 120, 135
Chester, Dominic, 118
Chester, Edward, 122
Chester, 85, 210, 226; Bishop of, 153, 204; diocese of, 131; Mayor of, 124
Chichester, Bishop of, 142, 223

Chief justices, as members of Star Chamber, 13
Cholemeley, Sir Hugh, 131
Christchurch, Oxford, 226
Christmas, John, 208
Christmas, Robert, 118
Cinque Ports, 163, 183, 218, 225, 248
Cirencester, laxity of the clergy at, 203
Civilians, use of, 33, 160
Civil war, 231
Clecher, Thomas, 143
Clere, Sir Edward, 122, 205, 249
Clerks of the council, 4, 52, 89, 156, 157, 208, 218; fees of, 169–171; oath of, 160; rotation of, 160. See also Beale, Robert; Cheke, Henry; Tremayne, Edmund; Wilkes, Thomas
Cleves, Anne of, 37
Clinton, Lord. See Fiennes, Edward de
Coal, burning of instead of wood, 146
Coastal defense, 105
Cobham, Lord, 79, 104–108 passim, 115, 117, 124, 222; and export of grain, 217; reports on overseas travel, 224; avoids blame, 248
Colby, Anthony, 183
Colchester, 126, 218; Sheriff of, 121
Cologne, 90, 147
Common law, 80, 81
Common law courts: chief justices of, 81; at Westminster, 9
Common Pleas, court of, 80
Communications, 221
Comptroller of the Household, 34, 36, 79
Congressional Record, 100
Cordell, Sir William, master of the rolls, 85, 214
Cornwall, 141, 142, 218, 220; Duchy of, 88
Council: as a court, 13; as precursor of Star Chamber, 13; inner ring of, 11, 54, 58; under Henry VI, 10; under Edward IV, 10; under Henry VII, 10–12; under Henry VIII, 10, 11, 13; Wolsey's attitude towards, 12. See also Privy Council; Privy councillors; Whole Council
Council chamber, 156
Council chest, 155, 127, 220
Council in the Marches of Wales, 25, 39, 109, 121, 154, 163, 192, 204
Council of the North, 26, 39, 56, 70, 87, 154, 163, 179, 192, 221, 238,

247; Beale as clerk of, 170
Counter, the, 211
Courtenay, Edward, 157
Courts. *See* Arches, court of; Common law courts; Common Pleas, court of; Exchequer; King's Bench, court of; Prerogative courts; Requests, court of; Star Chamber, court of; Wards, court of
Credit, maintenance of, 147–148
Crips, William, 84
Croft, Sir James, 17, 20, 23, 34, 35, 40–47 *passim*, 60, 79, 92, 98, 100, 115, 157, 166, 168, 169; as member of parliament, 22; loyalty of suspected, 35, 36
Cromer, William, 84
Cromer, 237
Cromwell, Thomas, 38, 230, 236; and the Privy Council, 13–14
Cumberland, 138, 179; copper deposits, 215
Curia Regis, 9, 10, 243
Customs, 145, 190

Dale, Dr. Valentine, 79, 158, 160, 194
Darcy, Lord, 110, 124, 208
Dartford, 215
Da Silva, Spanish ambassador, 116, 220
Daubeny, Lord, 11
De la Marck, Count William, 115, 220
Delaware, Lord, 106, 142, 182, 246
Denbighshire, 226
Denmark, King of, 144, 219
Denny, Richard, 83
Deputy-lieutenants, 225–226
Derby, Earl of, 79, 112, 204
De Republica Anglorum of Sir Thomas Smith, 32
Derynge, Edward, 216
De Spes, Spanish ambassador, 51, 144, 238
Devon, 141, 142, 147, 191, 196, 222; Sheriff of, 107, 120
Digges, Thomas, 213
Diplomacy, 143–144, 192
Doncaster, 70
Dorchester, 177
Dorset, 142, 196, 206
Dover, 105, 138; harbor repair at, 137, 218
Drake, Sir Francis, 43, 195
Drayton Basset, 152
Dudley, Ambrose, 1st Earl of Warwick, master of the ordnance, 17, 20, 28,

29, 35, 39, 43, 45, 47, 70, 71, 73, 106, 166, 170, 181; and the northern rebellion, 70
Dudley, Charles, 81
Dudley, John, Duke of Northumberland, 15, 24, 25, 27, 30, 38
Dudley, Robert, 1st Earl of Leicester, 17, 20, 28, 37–49 *passim*, 53, 58, 59, 79, 85, 88, 91, 92, 100, 106, 107, 115, 118, 127, 152, 158, 166, 168, 179, 180, 185, 194, 210, 215, 228, 239, 240, 245, 246; as go-between, 240; as Lord Lieutenant, 22; as master of the horse, 38; and Dr. Wilson, 33; special relationship with queen, 28–29, 79, 239–240; death of 135
Dunham, W. H., 12
Dunse, Richard, 84, 176
Dunye, Thomas, 246
Dutton, Mr., 84

Earl Marshall, 38, 221
Economic regulation, 139–149, 213–220; in Lent, 134, 140, 146, 206; of brewing, 139; of butter and cheese sales, 141; of flax growing, 139, 145; of glass manufacture, 145; of hemp production, 139, 145; of leather trade, 139, 141; of monopolies, 143; of prices, 141, 146, 215–216, 218; of printing, 139, 146; of timber trade, 145; of tree-felling, 139; of wax-making, 140; of wheat trade, 140–147 *passim*, 214, 220; of woad growing, 139, 145, 219; of wool trade, 140, 146, 147
Eden River, 203
Edgecumbe, Mr., loan collector, 184
Edinburgh, Treaty of, 69, 75, 76
Edmund (in *King Lear*), 230
Edward I, King of England, 237
Edward IV, King of England: council under, 10
Edward VI, King of England, 15, 24–38 *passim*, 228
Egerton, Sir Thomas, 86
Elizabeth I, Queen of England, 43–99 *passim*, 114, 125, 164, 169, 180, 204, 211, 212, 225, 226, 231–250 *passim*; associates self with council, 246; bypassed by council, 101; character of, 42, 152, 185, 211, 220, 246, 248–249; consults non-councillors, 53; consults with council, 110; court-

ships of, 77; discretion of, 53, 54, 61–62; economy of, 104; freedom of choice of, 61; harmony with council, 62; holds first council meeting, 17; imprisonment of, 35; council attempts to influence, 241; as judge of men, 24, 37–38; legal position of, 227; not a great "builder," 236; philosophy of, 248–249; childlessness of, 242; relations with advisers, 11, 102, 112, 152; sits in council, 59; authority of, 61, 238, 241; touchiness of, 61; view of conciliar responsibilities, 62–63, 67; views on torture, 211; listens to advice, 17, 21; youthful associations of, 35

Elizabethan world, 243
Ely, Isle of, 138
Englefield, Sir Francis, 124
Essex, 142
Evans, Richard, 207
Ewelme, 226
Exchequer, 86, 89, 108, 177, 184, 186, 190; and council, 9; at Westminster, 9; tellers of the, 87; Chancellor of the, 36, 87, 93; court of the, 80, 81; chamber, 165
Exeter, 179
Ex officio councillors, 36

Falmouth, 117, 124
Faunt, Nicholas, 152, 155; describes secretaryship, 150
Fees of council clerks, 170–171
Fenner, Thomas, 219
Fenton, Edward, 214, 215
Ferrybridge, 88
Fiennes, Edward de, 9th Baron Clinton and Saye, 1st Earl of Lincoln, 17–25 passim, 34, 43–48 passim, 56, 70–80 passim, 92, 101–118 passim, 127, 133, 166, 168, 171, 188–194 passim, 213, 231; appointed Lord Steward, 34; and northern rebellion, 70
Fifteen-seventies, characteristics of, 4, 232
Fish days, act of 1563, 206
Fitzalan, Henry, 19th Earl of Arundel, 18–28 passim, 39, 45–48 passim, 74, 78, 116; Catholic leanings of, 43; councillor under Mary I, 16
Fitzwilliam, William, 213
Flanders, 117, 142, 159, 194
Fleet, the 122, 130, 209, 211, 223

Fleetwood, William, recorder of London, 85, 96, 139
Florence, Duke of, 117
Flushing, port of, 190
Foix, M. de, 115
Forced loans, 182, 216
Fotheringay, 57, 159
France, 158, 198, 237, 245, 247; English policy towards, 23; immigration from, 125
France, King of. See Charles IX; Henry II; Henry III; Henry IV
French secretary, 156
Frobisher, Martin, 149, 214, 215
Furvill, Mrs. Bridgitt, 202–203

Garter, Order of the, 30, 131
Gaudy, Bassingbourne, 81, 177
Gearinge, Alexander, 203
Geneva, 28, 37
Gentry, willingness to serve Crown, 246
Gerard, Father John, 32, 132, 203, 237
Gerrard, Sir Gilbert, 32, 84, 147, 177
Gilbert, Sir John, 223
Gillingham, 104
Gloucester, 108
Gloucester, Earl of (in King Lear), 230
Gloucestershire, 83, 205; grain commissioners in, 218
Goodwyn, Christopher, 149
Goringe, George, 223
Gravesend, 104
Great Contract, 230
Great Seal. See Seal, Great
Greenwich, 88, 164, 165, 166
Gresham, Sir Thomas, 90, 92, 93, 149, 182, 219
Grevill, Lodowick, 83
Grey, Lady Catherine, 42
Grey, Lady Jane, 24
Grey, Lady Mary, 42
Grindal, Edmund, Bishop, 130, 152, 236
Guaras, Antoniode, 47
Guernsey, 86, 155
Guildford, Richard, 11
Guildford, 128

Hall, Arthur, 96
Halsted, Essex, 126
Hamburg, 90, 143, 147, 199
Hamlet, Prince of Denmark, 229
Hampshire, 126, 142, 177, 246
Hampton Court, 164, 165

Hanaper, 88
Hansard, 100
Hanse, 147, 250
Happisburgh, 237
Harpesfield, John and Nicholas, 208–209
Harpur, Justice, 178
Harwich, 124
Hastings, Francis, 120
Hastings, 124; building of harbor, 137; funding of new harbor, 178
Hatfield, 17, 55, 62
Hatton, Sir Christopher, 18, 20, 37–49 passim, 80, 85, 97, 179, 230, 240; member of parliament, 22; queen's judgment of, 37–38
Hawkes [Haukes], Mr., of Walmer Castle, 84, 176
Hawkins, John, 144
Hendrie, John, 220
Heneage, Sir Thomas, 53–54, 184–185
Henly, Margery, 182
Henry VI, King of England, council under, 10
Henry VII, King of England: council under, 10, 12; Elton's description of, 14; personality of, 13; view of council's function, 14
Henry VIII, King of England, 19–27 passim, 35–42 passim, 182, 193, 216, 236, 237; death of, 15; dominates council, 15; insecurity of, 14; and origin of Privy Council, 13–14; as patron of the Russells, 19; characteristics of, 12, 14; resembles Henry VII, 14
Henry II, King of France, 25
Henry III, King of France, 77
Henry IV, King of France, 75
Henry, Lord Darnley, 62
Herbert, William, 1st Earl of Pembroke, 18–26 passim, 39, 40–48 passim, 78, 217
Hereford, 197
Hereford, Bishop of, 202
Herle, William, 122
Hertford, Earl of. See Seymour, Edward
Hertford, Earl of (son of the Duke of Somerset), 85
Heydon, Sir Christopher, 126, 183
Heydon, William, 249
Heywarde, Sir Rowlande, 143
Higate, Reynald, 213
Higgins [Hyggins], George, 218

Highways, maintenance of, 137
Hillis, Thomas, 210
Hippesley, John, 81
Hitchcock, Robert, 179
Holinshed, Raphael, 237
Holland, Parts of, Lincolnshire, 133, 138
Holocrest, Mrs. Julian, 183
Hopton, Sir Owen, 139
Horsemen, 111
Horsey, Edward, 104, 106, 246
Hoseley, 208
Household, royal: function of, 34; treasury of, 86; vice-chamberlain of, 37, 88
House of commons, 94–100, 242
Howard, Catherine (Queen), 25
Howard, Lord Henry, 122, 129
Howard, Thomas, 2nd Duke of Norfolk, 25
Howard, Thomas, 4th Duke of Norfolk, 18, 19, 23–29 passim, 39, 43–48 passim, 58, 59, 73, 74, 78, 119, 122, 159, 187, 211, 212; Catholic leanings of, 42–43; trial of, 32; treason of, 34, 122
Howard, William, 1st Baron Howard of Effingham, 18–25 passim, 34, 39–48 passim, 78, 79, 166
Howard of Effingham, Lord. See Howard, William
Hunsdon, Lord. See Carey, Henry
Huntingdon, Earl of, 44, 87, 182, 238, 241, 247; consulted by queen, 53
Huntingdonshire, 138

Immigration, control of, 125
Imprisonment, arbitrariness of, 210
Inns, 134
Inns of Court, councillors at, 18, 30–37 passim, 236
International affairs, 115, 143–144
Ipswich, 149
Ireland, 39, 87, 90, 101, 121, 137, 152–154 passim, 157, 172, 192, 206, 219, 226, 238; Lord Deputy of, 38
Iron mining, 215
Isham, John, 84, 176

James I, King of England, 156
James VI, King of Scotland, 69
Jeffreys, Sergeant, 177
Jersey, 155
Jobson, Sir Francis, 122
Johnson, John, 149

Judges, 176–179
Justices of Assize, 141, 147, 176–178, 213
Justices of the peace, 21–22, 79, 102, 105, 107, 108, 120–141 *passim*, 146, 147, 155, 178, 203–204, 207, 214, 215, 218, 222, 224, 245

Katherine of Aragon, Queen of England, 27
Keeper of the Great Seal, Lord, 19, 21, 36, 82, 93, 96, 109, 115, 119, 121, 125, 141, 142, 165, 186, 194, 197, 215, 230, 238, 239. *See also* Bacon, Sir Nicholas; Seal, Great
Kendall, 138
Kennedy, Robert, 37
Kenninghall, 120
Kent, 126, 142, 196, 205; Sheriff of, 105
King's Bench, court of, 80, 178–179, 228
Kingsmill, Sir William, 107, 199, 203
Knight, Richard, 84, 176
Knight Marshall, 210, 213
Knole, 143
Knollys, Sir Francis, 18, 20, 34, 37, 38–48 *passim*, 55, 57, 60, 61, 67, 68, 69, 80, 82, 94–100 *passim*, 125, 165, 168, 169, 230; leads house of commons, 97; as Lord Lieutenant, 22; as member of parliament, 22
Knollys, Henry, 212
Kynde, John, 200

Lacie, John, 82
Lancashire, 120; Catholicism in, 204
Lancaster, Duchy of, 88, 138
Langham, Robert, 88
Latin secretary, 156
Law, slowness of, 228; supremacy of, 227
Lee, Sir Richard, 21
Le Havre, 29
Leicester, 70, 120
Leicester, Earl of. *See* Dudley, Robert
Leicestershire, 197
Leighton, Sir Thomas, 86
Levant, the, 144
Lewes, Dr. David, 118, 160, 193, 194
Libri pacis, 155
Lincoln, 22
Lincoln, Earl of. *See* Fiennes, Edward de
Lincolnshire, 142, 222

Loan collectors, 205, 216
Lock, Michael, 149, 215
London: 90, 104, 129, 130, 199, 205, 218, 239; subsidy commissioners of, 218; Bishop of: 83, 126, 217, consulted by queen, 53; Lord Mayor of, 93, 117, 121, 125, 141, 143, 180, 214, 218; Recorder of, 180; see of, 83. *See also* Tower of London
Lopez, Dr., 122
Lords Lieutenants, 22, 28, 70, 79, 102, 109, 110, 120, 127, 132, 133, 226; ordered to prevent grain exports, 214
Love, John, 210, 211
Lovell, Thomas, 11
Lucatelli, Innocent, 82
Lumley, Lord, 142
Lydd, 103
Lynn, 197

MacCaffrey, Wallace, 228
Maignare, Julian, 191
Maignewe, Andrew, 82
Mails, inefficiency of, 221
Manwood, Sergeant, 183
Marguerite de Valois, 75
Marksmen, proposed corps of, 200
Marshall, Earl, 38, 221
Marshalsea, the, 194, 211, 213–214
Martyn, William, 193
Mary I, Queen of England, 16, 24–30 *passim*, 33, 38, 95, 157, 228, 245; council under, 15
Mary, Queen of Scots, 23, 24, 26, 29, 43, 57–62 *passim*, 70, 74, 76, 95, 122, 135, 159, 238, 240, 247; flees to England, 3; as source of divisions in council, 43; subject of extra-conciliar consultation, 53; under conciliar surveillance, 67–69
Mary Stuart. *See* Mary, Queen of Scots
Mary Tudor. *See* Mary I, Queen of England
Masselin, Nicholas, 117
Mauvissiere, M. de, 218
Medway, 104
Mendips, 81
Mendoza, Spanish ambassador, 123
Merchant Adventurers, Company of, 142, 143, 144, 147, 188–195, 207
Merchant groups, control of, 147
Merchants of the Hanse, 147, 250
Merchants, Turkey, 144
Middlesex, 196

Mildmay, Sir Thomas, 140
Mildmay, Sir Walter, 18, 36, 39–49
  passim, 57, 73, 74, 76, 85, 86, 93–
  100 *passim*, 115, 118, 120, 127, 143,
  162, 168, 185, 206, 213, 230, 236,
  247; arbitrates dispute, 213; and
  Mary, Queen of Scots, 247; defends
  parliamentary privilege, 96; as Lord
  Lieutenant, 22; in parliament, 22, 94
Military affairs, 109–113, 196–201,
  231
Mills, Francis, 155
Minerals, exploitation of, 215
Monasteries, dissolution of, 19
Monopolies, 143, 144, 147, 207
Montague, Viscount, 106, 142
Montmorency, Duke of, 115
Mordaunt, Agnes, recusant, 226
More, Sir William, 84, 122, 128, 134
Motte, M. la, 115
Moyle, Thomas, 179
Muelen, Henrick von, 147
Murray, Earl of, 68–69, 73
Musters, 109–113, 147, 155, 196–201,
  206

Nantwich, 135–136, 138, 202
Naunton, Robert, 238
Naval affairs, 101–102, 154–155, 230–
  231, 238; shipbuilding, 145
Neale, Sir John, 228
Needham, Humphrey, 212
Netherlands, 114, 125, 133, 143, 147,
  158, 207, 220, 226, 232
Nevell, Sir Henry, 122
Newgate, 211
Newhall, 49
Newington Green, 127
New Romney, 103, 209
Nippevyle, 237
Norfolk, 122, 131, 138, 142, 177, 197;
  grain commissioners of, 218; plague
  in, 196
Norfolk, Duke of. See Howard, Thom-
  as.
Norris, Sir Henry, 33, 76
Northampton, Marquess of. See Parr,
  William
Northamptonshire, 138, 139, 206
Northern rebellion of 1569–1570, 29,
  30, 69, 108, 110, 131, 180, 232
Northumberland, Duke of. See Dudley,
  John
Northumberland, Earl of, 53
Northwich, 131

Norton, Thomas, 96, 122, 212
Norwich, 126, 127, 197; diocese of, 208
Nottingham, 57

Oatlands, 165
Offley, Sir Thomas, 93
Old Romney, 103
Orange, Prince of, 115, 192, 194
Ordance, 107, 219; master of the, 29;
  office, 155
Oxfordshire, 196

Palmer, Henry, piracy commissioner,
  192
Paris, 75, 127, 158
Parliament, 86, 92–100; bill for inter-
  regnum powers, 242; council and, 9,
  159, 186–187; decision to summon,
  238; of 1576, 248
Parr, Catherine (Queen), 27, 40
Parr, Sir William, 1st Marquess of
  Northampton, 18, 20, 27, 28, 39, 45,
  47, 74, 78, 116
Paulet, Sir Hugh, 212
Paulet, Sir William, 81–82
Paulet, William, 1st Marquess of Win-
  chester, 17, 18, 20, 27, 31, 36, 40,
  44–48 *passim*, 56, 60, 78, 87, 90,
  103, 105, 106, 189; councillor un-
  der Mary I, 16
Peckham, Sir George, 122
Pelham, William, lieutenant of the ord-
  nance, 105, 108, 149
Pembroke, Earl of, 214, 217. *See also*
  Herbert, William
Percy, Henry, 180
Perrot, Sir John, 103, 121, 193, 206
Peter, John, 140
Peter, Robert, 90
Petre, Sir William, 151n
Philip II, King of Spain, 24, 38, 44, 51,
  116, 117, 144, 184, 220, 238
Pickering, Sir William, 239
Pildrim, John, 122
Piracy, 188–195, 208, 219, 222
Pistor, Tristram, 99
Plays, payment for, 88
Popham, Sir John, 11
Popinjay, Richard, 107
Portsmouth, 105, 106, 107, 133
Portuguese matters, 115, 143–144, 149
Posts, 221
Precedent books, of council clerks, 110,
  162, 216, 218
Prerogative courts, and council, 82

President of the council, Lord, 27, 153
Prestall, John, 82
Prices: control of, 141, 146, 215–216, 218; causes of rise, 146, 147
Privy Council: definition of, 15, 243; origins of, 14; advisory function, 52–63, 110; aims of, 249; as arbitrator, 144; checks on own agents, 206; communication within, 72; composition of, 15, 17–18; concerns of, 3, 80, 114, 202; conservatism of, 148–149, 228–232, 236–237, 245–246; and conspiracy, 122; as coordinator, 113; as court of first instance, 83; and court of requests, 11; and *curia regis*, 9; delegation of authority, 84, 102; thrift of, 103–104; educational views of, 138; superficiality of, 139, 194–195; and finance, 86–100; and foreign policy, 114–115; full session, 59; as governing committee, 15; grandeur of, 74, 103, 209–210; how well-informed, 102–103, 154–155, 198, 217; humaneness of, 138; independence of, 101; inefficiency of, 217, 221–225; and the law, 80–86, 175–181, 227–228; as legislative body, 180; letters of, 161–163; Lord President of, 27, 153; meetings of, 17, 52, 164–168; membership in, 3, 31–34, 36; methods of business of, 150–172, 192, 207, 213, 217; moral attitude of, 138; and the navy, 101–105; openness to ideas, 149; and parliament, 9, 92–100, 159, 186–187; petitions to, 211; philosophy of, 149, 227, 246, 249–250; power and effectiveness of, 5, 111, 235, 242, 246; pragmatism of, 143, 197; and private interests, 116, 175–176; as queen's mouthpiece, 247; relationship to monarch(y), 62–63, 111–112, 246–248; and religious doctrine, 131; remuneration for services to, 171–172; as royal scapegoat, 247–248; and sedition, 119–121; self-confidence of, 39; size of, 15, 17; source of strength, 21; and queen's general orders, 107; and Star Chamber, 11, 81–82; summonses by, 143, 207; as supreme court, 82; and treason, 122–123; treatises touching on, 150, 168, 176; and violence, 83; warrant-counterfeiting, 209. *See also* Council; *Curia regis*; Privy Councillors; Privy Council registers

Privy Councillors: advise queen individually, 55; age differences of, 44–46; as diplomats, 75, 79; as interrogators, 73–75; as agents of the queen, 68; as special pleaders, 179; as subsidy commissioners, 186–187; burial places of, 47; clerics as, 13, 15, 18; communications among, 55–57; comparative status of, 153; self-confidence of, 55–56, 61; consultation among, 60–61; differences among, 42–44, 46, 48, 53, 58, 71; family ties of, 39–42, 158, 159; financial standing of, 92; harmony among, 46, 48, 49, 50, 51, 54, 71, 73; initiative of, 68–69, 71; meeting attendance, 165–167; methods of summoning, 59; oath of, 52; on full-time duty, 73–74, 168; pettiness of, 39, 43, 44, 48; relationship with queen, 68; religious attitudes of, 43, 46–48; remuneration of, 169; restriction on movements of, 131; sophistication of, 229; subordination of to Privy Council, 55, 102–103; territorial influence of, 19–21, 47; unique authority and position of, 67, 75–76
Privy Council registers, 4, 12, 13, 16, 52, 84, 86, 93, 101, 105, 109, 157, 160, 164, 192, 197, 208, 219
Privy Seal. *See* Seal, Privy
Privy Seal, Lord, in Star Chamber, 13
Proby, Peter, 224
Proclamations, 62, 247
Propaganda, 131
Puckering, Sergeant John, 84–85
Puttenham, George, 207

Queenborough, 105

Radcliff, Edward, 106
Radcliff, Sir Henry, 4th Earl of Sussex, 106, 133, 194, 196
Radcliff, Thomas, 3rd Earl of Sussex, 18, 20, 25, 26, 39, 40–49 *passim*, 53–61 *passim*, 70–79 *passim*, 85, 87, 88, 92, 106, 110, 115, 118, 131, 159, 166, 168, 171, 179, 194, 213, 239; as diplomat, 38–39; as Lord Chamberlain, 34; as Lord Deputy, 38; and northern rebellion, 70
Raleigh, Sir Walter, 3
Randolph, Thomas, 50, 89, 132; as interrogator, 211, 212; ordered to discharge posts, 221

Read, Conyers: on conciliar dissension, 44

Reading, 167

Rebellion of 1569. See Northern rebellion

Recusants, 111, 127, 154, 226; disarming of, 200; release of, 129

Reform, absence of, 230

Requests, court of, 11, 30, 34, 80; and council, 11

Richmond, 165

Richmond, Duke of, 24

Rivers, exploitation of, 137

Robsart, Amy, 28

Roddi, Malachias, 89

Rogers, Daniel, clerk of the council, 160

Rogers, Francis, 194

Rogers, Sir Richard, 194

Rogues and vagabonds, 134

Rouen, 116

Rowlett, Sir Rafe, 21

Russell, Francis, 2nd Earl of Bedford, 18, 19, 26, 27, 28, 39–48 passim, 70, 75, 89, 102, 106, 150, 151, 157, 165, 166, 179, 180; and northern rebellion, 70

Rye, 109, 133, 147

Sackford, Sir Henry, 103

Sadler, Sir Ralph, 18, 20, 23, 38, 40–48 passim, 55, 57, 69, 70–75 passim, 89, 98, 100, 115, 118, 120, 122, 127, 131, 159, 165, 166, 169, 179, 187, 239; as Lord Lieutenant, 22; as member of parliament, 22; as scottish expert, 69; sponsors Croft, 35; tact of, 71–72

Saint Andrew's castle, 106

Saint Bartholomew's day massacre, 33, 75, 77, 101, 110, 198, 247

Saint David's, Bishop of, 204

Saint Jean de Luz, 116

Saint Mawes, 106

Saint Michael's Mount, 106

Saint Paul's Cathedral, dean of, 121

Salisbury, 178; Bishop of, 122

Sandwich, 213; Mayor of, 74

Sandys, Edwin, Bishop, 126

Scilly Isles, 104

Scotland, 35, 39, 68, 75, 192–193; English policy towards, 23

Scotland, King of. See James VI

Scott, Sir Thomas, 84

Scrope, Lord, 68, 69, 212

Seal, Great, 16, 31, 91, 92, 93, 109,

125, 142, 178. See also Bacon, Sir Nicholas; Bromley, Sir Thomas; Chancellor, Lord; Keeper, Lord

Seal, Privy, 16, 89–90, 108, 112, 184, 185, 205, 219, 249

Seal of the Privy Council, 16, 163

Secretary, principal, 4, 88; as council coordinator, 56–57; as council functionary, 84; diplomatic role of, 76–78; as ex officio councillor, 36; function of, 150–155; importance of, 32; between queen and council, 32; operating methods of, 153–154; pivot man, 72; reputation of, 151; role of in parliament, 98; use of Signet, 156. See also Cecil, William; Smith, Sir Thomas; Walsingham, Sir Francis; Wilson, Dr. Thomas

Sefton, Richard, 226

Seymour, Edward, Earl of Hertford, Duke of Somerset, Lord Protector of England, 15, 25, 27, 30, 32, 38

Shakespeare, William, 229, 237

Shastre, M. le, 104

Sheepshearing, 147

Sheerness, 105

Shelley, Richard, 223

Shelley, William, redoubtable recusant, 130, 223

Sheppey, Isle of, 104–105

Sheriff: of Kent, 205; of Lancashire, 204; of Somerset, 213; of Surrey, 120; of Sussex, 219

Sheriffs, 204, 245; council nominates, 21; queen chooses, 21

Shirley, Sir Thomas, 223

Shoreham, 219

Shrewsbury, 108

Shrewsbury, Earl of. See Talbot, George

Sidney, Sir Henry, 18, 20, 35, 38–47 passim

Sidney, Philip, 16, 40

Signet, 16, 32, 90, 125, 156, 163, 185, 218; application of, 163; controlled by principal secretary, 32

Smith, Sir Thomas, 4, 18, 20, 32, 33, 40, 45, 47, 73, 74, 76, 98, 127, 128, 150, 151, 152, 159, 166, 203, 205, 212, 215, 238, 239, 247; appointed principal secretary, 32; as secretary, 151; death of, 34; failure as diplomat, 32; personality of, 151; as self-made man, 32

Smithes (property), 226

Sneyde, Sir William, 182

Social structure: upheld by design, 146, 245–246
Society, views of, 243–244, 248
Society of Antiquaries, 19
Somerset, 142, 196, 212, 213, 218; murder in, 212
Somerset, Duke of. *See* Seymour, Edward
Southampton, Earl of, 21
Southcote, John, 122
Southsea, 106
Sovereignty, nature of, 242
Spain, 143, 144; war with, 232
Spain, King of. *See* Philip II, King of Spain
Spanish Armada, 112
Special considerations: council attitude towards, 218, 219
Speculation, in foreign ore, 214
Spencer, John, 91
Spencer, Robert, 122
Spinola, Benedict, 92, 93
Standley, Thomas, 249
Stanhope, Sir Thomas, 184
Stanley, Thomas, 122
Stapleton, Thomas, 124
Star Chamber, court of, 11, 13, 80, 81; and Privy Council, 11, 81–82
Star chamber (meeting place), 13, 119, 165, 177, 210
Steward, Lord, 34, 217
Stoke, lordship of, 226
Stone, Lawrence, 228
Stowel, Mr., 213
Strasbourg, 37
Stuart, Mary. *See* Mary, Queen of Scots
Subsidies, 186–187, 218
Subsidy commissioners, 218
Suffolk, 122, 138, 142, 178, 197, 208; Duchess of, 33
Surrey, 111, 122, 133, 134, 142, 146, 196, 197, 226; ordnance production forbidden in, 108; Sheriff of, 120
Sussex, 122, 126, 127, 129, 133, 134, 142, 196, 219, 226; musters in, 222
Sussex, Earl of. *See* Radcliff, Sir Henry; Radcliff, Thomas

Tables: the queen's relationship to councillors, 41; Ages of Elizabeth and Her Councillors, 45; Average and Median Ages of Queen and Council, 45
Talbot, George, 6th Earl of Shrewsbury, 18, 19, 25, 26, 45, 47, 67, 69,

70, 112, 128, 150, 240; as Earl Marshall, 38
Talbot, Gilbert, 240
Tanner, John, 84, 176
Taxation, 186–187
Theobalds, 92, 165
Thirty-nine articles, 42
Throckmorton, Anthony, 129
Throckmorton, Sir John, 207
Tilbury, 199
Torture, 211–212
Tower of London, 82, 108, 122, 160, 211, 215
Trading companies, 142–144, 147, 207
Trained bands, 112
Travel, controls over, 123, 189, 220; within England, 131–133
Treasurer, Lord, 27, 31, 36, 57, 85–93 *passim*, 103, 115, 143, 151, 154, 190, 194, 217, 219, 238, 239, 242; in Star Chamber, 13
Treasurer of the Household, 34
Treasury, 31
Tremayne, Edmund, clerk of the council, 4, 120, 126, 142, 157, 239; as interrogator, 211; precedent book of, 162
Tudor, Mary. *See* Mary I, Queen of England
Turner, Edward, 84, 85
Tyrwhitt, Sir Robert: sons of, 129

Universities, councillors at, 18, 19, 30, 31, 32, 33, 36, 37, 236
Ushant, 104

Vaughan, John, 104
Venice, 157, 209
Vienna, 26

Waad, William, clerk of the council, 86
Wages, control of, 141, 146, 215
Waldegrave, William, 126
Wales. *See* Council in the Marches
Wallop, Sir Henry, 106, 149, 199, 203, 246
Wallop, Lady, 217
Walpole, Sir Robert, 149
Walsingham, Sir Francis, 4, 20, 33, 39, 40–47 *passim*, 56–61 *passim*, 76, 78, 80, 85, 87, 98, 101, 112, 116, 120, 123, 127, 134, 150–158 *passim*, 166, 192, 194, 209, 211, 212, 217, 224,

225, 230, 238, 240–247 *passim;* as member of parliament, 22; as the queen's servant, 241

Wards, court of, 18, 46, 85

Warwick, Earl of. *See* Dudley, Ambrose

Waterford, Mayor of, 115

Wekes, Robert, 83

Wentworth, Lord, 85

Wentworth, Paul, 97

Wentworth, Peter, 99

Wentworth, Thomas, 56

Westminster, 81, 93, 165, 166, 177

Westminster Palace, 146

Westmoreland, Earl of, consulted by queen, 53

Weston, John, 223

Weston, Sergeant, 178

Whitehall, 165, 208; fire at 156

Whitgift, John, Bishop, 139, 158

Whole Council, 12–13

Wight, Isle of, 106, 108, 196, 198

Wilkes, Thomas, clerk of the council, 157–159; treatise of on councillorship, 158

Wilson, Dr. Thomas, 18, 19, 20, 33, 40, 45, 47, 73–80 *passim,* 96, 98, 118, 143, 144, 152, 157, 159, 212; as member of parliament, 22; personality of, 152

Wilton, 19, 92

Wiltshire, 19, 177, 196

Winchester, Bishop of, 128

Winchester, Marquess of. *See* Paulet, William

Winchester, Warden of, 153

Windsor, 151, 165, 247

Wingfelde, Robert, 213

Winter, William, 105, 115

Wisbech River, 138, 203

Wolsey, Thomas, 12, 13, 14

Woodstock, 141

Wootton, Sir Edward, 153, 154

Wray, Sir Christopher, CJKB, 177

Wriothesley, Thomas, 38

Wylbraham, Mr. 85

Yarmouth, 126, 197, 237

York, 179

York, Archbishop of, 57

Young, Sir John, 81, 82

Zouche, Sir John, 134